A Companion to the Works of Walter Benjamin

Studies in German Literature, Linguistics, and Culture

Camden House Companion Volumes

The Camden House Companions provide well-informed and up-to-date critical commentary on the most significant aspects of major works, periods, or literary figures. The Companions may be read profitably by the reader with a general interest in the subject. For the benefit of student and scholar, quotations are provided in the original language.

A Companion to the Works of
Walter Benjamin

Edited by
Rolf J. Goebel

 CAMDEN HOUSE
Rochester, New York

First published 2009
by Camden House

Camden House is an imprint of Boydell & Brewer Inc.
668 Mt. Hope Avenue, Rochester, NY 14620, USA
www.camden-house.com
and of Boydell & Brewer Limited
PO Box 9, Woodbridge, Suffolk IP12 3DF, UK
www.boydellandbrewer.com

ISBN-13: 978-1-57113-367-0
ISBN-10: 1-57113-367-4

Library of Congress Cataloging-in-Publication Data

A companion to the works of Walter Benjamin / edited by Rolf J. Goebel.
    p. cm. — (Studies in German literature, linguistics, and culture)
Includes bibliographical references and index.
ISBN-13: 978-1-57113-367-0 (hardcover: alk. paper)
ISBN-10: 1-57113-367-4 (hardcover: alk. paper)
    1. Benjamin, Walter, 1892–1940—Criticism and interpretation. I. Goebel,
Rolf J., 1952–II. Title. III. Series.

PT2603.E455Z595 2009
838. '91209—dc22

2009017322

A catalogue record for this title is available from the British Library.

This publication is printed on acid-free paper.
Printed in the United States of America.

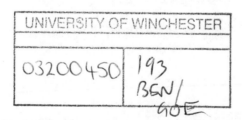

Contents

Contents

Preface

SIXTY-NINE YEARS AFTER HIS DEATH, the reputation of Walter Benjamin as a leading cultural critic, literary scholar, and philosopher of the twentieth century has been firmly established on a global scale. And yet his canonicity, lest it be relegated to the safe havens of the cultural archive, requires that we reread him in the changing context of our times, ask new questions of his texts, and interrogate him critically. To this end, the *Companion to the Works of Walter Benjamin* seeks to offer an advanced introduction to his major works and their recurrent themes while probing into his relevance for today from a variety of innovative perspectives, critical approaches, and interdisciplinary positions.

I have been very fortunate to work with an excellent team of international scholars, and I thank them for their contributions. Special thanks go to Wolfgang Bock and Dominik Finkelde, who checked the introduction and made valuable suggestions. Karl Ivan Solibakke kindly provided an excellent translation of Bernd Witte's essay and assisted with the editorial work. Last but not least, I wish to express my gratitude to Camden House's Editorial Director, Jim Walker, who responded enthusiastically to my plans for editing this volume and who guided the production process with exemplary patience, encouragement, and wisdom. I also wish to acknowledge the support of The University of Alabama in Huntsville, which granted me a sabbatical leave during the spring semester 2008 so that I could complete the *Companion*.

R. J. G.

Sources of Benjamin's Works

Gesammelte Schriften. Edited by Rolf Tiedemann and Hermann Schwep-penhäuser. 1972–89. Paperback edition, 7 vols., Suhrkamp Taschen-buch Wissenschaft 931–37. Frankfurt am Main: Suhrkamp, 1991. According to the editors, this edition contains corrections of printing errors in the cloth edition (VII.2:885). Cited as *GS* by volume and sub-volume. The *Passagen-Werk* (*GS* V.1/2) is cited by convolute number.

Gesammelte Briefe in 6 Bänden. Edited by Christoph Gödde and Henri Lonitz. Frankfurt am Main: Suhrkamp, 1995–2000. Cited as *GB*.

Selected Writings. Edited by Michael W. Jennings et al. 4 vols. Cam-bridge, MA, and London: Belknap P of Harvard UP, 1996–2003. Cited as *SW*.

The Origin of German Tragic Drama. Translated by John Osborne. Lon-don: NLB, 1977; London: Verso, 2003. Cited as *Origin*.

The Arcades Project. Translated by Howard Eiland and Kevin McLaugh-lin. Cambridge, MA, and London: Belknap Press of Harvard UP, 1999. Cited as *AP* or by convolute number. These references are identical for the German original and the English translation. Use of the "Guide to Names and Terms" (pages 1016–53) throughout the *Companion* is gratefully acknowledged.

Chronology of Benjamin's Major Works

1913–14   "Metaphysik der Jugend," *GS* II.1:91–104; "The Metaphysics of Youth," *SW* 1:6–17.

1914–15   "Zwei Gedichte von Friedrich Hölderlin," *GS* II.1:105–26; "Two Poems by Friedrich Hölderlin," *SW* 1:18–36.

1916   "Über Sprache überhaupt und über die Sprache des Menschen," *GS* II.1:140–57; "On Language as Such and on the Language of Man," *SW* 1:62–74.

1918–19   *Der Begriff der Kunstkritik in der deutschen Romantik, GS* I.1:7–122; *The Concept of Criticism in German Romanticism, SW* 1:116–200. Published 1920.

1919   "Schicksal und Charakter," *GS* II.1:171–79; "Fate and Character," *SW* 1:201–6. Published 1921.

1920–21   "Theologisch-politisches Fragment," *GS* II.1:203–4; "Theo-
(1937–38?)   logical-Political Fragment," *SW* 3:305–6.

1921   "Zur Kritik der Gewalt," *GS* II.1:179–203; "Critique of Violence," *SW* 1:236–52. Published 1921.

1921   "Die Aufgabe des Übersetzers," *GS* IV.1:9–21; "The Task of the Translator," *SW* 1:253–63. Published 1923.

1921   "Kapitalismus als Religion," *GS* VI:100–103; "Capitalism as Religion," *SW* 1:288–91.

1921–22   "Goethes Wahlverwandtschaften," *GS* I.1:123–201; "Goethe's Elective Affinities," *SW* 1:297–360. Published 1924–25.

1923–25   *Ursprung des deutschen Trauerspiels, GS* I.1:203–430; *The Origin of German Tragic Drama.* Published 1928.

1923–26   *Einbahnstraße, GS* IV.1:83–148; *One-Way Street, SW* 1:444–88. Published 1928.

1924   "Neapel" (coauthor: Asja Lacis), *GS* IV.1:307–16; "Naples," *SW* 1:414–21. Published 1925.

1927   "Moskau," *GS* IV.1:316–48; "Moscow," *SW* 2:22–46. Published 1927.

1927–40   *Das Passagen-Werk; GS* V.1/2; *The Arcades Project.*

1928   "Haschisch in Marseille," *GS* IV.1:409–16; "Hashish in Marseilles," *SW* 2:673–79. Published 1932.

1929   "Der Sürrealismus: Die letzte Momentaufnahme der europäischen Intelligenz," *GS* II.1:295–310; "Surrealism: The Last Snapshot of the European Intelligentsia," *SW* 2:207–21. Published 1929.

1937–38	"Das Paris des Second Empire bei Baudelaire," *GS* I.2:511–604; "The Paris of the Second Empire in Baudelaire," *SW* 4:3–92.
1938	"Berliner Kindheit um neunzehnhundert" (Fassung letzter Hand), *GS* VII.1:385–433; "Berlin Childhood around 1900" (Final Version), *SW* 3:344–86.
1938–39	"Zentralpark," *GS* I.2:655–90; "Central Park," *SW* 4:161–99.
1939	"Über einige Motive bei Baudelaire," *GS* I.2:605–53; "On Some Motifs in Baudelaire," *SW* 4:313–55. Published 1940.
1940	"Über den Begriff der Geschichte," *GS* I.2:691–704; "On the Concept of History," *SW* 4:389–400.

Introduction: Benjamin's Actuality

Rolf J. Goebel

I

IS OUR TIME — LATE CAPITALIST POSTMODERNITY in the age of globaliz-
ing politics and digital media — particularly destined to actualize Walter Benjamin?[1] If one understands actuality (*Aktualität*) to be a critical
moment in which something or somebody in the past becomes simultaneously real and current for the present, and by actualization (*Aktualisierung*) the historically contingent process of bringing about this actuality,
then the answer seems to be a resounding "yes." As even the most casual
Internet surfing will show immediately, Benjamin's texts and images are
everywhere, at least in cyberspace. But as with any apparently obvious
answer, the very terms of this one need to be continually reexamined and
reconfirmed in order to retain their legitimacy. Indeed, the question and
its answer require the posing of other questions: How do we make Benjamin our intellectual contemporary without resorting to the clichés of
the timelessness and universality of great thinkers or ideas? On the other
hand, how do we historicize him — read him in the context of his own
cultural time and space — without reducing him to a passive object of
seemingly dispassionate research agendas? Which of Benjamin's own theories and critical concepts can we employ for an innovative understanding
of his thinking in his original context and in our own? And, finally: are
the notions of actuality/actualization as employed here akin to the ideal
of self-actualization, commonly known as the realization of one's innate
potential? In other words, *how* do we actualize Benjamin?[2]

It may be wise to begin tackling such questions by reviewing some
rather obvious reasons why Benjamin ought to resonate particularly
well with our times. First of all, there is the immense spectrum of his
writings, which encompass literary criticism and metaphysical speculations on language; political theory, and the philosophy of history;
analyses of photography, film, and other media; autobiographical writings and travel essays; radio talks for young people; and translations.
Equally diverse are the traditions from which he borrowed eclecti-
cally for his own syncretistic thought: classical philosophy and idealist aesthetics, Jewish mysticism and Marxist materialism, surrealism and

the avant-garde. The historical context of these intellectual explorations — the modern European metropolis between the end of the bourgeois materialism of the Wilhelminian Empire and the demise of the Weimar Republic's liberal democracy in the cataclysms of the Third Reich and the Second World War — continues to fascinate and terrify us, even though it is always threatened by collective repression and oblivion. Paradoxically, however, the very terms in which Benjamin focused on this particular cultural territory contain anticipatory moments and even dialectical reversals that transcend the particular space and time of their origins and allow for a conceptual re-translation into other times, other cultures, other histories.

This is why the diversity of Benjamin's themes, categories, and methodologies appeals to the increasingly interdisciplinary directions in today's literary criticism, media studies, sociology, political science, urban studies, feminism, and postcolonial theory. Philologically, Benjamin's presence depends on Rolf Tiedemann's and Hermann Schweppenhäuser's standard edition of the *Gesammelte Schriften* (Suhrkamp Verlag, 1972–89),[3] three supplementary volumes of translations (1987,1999), and the *Gesammelte Briefe,* edited by Christoph Gödde and Henri Lonitz (1995–2000). The Walter Benjamin Archiv (part of the Akademie der Künste) in Berlin (Erdmut Wizisla, director) is of inestimable value for any scholarship that directly depends on original manuscripts. It has collected approximately 12,000 sheets of manuscripts, letters, photographs, and notebooks. These documents include materials that Benjamin took with him when he fled from his Paris exile in June 1940; they were obtained after his death by his friend and collaborator Theodor W. Adorno. The collection also includes a number of important documents of Benjamin that were discovered in 1981 after the philosopher Georges Bataille had hidden them from the German occupation troops in the Bibliothèque Nationale in Paris. Finally, the archive maintains materials that were confiscated by the Gestapo from Benjamin's last apartment in Paris and then taken to Moscow by the Red Army after the Second World War. After being deposited in the German Central Archive of the GDR and later in the Academy of the Arts (East Germany), they ended up in Frankfurt am Main in 1996 before being transferred to Berlin.[4] Benjamin's reception in the United States and beyond also benefits from the new translations of the *Selected Writings* for Harvard University Press under its general editor Michael W. Jennings (1996–2003). Numerous critical introductions[5] and collections of essays[6] address the academic specialist and the general reader alike. The monumental *Benjamin-Handbuch,* edited by Burkhardt Lindner, offers probably the most wide-ranging and reliable assessment to date of the writer's life, work, historical context, and scholarly reception.[7] An international conference titled "NOW — The Now of Recognizability: Locations of Walter Benjamin in Culture, Art, and Scholarship" (Berlin,

17–22 October 2006) combined critical lectures with musical theatre, performance art, public readings, film screenings, and exhibitions to mark Benjamin's cultural impact in the public sphere.

Moreover, the man himself and his biography have acquired an "aura" of authority and even mystique that go far beyond his texts' reception in academic circles. Indeed, Benjamin has also become something of an icon in popular culture and mass consumption. Jay Parini has written an intriguing novel titled *Benjamin's Crossing* (1997), which combines a fictional account of Benjamin's life with critical comments on his work, "interweav[ing] the thrilling tale of [his] escape [from the Nazis] with vignettes of Benjamin's complex, cosmopolitan past."[8] In *Walter Benjamin at the Dairy Queen: Reflections at Sixty and Beyond,* Larry McMurtry asks whether the art of storytelling, whose demise in modernity Benjamin analyses in his essay "Der Erzähler" ("The Storyteller"), can survive among the oilmen, cowboys, roughnecks, and other patrons of the Dairy Queen drive-up eateries in the arid small towns of west Texas — places seemingly remote from Benjamin's cosmopolitan European past.[9] Combining acoustic instruments and live electronic sound projection, Luigi Nono's *Prometeo — Tragedia dell'ascolto* (Prometheus — Tragedy About Listening, 1984/85) cites and reconfigures fragments from Benjamin's last text, "Über den Begriff der Geschichte" ("On the Concept of History," 1940), for instance by associating Prometheus with Benjamin's allegorical Angel of History, who is blown away by the storm of catastrophic history into an uncertain future and whose gaze wants to awaken the broken shards (of the past). Similarly, the avant-garde opera *Shadowtime,* by Brian Ferneyhough (2004), with a libretto by Charles Bernstein, focuses on Benjamin's final moments before his suicide. Allusively referencing musical idioms from such diverse sources as the madrigal and the Second Viennese School, the composition freely evokes key concepts of Benjamin, such as redemptive time, memory, the doctrine of similarity, and the Angel of History as Melancholia.[10] A documentary film, *Who killed Walter Benjamin?* (2005), by David Mauas, gives, according to the movie's Web site, "not just a reconstruction of a death but the living portrait of the scene of the crime."[11] The album *Banda Sonora* by Manel Camp contains a moody "Rèquiem A Walter Benjamin," and the album *Wørk,* by the Norwegian electropop band Elektrofant, features the edgy rap sound of "Walter Benjamin's Aesthetics." The visually appealing volume *Introducing Walter Benjamin,* by Howard Caygill, Alex Coles, and Andrzej Klimowski, published — *nomen est omen* — by Icon Books UK and Totem Books USA, offers an easy read about his life and work, combining scholarly text with comic-strip and collage illustrations to "help the reader through the dazzling maze of Benjamin's work" in order to find, at the end, "Benjamin the *allegorist.*"[12] The volume picks up on the idea of actualization by linking, for instance, Benjamin's notion of the "porosity" between the public and the private sphere in the city of Naples with the design *Alteration to a Suburban House* by the Jewish American conceptual artist Dan Graham (b. 1942), who criticized New York City's regressive demarcation of the public and the private in its reflecting glass architecture (91). *Introducing Walter Benjamin* also traces Benjamin's foreseeing of a "picture-writing of the future" in *Einbahnstraße* (*One-Way Street*, 1928) from print culture, film, and advertisement= to "future graphic regions: statistical and technical diagrams — an international *moving script* — and into the 'ether' of the internet" (116–17); and the volume hints at the obvious echoes of Benjamin's notion of the destruction of classical art's "aura" by technological reproduction in Andy Warhol's Campbell's soup cans (137).

Indeed, so ubiquitous is Benjamin's presence in the international arena that his texts are sometimes turned into cultural commodities. This happens in the popular area as well as in some scholarly circles, which seem more interested in Benjamin as a legitimizing authority for their own work rather than as an object of meticulous textual criticism.[13] Especially some of his key concepts — "aura," "technological reproduction," "dialectics at a standstill," "the now of recognizability," "homogeneous empty time" — seem prone to infinitely new re-citation, recycling, and reconfiguration because they combine intellectual depth and multi-layered ambiguity with a rhetorical force that can turn these philosophical terms into all-too-fashionable catch phrases. Ultimately, however, Benjamin's work refuses to be instrumentalized for pragmatic programs and ideologies, because it eludes all later generations' will to grasp his work in universalizing gestures of interpretive mastery.[14] Ironically, some of the same qualities that account for his diverse appropriation by today's cultural studies paradigms also subvert any attempt to press him into a unifying theory or a totalizing analytic framework. Often reading the truth claims of cultural traditions against the accepted grain of academic orthodoxy, and critical of systematic philosophy, Benjamin's texts favor non-linear montage techniques and fragmentary argumentation filled with unpredictable gaps and reversals. His essayistic style usually combines highly abstract reflection with deliberately esoteric metaphors and idiosyncratic comparisons to reveal secret affinities between seemingly remote ideas and minute reality details, which he forges into dialectical thought-images exploring a subject matter through its extreme aspects. As a result, any reading of Benjamin's texts will sooner or later stumble across (apparently) irresolvable contradictions (at first glance), inexplicable terminologies, or (for the moment) inconclusive arguments that continually force readers to revise their hermeneutic perspectives and critical categories. Although necessarily marked by contingency and partiality — in the double sense of bias and incompleteness — each rereading of Benjamin's texts thus yields new insights while opening up new interpretive uncertainties. Rarely, then, is the reader's sense of going astray and getting lost in the labyrinth of textual signifiers more frustrating and yet more profoundly satisfying than in Benjamin's case. Thus it seems that Benjamin's actuality today is not a natural given, not something that can or should be taken for granted. Instead, it may be the uneven and unsteady index of a continual process marked by fashionable appropriation as well as by serious interrogation, by market forces, and by genuine interest. Benjamin's actuality seems real and phantasmagoric at the same time, an ambivalent phenomenon that requires continual self-reflection and self-critique. But for all its achievements and drawbacks, Benjamin's actuality seems to restore posthumously at least some aspects of the leading reputation as a critic that Benjamin aspired to but was prevented from achieving fully by the circumstances of his life.

Let us therefore recapitulate some of its bare facts.[15] Walter Bendix Schoenflies Benjamin was born on 15 July 1892 as the oldest of three children of Emil Benjamin, an art dealer and investor, and his wife Pauline, née Schoenflies. He grew up in the upper-bourgeois milieu of the largely assimilated Jewish population of Berlin during the economic boom years of the *Gründerzeit*. Rebelling against his father's expectations that he pursue a "respectable" bourgeois life, he also detested the authoritarian stuffiness and scholarly pedantry of the school and university life of his days. As a result, Benjamin was active in the progressive Free School Community and the Free Student Movement, advocating a non-hierarchical community in the service of intellectual freedom and "pure spirit," but soon became disillusioned with nationalistic tendencies in the movement and the support of the First World War by one of their leaders, Benjamin's former teacher Gustav Wyneken. After studying in Freiburg im Breisgau, Berlin, and Munich, Benjamin, who had married Dora Sophie Pollak in 1917, moved to Bern, where he received his doctorate with a dissertation titled *Der Begriff der Kunstkritik in der deutschen Romantik* (The Concept of Criticism in German Romanticism, 1918–19). Perhaps the most important essay of these early years is his interpretation of Goethe's novel *Die Wahlverwandtschaften* (*Elective Affinities*, 1921–22). Despite his reservations against its institutional limitations, Benjamin considered pursuing a formal university career, but his plans were dramatically cut short in 1925, when his *Habilitation* thesis (the prerequisite for attaining a professorial position), titled *Ursprung des deutschen Trauerspiels* (The Origin of the German Mourning Play) was rejected because his supervisor found the language of its daring combination of metaphysical speculation and philological exegesis utterly incomprehensible.

A restless traveler throughout his life (Paris, Capri, Naples, Spain, Riga, Moscow, Norway, Ibiza, and so on), Benjamin now embarked on a rootless life as a freelance literary critic, book reviewer, translator (Proust, Baudelaire, Aragon, and others), and radio broadcaster. Although constantly plagued by financial problems and personal difficulties (divorce, unfilled love affairs, severe depression, suicidal tendencies), Benjamin published a large amount of work during the late 1920s and early 1930s, including his *Habilitation* and the aforementioned avant-garde collection *Einbahnstraße*, as well as important essays on surrealism, Proust, Karl Kraus, and photography. Benjamin benefited intellectually and personally from his precarious friendship, dating back to 1915, with the preeminent scholar of Jewish mysticism, Gershom Scholem, and his tortuous love relationship with the Communist revolutionary Asja Lacis. His knowledge of materialist philosophy and socialist politics was also significantly enriched through his friendship (from 1929) with Bertolt Brecht, with whom he stayed repeatedly in the latter's Danish exile during the 1930s.

When the National Socialists seized power in 1933, Benjamin left Germany for ever. He avoided following Scholem's example of going to Palestine, instead opting for the cultural Zionist exploration of the intellectual potential of Jewishness in the heart of the Western European metropolis. He relocated to Paris, where he much preferred solitary work in the Bibliothèque Nationale to socializing with other émigrés. Despite the specters of political persecution and material poverty, he managed to complete some of his most important works during that time: "Franz Kafka: Zur zehnten Wiederkehr seines Todestages" ("Franz Kafka: On the Tenth Anniversary of His Death," 1934); "Das Kunstwerk im Zeitalter seiner technischen Reproduzierbarkeit" ("The Work of Art in the Age of Its Technological Reproducibility," three versions, 1935–39); "Der Erzähler: Betrachtungen zum Werk Nikolai Lesskows" ("The Storyteller: Observations on the Works of Nikolai Leskov," 1936); *Deutsche Menschen: Eine Folge von Briefen* ("German Men and Women: A Sequence of Letters," 1931–36); "Eduard Fuchs, der Sammler und der Historiker" ("Eduard Fuchs, Collector and Historian," 1934–37); "Berliner Kindheit um 1900" ("Berlin Childhood around 1900," 1938); his work on Charles Baudelaire: "Das Paris des Second Empire bei Baudelaire" ("The Paris of the Second Empire in Baudelaire," 1937–38); "Über einige Motive bei Baudelaire" ("On Some Motifs in Baudelaire," 1939); and "Zentralpark" ("Central Park," 1939). And he continued assembling his monumental collection of citations and reflections on Paris as the capital of the nineteenth century, known as *Das Passagen-Werk* (*The Arcades Project*, 1927–40).

In 1939 Benjamin lost his German citizenship, and from September to November he shared the fate of other non-French foreigners by being interned in Clos St. Joseph, Nevers. Through Scholem he tried to obtain a visa to Palestine, while also hoping to escape to the United States, largely because Theodor W. Adorno's and Max Horkheimer's Institute for Social Research, which had financially supported him and had published some of his work, had by then relocated to New York. In 1940, when Benjamin wrote "Über den Begriff der Geschichte," the German troops caught up with him. He fled to Lourdes and Marseille and, with Adorno's help, obtained an entry permit to the United States, but he was unable to get an exit visa from France. This meant that he and his travel companions would likely end up in an internment camp. After secretly crossing the border into the small Spanish town of Port Bou, Benjamin was told that he was to be returned to France, where he would most certainly fall into the hands of the Nazis. Ill with heart disease and emotionally devastated, he took his own life through an overdose of morpheme during the night of September 26. His grave at the small Port Bou cemetery remains unidentified, but a monument by the Israeli artist Dani Karavan was installed in 1994 to commemorate Benjamin's death.

II

As even this very selective survey of biographical data suggests, Benjamin's life was, by choice and circumstance, predicated on the perennial experience of dislocations, exile, and ruination. His fate is typical of that of countless victims of Fascism and the Holocaust, but beyond the immediate threat to his physical existence that was common to so many, his life also reflects the predicament of the modern European intellectual generally, who is no longer at home in a particular nation-state or tradition but must time and again renegotiate his self-identity in the hybrid space of cosmopolitanism, migration, and transcultural affiliations. Benjamin's preoccupation with allegory, montage, translation, critique, citation, and the dialectical image can be regarded as the formal equivalent of this experiential space, even though it would be reductive to take these genres and concepts simply as direct expressions of their author's personal biography.

Benjamin views the fallen state and ruination of European modernity in allegorical images that hark back to the era of the Baroque and that he saw recurring in the commodity culture of high industrial capitalism. In contrast to the symbol in idealist aesthetics, where the sensuously beautiful particular incarnates the universal idea, the fragmentary meaning of Baroque allegory is the product of a willfully subjective and artfully arbitrary projection by the mournful intellectual's melancholic gaze. In Benjamin's analysis of the mythical ever-same behind illusory innovations, this allegorical structure uncannily corresponds to the modern commodity, whose price does not represent true value but changes according to the fashionable mechanism of manipulative market forces. As he writes in the *Passagen-Werk:* "Die Moden der Bedeutungen wechselten fast so schnell wie der Preis für die Waren wechselt" ("The fashions of meaning fluctuated almost as rapidly as the price of commodities," J80,2/ J80a,1, translation modified). Believing that historical progress had merely brought about technological advances without furthering true human liberation, Benjamin had little faith in political revolutions, especially in the wake of the National Socialist catastrophe, harboring instead a messianic hope for a sudden redemptive intervention to restore the lost order of displaced things.

Benjamin's view that reality is fragmentary and its meanings an arbitrary projection corresponds in a way to his fascination with the incompleteness of the work of art and the subsequent function of criticism. In his dissertation Benjamin shows that for Friedrich Schlegel and other early Romantics the task of criticism was to initiate the work of art's internal self-reflection, through which the work attains consciousness and knowledge of itself (*GS* I.1:65; *SW* 1:151). Criticism transforms each artwork, which is finite, limited, and incomplete, into the absolute idea of art as a medium of reflection, which is by nature infinite (*GS* I.1:67; *SW* 1:152). In so doing, criticism supplements, rejuvenates, and reconfigures the secret tendencies and hidden intentions of the work of art (*GS*, 69–70, *SW* 1:153–54): "Kritik ist also, ganz im Gegensatz zur heutigen Auffassung ihres Wesens, in ihrer zentralen Absicht nicht Beurteilung, sondern einerseits Vollendung, Ergänzung, Systematisierung des Werkes, andererseits seine Auflösung im Absoluten" (*GS* I.1:78; "Thus, in complete antithesis to the present-day conception of its nature, criticism in its central intention is not judgment but, on the one hand, the completion, consummation, and systematization of the work and, on the other hand, its resolution in the absolute," *SW* 1:159).

While modernism radicalizes the incompleteness of the work of art and the radically contingent infinitude of criticism, it usually abandons the idealist metaphysics of the absolute idea of art, especially under the influence of the avant-garde movements. Hence Benjamin's interest in the Baroque mourning play, which does not conform to classical aesthetics and whose allegorical form he interprets through a direct application of the avant-garde aesthetics of montage, which juxtaposes disparate elements without forging them into a symbolic whole.[16] In the "Epistemo-Critical Prologue" to *Ursprung des deutschen Trauerspiels*, Benjamin posits that the truth content of a subject matter can only be discerned through the philosophical contemplation of the disparate fragments of thought details that make up its material content. The object of this contemplation is the representation of the ideas, in which truth presents itself, even though the unity of truth evades any kind of projection into the realm of cognition, which deals with the possession of knowledge rather than the being (essence) and unity of truth (*GS* I.1:208–10; *Origin*, 28–30).

Similarly, in his programmatic essay "Die Aufgabe des Übersetzers" ("The Task of the Translator," 1921), written as the preface for his translations of Charles Baudelaire's poetry cycle *Tableaux parisiens*, Benjamin proposes that the task of literary translation is not to convey a specific sense, information, or intention but to release the "reine Sprache" ("pure language") — an ideal language of the "ausdrucksloses und schöpferisches Wort" ("expressionless and creative Word"): "Jene reine Sprache, die in fremde gebannt ist, in der eigenen zu erlösen, die im Werk gefangene in der Umdichtung zu befreien, ist die Aufgabe des Übersetzers" (*GS* IV.1;19; "It is the task of the translator to release in his own language that pure language which is exiled among alien tongues, to liberate the language imprisoned in a work in his re-creation of that work," *SW* 1:261). It is striking how Benjamin's rhetoric of imprisonment, exile, and liberation here anticipates metaphorically his all-too real exile twelve years later, even though his theoretical reflections obviously transcend the parameters of his own life story.

Like pure language, the cultural past itself appears exiled in Benjamin's *Passagen-Werk*. In nineteenth-century capitalist commodity culture, the Passage de l'Opéra appears as a surrealistic dream-space of "raumgewordene Vergangenheit" (*GS* V.2:1041; "a past become space," *AP*, 871). It assembles all kinds of strange, outdated, and discordant trades and commodities: a shop sign possibly advertising a hairdresser; a store selling "Theatrical Tights"; forbiddingly dilapidated stairs leading to a beauty salon; mosaic thresholds possibly announcing some kind of restaurant. These wayward venues cannot be understood as a totality of determinate meaning; rather, they function as allegories of modernity's spiritual fragmentation and social alienation: "Veraltende Gewerbe halten sich in diesen Binnenräumen und die ausliegende Ware ist undeutlich oder vieldeutig" (*GS* V.2:1041; "Antiquated trades survive within these inner spaces, and the merchandise on display is unintelligible, or else has several meanings," *AP*, 871).

Like the arcades, all of Benjamin's Paris figures as a topographical allegory of high capitalist commodity society. Here, the elusive past — ancient catacombs and grottoes, fancy imitations of historic styles, a craze for collecting antiques, exotic imports from faraway colonies — intrudes into the signs of technological innovation, such as new boulevards and widened sidewalks, world exhibitions, railroad stations, iron construction, and electric light fixtures. In this way, the presence of the past deconstructs the totalizing master-narrative of linear, teleological progress. To represent this urban heterogeneity, the *Passagen-Werk* employs literary montage to assemble shock-like juxtapositions of marginal, neglected, or half-forgotten details of reality and textual fragments without a unified totality of meaning:

> Methode dieser Arbeit: literarische Montage. Ich habe nichts zu sagen. Nur zu zeigen. Ich werde nichts Wertvolles entwenden und mir keine geistvollen Formulierungen aneignen. Aber die Lumpen, den Abfall: die will ich nicht inventarisieren sondern sie auf die einzig mögliche Weise zu ihrem Rechte kommen lassen: sie verwenden.

[Method of this project: literary montage. I needn't *say* anything. Merely show. I shall purloin no valuables, appropriate no ingenious formulations. But the rags, the refuse — these I will not inventory but allow, in the only way possible, to come into their own: by making use of them. (N1a,8)]

The topographic montage of Paris is principally constructed through the viewpoint of the *flâneur*. Deriving from the nineteenth-century dandy and aesthete leisurely strolling through the city, Benjamin's *flâneur* is less a historical figure or individual subject than a perspectival medium, reading the collective memory of his city from the silent surfaces of churches, thresholds, and paving stones: "Beim Nahen seiner Tritte ist der Ort schon rege geworden, sprachlos, geistlos gibt seine bloße innige Nähe ihm Winke und Weisungen" ("At the approach of his footsteps, the place has roused; speechlessly, mindlessly, its mere intimate nearness gives him hints and instructions," M1,1). Thus the *flâneur* functions as the translator of the silent language of topographic sites into the conceptual language of the modern urbanite. In this sense he relates to Benjamin's magic philosophy of language, which proposes, in "Über Sprache überhaupt und über die Sprache des Menschen" ("On Language as Such and on the Language of Man," 1916), that there is no event or thing in animate or inanimate nature that does not participate in language in order to communicate its mental content (*GS* II.1:140–41; *SW* 1:62). The classical *flâneur's* movements still negotiate the physical confines of real urban topographies and the visible traces of their local histories. By contrast, the stationary Internet surfer of today's digital communication age is sucked into an ever expanding virtual reality that represents the opening of geopolitical boundaries, the flow of transnational capital, and the seemingly universal dissemination of data typical of the age of globalization, but seems to subvert the authentic experience of material reality and its spatial depth of field.[17]

This virtualization of topographic space today harks back to Benjamin's theory of the loss of "aura" in the age of technological media.[18] By reproducing unique and faraway things, photography and film bring them closer to any audience, no matter where and when, thus satisfying modern desires of mass consumption and entertainment distraction. Like textual translation, these media are less bound to the authority of an original than to the function of transmittance and change itself. In fact, by reproducing the original for new audiences, photography and film destroy the aura of the original, its mysterious authenticity and uniqueness, which seems to remove the object perceptively even when it is physically close. As Benjamin notes in "Kleine Geschichte der Photographie" ("Little History of Photography," 1931): "Was ist eigentlich Aura? Ein sonderbares Gespinst von Raum und Zeit: einmalige Erscheinung einer Ferne, so nah sie sein mag" (*GS* II.1:378; "What is aura, actually? A strange weave of space and time: the unique appearance or semblance of distance, no matter how close it may be," *SW* 2:518). The object whose aura is destroyed by technological reproduction can be the classical work of art and its aesthetic autonomy, or it can be the architectural space of a city like Paris. Benjamin regards the French photographer Eugène Atget (1857–1927) as a pre-surrealist artist because his pictures focus on seemingly banal, wayward, and obscure sites rather than on famous and glittering landmarks, and he shot them without any people in them, thus cleansing Paris of its romantic aura. As a result, photography promotes a new way of perceiving reality, which promises to be politically liberating: "Surrealistische Photographie . . . macht dem politisch geschulten Blick das Feld frei, dem alle Intimitäten zugunsten der Erhellung des Details fallen" (*GS* II.1:379; "Surrealist photography . . . gives free play to the politically educated eye, under whose gaze all intimacies are sacrificed to the illumination of detail," *SW* 2:519).

What began with film and photography in Benjamin's era accelerates in our age of digital communication technologies.[19] Today the aura of authenticity and uniqueness — both with respect to works of art and topographic sites — seems increasingly to disappear in virtual reality scenarios that can be received all over the world. As television and Internet images circulate all over the global map, these media effectively demystify the terrifying or intriguing strangeness of faraway lands, potentially leading to a salutary subversion of stereotypical notions of the other. However, the visual image surplus promoted by telecommunications media may also lead to the uncanny re-auratization of distant places and figures.[20] Think, for instance, of the anonymous man defying a military tank in Beijing during the Tiananmen Square pro-democracy student revolt in the spring of 1989, closely followed by the East German woman screaming at a stolid-looking border guard during the equally emotionally charged and visually overwhelming fall of the Berlin Wall in November of the same year. Recycled by the mass media, these people's actions, initially motivated by individual emotions and political opinions responding directly to a particular time and place, seem transfigured into symbolic imagery of universal significance. In contrast to Benjamin's identification of political aura with Fascism, this kind of aestheticizing of politics by the mass media is now coded as democratic self-articulation and anti-authoritarian defiance, but the paradox of aura — the appearance of (heroic, almost larger-than-life) distance, no matter how close the technologically mediated image actually is in our living rooms, has been powerfully reinstated for our times.

III

These principles of translation, criticism, and mediation typical of Benjamin's life and work help us to understand his philosophy of actualizing the past for the present. In no unclear terms, Benjamin himself rejects appropriations anchored primarily in the recipient's subjectivity and the cultural horizon of the present rather than in the truth claims of the past text itself. In his translator essay, he asserts: " . . . kein Gedicht gilt dem Leser, kein Bild dem Beschauer, keine Symphonie der Hörerschaft" (*GS* IV.1:9; "No poem is intended for the reader, no picture for the beholder, no symphony for the audience," *SW* 1:253). Of course, Benjamin does not deny the fact that works of art must be read, watched, or listened to; rather, for him, works of art, like language, have a life of their own and therefore their unfolding legacy does not depend on the merely subjective and arbitrary reception by changing audiences. In this sense, translations do not serve the afterlife of great works of art but, on the contrary, owe their very existence to the work's fame: "In ihnen erreicht das Leben des Originals seine stets erneute späteste und umfassendste Entfaltung" (*GS* IV.1:11; "In them the life of the originals attains its latest, continually renewed, and most complete unfolding," *SW* 1:255).

Accordingly, in his *Passagen-Werk* Benjamin detects in the images of the past a "historische Index" (historical index), which says that these images do not merely belong to their own time but attain their "Lesbarkeit" (legibility) at a particular later time:

Und zwar ist dieses "zur Lesbarkeit" gelangen ein bestimmter kritischer Punkt der Bewegung in ihrem Innern. Jede Gegenwart ist durch diejenigen Bilder bestimmt, die mit ihr synchronistisch sind: jedes Jetzt ist das Jetzt einer bestimmten Erkennbarkeit.

[And, indeed, this acceding "to legibility" constitutes a specific critical point in the movement at their interior. Every present day is determined by the images that are synchronic with it: each "now" is the now of a particular recognizability. (N3,1)]

On the other hand, in "Über den Begriff der Geschichte" Benjamin insists that past cultural objects do not simply present themselves to later generations as timeless treasures. Rather, in opposing the archival complacency of nineteenth-century historicism, the materialist historian must blast specific moments of the past, moments that are in danger of being forgotten or marginalized by the course of history, out of the continuum of the "homogene und leere Zeit" (*GS* I.2:702; "homogeneous, empty time," *SW* 4:396) of universal history. This act of rescuing elements of the past is not an arbitrary and subjective act but only facilitates or completes the internal dynamic of images, texts, and events, which attain their full understanding in a shock-like constellation of past and present forged by the critic as a "Dialektik im Stillstand" ("dialectics at a standstill," N3.1).[21]

Benjamin's theory of actualizing the past raises the important question of whether *our* time qualifies as the "now of recognizability" in which Benjamin's legacy may come to fruition. In a recent essay on the possibilities and limitations of actualizing Benjamin's theory of art, Peter Bürger has proposed that our era may not be the one in which Benjamin's thoughts can attain a higher degree of actuality than in their own time.[22] In Bürger's opinion, the May 1968 uprisings in Paris, when students and workers appropriated surrealist calls for the integration of imagination and desire into political reality, may have been the last Benjaminian "now-time" to date. At that critical moment, surrealist theory, Bürger believes, did attain a higher degree of actuality than it had achieved in the 1920s, when the first surrealist manifesto was written. He maintains that no such past is in sight that could be redeemed in our own time, because a comprehensive perspective on how to rescue a segment of tradition seems to be shrinking. Bürger's example is the faithfully reconstructed Frauenkirche in Dresden. For him, this famous centerpiece of Dresden's celebrated Baroque panorama appears like an isolated monument within Socialist prefabricated housing complexes and the clumsy 1990s architecture surrounding it. Although he concedes that the church (which was financed by a huge popular fund-raising initiative) has promoted a sense of social collectivity among the population, he denies that it is the spirit of the Baroque that has contributed to this collective identity formulation.

Bürger's pessimistic position rests largely on his assumption that Benjamin lived at a time when, in the organic growth through history of cities like Paris, the experience of tradition as a lived reality could still be taken for granted. It was precisely this ubiquitous presence of genuine tradition, Bürger argues, that allowed Benjamin to propose radical breaks with the past. By contrast, he contends, our own time has lost this sense of a lived tradition. Instead of detecting a period of the past whose analysis would really enlighten the present, cultural studies, unable to resist political interference in educational institutions and capitalism's commodification of culture, has lost its faith in the power of tradition and instead appropriates its objects arbitrarily. Consequently, Bürger doubts that the entire oeuvre of Benjamin, in all its diversity and contradictions, can be incorporated into our present; rather, only selected motifs of this thought may be taken up and continued. Thus Benjamin's methodological reflections, for instance his theoretical analysis of the historicity of auratic art, may promote new ways of thinking about culture. Bürger appeals to the academic establishment to face this dire situation in order to regain a concept of tradition that allows for a new, meaningful engagement with works of the past. He concludes rather vaguely with the unanswered question of how Benjamin, an advocate of historical rupture who nonetheless thinks in terms of a lived tradition, might have responded to our petty-minded attitude ("Kleinmütigkeit").[23]

Bürger's ambivalence toward Benjamin's actualization, it seems to me, stands on shaky feet. Problematically equating a meaningful attitude toward the past with continuity and organicity of tradition, he misconstrues Benjamin's notion of the past. For Benjamin, traditions are not organically grown presences to be taken for granted; instead, the commodification of cultural substance by high capitalism in modern cities like Paris indicates a profound crisis in the relation between past and present. People try to compensate for this historical alienation by resorting to simulations, haphazard borrowings, and the frantic collecting of bits and pieces from the past. Benjamin notes, for instance, that among the "Traumhäuser des Kollektivs" ("dream houses of the collective," L1,3) — arcades, winter gardens, panoramas, factories, and so on — the museums combine scientific research with a dreamlike nostalgia for bad taste and a "Durst nach Vergangenheit" ("thirst for the past," L1a,2).

In this respect Benjamin's nineteenth century is not at all different from our own; indeed, it anticipates it strikingly. Certainly Bürger is justified in doubting that the Dresden Frauenkirche can "rescue" the genuine spirit of the Baroque. But in a different sense, the edifice — with its combination of old and new stones, reassembled through authentic building techniques for contemporary uses (worship, concerts, and tourism) — is nonetheless a striking allegory (in Benjamin's sense) of our time. The church's visually overwhelming presence — one is tempted to call it its resuscitated aura — signifies contradictions that are as significant for Dresden's self-identity as they are for the self-understanding of Germany as a reunited nation. Like few other recent architectural landmarks, the Frauenkirche signifies the tensions between the terrors of Second World War destruction and the popular desire for redemptive healing; between the need for commemorating a grand period of art history and the vision for new beginnings; between the desire for "authentic" reconstruction and the recognition that recovering the past must necessarily remain a process of artful simulation.[24]

This dialectic seems to haunt cities worldwide. Post-reunification Berlin proudly displays the historic Reichstag façade with its high-tech dome not far from the corporate futurism of Potsdamer Platz surrounding the old-fashioned Weinhaus Huth and the remnants of the Hotel Esplanade. In New York's post–Rudy Giuliani phase, Times Square, Greenwich Village, SoHo, and other parts of gentrified Manhattan begin to resemble nostalgic theme parks, where historic building substance is restored to satisfy nostalgic desires as well as commerce and tourism. Signifying China's international presence, Shanghai showcases a particularly uncanny collage of European colonial architecture and ultra-futuristic skyscrapers that especially in photographic and cinematic night shots look totally unreal. Thus we are witnessing everywhere a global city culture that radicalizes Benjamin's modernist analysis of the dynamic simultaneity of different time-layers, the translation of the receding past into the uncertain present, and the intrusion of authentic historical remnants into image-driven urban renewal projects.[25]

In this sense our time seems actually quite capable of opening up the "now of recognizability" in which Benjamin's thought attains new legibility. Strictly speaking, however, Bürger's question — whether our time is the now-time in which Benjamin's thoughts attain a *higher* legibility than they did in their own era — must indeed be answered in the negative. But this is not, as Bürger suggests, because our time appropriates the past only in haphazard and fragmentary ways; as I have argued, this is an attitude that we thoroughly share with Benjamin's era. The true reason, rather, is that according to Benjamin's "Über den Begriff der Geschichte," *any* truly authentic and complete reading of history must remain a utopian projection, one that can be accomplished only in a messianic future: "Freilich fällt erst der erlösten Menschheit ihre Vegangenheit vollauf zu. Das will sagen: erst der erlösten Menschheit ist ihre Vergangenheit in jedem ihrer Momente zitierbar geworden" (*GS* I.2:694; "Of course only a redeemed mankind is granted the fullness of its past — which is to say, only for a redeemed mankind has its past become citable in all its moments," *SW* 4:390). From this messianic perspective, any present — not just our own late-capitalist postmodernity — can only attain a partial, distorted, and temporary understanding of its past. But if this is true, then we may perhaps conclude that every present's engagement with endangered and neglected facets of history contributes in its own modest way to the fullness of the past attaining its legibility in a future that is unpredictable but may surprisingly occur at any moment. Thus each and every one of our readings of Benjamin, incomplete as it necessarily is, may add a tiny bit to a utopian legibility of his texts in their full significance at some other, later, time that lies beyond our own horizons of comprehension and thus remains unfathomable.

IV

Benjamin's reflections on translation, legibility, the now of recognizability, and dialectics at a standstill outline his recurrent master-trope of actualization/actuality. I have reviewed it here as the programmatic framework for the kind of reading of Benjamin's writings themselves that is espoused by the contributions to this *Companion*. The guiding principle for selecting the topics of this volume has been the assumption that Benjamin's work can be made significant for today in a manner that accords with, and often draws directly on, his own notion of actuality. If, for Benjamin, moments of the past contain an internal dynamic of meaning that when blasted out of the continuum of homogeneous and empty time attains new meaning in a later time, then the contributions to this volume pursue a similar task with respect to Benjamin's own work. As advanced introductions they examine Benjamin's central texts, themes, terminologies, and genres in their original contexts — cultural, sociopolitical, literary, philosophical, and so on — while simultaneously pursuing an actualization of these subjects within the changed parameters of our time, such as contemporary media, memory culture, constructions of gender, postcoloniality, and theories of urban topographies. These two interpretive perspectives — historicization and actualiziation — are not categorically separable but mutually illuminating. Actualization anchors the historicizing analysis in some of the pressing concerns of today, from where all questioning of the past must necessarily start, while the hermeneutic grounding of Benjamin's work in its original cultural contexts and intentions prevents the actualizing dynamic from lapsing into mere presentist projections of today's preoccupations onto the past.

Working in Brazil, Canada, Europe, and the United States, the contributors to this volume explore this two-pronged approach to Benjamin from a variety of methodologies, political concerns, and cultural values. The essays focus on Benjamin texts of canonical status but also engage relatively unknown or neglected ones. Even the ratio of philological exegesis to actualization varies considerably from essay to essay, depending on the internal difficulty of Benjamin's texts and the hermeneutic questions asked of them. Thus the significance of Benjamin today emerges, not as a uniform presence of established texts and their accepted readings, but as a dynamic network of his work's affiliations with other texts, other cultures, and other times.

In his wide-ranging essay on Benjamin's language theory and literary criticism, Wolfgang Bock identifies several themes and categories uniting these two strands of intellectual activity. Benjamin's construction of language encompasses several interconnected elements, such as the idea of a pure language, nonsensuous similarity, attention to form, the elements of untranslatability in textual artifacts, and the idea of a historical after-maturity of artworks as a central aspect of their reception. Bock also shows that the secret unification of cultures envisioned by Benjamin is a category that is of potential significance to contemporary critiques of globalization. But while Benjamin is an important source of inspiration for today's literary and cultural critics, Bock also warns against overly facile forms of identification with Benjamin, an ever-present danger since he has become an object of reference, quotation, and cultural power games.

Continuing the focus on Benjamin's literary criticism, Dominik Finkelde provides a close reading of Benjamin's *Trauerspiel* book, analyzing such themes as mourning and melancholia, the allegory, fragment, and ruin, and the sovereign and the martyr. Finkelde draws on the radical immanence of Gilles Deleuze's philosophy, which opposes Benjamin's messianic thinking. He also proposes that Benjamin was the inspiration for the German writer W. G. Sebald's preoccupation with the fragment and the ruin. Reflecting a new constellation between Benjamin's Baroque and postmodernism, Sebald's protagonists meander like Baroque melancholics through a catastrophic world that stands in the wake of Auschwitz as if under the ethereal influence of Saturn.

Wolfgang Bock offers a detailed reading of Benjamin's avant-garde collection *Einbahnstraße*, which was published in the same year as his *Trauerspiel* book, 1928, explaining it as a montage of literary programs, surrealistic associations, reports of dreams and drug-inspired experiments, dramatic scenes of daily life, travel-diary inscriptions, and so on. Although the text breaks with traditional narrative forms and explores the influence of media on (written) culture, Bock argues that Benjamin's modernist aesthetics is far removed from a simplified preoccupation with the new media of the Internet: hypertext, virtual reality scenarios, and digital communication.

Bernd Witte focuses on Benjamin's reflections on literature as a medium of collective memory and political experience. He connects *Einbahnstraße* with Benjamin's *Erzähler* essay on the loss of oral storytelling in the age of the modern novel and his interpretation of Baudelaire as the representative of the loss of poetic experience in the shock-like encounters of information-dominated modernity. Witte inscribes Benjamin's media reflections into our telematic age, proposing that the computer's merging of text, image, and sound may yield a new pedagogy of reading and writing that integrates the technological possibilities available today.

Like other contributors to this volume, Lutz Koepnick warns against an uncritical use of Benjamin's theory of aura and technological reproduction for the sake of theorizing new media today. Nevertheless, his essay upholds the viability of Benjamin's writings as a compelling model of how to think about the relationship between technological change, the aesthetic, and how media engage the user's body. For a case study, Koepnick compares Benjamin's theories with today's computer-driven animation techniques such as rotoscoping and their impact on the mediation of corporeality on and beyond the screen.

Eric Jarosinski finds that Benjamin's autobiographical texts stage many of the key concerns he articulates elsewhere, including the status of the subject in modernity, the interpolation of past and present, and the interplay of technology and experience. Jarosinski reconstructs the complex changes from "Berliner Chronik" ("A Berlin Chronicle") to "Berliner Kindheit um 1900" ("Berlin Childhood around 1900"), exemplified, for instance, by the shift from the digging hand of the archaeologist to the hovering eye resembling a movie camera. Connecting these images to the figure of the book collector in Benjamin's essay "Ich packe meine Bibliothek aus" ("Unpacking My Library"), Jarosinski insists that in following Benjamin's excavations of his life, we are forced to rethink our own critical categories, theoretical assumptions, and representational modes.

Next to the childhood texts, perhaps the greatest product of Benjamin's years of exile is the *Passagen-Werk*, whose conceptual structure Karl Ivan Solibakke analyzes from synchronic and diachronic perspectives, reading its montage-like topography of Paris as the capital of nineteenth-century commodity capitalism in the context of Benjamin's historical materialism, philosophy of history, and views on cultural memory. He argues that Benjamin's *opus maximum* constitutes a pivotal link between Heinrich Heine's post-Romantic representation of Parisian modernity and Paul Virilio's postmodern critique of the global city in the age of tele-communication and virtual reality.

Focusing on Benjamin's last text, "Über den Begriff der Geschichte," Marc de Wilde engages the writer's political texts through the "experience of disillusion." It allowed Benjamin to formulate a radical critique of totalitarian ideologies, whose forgetting of the past led to their complicity with political violence. Critiquing former German foreign minister Joschka Fischer's ideologically pragmatic use of the slogan "Never again Auschwitz" to justify his country's engagement in the Kosovo conflict, de Wilde differentiates Benjamin's "politics of remembrance," which focuses on rescuing images of the past that refuse appropriation for dogmatic ends, from a questionable "politics of commemoration" that reifies the past for partisan political interests of the present.

Addressing a closely related theme, Vivian Liska analyses the radical rereading of Benjamin's messianic juxtaposition of theology and politics by Giorgio Agamben, the Italian editor of Benjamin's collected works and a leading figure in contemporary European political philosophy. Agamben seeks to liberate Benjamin from the views of previous commentators such as Gershom Scholem, Theodor W. Adorno, and Jacques Derrida. From Agamben's vantage point, Liska arrives at a fresh interpretation of Benjamin's key theories of quotation, collecting, and historical tradition, the "idea of prose," and his paradigmatic reading of Kafka.

From a postcolonial perspective, Willi Bolle analyzes the significance of Benjamin's study of Paris as the quintessential European metropolis of modernity for a new understanding of megacities on the "periphery" of the global map, such as Ciudad de Mexico, Buenos Aires, Rio de Janeiro, São Paulo, and also of Belém and Manaus, which claimed to be a "Paris on the Amazon." Drawing on the modernist Brazilian writer Mário de Andrade, on a contemporary São Paulo rap band, and on the Amazonian playwright Márcio Souza, Bolle explores interpretive categories that take account of the different histories and present situations of these new metropolitan sites while questioning the Eurocentricity of older hegemonic centers.

Dianne Chisholm charts the unexamined "perversity" with which Benjamin imagines issues of gender, sex, and Eros in conjunction with his themes of language, history, and technology in modernist society. Her essay suggests radically new approaches to Benjamin in areas such as androgyny, transsexual architecture, the work of sex in the age of technological reproducibility, and the notion of an eco-technological Eros. Even though Benjamin did not formulate an explicit theory of sexuality and gender, his remarks may advance contemporary feminist and queer theory and even have implications for social/sexual emancipation.

Exploring Benjamin's actuality may also involve broadening the scope of his concepts in intermedial ways. With recourse to Theodor W. Adorno, Adrian Daub frees Benjamin's notions of *flânerie* and phantasmagoria from their predominantly and one-sidedly visual focus to explore acts of auditory *flânerie* as an avenue into the investigation of operatic phantasmagoria, by which he understands a type of illusory performativity that conceals its own material conditions of production. Daub discusses two operas of Franz Schreker (1878–1934) as instances where the technological and aesthetic aspects of phantasmagoria are self-reflectively built into the very structure of the modern artwork itself. Thus Daub's contribution helps fill the gap in the largely unexplored territory of Benjamin's relevance for aural phenomena and musical culture.

As these brief synopses suggest, the goal of the contributions is not to appropriate Benjamin's positions to justify the fashionable tendencies of today's culture. Rather, the essays work through specific differences and similarities that define the historically contingent constellations between Benjamin's texts and our time. In order to allow these constellations to emerge, the arrangement of the contributions does not strictly follow the chronological timeline of Benjamin's writing career. Benjamin's writing, although obviously changing in themes and methods, does not really follow a linear intellectual development but moves, spiral-like, among recurrent and yet variable concerns, themes, and categories. In fact, Benjamin frequently borrows entire passages from his earlier writings for later texts while revising earlier definitions of key concepts. His work remains a ruin in the negative sense — damaged by persecution, misunderstanding, and suicide — and in the positive sense — as an assemblage of fragments and torsos that point into a void that stimulates the readers' interpretive imagination without being filled by it. Correspondingly, the essays in this volume sometimes overlap in some aspects while offering different, perhaps even contradictory viewpoints in other instances. Needless to say, the *Companion* does not pursue some kind of illusory completeness. Rather, the volume's intersections and interstices, including the gaps — the texts or issues not addressed by any of the essays — are intended to spur readers' own interpretive interrogations without aiming at a hermeneutic closure with definite answers and permanent explications. In this sense, the question raised at the beginning — whether actualization is akin to the common notion of self-actualization, in the sense of realizing or fulfilling one's own innate potential — must be answered in the negative. But recognizing that Benjamin's potentiality can never be fully realized — least of all by this *Companion* — is not such a bad thing at all. For ultimately, the *Companion* wants to send the reader back to where any study of Benjamin must, of course, begin and end: to the inexhaustible texts themselves.

Notes

[1] In this book the terms actualize and actuality are not used in their usual meaning in English but instead to reflect Benjamin's German usages *aktualisieren* and *Aktualität*.

[2] See also *The Actuality of Walter Benjamin,* ed. Laura Marcus and Lynda Nead (London: Lawrence & Wishart, 1998), especially the programmatic essay by Irving Wohlfarth, "The Measure of the Possible, the Weight of the Real and the Heat of the Moment: Benjamin's Actuality Today," 13–39, which, like this introduction, takes Benjamin's notion of actuality as the basis for exploring the continuing significance of his own writings today.

[3] A new critical edition is currently being prepared by Suhrkamp Verlag: *Werke und Nachlaß: Kritische Gesamtausgabe.*

[4] http://www.adk.de/de/archiv/archivbestand/literatur/kuenstler/informationen_walter_benjamin_archiv.htm.

[5] Two of the best introductions in English are Richard Wolin, *Walter Benjamin: An Aesthetic of Redemption* (New York: Columbia UP, 1982) and Susan Buck-Morss, *The Dialectics of Seeing: Walter Benjamin and the Arcades Project* (Cambridge, MA, and London: MIT Press, 1989); on actualization, see 331–75.

[6] Representative English-language collections are Gary Smith, ed., *On Walter Benjamin: Critical essays and Recollections* (Cambridge, MA: MIT Press, 1988); Gerhard Richter, ed., *Benjamin's Ghosts: Interventions in Contemporary Literary and Cultural Theory* (Stanford, CA: Stanford UP, 2002); David S. Ferris, ed., *The Cambridge Companion to Walter Benjamin* (Cambridge: Cambridge UP, 2004); and Beatrice Hanssen, ed., *Walter Benjamin and The Arcades Project* (London and New York: Continuum, 2006). Richter's volume is especially noteworthy for its emphasis on Benjamin's actuality, seen as a form of textual ghostliness that "speak[s] to us from a time and space . . . that is no longer our own but with which we are always seeking to catch up" (1).

[7] Burkhardt Lindner, ed., *Benjamin-Handbuch: Leben — Werk — Wirkung* (Stuttgart and Weimar: Metzler, 2006).

[8] Jay Parini, *Benjamin's Crossing* (New York: Henry Holt, 1997), dust jacket.

[9] Larry McMurtry, *Walter Benjamin at the Dairy Queen: Reflections at Sixty and Beyond* (New York: Touchstone — Simon & Schuster, 1999).

[10] Luigi Nono, *Prometeo — Tragedia dell'ascolto,* Solistenchor Freiburg, Ensemble Modern, Ingo Metzmacher, Peter Rundel, EMI Classics 7243 5 55209 2 0 (1995). Brian Ferneyhough, *Shadowtime,* Nieuw Ensemble, Neue Vocalsolisten Stuttgart, Jurjen Hempel, NMC D123 (2006).

[11] http://www.whokilledwalterbenjamin.com/.

[12] Howard Caygill, Alex Coles, and Andrzej Klimowski, *Introducing Walter Benjamin* (Cambridge: Icon Books, n.p.: Totem Books, 1998), 3.

[13] See Jeffrey Grossman, "The Reception of Walter Benjamin in the Anglo-American Literary Institution," *The German Quarterly* 65.3–4 (Summer–Fall 1992): 414–28.

14 On the dialectics of Benjamin's appropriation by popular culture and his resistance to assimilation see also Gerhard Richter's "Introduction: Benjamin's Ghosts," in *Benjamin's Ghosts*, 2–3.

15 See Nadine Werner, "Zeit und Person," in Lindner, *Benjamin-Handbuch*, 3–8. Standard biographies are Bernd Witte, *Walter Benjamin: An Intellectual Biography*, trans. James Rolleston (Detroit, MI: Wayne State UP, 1991); Momme Brodersen, *Walter Benjamin: A Biography*, ed. Martina Derviş, trans. Malcolm R. Green and Ingrida Ligers (London and New York: Verso, 1996); Willem van Reijen and Herman van Doorn, *Aufenthalte und Passagen: Leben und Werk Walter Benjamins; Eine Chronik* (Frankfurt am Main: Suhrkamp, 2001).

16 For an analysis of Benjamin's concepts of allegory and montage in the context of the avant-garde critique of classical aesthetics and the bourgeois "institution of art," see Peter Bürger, *Theory of the Avant-Garde*, trans. Michael Shaw (Minneapolis: U of Minnesota P, 1984), 68–82.

17 See Janet Ward, *Weimar Surfaces: Urban Visual Culture in 1920s Germany* (Berkeley and Los Angeles, London: U of California P, 2001), 14–18. For a more detailed discussion of the *Passagen-Werk* and its significance today, see Karl Solibakke's contribution in this volume. Ward and Solibakke both refer to Paul Virilio's critique of the subversion of the real by electronic communication media.

18 For a critique of Benjamin's theory of art see Bürger, *Theory of the Avant-Garde*, 27–34.

19 See also Wolfgang Bock, *Medienpassagen: Der Film im Übergang in eine neue Medienkonstellation. Bild — Schrift — Cyberspace II* (Bielefeld: Aisthesis, 2006).

20 On the return of the aura in the postmodern culture of commodity capitalism and digital communication, see Lutz Koepnick, "Aura Reconsidered: Benjamin and Contemporary Visual Culture," in Richter, *Benjamin's Ghosts*, 95–117, as well as his contribution in this volume.

21 See also Samuel Weber's recent discussion of Benjamin's notions of history and actuality in the context of "recognizability" and other such "–abilities" (*Benjamin's –abilities* (Cambridge, MA, and London: Harvard UP, 2008), 48–52). The difference between Benjamin's notion of –abilities and comparable terms in Kant "can be interpreted negatively, as the impossibility of ever realizing, in a full and self-present act of cognition, the 'abilities' involved; or it can be interpreted positively, as a *virtuality* that, precisely because it can never hope to be fully instantiated or exhausted in any one realization, remains open to the future" (14). As Weber explains, "Benjamin's concept of history knows neither goal nor 'global integration' [Deleuze's notion of the "actualization of the virtual," 32] but at best, an 'end.' This end does not come 'at the end'; rather it is always *actual*, always *now*" (51).

22 Peter Bürger, "Benjamins Kunsttheorie: Möglichkeiten und Grenzen ihrer Aktualisierbarkeit," in *Schrift Bilder Denken: Walter Benjamin und die Künste*, ed. Detlev Schöttker (Berlin: Haus am Waldsee; Frankfurt am Main: Suhrkamp, 2004), 168–83.

23 Bürger, "Benjamins Kunsttheorie, 180–83.

[24] See also Rolf J. Goebel, "*Gesamtkunstwerk* Dresden: Official Urban Discourse and Durs Grünbein's Poetic Critique," *German Quarterly* 80:4 (Fall 2007): 492–510.

[25] See Andreas Huyssen, *Present Pasts: Urban Palimpsests and the Politics of Memory* (Stanford, CA: Stanford UP, 2003).

1: Walter Benjamin's Criticism of Language and Literature

Wolfgang Bock

Benjamin's Language Criticism: Introduction

IN WALTER BENJAMIN'S INTELLECTUAL PHYSIOGNOMY, criticism plays a leading role: one finds the term in many of his writings, and many of the books and articles about him bear the words "critique" or "critic" in their titles.[1] He established himself as a leading critic of language as well as of literature and art during the Weimar Republic until his suicide in 1940. Every text by Walter Benjamin is a text *on* language, expressed in a certain way *in* language. In "Notiz über ein Gespräch mit Béla Ballasz" ("Notes on a Conversation with Béla Balász") he refers to a characterization of his own style by the Austrian journalist Alfred Polgar, in which Polgar proposed that he, Benjamin, uses even German words as if they were foreign (*GS* VI:418; *SW* 2.1:276–77).[2] That makes Benjamin a kind of deconstructionist *avant la lettre*, who anticipated the later theories of Jacques Derrida, Paul de Man, and others, although in a different context.

One may divide his explicit expressions about language into an official and published part and an unofficial one that was only meant for a dialogue with himself and some close friends. Benjamin's writings about language published in his lifetime include the introduction to *Ursprung des deutschen Trauerspiels* (Origin of the German Mourning Play; written 1924, published 1928; *GS* I:203–430); here one finds relics of a *Habilitation* project, planned in 1920/21 but not realized, on the language theory of the Scholastic John Duns Scotus — a subject about which Martin Heidegger wrote his own *Habilitation* thesis in 1916.[3] The second important essay is another introduction, this one to his translation of Charles Baudelaire's cycle of poems *Tableaux parisiens,* bearing the title "Die Aufgabe des Übersetzers" (*GS* IV.1:9–21; "The Task of the Translator," *SW* 1:253–63); published in 1923, it is today a classic among the theories of translation. Even though he wrote it in language close to that of Stefan George, it still has relevance for today's globalized world, as we will see below. A third essay was published 1934 in the *Zeitschrift für Sozialforschung:* "Probleme der Sprachsoziologie. Ein Sammelreferat" (*GS*

III, 452–80; "Problems in the Sociology of Language," *SW* 3, 68–93). In this text Benjamin discusses his own ideas in a wider context; his interest is spurred by a mimetic and onomatopoetic function, which he tries to detach from its "primitive" context and actualize in the contemporary state of language.[4]

The subjects Benjamin addresses in these writings are related to two versions of his own reflections on language, which he discussed mainly with Gershom Scholem (*GS* II.3:934). The first one, "Über Sprache überhaupt und die Sprache des Menschen" ("On Language as Such and on the Language of Man"),[5] which he wrote in Munich in 1916, was only meant to circulate among a small group of adepts, and deals mainly with words, the written text, and sound-images from the perspective of a comparatist. Seventeen years later he shifted slightly to a point of view that pays more attention to images and media phenomena, and this led to the second version (written early in 1933) of his theory of language, with the title "Lehre vom Ähnlichen" (*GS* II.1:204–13; "Doctrine of the Similar," *SW* 2:694–98), which that same year was condensed into a shorter adaptation titled "Über das mimetische Vermögen" (*GS* II.1:210–13; "On the Mimetic Faculty," *SW* 2:720–22). Unfortunately his friend Scholem, being himself a historian and specialist of the Jewish cabala, who had recognized the allusions to the cabala in the first theory, could not understand the transformation of these motifs to the second version, although Benjamin sent him a comparison of both theories (*GS* VII.2:795–96; *SW* 2:717–19). Only after Benjamin's death did Scholem realize the complicated relationship between the different versions.[6]

Naming and Translation

In this essay we will focus on the development of Benjamin's language theory from the first version of 1916 to the second of 1933 and then, in reverse chronological order, point out connections to the work "Die Aufgabe des Übersetzers" of 1923. Benjamin's theory of modernity had at the beginning of the century made space in his own thinking for motifs from other cultures, not as a kind of exotic decoration but as a sign of his affinity with these cultures. Indeed, his texts often anticipate the present-day debates on postcolonialism. Because it deals with the interrelations among cultures and languages, his essay on the translator is of especial interest in this context. Benjamin himself prepared translations of Charles Baudelaire, Marcel Proust, Gabriele D'Annunzio, and others.[7] His various reflections on language theory originate from diverse starting points in each case, but follow more or less the same line of thought. In this chapter I will reconstruct this train of thought in its broad outlines in order to show its relevance today. Since Benjamin's reflections are among the most difficult in the German language, certain simplifications cannot be avoided in the interest of overall clarity; perhaps they will also allow us to illustrate a similarity of thought running through his works, one that remains hidden to other interpretations.

"Über Sprache überhaupt und die Sprache des Menschen"

In his first work about language (in English: "On Language as Such and On the Language of Man"), Benjamin understands language as expression and medium in a spiritual sense but nevertheless criticizes mystical theories of language. The text begins with the programmatic sentences:

> Jede Äußerung menschlichen Geisteslebens kann als eine Art der Sprache aufgefaßt werden, und diese Auffassung erschließt nach Art einer wahrhaften Methode überall neue Fragestellungen. Man kann von einer Sprache der Musik und der Plastik reden, von einer Sprache der Justiz, die nichts mit denjenigen, in denen deutsche oder englische Rechtssprüche abgefaßt sind, unmittelbar zu tun hat, von einer Sprache der Technik, die nicht die Fachsprache der Techniker ist. Sprache bedeutet in solchem Zusammenhang das auf Mitteilung geistiger Inhalte gerichtete Prinzip in den betreffenden Gegenständen: in Technik, Kunst, Justiz oder Religion. Mit einem Wort: jede Mitteilung geistiger Inhalte ist Sprache, wobei die Mitteilung durch das Wort nur ein besonderer Fall, der der menschlichen, und der ihr zugrunde liegenden oder auf ihr fundierten (Justiz, Poesie), ist. (*GS* II.1:140)

> [Every expression of human mental life can be understood as a kind of language, and this understanding, in the manner of a true method, everywhere raises new questions. It is possible to talk about a language of music and of sculpture, about a language of justice that has nothing directly to do with those in which German or English legal judgments are couched, about a language of technology that is not the specialized language of technicians. Language in such contexts means the tendency inherent in the subjects concerned — technology, art, justice, or religion — toward the communication of the contents of the mind. To sum up: all communication of the contents of the mind is language, communication in words being only a particular case of human language and of the justice, poetry, or whatever underlying it or founded on it. (*SW* 1:62)]

Benjamin is using a concept of language here that includes every significant utterance. However, everything existing in the world expresses itself in some sort of language. Things express themselves in their language, which is not the language of man like words and writing, but it is nonetheless the signature of the thing, which Benjamin calls *its* language. Yet there are certain differences, because in such a conception of language as a medium, the expressions of objects, plants, and animals are more or less mute. This indicates for him a lower kind of language. In the following paragraphs Benjamin constructs a kind of story that creates a mythos of its own. He argues that God's language is inclusive in the sense that when he speaks, as he does in the first book of Genesis, he creates holistic, complete figures at the same time. Benjamin here sees two potentials for divine language: creation and reflection, as when the Bible turns to the formula repeated at the end of each day of creation: "And he saw that it was good." For Benjamin, this second faculty of language, as a reflection of successful creation, now characterizes human language as it was spoken in paradise, when Adam received the task of naming everything. This faculty was lost when paradise was lost to humankind, but it was not completely destroyed. It can be developed even in today's multilingual world, as part of the future evolution of our culture.

Benjamin goes on to argue that in paradise Adam gets the task of naming things and living beings in the specifically human idiom, an element of God's own language, which he had given to man. Thus human language is primarily a medium between God and nature, in the sense of a translation from one world to the other. According to this understanding, words originally are names. For instance, a genitive relation is an expression of hierarchies between a subject and an object that only exists after the fall of language. These names are not completely understandable either to the named object or to the naming humans; their enigmatic core is fully understandable only to God and has no other meaning in itself.

It has to be said that Benjamin's account, which can be read like one of Jorge Luis Borges's or Franz Kafka's fictions, in contradiction to magical or mystical theories of language, opens up a heterogeneous Jewish theological horizon. Benjamin does not stay within this theological field, but he does not give it up either; instead he argues in theological and secular ways at the same time. The effect is antinomic: one may say that by openly relating his theory to a religious context Benjamin gains a kind of contradictory "secularization of a second degree," because it relates to materialistic elements as inherent aspects of theology itself.

Another similarly contradictory moment is Benjamin's notion of a "non-hierarchic hierarchy" of the diverse expressions of the different languages of beings. Here Benjamin on one hand establishes an order among the different languages of things and man, but on the other hand says that all things are part of creation and their expressions are also of a profound equality. With this statement he forecasts the development of different languages throughout the world. He opens up a line of thought beginning with the divine language of creation, which speaks in holistic images where all meaning is transparent and signifiers coincide with what is signified, followed at the next, lower, level by Adam's language of sounds and names, and finally by the fallen language of the mute expressions of objects and nature. The human position is especially privileged in this scheme because it participates in both spheres, that of God and that of nature.

For Benjamin, Adam's language of paradise is an ideal point of departure and, at the same time, the final destination. He therefore relates the biblical episode of the construction of Tower of Babel (Genesis 11:1–9) to Adam and Eve's expulsion from paradise and interprets the Babylonian confusion of language and humankind's scattering about the earth as the actual banishment from paradise. Benjamin here sees the loss of paradise and the loss of the language of Adam in paradise as one. In the usual Christian version paradise is lost because Adam and Eve are desirous of knowledge, both general and sexual. Benjamin now refers to a Jewish interpretation according to which paradise is lost not because of sexual desire, but only because Adam tries to use language for his own purposes and his own messages. For Benjamin, this is the moment when signs — the relation between signifier and signified — became arbitrary, a development that leads to language theories like that of de Saussure, which Benjamin calls the "bourgeois conception of language":

> Diese Ansicht ist die bürgerliche Auffassung der Sprache, deren Unnahbarkeit und Leere sich mit steigender Deutlichkeit im folgenden ergeben soll. Sie besagt: Das Mittel der Mitteilung ist das Wort, ihr Gegenstand die Sache, ihr Adressat ein Mensch. Dagegen kennt die andere kein Mittel, keinen Gegenstand und keinen Adressaten der Mitteilung. Sie besagt: im Namen teilt das geistige Wesen des Menschen sich Gott mit. (*GS* II.1:144)

> [This view is the bourgeois conception of language, the invalidity and emptiness of which will become increasingly clear in what follows. It holds that the means of communication is the word, its object factual, and its addressee a human being. The other conception of language, in contrast, knows no means, no object, and no addressee of communication. It means: in the name, the mental being of man communicates itself to God. (*SW* 1:65)]

In the Greek and Jewish traditions, the concept of the catastrophe as the fall of paradise, including the moment when signs became arbitrary, is deeply ambiguous: every accident carries at the same time a hidden ontological purpose. In the same way, Benjamin wants to see an ambivalent and opposite development beyond this fall of the original language, which caused its dispersal into many different idioms. Because of this common origin, even in the most distracted and fragmented human idioms something of the original language still remains. The reasons for the division of languages and the unintelligibility of the languages to each other lie in the collective apparatus of the human language, which Benjamin sees as a hidden project of human culture. In other words, Benjamin assesses the Babylonian disintegration of language not only in a negative but also in a hidden positive light, because every single language is locatable in its development from the original language to the coming unifying language. In this construction Benjamin places the origin somehow beyond the flow of time.[8] When we examine Benjamin's first language theory, it is essential to be mindful of this dialectic of the development of language as obvious dispersal and unintelligibility and at the same time as a secret collection and clarification. Misapprehension, translatability, and untranslatability are to Benjamin a complex constellation.[9]

"Lehre vom Ähnlichen"/ "Über das mimetische Vermögen"

In the essay of 1933, "Über das mimetische Vermögen," which Benjamin referred to in his correspondence with Gershom Scholem as his "new theory of language," he chose another starting point (*GB* IV:163). Here he began not with a biblical myth but with its anthropological prerequisites, understanding language and writing as imitations of nature and its phenomena. They appear as extensions of a tendency of early human beings to assimilate themselves to the world:

> Die Natur erzeugt Ähnlichkeiten. Man braucht nur an die Mimikry zu denken. Die höchste Fähigkeit im Produzieren von Ähnlichkeiten aber hat der Mensch. Die Gabe, Ähnlichkeit zu sehen, die er besitzt, ist nichts als ein Rudiment des ehemals gewaltigen Zwanges, ähnlich zu werden und sich zu verhalten. Vielleicht besitzt er keine höhere Funktion, die nicht entscheidend durch mimetisches Vermögen mitbedingt ist. (*GS* II.1:210)

> [Nature produces similarities — one need only think of mimicry. The very greatest capacity for the generation of similarities, however, belongs to the human being. The gift he possesses for seeing similarity is nothing but a rudiment of the formerly mighty compulsion to become similar and to behave in a similar way. Indeed there may be no single one of his higher functions that is not codetermined by the mimetic faculty. (My translation. The *Selected Writings* translates the second version; cf. *SW* 2.2:694)]

In this sense, humans imitate the world in their gestures, in speaking, and in writing. According to Benjamin, however, these reproduce not only elements of nature like mountains or wind but also more abstract phenomena, such as the flight of birds or the constellations of stars. He goes on to say that a clear expression of these tendencies, which have exerted strong effects throughout the history of humankind, can still be seen in the play of children, which habitually includes imitations and forms of make-believe. With this thesis Benjamin is no longer arguing within the area of theology; already in his introduction to the *Trauerspiel* book Benjamin shifts the terms into the philosophical field: things become phenomena, the names are now called concepts and instead of God he speaks about ideas (*GS* I:214–18; *Origin* 34–38). In the *Mimesis* essay he now takes his examples from magic and occult knowledge. This genealogy of imitation includes the spoken language and the written word as late ramifications of this development; they also originally followed relations of similarity, but later developed a kind of independence and freedom from their origin.

So we see that Benjamin now uses an anthropological myth as his point of departure. In this case he can also lean, without mentioning it directly, on psychoanalytical examinations of magic. In his text *Totem and Taboo* of 1912–13 Sigmund Freud follows the anthropologists James George Frazer (1854–1941) and Lucien Lévy-Bruhl (1857–1939), describing a form of magic that simply enacts the desired effect of the ritual on a smaller scale. For instance, in Japan, water is poured onto the ground to try to conjure rain; the Javanese have sex in the paddy to increase the fertility of the plants.[10] From this type of magic a second form originates, more developed and symbolic, working with certain so-called nonsensuous similarities and correspondences, assuming forms that replace the previous symbol instead of the original. "Nonsensous similarity" is a difficult and enigmatic term, which may cause some misunderstanding because Benjamin uses "nonsensuous" very differently from the ordinary meaning of "not having a relation to the senses." The concept can be clarified by relying on concrete examples from other scholars. According to the art historian Aby Warburg, the Navajo Indians of North America perform a serpent ritual in which the handling of the snake is supposed be similar to the handling of lightning in a thunderstorm. The strong force of the flash still appears in the power of the snake, and for the Indians it can also be found in the holy pictures that they use in their ceremonies. This similarity is supposed to work both ways: when the people of these tribes draw a snake, they relate to the forces of lightning by imitating them. For Warburg all kind of images retain the character of banning mythological forces as a enigmatic similarity, although during the process of civilization they become more and more hidden until they are no longer to be seen.[11]

Benjamin conceives of his idea of nonsensuous similarity — hidden but still to be released — only in very specific situations, in which a historian, a painter, or a poet actualizes these forces. This implementation is again close to magic and shows how magic gestures and spoken or written formulas operate. Freud calls this developed form of magic, in which one can hardly recognize the original act that the ritual is replacing, *sympathetic* or *homoeopathic,* because its resembles a specially prepared homeopathic medicine, where almost nothing of the healing substance is left to be analyzed chemically, but nonetheless keeps its great power of healing. Also, in Benjamin's idea of similarities there is no longer an obvious reference to an original; rather, the independence of the new reference is emphasized, without, however, its being completely severed from the original.

In Benjamin's second theory of language, as in his first, a surface and a hidden tendency are available side by side. Especially asymmetrical or *nonsensuous similarity* has much in common with the concept of mimesis developed by Aristotle in his *Poetics*.[12] Aristotle was the first to develop a philosophy in which aesthetics tends to gain an autonomous position and is no longer dependent on references to a prior original depicted in representations. According to this theory, mimesis in the arts does not mean a simple imitation; rather, in the representation something new arises. It is no longer a relationship of model and copy; instead, the representation has its own autonomous meaning.

If one transfers these complex connections to Benjamin's construction of the development of language in his second theory, one sees a change in the role of spoken and written language from imitation and representation of the original to a self-representation in the medium itself. Thus linguistic representation attains a logic of its own, independent of the faithfulness to an original. What linguists like Ferdinand de Saussure call an arbitrary relation of word and meaning, signifier and signified, is for Benjamin just a hidden relation that still is active but gives the signifier a particular kind of freedom.[13] This new independence also implies a distance from both magic and theology and a move toward the secularization of culture. In this regard Benjamin's second theory of language posits the reverse case of the first: in the first, the spreading of language appears as a dilution of the true language of the original, while with the secularization of magic in the second theory a more autonomous perspective on aesthetics is won. This important shift from the first to the second theory was difficult for Scholem to understand; maybe because it includes also a criticism of religion's transformation into art.

However, in both cases an enigmatic element is present in the relation of word and thing. This adherence to a hidden opposite element remains characteristic of Benjamin's thinking: in the first theory there remains a sense that there was still something standard about language, even as it was being "spun apart" as if by centrifugal force in the same way that in the second one the hidden relationship between the mundane forms and their magic references is still kept. In other words, even a nonsensuous similarity is a similarity and a reference.

In this way Benjamin uses the image of an ellipse — a geometric figure or curve that is defined by the distance of its points from *two* fixed foci — to capture the relation between the two elements — tradition and innovation; imitation and creation — that does not neatly distinguish between religion or magic and secularization; rather, he wants to let both poles have their due in an uncommon constellation. In this way Benjamin also breaks, to borrow a phrase from Herbert Marcuse, with a one-dimensional idea of historical progress. Benjamin believes that the creative artist always relies on a certain continuance of forms that updates traditional motifs and thus rescues them from the danger of being forgotten.[14]

"Die Aufgabe des Übersetzers"

These motifs are already summarized in Benjamin's essay of 1923, "Die Aufgabe des Übersetzers" ("The Task of the Translator"), which was one of the most important works published in his lifetime and is frequently quoted in present-day debates in cultural studies. Benjamin here posits an enigmatic element in language that is not translatable from one culture into another. These idiosyncratic elements of the texts in their original language not only resist translation into another language but often cannot be assigned a definitive meaning even within their own culture. Therefore Benjamin programmatically asserts that works of art are not produced for their consumption by readers, viewers, or listeners:

> Nirgends erweist sich einem Kunstwerk oder einer Kunstform gegenüber die Rücksicht auf den Aufnehmenden für deren Erkenntnis fruchtbar. Nicht genug, daß jede Beziehung auf ein bestimmtes Publikum oder dessen Repräsentanten vom Wege abführt, ist sogar der Begriff eines "idealen" Aufnehmenden in allen kunsttheoretischen Erörterungen vom Übel, weil diese lediglich gehalten sind, Dasein und Wesen des Menschen überhaupt vorauszusetzen. So setzt auch die Kunst selbst dessen leibliches und geistiges Wesen voraus — seine Aufmerksamkeit aber in keinem ihrer Werke. Denn kein Gedicht gilt dem Leser, kein Bild dem Beschauer, keine Symphonie der Hörerschaft. (*GS* IV.1:9)

> [In the appreciation of a work of art or an art form, consideration of the receiver never proves fruitful. Not only is any reference to a particular public or its representatives misleading, but even the concept of an "ideal" receiver is detrimental in the theoretical consideration of art, since all it posits is the existence and nature of man as such. Art, in the same way, posits man's physical and spiritual existence, but in none of its works is it concerned with his attentiveness. No poem is intended for the reader, no picture for the beholder, no symphony for the audience. (*SW* 1:253)]

Seen from this point of view, the original stays hermetic in itself and has no clear message for a reader. It is primarily not meant for a communication with the outside, but follows a line of *l'art pour l'art* relations, which combines it with other artworks in an internal relation of self-reference. We might relate this point to Derrida's notion of deconstruction, where we find a similarly incommensurate relation of word and meaning. In order to make the relationship between the work of arts' untranslatability and their communication plausible, Benjamin nevertheless develops an enigmatic or hidden correspondence between tradition and topicality. He argues that the aesthetic life of works of art lets itself be decided historically, that is, within the context of its later development. But especially this relation between the work of art's origin and its development remains obscure. What the text meant in the context of its origin and the intention of the author is something that one can hardly know later. Although the written and printed text is fixed, a "Nachreife auch der festgelegten Worte" ("after-maturity of the established words") nevertheless arises through the readings of later readers in which they update meanings in the text that were not accessible to contemporary readers and not even to the writer (*GS* IV.1:12; *SW* 1:256). These later readers make what one may call certain prophetically positioned parts of the text relevant for their own time; in this way they put parts of the text in a tradition that becomes recognizable only later.

According to Benjamin, tradition is always something that succeeding generations project backward onto the past, forming it like a historical and rhetorical dress.[15] The translator has to proceed in much the same way as the later reader. However, he must not only direct his activity toward the past but must use it to lead to a future already latently present. Combining fidelity to the text with the freedom of his own creation, he maintains the integrity of the original through the alignment of the translation with a future element that is already positioned as a hidden quality in the text of the original. A translation, as Benjamin proposes with reference to the concept of the *medium* in Goethe's theory of colors, must in this way increase the signification of the original and its effects, instead of hiding it behind a purely historical view.

Here again Benjamin puts two superficially opposite elements together: the translation enters into the service of the original by taking itself and its freedom seriously. Original and translation therefore refer to a third element, which is the original language that we already know from Benjamin's first theory; he also speaks about the *pure* or the *true* language in the same sense. In this way original and translation form necessary variations related to the pure language. These variations are defined by their differences — in much the way in which the concrete and singular phenomenon of the table broadens the idea of a table, but, as a phenomenon, remains detached from it at the same time.[16] The differences between the respective languages occur as variations between them and also in relation to signification. But this ontological alienation is necessary because the commonality of different languages today is not always recognizable, as can be seen, for instance, in Benjamin's illustration of the difference and similarity between the image that the word *pain* conjures up for a French person and the image that the word *bread* evokes for an English person.

Benjamin arrives at this vantage point of his theory by joining the motif of representation from his second theory of language and magic with the concept of pure language from his first, theological, one. The idea of the divine and pure language of names is meaningful not only at the beginning of the history but also at its anticipated end, because only in the case of a messianic deliverance of history in the form of a resurgence of the pure language would the hidden meanings nowadays slumbering in the words become visible. And in such an event, according to Benjamin, language would relinquish all forms of communication and all sense and would become simply literal, pure, and clear. This development is not yet fully evident. A translation therefore has to search for an "echo of the original" in the new language; however, this echo does not come from the past but calls from the future (*GS* IV.1:16; *SW* 1:258). Thus for Benjamin the task of the translator finally consists in the contradictory act of ripening the seed of pure language in a translation (*GW* IV.1:17; *SW* 1:259). However, this should not be confused with the task of communicating between a sender and a receiver through a medium. Rather, the translation in a mimetic sense has to be true to the untranslatable.[17] This process necessarily remains enigmatic under the circumstances of the present day, because according to this theoretical position its time has not yet come.

One doesn't need to accept this view of language and translation in all its aspects. As we have seen, Benjamin uses highly speculative theological and neo-mythological conceptions that have prerequisites and bring with them implications. In the field of intercultural relations, however, we would do well to hold on to Benjamin's belief that the original and its translation mutually support each other's representation, a belief that runs through the three texts I have discussed. The original needs a translation in order to become represented, and the translation needs the reference to the hidden meaning of the original, which, however, unfolds according to the further development of the languages.

What does this mean for the development of cultures? In his translator essay Benjamin first derives this relationship between the original and the translation from classical texts in languages no longer spoken, such as Greek, ancient Hebrew, or Latin. At the same time, however, the concept is very modern and is related to what the French call, in their term of globalization, a *mondialisation:* to come to the world means in this case also to come to language. Everything in the world must be named in order to become real. The work of translation, then, is a unification of languages into a projected one that includes all the others. The translator of today pursues the present version of an Adamitic and divine faculty by giving new names to the texts and referring to elements of the original language, spoken in paradise, at the same time. This process works in both directions, forward and backward. Benjamin believes that confrontation with a foreign language is necessary for the development of one's own language, without which it will die out.

Criticism and New Readings of Benjamin's Theories

Benjamin's construction of language includes a range of interconnected elements: the idea of a pure language, nonsensuous similarity, attention to form, and the untranslatability of works, as well as the idea of a historical after-maturity of the aesthetic life of the works of art as a central aspect of their reception. In this way he develops a picture of how the original passes from the past to the present and to the future and at the same time obtains a new freedom in the translation: work of art and translation, object and subject, fidelity and freedom, the revealed and the obscured — for him these are not contradictions but necessary poles of tension in the lively development of language and culture.

It is crucial to point out that Benjamin lays out his theory in deliberately contradictory and hermetic ways. He directs his hope toward a projected messianic end of history when pure language will appear again. This is an idealistic construction not unlike Anselm of Canterbury's medieval proof of the existence of God, which Descartes applied to modern times: God is always the ideal that human beings are striving toward. Using this idealization, Benjamin, as argued above, constructs in his theories a new myth of language, but here there is also another implication to consider.

With his theological theory, Benjamin also performs implicitly a criticism of positivist semiotics. In his above-mentioned "Probleme der Sprachsoziologie" he directly refers to Rudolf Carnap.[18] But also the father of modern linguistics, Ferdinand de Saussure, posited that the connection between the signifier and the signified is arbitrary, because it is not accessible to human beings. This leads him to focus on the system of signs and their relationships.[19] This is a basic concept of structuralism; but when de Saussure presents his model of the relationship between signifier and signified, it is not really an alternative to the theological one he intends to criticize, because it is missing the utopian character that is to be found even in metaphysics (if beneath the surface). So one may say that de Saussure has a tendency to proclaim the existing world as the norm. While de Saussure leads secular semiotics back into the realm of the theological, Benjamin, working from an open theological perspective, develops a reverse secularization by pointing out profane elements in theology itself.

At the same time, however, it is valid to argue that the enigmatic unification of cultures hinted at by Benjamin is something to which recent critics of globalization usually pay too little attention. Therefore Benjamin's theory is of particular importance in today's academic debates.

For example, the American Germanist Rolf J. Goebel has recently shown how Benjamin, far ahead of his time, developed a postcolonial pattern of thought. Goebel reads Benjamin in the context of migration, otherness, traveling, media, and the city. Willi Bolle, teaching in São Paolo, Brazil, employs Benjamin for his critical discourse on the South American metropolis.[20] The Indian Homi K. Bhabha, originally from Mumbai, who today teaches in the United States, turns frequently to Benjamin's translator essay in his books. His particular interest is the category of untranslatability, which he interprets in the context of a model for cultural life in the process of migration. One may also mention the Chinese scholar Rey Chow, who also lives and teaches in the United States, and who interprets Benjamin's essay as a theory of intercultural translation with a focus on anti-ethnocentric politics.[21]

It remains to be decided whether these projects are faithful to Benjamin's own intention. At the end of his translator essay Benjamin points out that all potential forms of translation already lie in the original: in the so-called interlinear version (*GS* IV.1:21; *SW* 1:263). In this case, freedom of interpretation and the need to adhere strictly to the original, which usually are in conflict with one another, coincide for Benjamin.

Benjamin as a Critic of Literature and Art: Reviews, Essays, Aphorisms

At the beginning of this chapter I pointed out that Benjamin was thinking not only *about* language but also *in* language. His criticism testifies to the process of signification that Benjamin practiced in his own writing style, which reflected on and problematized the production of meaning itself. According to the critic and biographer Momme Brodersen, Benjamin was among the most influential public and freelance critics in Germany between the two world wars.[22] After the failure of his *Habilitation* at the University of Frankfurt in 1925 he had to earn his living outside the establishment of the academic world. He began publishing small texts on literature in the *Frankfurter Zeitung* and the *Literarische Welt,* the most important German *feuilletons* of the time. His more than 170 book reviews of the period from 1926 until 1940 fill over 600 pages in the third volume of the *Gesammelte Schriften.*

Among the reviews one finds programmatic titles, some of which attained late fame, such as "Neues von Blumen" ("News about Flowers"), on the photographer Karl Bloßfeld; "Rückblick auf Chaplin" ("Chaplin in Retrospect"); "Krisis des Romans" ("The Crisis of the Novel"), about Alfred Döblin's *Berlin Alexanderplatz;* "Linke Melancholie" ("Left-Wing Melancholy"), on Erich Kästner; and "Nietzsche und das Archiv seiner Schwester" ("Nietzsche and the Archive of His Sister").[23] In a revised version of his 1931 review essay "Wie erklären sich große Bucherfolge?"

("How Can Big Book Successes Be Explained?," *GS* III:294–300) Benjamin gives an ironic panorama of the small rural world of Swiss naturopaths, which may still be highly topical in the context of today's ecologists and devotees of naturopathy. In this essay, as in his later well-known article "Der Autor als Produzent" (*GS* II.2:683–701; "The Author as Producer," *SW* 2.2:768–82) of 1934, he calls for a new materialistic criticism, but in both texts he uses the term materialistic more or less as a cover for his own method of writing, which is mainly influenced by the German Romantics and their ideas of metaphysics. As I will explain below, Benjamin also displays this idea of criticism in his major essays on certain authors and their connection to literature, politics, and aesthetics. The authors' names often provide the titles of the pieces: Karl Kraus, Franz Kafka, Nikolai Leskov, Eduard Fuchs.[24] The *Einbahnstraße* (One-Way Street) collection of 1928 also contains shorter and longer aphorisms and reflections about the art of the critic, such as "Die Technik des Kritikers in dreizehn Thesen" (*GS* IV.1:106–7; "The Writer's Technique in Thirteen Theses," SW 1:458–59). These texts are related to the fragments nos. 131–51 on literary criticism, — among them the important "Programm der literarischen Kritik" (*GS* VI:161–67; "Program for Literary Criticism," *SW* 2:289–96) and "Die Aufgabe des Kritikers" (*GS* VI, 171–72; "The Task of the Critic," *SW* 2:548–49). These are fragments of a larger work that Benjamin was planning on this topic (*GS* VI:161–84). He also planned two literary-critical journal projects: from 1921 to 1923, with Florens Christian Rang, *Angelus Novus,* which was intellectually related to the German *Jugendbewegung,* and in the early thirties *Krise und Kritik* (Crisis and Critique) with Bertolt Brecht, Georg Lukács, and Alfred Kurella, in a communist milieu. But both projects were too heterogeneous to be realized: in the first case the publishing company failed to make a realistic financial calculation at the time of German inflation, and in the second the editors were too diverse a group to sustain such a project in a time of crisis.[25]

On Romanticism and Goethe

Most of Benjamin's essays on canonical literary topics from Goethe and the Romantics to Franz Kafka and Karl Kraus are well known nowadays, and there is a blooming and fruitful secondary literature on them by scholars all over the world from Wuhan in China and Mumbai in India to Belém in Amazonian Brazil. But as Uwe Steiner points out, the status of criticism in Benjamin's work is registered less frequently.[26] The term "critique" in the period of Goethe and the Romantics is strongly influenced by Immanuel Kant and the neo-Kantians as well as by the Romantics and later by the left-wing Hegelians, as has been shown in the "critical theory" of Max Horkheimer and his colleagues at the Institute of Social Research, an extension of the Frankfurt School.

Benjamin forged his literary and philosophical style in the context of Kantian, Romantic, and Hegelian thought. Although he used the term in his very first writings, he turned toward the idea of criticism especially in his dissertation *Der Begriff der Kunstkritik in der deutschen Romantik* (*GS* I:7–122; *The Concept of Criticism in German Romanticism; SW* 1:117–200) and his essay on Goethe's novel *Die Wahlverwandtschaften* (*Elective Affinities*), written in the early 1920s (*GS* I:123–202; *SW* 1:297–360). In his work on the Romantics he follows the term as used in the writings of Johann Gottlieb Fichte, Friedrich Schleiermacher, Friedrich and August Wilhelm Schlegel, Friedrich Hölderlin, and, especially in the concept of natural science, of Novalis (Friedrich von Hardenberg). For Benjamin the task of the critic includes paying special attention to what Novalis called the *Reflexionsmedium* (medium of reflection) between the subject and the object, which allows both to enter an intersubjective evolution. Like Goethe, Novalis worked out his method in the field of natural sciences and literature, and he applied this poetic principle to Goethe's works; for him there exists neither fixed subject nor object. What we usually refer to with these terms are for Novalis two poles in an *a priori* unifying medium of reflection where the one does not exist without the other: the object only gives the knowledge that it intends to give, and the researcher himself has to initiate a new cognitive development to see it in a new way, then in the next step the object can offer something new, and so on. In this way both parties in this process, subject and object, are able to undergo a certain evolution.[27] Benjamin adopts this principle for his literary criticism but diverges from Novalis's process of endless romanticization, by which common things are given a higher meaning, the ordinary acquires a mysterious appearance, the known becomes unknown, and the finite takes on the aura of infinity. In contrast to this dynamic concept of romanticizing, Benjamin develops, following Friedrich Hölderlin, a concept of freezing and standstill, which he calls mortification. According to this notion, not only the endless shift from one position to the other becomes visible but also the medium of the shift itself (*GS* I.1:52 and 53–61; *SW* 1:142 and 143–48).[28]

In the first two pages of his essay about Goethe's *Die Wahlverwandtschaften* Benjamin immediately starts to explain why he distinguishes commentary from critique: the first has to follow the *Sachgehalt* (material content) of the literary work, while the second attends to what he calls the *Wahrheitsgehalt* (*GS* I:125–27; truth content: *SW* 1:297–99).[29] But the one does not exist without the other; the knowledge of the first is necessary to approach the second. He summarizes and defines this relation in the latter part of the essay as follows:

> Die Kunstkritik hat nicht die Hülle zu heben, vielmehr durch deren genaueste Erkenntnis als Hülle erst zur wahren Anschauung des Schönen sich zu erheben. (*GS* I:195)

[The task of art criticism is not to lift the veil but rather, through the most precise knowledge of it as a veil, to raise itself for the first time to the true view of the beautiful (SW 1:351)][30]

This idea of criticism, which here seems to have a more or less passive attitude, is however also related to the active concept of objective irony promulgated by the Romantics. It demands a certain destruction of the literary work's form to show its content of truth. In his book about the Romantic idea of art criticism Benjamin explains:

> Die formale Ironie ist nicht, wie Fleiß oder Aufrichtigkeit, ein intentionales Verhalten des Autors. Sie kann nicht, wie es üblich ist, als Index einer subjektiven Schrankenlosigkeit verstanden, sondern muß als objektives Moment im Werke selbst gewürdigt werden. Sie stellt den paradoxen Versuch dar, am Gebilde noch durch Abbruch zu bauen: im Werke selbst seine Beziehung auf die Idee zu demonstrieren. (*GS* I.1:87)

> [Formal irony is not, like diligence or candor, an intentional demeanor of the author. It cannot be understood in the usual manner as an index of a subjective boundlessness but must be appreciated as an objective moment in the work itself. It presents a paradoxical venture through demolition to continue building on the formation, to demonstrate in the work itself its relationship to the idea. (SW 1:165)]

One might say that in this sense critique is this destruction of the former context by the critic; the process of criticism can also be seen as a process of naming anew: the critics must point out the relevance and beauty of the work, must reveal its form, as a prerequisite for understanding it better. This task is similar to that of the translator. For this undertaking Benjamin, in a letter of 9 December 1923 to Florens Christian Rang, coins the formulation "Kritik ist Mortifikation der Werke" ("criticism is the mortification of the works"), a phrase that can be seen as a condensation of his thoughts on this subject.

The Letter to Rang

In this letter Benjamin combines in a unique manner his concept of the critic in the fields of literature and art, explaining in an enigmatic but original way what criticism means for him. First he discusses the relation of works of art to historical life. He argues that for works of art no history exists, because their physis is different from that of a living creature or a human being. The works of art affect other works of art, but these effects cannot be reconstructed, because the social context in which they were created is now lost. Therefore they remain enigmatic, and because of what Benjamin calls their muteness they stand outside the flow of time, which in Benjamin's theological diction can only be terminated by the appearance of the Messiah. This marks a relation between history and theological time. However, the moment a reader begins a hermeneutic interpretation of the work of art, the reference to historical time is restored (*GB* II:392–93; *SW* 1:388–89). After having expounded the intensive, timeless, and concealed character of works of art, Benjamin formulates the basic idea of his criticism with recourse to a metaphor of stars and sun, where stars are ideas, the sun, revelation:

> Bitte verzeihe diese dürftigen und vorläufigen Gedanken. Sie sollten mich nur hierher leiten, wo ich Dir zu begegnen hoffe: die Ideen sind die Sterne im Gegensatz zur Sonne der Offenbarung. Sie scheinen nicht in den Tag der Geschichte, sie wirken nur unsichtbar in ihm. Sie scheinen nur in die Nacht der Natur. Die Kunstwerke nun sind definiert als Modelle einer Natur, welche keinen Tag also auch keinen Gerichtstag erwartet, als Modelle einer Natur die nicht Schauplatz der Geschichte und nicht Wohnort der Menschen ist. Die gerettete Nacht. Kritik ist nun im Zusammenhange dieser Überlegung (wo sie identisch ist mit Interpretation und Gegensatz gegen alle Kurrenten Methoden der Kunstbetrachtung) Darstellung einer Idee. Ihre intensive Unendlichkeit kennzeichnet die Ideen als Monaden. Ich definiere: Kritik ist Mortifikation der Werke. Nicht Steigerung des Bewußtseins in ihnen (Romantisch!) sondern Ansiedlung des Wissens in ihnen. Die Philosophie hat die Idee zu benennen wie Adam die Natur um sie, welche die wiedergekehrte Natur sind, zu überwinden. (*GB* II:393)

> [Please forgive these skimpy and provisional thoughts. They are meant merely to lead me to where our ideas can meet: the ideas are stars, in contrast to the sun of revelation. They do not appear in the daylight of history; they are at work in history only invisibly. They shine only into the night of nature. Works of art, then, may be defined as the models of a nature that awaits no day, and thus no Judgment Day; they are the models of a nature that is neither the theater of history nor the dwelling place of mankind. The redeemed night. In the context of these considerations, where criticism is identical with interpretation and in conflict with all current methods of looking at art, criticism becomes the representation of an idea. Its intensive infinity characterizes ideas as monads. My definition is: criticism is the mortification of the works. Not the intensification of consciousness in them (that is Romantic!), but their colonization by knowledge. The task of philosophy is to name the idea, as Adam named nature, in order to overcome the works, which are to be seen as nature returned. (*SW* 1:389)]

Here Benjamin develops his image of night, stars, and nature on the one hand, to which the sun of revelation is opposed on the other. Although the ideas still burn unseen behind the glare of revelation, as the real stars do behind the light of the sun during the day, they nevertheless exist. Although Benjamin excludes works of art and nature from the "daylight of history," ideas are nevertheless still at work in them.

This relation between ideas and astronomical bodies is one that he transposes to the sphere of art and criticism. Works of art stand like the stars and nature; they are no longer intrinsically historical by themselves but receive this quality only through an interpretation from outside, which corresponds with their hidden contents, now named by criticism. The result of this process of naming Benjamin now calls "die gerettete Nacht" ("the redeemed night"), using a term reminiscent of the title of Novalis's poems *Hymnen an die Nacht* (Hymns to the Night). This redemption is now the work of the critic, because naming is always a kind of interpretation involving the representation of an idea. In this context Benjamin defines critique as a "mortification of the works." But, as has already been said, in contrast to Novalis and his concept of romanticization, Benjamin denies the never-ending movement of knowledge between the critic and his object implied in Novalis's concept, positing a static state instead of an infinite process (*GS* I:58; *SW* 1:147). The representational form of criticism has to refer to the work of art, which is enigmatic in itself, and which in this thought-picture is outshone by the light of revelation. This conception plays with the categories that Benjamin, in his later essay "Das Kunstwerk im Zeitalter seiner technischen Reproduzierbarkeit" (The Work of Art in the Age of Its Technological Reproducibility, 1936), would identity as the difference between "Kultwert," which is mainly directed to this internal history and "Ausstellungswert" (*GS* II:482; "cult value" and "exhibition value," *SW* 4:257), which deals with the perspective from outside: For Benjamin the "Kultwert" of the work of art relates to its internal value, which originates from a religious tradition, whereas the "Ausstellungswert" pays attention to the fact that in modernity there is a market, which also includes all works of art as commodities with a specific price. In the context of the letter to Rang, Benjamin identifies these categories as internal and external relations of the works of art, which the critic now has to use in his criticism.

Standstill is another term for what Benjamin refers to as mortification, which now has not only an aesthetic but also a theological implication. As we saw in Benjamin's reference to Hölderlin's critique of Novalis's model, in the aesthetic context not only the single reflection appears, but also the medium of the movement itself; the religious connotations of "mortification" now also includes the Messiah's redemption of the dead at the end of time.

So this standstill is related not only to Hölderlin's aesthetic idea of *das Ausdruckslose* (*GS* I:181; "the expressionless," *SW* 1:340) but also to Benjamin's works that focus on the element of religion, such as the "Theologisch-politisches Fragment" (*GS* II.1:203–4; "Theological-Political Fragment," *SW* 3:305–6), as well as to later works such as the *Passagen-Werk* (*GS* V; *Arcades Project*) and "Über den Begriff der Geschichte" (*GS* I.2:691–704; "On the Concept of History," *SW* 4:389–400). Here Benjamin argues that a messianic end of time not only stands outside the flow of time itself but, paradoxically, can only come about through a striving for secular happiness.

Benjamin's exposition of criticism in his letter to Rang combines almost all his ideas about language that we have already considered in this essay. We find here the already mentioned ideas, concepts, and phenomena that he would soon afterward explain in the introduction to the *Trauerspiel* book (*GS* I:214–18; *Origin* 34–38). Here the critic is an interpreter of the world, who, in describing its phenomena in terms of his concepts, represents them as ideas. As in the other works on language, here we also find the task of Adam in paradise identified as one of calling things by their right name. This faculty was lost after the fall of paradise, which was also the downfall of the language of divine origin, but may partly be resurrected in the act of critique and interpretation.

Criticizing Benjamin as a Critic

Benjamin employs a similar concept of criticism in the fields of literature, art, language, and religion. On one hand he constructs an idealistic system with a strong relationship to religion and myth; on the other hand, this system is also directed against metaphysics as well as against pure materialism. By emphasizing elements of fragmentation and destruction he hopes to avoid a mistaken idea of totality, while the construction of an end to history is meant to avoid a homogenic and empty concept of time — as he explains in "Über den Begriff der Geschichte" ("Anhang, These B," *GS* I.2:704; "B," *SW* 4:397). However, Benjamin's ideas on criticism are not beyond dispute. In the early 1970s in Germany, conservative literary *feuilletonists* of the Frankfurter *Allgemeine Zeitung* (*FAZ*) and *Die Zeit*, such as Marcel Reich-Ranicki, Fritz J. Raddatz, and scholars following their lead, tried to trivialize Benjamin's works, and Thomas Steinfeld's comments in the *FAZ* on the first volume of the *Gesammelte Briefe* (*Collected Letters*), published in 1995, have the same tendency.[31] Steinfeld, who today is in charge of the feuilleton section of the *Süddeutsche Zeitung*, at that time criticized Benjamin as a notorious pretender and someone who in a pathological sense always has to quarrel and is never able to work together with others in a rational way.

These judgments, which I suppose Steinfeld would not repeat identically today, are polemics and full of resentment; but nevertheless they draw attention to the fact that Benjamin has now become a kind of saint figure in the literary establishment. He also is now an object of reverence, quotation, and cultural power games. The South African writer J. M. Coetzee sees this similarly in his even-handed if irreverent review of the *Selected Writings* (vols. 1 and 2) and *The Arcades Project* in *The New York Review of Books,* under the programmatic title "The Marvels of Walter Benjamin." After telling the complicated story of the manuscript of the *Passagen-Werk* in the context of a marvelous new Benjamin mythology, he finally asks: "Why all the interest in a treatise on shopping in nineteenth-century France?"[32]

A Benjamin mythology of this sort contains several significant elements. The structure of Benjamin's texts seems to call up phantasmagorias in the mind of each critic, like a kind of private relation between the author and his interpreters. In this case the fact that there are other readers with different opinions leads to the question of whose interpretations of Benjamin's works are considered definitive or the best. This also leads critics to imitate Benjamin's language, a phenomenon of false identification that we also find in scholars of Adorno, Lacan, Deleuze, Foucault, and so on. Another recent trend is the tendency to relate facts of Benjamin's biography directly to his writings; Benjamin himself criticized this phenomenon as it occurred in the work of other critics, for instance, as applied by Friedrich Gundolf to the life and works of Goethe: "daß unter allen Goetheschen Werken das größte sein Leben sei — Gundolfs *Goethe* hat es aufgenommen" (*GS* I.1:160; "asserts that among all the works of Goethe the greatest is his life; Gundolf's *Goethe* took this up," SW 1:324). But because of Benjamin's closeness to melancholy we find that some critics identify with a figure that can be called "the poor Walter Benjamin." Today the task of a critic in the growing community of Benjamin scholars may be to avoid feeding the illusion of being Benjamin's only ideal reader; one should also not ignore the fact that mentioning Benjamin and quoting from his texts are no guarantees of the quality of one's own writings. As the critics of today move toward their independence, Benjamin might be an important way station but cannot be a final target of identification. I am reminded of Spike Jonz's 1999 film *Being John Malkovich;* one might make a film under the title "Being Walter Benjamin," but such a film cannot be a password for today's critic. Because Benjamin tried to anticipate the constant metamorphoses of culture, he can teach us to understand culture as always in motion, following certain rules of contradictions beyond a one-dimensional reading. Contradictory logic, skepticism, criticism, and open speculation are important aspects of the Benjaminian spirit that lives on in his followers.

Notes

[1] See, for example, Bernd Witte, *Walter Benjamin — der Intellektuelle als Kritiker* (Stuttgart: Metzler, 1976). See also Uwe Steiner, *Die Geburt der Kritik aus dem Geiste der Kunst* (Würzburg: Königshausen & Neumann, 1989), and "Kritik," in *Benjamins Begriffe*, ed. Michael Opitz and Erdmut Wizisla (Frankfurt am Main: Suhrkamp, 2000), 479–523.

[2] Benjamin writes Ballasz instead of Balász, as Herbert Bauer (1884–1994) used to call himself; cf. *GS* VI:791; *SW* 2:277. See also my other contribution in this volume: "Lost Orders of the Day: Benjamin's *Einbahnstraße*."

[3] See Martin Heidegger, "Die Kategorien- und Bedeutungslehre des Duns Scotus (1916)," in *Frühe Schriften* (Frankfurt am Main: Vittorio Klostermann, 1972), 133–354. Notes of Benjamin's project can be found in the "Schemata zur Habilitationsschrift" (*GS* VI:21–23; "Outline for a *Habilitation* Thesis," *SW* 1:269–71); "Sprache und Logik" (*GS* VI:23–26; "Language and Logic I–III," *SW* 1:272–75); and "Wenn nach der Theorie des Duns Scotus" (*GS* VI:22; "According to the Theory of Duns Scotus," *SW* 1:228).

[4] See also Anja Lemke, "Zur späten Sprachphilosophie," in *Benjamin-Handbuch*, ed. Lindner, 643–53.

[5] *GS* II.1:140–57; *SW* 1:62–74. See also Benjamin's letter to Scholem of 11 Nov. 1916, *GB* 1:343–46.

[6] See *GS* II.3:953–58. *GS* VI contains more fragments about language philosophy; see 7–53.

[7] See the supplement, vols. I and II of the *Gesammelte Schriften*.

[8] This usage of the term "origin" is also related to Benjamin's usage in the introduction to the *Trauerspiel* book (*GS* I.1:226). See also Jacques Derrida's criticism of the eschatological use of the term, which is close to Benjamin's version, in "Zeugnis, Gabe: Jacques Derrida," in *Jüdisches Denken in Frankreich*, ed. Elisabeth Weber (Frankfurt am Main: Jüdischer Verlag im Suhrkamp Verlag, 1994), 63–90, esp. 64–65.

[9] Within the permutation of words and letters, which the practice of the cabala allows in all possible combinations, there is an important reference to the works of Spanish cabalist Abraham Abulafia (1240–90). Benjamin also links this development of culture and language in a way that ties them to the cabalistic version of the Sephardic Jews Isaac Luria (1534–72) and Moses Cordovero (1522–70). They founded the school of Safed in the north of Galilee and on the authority of Genesis interpreted the expulsion of the Sephardic Jews from Spain in 1492 in a similarly ambiguous way as disaster and purpose at the same time. The diaspora of the Jews picks up motifs of the migrant world. See Gershom Scholem, *Die jüdische Mystik in ihren Hauptströmungen* (Frankfurt am Main: Suhrkamp, 1980), 267–314; in English, *Major Trends in Jewish Mysticism* (New York: Schocken Books, 1976), chapter 7.

[10] See Sigmund Freud, *Totem und Tabu*, student edition, ed. Alexander Mitscherlich, Angela Richards, James Strachey (Frankfurt am Main: Fischer, 1972), 9:369; cf. James Georges Frazer, *The Golden Bough: A Study in Magic and Religion. Part 1: The Magic Art and the Evolution of Kings*. Vol. 2 (3rd ed., Macmillan: London, 1911), 98).

[11] See Aby Warburg, *Schlangenritual: Ein Reisebricht* (Berlin: Wagenbach, 1992) and Ernst Cassirer, *Die Begriffsform im mythischen Denken* (1922), in *Wesen und Wirkung des Symbolbegriffs* (Darmstadt; Wissenschaftliche Buchgesellschaft, 1956), 1–70.

[12] Cf. Aristotle, *Poetik* (Stuttgart: Reclam, 1982), 1448a–1448b, 11–14.

[13] Ferdinand de Saussure, *Grundfragen der Allgemeinen Sprachwissenschaft* (1916; 2nd ed., Berlin: De Gruyter, 1967), 79.

[14] Inspired by reflections not only on language but also on ritual, memory, and the innovation of images, this procedure of negotiating between the past and the current relevance of the arts brings Benjamin into close proximity with the protagonists of the Warburg School, such as Ernst Cassirer, Erwin Panofsky, and Aby Warburg himself. See Aby Warburg, *Schlangenritual* and *Der Bilderatlas Mnemosyne* (Berlin: Akademieverlag, 2008). But there remains a certain difference, which is to be found in a strong element of subjectivity and an open relation to Judaism in Benjamin, which the Warburgians are missing.

[15] Benjamin refers to this connection more extensively in "Über einige Motive bei Baudelaire" (On Some Motifs in Baudelaire, *GS* II.1:638–39, note; *SW* 4:352–53, note 63).

[16] Benjamin explains the relation between ideas, concepts, and phenomena extensively in the introduction of the *Trauerspiel* book and in the letter to his friend Florens Christian Rang of 9 Dec. 1923 (*GS* I.3:889–90; *SW* 1:387–90).

[17] This would probably coincide with Paul Valéry's formulation, referred to by Benjamin (*GS* I.2:639; *SW* 4:352): "Beauty may require the servile imitation of what is indefinable in things." Translated from Valéry, *Autre rhumbs* (Paris: Gallimard, 1934), 167.

[18] *GS* III:466–68; *SW* 2:77–78; cf. Rudolf Carnap, *Logische Syntax der Sprache*, Schriften zur wissenschaftlichen Weltauffassung, vol. 8 (Vienna, 1934).

[19] See Ferdinand de Saussure, *Grundfragen der allgemeinen Sprachwissenschaft*, 19. This critical position of de Saussure's is in contrast to that of Lacan.

[20] See Rolf Goebel, *Benjamin heute* (Munich: Iudicium, 2001) and Willi Bolle, *Physiognomik der modernen Metropole: Geschichtsdarstellung bei Walter Benjamin* (Cologne, Weimar, and Vienna: Böhlau, 1994).

[21] See Homi K. Bhabha, *The Location of Culture* (London and New York: Routledge, 1994) and Rey Chow, *Primitive Passions: Visuality, Sexuality, Ethnography and Contemporary Chinese Cinema* (New York: Columbia UP, 1995), 186; see also Rey Chow, *Writing Diaspora: Tactics of Intervention in Contemporary Cultural Studies* (Bloomington and Indianapolis: Indiana UP, 1993). For a conservative criticism of the practice of quotation and interpretation see also Jeffrey Grossman, "The Reception of Walter Benjamin in the Anglo-American Literary Institution," *German Quarterly* 65.3–4 (Summer-Fall 1992): 414–28.

[22] See Momme Brodersen, *Spinne im eigenen Netz* (Bühl-Moos: Elster-Verlag, 1990) and *Walter Benjamin* (Frankfurt am Main: Suhrkamp, 2005), 100–104.

[23] For a good overview of the order and the subjects of Benjamin's reviews in general see Michael Opitz, "Literaturkritik" in *Benjamin Handbuch: Leben — Werk — Wirkung*, ed. Burkhardt Lindner with Thomas Küpper and Timo

Skrandies (Stuttgart: J. B. Metzler, 2006), 311–32. For the reviews themselves, see, for Bloßfeld, *GS* III:151–53; *SW* 2:155–57; for Chaplin, *GS* III:157–59; *SW* 2:222–24; for Döblin, *GS* III:230–35; *SW* 2:299–304; for Kästner, *GS* III:279–82; *SW* 2.2:423–27; and for Nietzsche, *GS* III:323–26.

24 The *Selected Writings* list the works chronologically. For Kraus, see *GS* II:334–38; *SW* 2:433–58; for Kafka, *GS* II:409–38; *SW* 2:794–820; for Fuchs, *GS* II:465–505; *SW* 3:260–304; for Leskov, *GS* II:438–65; *SW* 3:143–66.

25 See "Memorandum zu der Zeitschrift 'Krisis und Kritik'" (*GS* VI:619–21). See also Uwe Steiner, "'Ankündigung der Zeitschrift Angelus Novus.' 'Zuschrift an Florens Christian Rang,'" in *Benjamin Handbuch*, ed. Lindner, 301–11, and Erdmut Wizisla, *Benjamin und Brecht: Die Geschichte einer Freundschaft* (Frankfurt am Main: Suhrkamp, 2004), 298–328.

26 See Steiner, "Die Geburt der Kritik," 479.

27 In his Fragment 232 Novalis points out: "Die Welt muß romantisiert werden. So findet man den ursprünglichen Sinn wieder. Romantisieren ist nichts als eine qualitative Potenzierung. Das niedre Selbst wird mit einem bessern Selbst in dieser Operation identifiziert" (The world must be romanticized. In this way one recovers the original sense. Romanticizing is nothing but a qualitative potentiation. The lower self will be identified with a higher one in this operation). Novalis, "Fragmenten vermischten Inhalts (aus den Schlegel-Tieckschen Ausgaben)" in *Werke in zwei Bänden*, ed. Rolf Toman (Cologne: Könemann, 1996).

28 See also Benjamin's "Theorie der Kunstkritik" (*GS* I.3:833–35; "The Theory of Art Criticism," *SW* 1:217–19), written during this period, 1920–21.

29 On material content and truth content in the context of the visual arts see also the two versions of Benjamin's article "Strenge Kunstwissenschaft" (*GS* III:363–69 and *GS* III:369–74; "Strict Art-Science").

30 Sigrid Weigel has shown that Benjamin, when writing the *Arcades Project*, developed a tendency to substitute a content of meaning for a content of truth; in the context of allegory for him everything becomes writing. Sigrid Weigel, *Walter Benjamin: Die Kreatur, das Heilige, die Bilder* (Frankfurt am Main: Fischer, 2008), 228–64.

31 See Marcel Reich-Ranicki, "Auf der Suche nach dem verlorenen Echo," *Die Zeit*, 24 Nov. 1972; Fritz J. Raddatz, "Sackgasse, nicht Einbahnstraße," *Merkur* 27, 1973; and Steinfeld, "Wie ein Weichtier haust im neunzehnten Jahrhundert: Der ewige Sezessionist; Walter Benjamin im Spiegel seiner Briefe," *Frankfurter Allgemeine Zeitung*, Literature Supplement, 14 Nov. 1995.

32 J. M. Coetzee, "The Marvels of Walter Benjamin," *New York Review of Books*, 11 Jan. 2001.

2: The Presence of the Baroque: Benjamin's *Ursprung des deutschen Trauerspiels* in Contemporary Contexts

Dominik Finkelde

Introduction

DIE ARBEIT DES HERRN DR. BENJAMIN . . . ist überaus schwer zu lesen. Es werden eine Menge Wörter verwendet, deren Sinn zu erläutern der Verfasser nicht für erforderlich hält."[1] (The work of Dr. Benjamin . . . is excessively difficult to read. A lot of words are used whose sense the author does not feel obliged to explain.) These are the first words of a review written by the scholar Hans Cornelius in 1925, at a time when Benjamin was trying to obtain the academic title of professor at the University of Frankfurt.

And Cornelius's judgment is right. The text of Benjamin's *Ursprung des deutschen Trauerspiels* (The Origin of the German Mourning Play, 1928), conceived in 1916 and written down in the years 1924 and 1925, is in some ways unreadable. Max Horkheimer, who assisted Cornelius in his judgment and participated remotely in the academic process of Benjamin's unsuccessful candidacy, "failed" to recognize the importance of the text, as did Walter Brecht, Fritz Saxl, and Richard Alewyn. They refused to write a review of it after its publication by Rowohlt.[2] The fortunate discovery of the book by Benjamin scholars in the last decades has transformed the controversial *Trauerspiel* book into a kind of *summa philosophiae* of Benjamin's work, nowadays universally praised as Benjamin's most sustained and original masterpiece. It is the objective of the following article to show the appropriateness of this judgment on the basis of key ideas of the book and thereby to unfold new perspectives with cross-references to contemporary thought — represented here by W. G. Sebald and Gilles Deleuze.

However, before going into Benjamin's text, we need to ask *why* Benjamin opted for a diction that was viewed as excessively difficult by Cornelius. The question is legitimate because Benjamin at that time faced economic problems, and one may ask why a scholar should complicate his academic vocation when other texts of his prove that he did possess profound expertise in a discerning and skillfully pedagogical writing style. A possible answer could be that Benjamin situated his work in coordinates that, at first glance, look incompatible: Nietzsche's theory of Greek tragedy, Carl Schmitt's treatise of the sovereign, the writings of the Warburg school, and the reflections of Florens Christian Rang concerning the relation of mourning play and tragedy. But another answer might be more convincing: Benjamin had not solely the intention of writing an interpretation of the Baroque according to the academic standards of his time. His objective was to challenge the established epistemic coordinates in the humanities of the German university, which he contemptuously regarded as "philistine and idealistic"[3] performances of academic criticism. He not only desired to establish himself as an "expert" but also wanted to show that other experts founded their findings on poor and inadequate epistemological premises. Benjamin aimed at an avant-garde style of analytical thinking that progressed more in constellations than definitions. In this way the *Trauerspiel* book can be compared to the Warburg School, which — though in the academic field of the history of art — was almost at the same time working on the *Mnemosyne-Atlas*[4] with the goal of furnishing — like Benjamin — a cultural analysis that progressed in iconographic constellations to rework the assumptions and premises of cultural philosophy. It is clear that Benjamin was part of an avant-garde movement in the academic world of the Weimar Republic.

Benjamin wrote his book when the Baroque as an epoch torn up by flagrant conflicts was just being rediscovered[5] in the Weimar Republic, which was plagued by similar problems. The German Baroque was a period of estrangement and alienation. It does not fit into a progressive concept of history and cannot therefore be easily categorized in line with the Renaissance and the German classical period. Whereas these focus on a secularizing world with human beings discovering themselves in the center of creation (remember Da Vinci's *The Vitruvian Man*, 1492), the Baroque changes this perspective: death and morbid despair are ubiquitous, and mankind is deprived of its position at center stage. At the time of the religious wars, enchantment by the world is overshadowed by the knowledge of finitude. The hero of Grimmelshausen's book *Der abentheuerliche Simplicissimus Teutsch* (The Adventurous Simplicissimus, 1668) is thrown into a world of excessive violence, greed, and brutality, only to realize at the end of his *negative* education that every pursuit of prosperity is a vain illusion.

For the transcendent awareness of the epoch, everything worldly becomes deceptive and illusory. Nevertheless, it is not negated but becomes, due to a missing link to celestial transcendence, the object of an *increased curiosity*. Especially the protestant mourning play demonstrates this intensified curiosity in the context of excessive disenchantment, and it is to *this* literature that Benjamin devotes his attention. In the plays of Andreas Gryphius, for example in his *Leo Armenius* (1650), human history is not seen as a development; rather it is poetically depicted as finitude and futility. The failure of the play's characters is not caused by a tragic conflict, as in Greek tragedy; rather it happens with a somewhat transcendental necessity, because the striving for magnitude already entails the protagonist's downfall into perdition.

As one can see from this panoramic sketch, Benjamin's interest in the Baroque is embedded in the experience of a cultural predicament that he experienced as an intellectual and cultural philosopher of the Weimar Republic, but also of European modernity in general. This is evident throughout the book, for example when Benjamin studies weak "sovereigns" and powerful "intriguers," or when he unfolds a world experience detached from the eschatological hope for a final and divine affirmation of the world. Germany's defeat in the First World War and the failure of the first German republic transform the Baroque into a mirror-like era, where politics is doomed to fail and history emerges as *Naturgeschichte* (natural history): that is, as an anonymous process standing for the destruction of the Hegelian vision of World Spirit. With it allegory, as a key stylistic device of the Baroque, becomes a kind of "geschichts-philosophische Signatur" (historical-philosophical signature) of this era. On the one hand Benjamin sees in this figure of speech a breaking-apart between the "object" and its natural embeddedness in its world context, a split between signifier (form) and the signified (content, meaning). On the other hand, the *poetics of allegory* seems to give the Baroque poet, as Benjamin sees it, the possibility to put things permanently into new and heterogeneous arrangements. This heterogeneity and this *mise en scène* of the break of signification affect the Baroque but also a modern diction like the one typical of Benjamin's thinking. Benjamin presents the Baroque in a constellation of "erstarrte Unruhe" (petrified unrest) that takes form through his own restless diction, which breaks with a linear structure of thought in favor of assessments in sidesteps, fragments, and detours. This also makes explicit the modernity of the *Trauerspiel* book and its relation to postmodern thought. As is well known nowadays, postmodernity values the fragment over its totalizing *idea,* the discontinuity of history over a universal process, the particular discourse over an "ideal speech community." Especially the philosophy of the second half of the twentieth century takes up models that were developed by Benjamin no less than half a century before. Therefore it is not surprising that Paul de Man borrowed from Benjamin's *Trauerspiel* book the idea that allegory was bound to the law of non-correspondence and differentiality.[6] The allegorical sign always refers to another sign, never to the core of its own meaning. That means that the language of allegory leads — according to Benjamin and de Man — to the self-revocation of its enunciation.

Still, one can be tempted to describe Benjamin's diction as a kind of post-metaphysical mysticism (Bertolt Brecht),[7] a term that can be especially applied to the *Erkenntniskritische Vorrede* (Epistemo-Critical Prologue) and its cabalistic movements of thought. Nevertheless it is obvious that the *Trauerspiel* book (as opposed, for example, to the essays "Der Erzähler: Betrachtungen zum Werk Nikolai Lesskows" ["The Storyteller: Observations on the Works of Nikolai Leskov," 1936] and "Das Kunstwerk im Zeitalter seiner technischen Reproduzierbarkeit" ["The Work of Art in the Age of Its Technological Reproducibility," 1939]) has not yet been exhausted by interpretation. As is manifest throughout the reception of the book in the broad field of *cultural studies,* it can always be newly discovered despite, but probably even more *because,* of the fact that "it is excessively difficult to read."

The Epistemo-Critical Prologue: A Negative Theology of Perception

The epistemo-critical prologue introduces the reader to the *Trauerspiel* book and presents in the form of a philosophical-theological *tractatus* Benjamin's way of thinking, a thinking that progresses more in fractions and diversions than in classical dialectical deductions. The text is not an introduction to the Baroque. It sees its goal rather in inserting the reader into the context of Benjamin's epistemological assumptions. With it Benjamin refers back deliberately to notions like the Platonic "idea" or the Leibnizian "monad." Both carry a heavy philosophical heritage, associated with an occidental understanding of philosophy as a *Lehre vom Sein* (doctrine of being). In a way Benjamin does not care much about this philosophical burden. He takes these notions with an almost naive carelessness and transforms them into cornerstones of his *tractatus.* The epistemo-critical prologue stands as a continuation of Benjamin's reflections of his *philosophy of language,* which he had worked on before, particularly in the twenties. In the first years after his dissertation *Der Begriff der Kunstkritik in der deutschen Romantik* (The Concept of Criticism in German Romanticism, 1920) Benjamin wanted to write his postdoctoral thesis in the field of the philosophy of language. In a letter to Gershom Scholem he wrote that he hoped, with regard to this field of investigation, to find inspiring literature in the area of scholastic writings or in the period of scholasticism (*Briefe,* 230). Benjamin was affected by mystical traditions of language and hoped to find in them an opportunity to articulate experiences "die man synthetisch noch nicht darzustellen wüßte" (*Briefe,* 259; that could not yet be represented in synthetic ways). So the recourse to mystical traditions in the field of the philosophy of language can be understood as an experiment in developing a counter-discourse that directs itself against what Benjamin calls contemptuously the "philistine and idealistic"[8] academic epistemological activities. The prologue does not try to revive forms of uncritical, pre-Kantian metaphysics. Instead it reveals Benjamin's struggle to enlarge an undialectical and "bourgeois" notion of reason with metaphysical gestures of speech that reverberate in the words "monad" and "idea." One could even be tempted to say that Benjamin tries intentionally to stress and overburden the vault of intellectual (occidental) reason with these premodern terms of philosophy, in order to explore new lines of thought.

In 1924 he writes to Scholem: "Du wirst [in der Vorrede] seit der Arbeit 'Über Sprache überhaupt und über die Sprache des Menschen' zum ersten Male wieder so etwas wie einen erkenntnistheoretischen Versuch finden" (*Briefe*, 346–47; You will find [in the prologue] something like an epistemological essay for the first time again since my work "On Language as Such and on the Language of Man"). And after having finished the prologue, Benjamin writes: "Diese Einleitung ist eine maßlose Chuzpe — nämlich nicht mehr und nicht weniger als Prologomena zur Erkenntnistheorie" (*Briefe*, 372; This introduction is an excessive chutzpah — it is nothing less and nothing more than *prologomena* to a theory of cognition.) Of significance is, as mentioned before, the Platonic "idea." But in contrast to Plato, Benjamin tries to provide this term (which is traditionally associated with an abstract entity) with a new facet that takes into account, as Bernd Witte writes: "*history* . . . to a relevant degree."[9] Hence Benjamin converts the "idea" from a metaphysical and abstract notion into a model of an inductive procedure that starts from "historical fields of gravitation" (Winfried Menninghaus),[10] comprising constellations, which are considered more elusive than are static assemblages. In the elaboration of these never fixed or fixable "constellations" — which touch all kinds of different notions on which Benjamin will focus his attention: "melancholy," "honor," the "sovereign," or the "martyr" — it will become obvious that the visibility of these constellations does not lead the reader of the *Trauerspiel* book to clearly defined *classifications* of them, purified, so to speak, of historical arbitrariness. Benjamin says of these ideas/constellations that they are not "Inbegriffe von Regeln" (*GS* I.1:224; "simply the sum total of certain sets of rules," *Origin*, 44). They might even not be "einem jeden Drama . . . kommensurabel" (*GS* I.1:224; "to any and every drama . . . in a way commensurable," *Origin*, 44).[11] They make no claim "eine Anzahl gegebener Dichtungen auf Grund irgendwelcher Gemeinsamkeiten 'unter' sich zu begreifen" (*GS* I.1:224; "to embrace a number of given works of literature on the basis of certain features that are common to them," *Origin*, 44). By contrast, "ideas" become visible by constellations manifesting themselves through phenomena, but they cannot — through these same phenomena — be converted into propositional matter.[12] In a sense the notion of "idea" sends us back, as Menninghaus shows, to what Benjamin called in his early text "Über Sprache überhaupt und über die Sprache des Menschen" the "mental being," *das geistige Wesen,* of language. This "mental being" cannot be communicated *through* language, only *in* language. Peter Fenves notes that Benjamin, along with Gershom Scholem, says that there are two ways to truth — that is, metaphysical truth.[13] One of these ways is mathematical. The other is linguistic. The question is, are ideas given mathematically as Plato describes it in his simile of the divided line, or are they given in language? Plato's simile of the divided line — as it is described in book six of "The Republic" — is intended to clarify how the things we experience in the ordinary sensible world are less real than the ideal models (forms) which they rely on for their existence. Mathematics for Plato is, as it were, "more real" because it divests itself of the arbitrariness of human history and of language. Benjamin takes the opposite stance when he focuses on the inner intentions of language. In the *Trauerspiel* book truth is for Benjamin obviously linguistic and bound to the *way of meaning* (*die Art des Meinens*) of language. This does not refer to an external metaphysical substance, but to a metaphysical content *in* language, in its *folds,* as Gilles Deleuze later says in his book on Leibniz.[14] The French philosopher notes that for Leibniz the seemingly chaotic order of the world is always incorporated in a higher, superior order, an order, as Erich Kleinschmidt notes, whose "*foldings*" must be recognized.[15] Consequently every rational thought is in relation to what Deleuze calls "unthought," that is, making unthought therefore not external to thought but being folded into its very heart. The *fold* thus serves as a powerful symbol for overcoming the otherwise incompatible dualisms between rational and non-rational — or cognitive and precognitive — thinking, or any of the binary opposites for that matter. As Kleinschmidt shows, like Benjamin, Baroque culture is based essentially on a *reading-knowledge* (*Lesewissen*) that is marked by allegory and that functions free from principles of scientific causality (without eliminating these principles). This merges into a "formation of memory . . . whose 'implicative' foldings determine the associated assignments. A humanistic, allegory-based poetics of reference with its doctrine of signature [Signaturlehre] based on resemblance gains in the more complex context of the philosophy of the 17th century a cosmogonical significance."[16] In this sense, as Kleinschmidt says, the prologue can be called a "Verweisungspoetik" (poetic treatise of referentiality). By going back to the *tractatus* and its "Kunst des Absetzens im Gegensatz zur Kette der Deduktion" (*GS* I.1:212; "art of interruption in contrast to the chain of deduction," *Origin,* 32) Benjamin tries to take into account epistemic conceptions that are compatible with modernity, where all *that is solid [in a pre-modern world] melts into air* (Marx). In the *Vorrede* Benjamin wants to give a method to what for him is *Kunstphilosophie,* a working toward the truth via digression, marking new beginnings, returning in a roundabout way to its original object. The text is thus like a mosaic: a "Stückelung in kapriziöse Teilchen" (*GS* I.1:208; "fragmentation into capricious particles," *Origin* 28) that are distinct and disparate. Therefore the prologue explains that it is impossible for traditional criticism to go back in time and to take an epoch as an abstract, clear observable object of inspection. The *Trauerspiel* book lays bare what in the language of the mourning play comes to pass without being objectifiable *through* language. As Benjamin writes in "Trauerspiel und Tragödie" ("Mourning Play and Tragedy," 1916) the "idea" remains something that is "ein empirisches Unbestimmtes" (*GS* II.1:134; "something indeterminate empirically," *SW* 1:55) without being a metaphysical *abstractum* beyond language. The idea can — as a determining force — not be captured or reassembled by any empirical event, because it develops itself always in a *web of folds* and constellations.

Another notion of central importance in the *Vorrede* is the "monad," whose theoretical framework we have already mentioned with references to Leibniz and Deleuze. "Die Idee ist Monade" (*GS* I.1:228; "The idea is a monad," *Origin*, 48). With this perplexing equation he does not want to transform the monad into a transcendent category. Rather, he continues to pursue his goal of transforming epistemologically the "idea" into a world-*immanent* measure. With this thought he develops the picture of a world extended in never-ending foldings of pure immanence. In analogy to this he speaks of a limitless "Vertiefung der historischen Perspektive . . . ins Vergangene oder ins Künftige" (*GS* I.1:228; "investigations . . . that can be extended, into the past or future," *Origin*, 47) without being subject to any limits of principle. This gives the idea "das Totale" (*GS* I.1, 228; "its total scope," *Origin*, 47). That means that the idea is not "total" where it is untouched by historical arbitrariness and where it rules as a prototype for mimetic participation in a divine realm of entities, but it is "total," that is, marked by "totality" where it appears in concrete historical reference to the world and to history, a reference that does not — strictly speaking — know completion but progresses in foldings over time and also over the borders of scientific disciplines. This explains why Benjamin oversteps the margins of literary theory and creates a web of connections with political theory, art history, and metaphysics that touch both modernity and Baroque alike. The monad is his medium. It is not an intrinsic singularity, but, as Deleuze says about the fold, "[an] ambiguous sign"[17] exemplified across disciplines, as he points out in his own philosophy.[18] Under the guise of this ambiguous sign, "we go from fold to fold and not from point to point . . . There remains the latitude to always add a detour by making each interval the site of a new folding . . . Transformation [is] deferred . . . : the line effectively folds into a spiral."[19] The fact that the monad is closed and wrapped into itself means that with every monad there can be an incessantly new beginning, a new process of folding. In the same sense the monad sends us back to Benjamin's concept of "Ursprung," which stands "im Fluß des Werdens als Strudel und reißt in seine Rhythmik das Entstehungsmaterial hinein" (*GS* I.1:226; "[as] stream of becoming, and in its current it swallows the material involved in the process of genesis," *Origin*, 45). *Ursprung* is an Ur-*Sprung*, a leap, an offspring.[20] It does not stand for a first source (*Quelle*), or for a first logical category, but for a historical one (*GS* I.1:226; *Origin*, 46).

The idea as monad depicts an immanent dimension of historical relations. This essentially concerns not only the allegory as a key figure of Baroque literature that can unfold never-endingly into something new (the allegory has "lost" the force of the symbol to articulate stable signification), but it also concerns as pure immanence the loss of transcendence that is responsible for a basic mood of Baroque melancholy.

Baroque Mourning Play versus Greek Tragedy

In the middle of the first chapter of the *Trauerspiel* book Benjamin compares Greek tragedy and the Baroque mourning play; he contradicts the thesis that the mourning play could be put in a univocal affiliation with the former. He confutes this thesis through an analysis of the tragic itself, with the aim of interpreting the concept of mourning. He turns down the attempt to define tragedy as a timeless and ideal art form, which was the practice subsequent to Aristotle's *Poetics*. Instead he starts from the historical conditionality of tragedy and synthesizes a variety of theories by Ulrich von Wilamowitz-Moellendorff, Franz Rosenzweig, and Friedrich Nietzsche, but which he too had already drafted out in "Trauerspiel und Tragödie."

As is well known, the classical tragedy has its beginning in the Greek lyric of the dithyramb. But, as Hegel revealed, tragedy announces at the same time the downfall of the mythical world that is its indispensable background. The tragic hero is crucial in this first stage of a process of secularization, because he comes onstage as a challenger of the polytheistic cosmos, incorporating two decisive qualities: his "Trotz" (defiance) that repudiates an all-too-easy surrender to his destiny (that is, the providence assigned for him by the gods), and his "Schweigen" (speechlessness) that accompanies his tragic end. Franz Rosenzweig interprets this "speechlessness" in his book *Der Stern der Erlösung* (The Star of Redemption, 1921), which Benjamin cites several times. The "speechlessness" of the tragic hero transforms itself into a silent accusation. He overcomes his mythical destiny by manifesting through his "speechlessness" an inner repudiation of the divine world-order that before him was never put into question. But, on the other hand, he still confirms this mythical world even through his denial and hostile rejection and hence cannot break its rule entirely. Consequently his death is deeply ambiguous: it is announced as a new kind of human selfconsciousness, but the mythical order still lives on. In tragedy the human being becomes conscious that he is morally superior to his gods, but this knowledge cuts his voice. In combination with this thought the death of the hero is interpreted as a "sacrifice" that is given in favor of a *coming community*. While the tragic hero is still obliged to live under the demonic ambiguity of the myth, a new promise reverberates in his perdition, a promise to a coming community that might, one day, be freed from living exposed to mythic violence. What the tragic hero at the same time asserts against the mythical world is therefore the principle of individuation that he embodies, "a principle that challenges the multiplicity and ambiguity of the existing, mythical order."[21] Benjamin writes that "das alte Recht der Olympischen" (*GS* I.1:285; "the ancient rights of the Olympians," *Origin*, 107) is shattered through this half-sacrificial, half-tragic death, and that the coming of the "unbekannten Gott" (*GS* I.1:286; "the unknown god," *Origin*, 107) as the first fruit of a still-unborn harvest of humanity is proclaimed.

Benjamin puts tragedy and mourning play in relation before the background of his conceptualization of messianic time. "Tragedy has something to do with messianic time, not so the *Trauerspiel*."[22] He first offers this distinction in "Trauerspiel und Tragödie," which he had written in 1916. The structure of time in tragedy is "messianic," not in a religious or biblical sense but in the sense of a kind of "fulfillment" that lies bare in the "speechlessness" and the failing of the tragic hero. The mourning play, by contrast, cannot commit itself to the belief in a fulfillment-through-perdition.[23] When the silent hero in Greek tragedy does not find words to articulate, his muteness "speaks" a fatal judgment over the "old order" of the mythical world: he does not understand it any more. "Die Schroffheit des heroischen Selbst" (*GS* I.1:289, "The forthrightness of the heroic self," *Origin*, 110) that shines through the silence is not a character trait "sondern geschichtsphilosophische Signatur des Helden" (*GS* I.1:289; "but the historical-philosophical signature of the hero," *Origin*, 110). The muteness becomes a speaking dismissal of the old order and a triumph of the self: the hero who *dares to dare* stands first of all as individual and as a principle of individuation in opposition to a polymorphous cosmos of gods. At the same time he stands also for the multiplicity of individuals in a future community that will be free from myth one day. That he is an almost modern individual, a forerunner of this community, can be seen from the fact that his fight for the community takes place in the arena of the theatre. When Benjamin compares the performance of the tragedy with a court procedure and a lawsuit, it is for him no longer the tragic hero who stands at the bar; now it is the Olympians themselves who are confronted with a judging audience that fills the rows of the amphitheatre. The silence of the hero reflects like a speaking force the judgment that the community enunciates over the myth.[24] In this sense the "speechlessness" is performative, "an *act of defiance*, even if it is not fully understood as such by the hero."[25] It is a significant void. The audience is raised to an authority that passes judgment on the myth in the way of a *non liquet* ("it is not clear"), meaning the juridical process is disputed and the verdict given by the jury is to be deferred to another day of trial.

Nonetheless the myth does not encounter its own death-bringing end in Greek tragedy. It finds it, according to Benjamin, in the dialogues of Socrates and at the same time in the development of occidental philosophy. The latter voids the sky populated by the gods in the course of a dialectical ascent through erudite conversation. "Im sterbenden Sokrates ist das Märtyrerdrama als Parodie der Tragödie entsprungen" (*GS* I.1:292; "The martyr-drama was born from the death of Socrates as a parody of tragedy," *Origin*, 113). Socrates shares death with the tragic hero. But the death that Socrates suffers through acceptance of the cup of hemlock is of a thoroughly different quality than the death of the tragic hero. The Socratic death is, as Benjamin suggests, "aller tragischen Bindung [entledigt]" (*GS* I.1:293; "free of all tragic association," *Origin*, 114). Socrates confronts his death almost with irony as "der beste, der tugendhafteste der Sterblichen" (*GS* I.1:293; "the best and most virtuous of mortals," *Origin*, 114). But especially his moral and virtuous strength shows that this same virtue no longer knows the former arbitrary terror of the gods. For the tragic hero, death was not the beginning of *real reality*. He shrinks when confronted with death. Thus Benjamin can declare that the tragic hero is in a way "seellos" (*GS* I.1:293; "soulless," *Origin*, 114). We still cannot assign to him different parts of the soul, as Plato does in his dialog *Phaedrus*, that rise to an ethereal sky.

The mourning play stands in radical contrast to tragedy. As we saw in regard to tragedy, the speechlessness of the hero announced the beginning of a new era, a rupture with a cyclic mythical time and the beginning of "history" as a successive chain of localizable events. In the mourning play, by contrast, "[die] Folge der dramatischen Aktionen" (*GS* I.1:270; "[the] sequence of dramatic actions," *Origin*, 91) continues "wie in den Schöpfungstagen . . . , da Geschichte sich [nicht] ereignete" (*GS* I.1:270; "as in the days of creation, when it was not history which was taking place," *Origin*, 91). When Benjamin writes immediately after this statement that "Geschichte wandert in den Schauplatz [des barocken Trauerspiels] hinein" (*GS* I.1:271; "history merges into the setting [of the Baroque Trauerspiel]," *Origin*, 92), he means history as "Säkularisierung des Historischen" (*GS* I.1:271; "secularisation of the historical," *Origin*, 92). The mourning play is therefore very much caged in history, but in history that lapses back into a *Naturgeschichte* (*history of nature*). In the Protestant mourning play history becomes part of a fallen world. Instead of "heroes," the audience encounters human beings in the guise of "creatures," *Kreaturen*. For Benjamin, German Protestantism is responsible for this shift in perspective, especially where the latter, after having devalued the impact of "good works" in a divine creation, makes the salvation of the individual soul of the faithful dependent on belief, which was bestowed by an act of a God who almost arbitrarily distributes his "Gnade des Glaubens" (*GS* I.1:317; "grace through faith," *Origin*, 138) and makes the "weltlich-staatlichen Bereich zur Probestatt eines religiös nur mittelbaren . . . Lebens" (*GS* I.1:317; "secular-political sphere a testing ground for a life which was only indirectly religious," *Origin*, 138). With this, admittedly, Protestantism has instilled "im Volke . . . den strengen Pflichtgehorsam [. . .], in seinen Großen aber den Trübsinn" (*GS* I.1:317; "into the people a strict sense of obedience to duty but in its great men it produces melancholy," *Origin*, 138). With the devaluation of "good works," human actions are deprived of any kind of magnitude at all. "Etwas Neues entstand: eine leere Welt" (*GS* I.1:317; "Something new arose: an empty world," *Origin*, 139).

The *Trauerspiel* no longer knows any "heroes." It drifts through history as if through an arbitrary world (but not through History). The creature "hält an der Welt [fest]" (*GS* I.1:246; "clings so tightly to [this] world," *Origin*, 66), almost animal-like with all four legs on the ground, whereas the Greek tragic hero even in his defeat can set himself upright against divine destiny. Therefore the figures of the mourning play find themselves in constellations rather than in situations. The stage is a setting (*Schauplatz*) and no longer a courtroom as in Greek tragedy. At the same time death in the mourning play is no longer the climax/highlight of an interiority in a process of individuation. Instead it is marked by "vehemente[r] Äußerlichkeit" (*GS* I.1:315; "drastic externality," *Origin*, 137). In the mourning play it takes the form of a communal fate. The mourning play is conceptualized for repetition. It puts the lamentations of the creature "halb nur bearbeitet zu den Akten" (*GS* I.1:316; "only partly dealt with [aside]," *Origin*, 137). "Die Wiederaufnahme ist im Trauerspiel angelegt und bisweilen aus ihrer Latenz getreten" (*GS* I.1:316; "resumption is implicit in the *Trauerspiel* [mourning play], and sometimes it actually emerges from its latent state," *Origin*, 137).

Together with the notion of destiny, another notion of central importance is revealed. In the Protestant mourning play destiny is seen as "die elementare Naturgewalt im historischen Geschehen" (*GS* I.1:308; "the elemental force of nature in historical events," *Origin*, 129) which are not themselves entirely nature "weil noch der Schöpfungsstand die Gnadensonne widerstrahlt" (*GS* I.1:308; "because the light of grace is still reflected from the state of creation," *Origin*, 129). As Benjamin explains in "Schicksal und Charakter" ("Fate and Character"), in the context of ancient myth destiny was seen as a *Schuldzusammenhang des Lebendigen* (*GS* II.1:175; "guilt context of the living," *SW* 1:204). In the spirit of the restoration theology of the Counter-Reformation it now appears as the prehistoric sin that precedes every understanding of individual and moral misconduct. Destiny leads to death and confirms the "Verfallenheit des verschuldeten Lebens an das Gesetz des natürlichen" (*GS* I.1:310; "the subjection of guilty life to the law of natural life," *Origin*, 131). While the tragic hero breaks through the mythical cycle of time by individuating himself in his defeat, man in the mourning play is part of a repeatable process. All elements of the mourning play point to the fact that fate is now "die wahre Ordnung der ewigen Wiederkunft" (*GS* I.1:313; "the true order of eternal recurrence," *Origin*, 135). It "can only be described as temporal in an indirect, that is, parasitical sense" (*GS* I.1:313; *Origin*, 135). Whereas tragedy is completely released "von der Dingwelt" (*GS* I.1:312; "from the world of things," *Origin*, 134), in the mourning play this world of things "ragt . . . übern Horizont . . . beklemmend" (*GS* I.1:312; "towers oppressively over the horizon," *Origin*, 134). Because of this condition, the "world of things" becomes almost intrusive through its stage props. As props, inanimate things rule the events that take place in the setting.

Mourning and Melancholy

Benjamin concludes the first part of his *Trauerspiel* book with a treatise on melancholy, focusing his comments on the copperplate engraving *Melencolia I* by Albrecht Dürer and two art-historical treatises on it by the German scholars Karl Giehlow and Erwin Panofsky in cooperation with Fritz Saxl. They published their works in 1904 and 1923.[26] As will become come clearer below, Benjamin's annotations to this engraving and his concept of melancholy stand in a direct relation to the allegory as a Baroque stylistic device that no longer refers to a signification "inside the representation" — the way it did (according to Michel Foucault)[27] in the "classical" sign. Allegory is rather marked by outward appearance and pure externality. Melancholy mourns this externality and consequently a world that has become devoid of determinate sense, where "das Eidos verlischt" (*GS* I.1:352; "the *eidos* disappears," *Origin*, 176) and where nothing is left except "[die] dürren rebus, die bleiben [und in denen] Einsicht [liegt], die noch dem verworrenen Grübler greifbar ist" (*GS* I.1:352; "the dry rebuses which remain contain an insight, which is still available to the confused investigator," *Origin*, 176). The act of allegorical signification is seen here as a "deflation" of a profane world, and melancholy protests against and opposes a "Dasein als . . . ein Trümmerfeld halber, unechter Handlungen" (*GS* I:318; "existence as a rubbish heap of partial, inauthentic actions," *Origin*, 139). In doing so, the sentiment of mourning resists the psychology of an inner emotion as well. The mourning play does not evoke a "cathartic" feeling of an inside convulsion. "Mourning" in the word *Trauer*-Spiel rather represents a play in front of the mournful spectators (*GS* I.1:298; *Origin*, 119). It is not a play that *renders* the audience sorrowful or that captures it in a psychological and emotional way. The mourning play is characterized by "ostentation" (*GS* I.1:298; *Origin*, 119). "Ihre Bilder sind gestellt, um gesehen zu werden" (*GS* I.1:298; "[The] images [of the mourning play] are displayed in order to be seen, arranged in a way they want them to be seen," *Origin*, 119). However, the pictures in the setting, i.e. the stage props, resemble the objects that are lying scattered around Dürer's angel in *Melencolia I*. These are not placed on the floor to be taken up as utensils for future pursuits. Instead, Dürer's angel contemplates them. For Benjamin, this engraving antici-pates the Baroque in various ways (*GS* I.1:319; *Origin* 140). The instru-ments that are scattered around the angel lie there in an unused state as objects for contemplation (*GS* I.1:319; *Origin*, 140). They are stripped of practical utility and become allegories of melancholy so that they have to be encoded now and read while the melancholic viewer loses himself in gazing at them. In the melancholic gaze the object is devalued and becomes "rätselhafte Wahrheit" (*GS* I.1:319; "a symbol of some enig-matic wisdom," *Origin*, 140).

In Dürer's angel, modern brooding and scholarly investigation are announced. The scholar transforms the world into the "book of nature" (*GS* I.1:320; *Origin*, 141), in the sense of an enigmatic, riddle-like scrip-ture that must be unfolded in a never-ending manner: "Die Renaissance durchforscht den Weltraum, das Barock die Bibliotheken" (*GS* I.1:319; "The Renaissance explores the universe; the Baroque explores libraries," *Origin*, 140). One effect is an interrelation of melancholic gaze and the allegorical written word.[28] *Acedia*, considered in Christian ethics to be a mortal sin, is "pathologische . . . Verfassung, in welcher jedes unschein-barste Ding . . . als Chiffer einer rätselhaften Weisheit auftritt" (*GS* I.1:319; "a pathological state, in which the most simple object appears to be a symbol of some enigmatic wisdom," *Origin*, 140). Things no longer refer to a practical engagement, in the sense of being "ready to hand" (Heidegger speaks of *Zuhandenheit*). As emblems they stand for some-thing else whose absence they designate. Whereas Sigmund Freud defined melancholy in his text *Mourning and Melancholy* (1917) as a grieving that is not ready yet to remove emotions from the dead, and that is character-ized by a problematic relation to the object, for Benjamin melancholy becomes a paradigm that does not yield a "straightforward compensa-tion"[29] for the dead object. Melancholy describes an attitude of perceiving the world in a state of permanent self-reflection. This motive is explained with reference to *Hamlet*. Shakespeare's prince of Denmark is not only an actor onstage *for the audience,* but in a certain way *for himself.* He is a self-reflecting observer or theater spectator of his own action[30] and as a result dissolves, as it were, the dramatic presence of represented stage action.[31] In *Hamlet* the spectacle becomes a "play" in which the audience is imbued with an attitude of self-reflection. That is why melancholy on an existential level refuses what allegory refuses in language: the integration into a wholeness that is associated with an aesthetics of the symbol. The stone-like physicality that Dürer gives his angel and in which the "Tiefsinn" (pensiveness) of the angel transforms itself to "Gravität" (*GS* I.1:319; "gravity," *Origin*, 140), is not comparable to the symbolic beauty of the German classical period, where the beautiful ascends like a feather "bruchlos ins Göttliche" (*GS* I.1:337; "[into the realm of] the divine [as] in an unbroken whole," *Origin*, 160, translation modified). The "Grübeln" (brooding) equals a founding in and a "Depersonalisation" (*GS* I.1:319; "depersonalization," *Origin*, 140), through which the pensive person dissolves in a world of things. And yet, following an interpretation by Florens Christian Rang, Benjamin confirms a significant difference between the melancholy of the Baroque mourning play and the melancholy of *Hamlet*, when he maintains that "[allein] Shakespeare vermochte [es,] aus der barocken, unstoischen wie unchristlichen . . . Starre des Melancholikers den christlichen Funken zu schlagen" (*GS* I.1:335; "only Shakespeare was capable of striking Christian sparks from the Baroque rigidity of the melancholic, un-stoic as it is un-Christian," *Origin*, 158). With this Benjamin refers back to a "playful" handling of Hamlet, a playfulness he misses in the German mourning play. In contrast to *Hamlet*, the German mourning play "[blieb sich] selbst erstaunlich dunkel" (*GS* I.1:335; "remained astonishingly obscure to itself," *Origin*, 158).

Allegories and Dead Things

Probably the most-cited and most interpreted section of the *Trauerspiel* book is Benjamin's analysis of Baroque allegory. It accompanies his entire theory of modernity with an impact that reverberates in his interpretations of the works of Baudelaire and Proust.[32] For Benjamin it is especially in the area of allegory that the German Baroque can stand up to the German classical period, an honor that has hitherto been given, as Benjamin stresses, only to Romanticism (*GS* I.1:352; *Origin*, 176). Hence Benjamin responds to prejudices that limit the Baroque to a preliminary stage of German classicism and that discard the suggestion that an aesthetic evaluation of the Baroque would be worth the effort. Even when Benjamin consequently acknowledges that the Baroque achieved its only and singular mastery in the theatre plays of the Spanish Golden Age, he nevertheless shows how — with allegory — a figure of speech enters the history of European literature whose importance is not only equal to, but even surpasses, the symbol. The explicit anti-humanistic and premodern moments in allegory elucidate why it (and not the symbol) regains prominent position in the works of Baudelaire and Proust.[33] Of importance for Benjamin's statements is the inability of classicism "Unvollendung und Gebrochenheit . . . zu gewahren" (*GS* I.1:352; "to behold . . . the imperfection, the collapse of the physical," *Origin,* 176). Winckelmann, with his veneration of Greek sculpture, saw in the symbol the "höchste 'Fülle des Wesens'" (*GS* I.1:341; "highest 'fullness of being,'" *Origin,* 164), that is, a figure of speech that incorporates a knowledge of the absolute, an almost divine or cosmic plenitude. Humankind was the accomplishment of creation, and the individual was invited to perfect this fulfillment through the ideal of *Bildung.* Such an ideal was spiritually akin to the symbol and an image of a world ruled by wholeness and harmony. The artwork and the artist stood for a symbolic totality in the same way that humanism worshipped *human*kind as the top of the chain of beings. This explains why Goethe saw in allegory only a low-grade artistic technique. Schopenhauer saw in it only the expression of a concept (*GS* I.1:338; *Origin,* 161), while the symbol was for him the carrier of an "idea" (*GS* I.1:338; *Origin,* 161). The "*art* of the symbol" stood in contrast to the mere "technique" of allegory. This view dominated the aesthetic coordinates of the classical period. Benjamin by contrast insists on the independent expertise that the Baroque allegory incorporates. The repudiation of signification is what gives the allegory its delicate and elusive tenseness. While the symbol incorporates "das Momentane, das Totale" (*GS* I.1:340; "the momentary, the total," *Origin,* 163) allegory incorporates a discontinuous series of void moments, a sequence of "failed" representations. It brings life and credence to historical experiences that for the symbol seem to be without weight: the experience of the outdated, the grief-stricken and unsuccessful — in brief, all that cannot be put into relation with the wooing of a resplendent knowledge of the absolute. Allegory grants these unsuccessful and "creaturely" elements of human existence "justice" by rejecting meaningful unity: "Produktion der Leiche ist, vom Tode her betrachtet, das Leben" (*GS* I.1:392; "Seen from the point of view of death, the product of the corpse is life," *Origin,* 218). Consequently Benjamin, by rehabilitating allegory, also criticizes the symbol as an incorporation of optimism that through features like timelessness and perfection regains access into the mentality of nineteenth-century positivism.

Benjamin makes allegory a historical signature of an epoch. He does not want to know what a particular allegory signifies. In his review of Hans Heckel's *History of German Literature in Silesia,* he does not want to know "ob sie beim einen aufrichtiger, psychologisch vertiefter, entschuldbarer, formvollendeter als beim anderen sind" (*GS* III:192; whether in the work of one author it is more authentic, psychologically deeper, more justifiable, more perfect than in the work of another). He wants to know: "Was sind sie selbst? Was spricht aus Ihnen? Warum mußten sie sich einstellen?" (*GS* III:192; What are they of themselves? What is speaking through them? Why did they have to come to mind?) With these claims Benjamin remains on the path of his early texts on language, where he engaged in analyzing its "magical" and physiognomic dimension aside from its verbal propositional content. Similarly, in his analysis of the mourning play he looks for a shaping principle that manifests itself, like an "idea," from combined and determining historical forces. The notion of the "idea" refers — as we have already seen in relation to the prologue — not to a Platonic heaven composed of abstract entities but to historical potentials as gravitational fields that are not maneuvered or influenced by the human subject. The "idea" does not designate an item in an individual allegory but belongs to a "grundsätzlich anderen Bereich . . . als das von ihr Erfaßte" (*GS* I.1:214; "fundamentally different world from that which it apprehends," *Origin*, 34). As Heymann Steinthal says, Benjamin inspects what takes place in language without defining this movement of language as a segregated "content" of language.[34] The "idea" appears as a shaping force only *in* phenomena, not beyond them. The "Allegorisierung der Physis" (*GS* I.1:391–92; "allegorization of the physis [i.e. of 'natural things']," *Origin*, 217), the way it is expressed in the dead body but also in "scenes of cruelty and anguish" (*GS* I.1:389; *Origin*, 216) is therefore of structural nature and not a leitmotif. "Die Personen des Trauerspiels sterben, weil sie nur so, als Leichen, in die allegorische Heimat eingehen" (*GS* I.1:391; "The characters of the *Trauerspiel* die, because it is only thus, as corpses, that they can enter into the homeland of allegory," *Origin*, 217).

The definitions of the allegory, as the German classical period conceptualized them, saw in it only an arbitrary sign. For Benjamin it will become the essence to be recovered or redeemed, as he writes in a letter to Scholem in 1924 (*GS* I.3:881). While in the symbol the relation between sign (sound, the written word) and signification (content, referent) is based on an original link between these two elements; this link, which warrants a fixable content of signification, breaks down in allegory.[35] One effect is that the "content" melts into nothing. If we take in combination with this statement Karl Marx's diagnosis of modernity: "Alles Ständische und Stehende verdampft"[36] (all that is solid melts into air) one can understand why in the writings of Baudelaire and Proust Benjamin rediscovers the allegory as a primordial stylistic device of modernity.

Even ancient rhetoric referred to a tension between sign and signification, and it is this that Benjamin takes up as the particular nature of the allegory in the Baroque mourning play. Benjamin interprets the allegorically visualized transitoriness of worldly things as an allegorical sign[37] that can even signify the contrary of itself. "Any person, any object, any relationship can mean absolutely anything else" (*GS* I.1:350; *Origin*, 175).[38] Allegory refers as an emblem, auto-poetically, *to its own referentiality,* a referentiality that cannot be decoded on the side of signification. The significations do not keep their concrete meaning in dialogue but replace one another mutually. Instead of being "effaced" and "stopped" by concrete signification, the allegorical image remains vivid in this play and counterplay of meaning with the result that the allegorical image unfolds "ein erregendes Spiel" (*GS* I.1:352; "a stirring game," *Origin,* 176) and metamorphosis itself becomes the "scheme" (*GS* I.1:403; *Origin,* 229) of the epoch. In the same way that allegory unfolds *ad infinitum* by new "folding," the Baroque comprises also the experience of an infinitely pleated human *soul* (Leibniz). Grimmelshausen's character "Baldanders" ["soon different"] in his picaresque novel *Der abentheuerliche Simplicissimus Teutsch* can be seen in this context as a Baroque figure of perpetual transformation and metamorphosis.

The possibility of seeing in this never-ending "folding" a positive process of continuous creativity (and not only a loss of eternal knowledge) is endorsed by the philosophy of Gilles Deleuze and his postmodern adaptation of Leibniz's philosophy. The radical immanence of Deleuze's philosophy (which in a way opposes Benjamin's profound messianic and theological thinking) opts for an unending creative process through which reality — because of its being detached from Platonic ideastic prefigurations — is seen as a virtual sphere of permanent mutation. In a Deleuzian perspective Benjamin's allegorist would no longer possess a melancholic temper, mourning the loss of metaphysical eschatology and a world devoid of stable signs, but would be a Proust-like artist of always-new creation that arises out of the infinitude of world-immanent signifying procedures.[39] The entire world, for Deleuze, is "pure virtuality." It exists and creates itself anew also in the "folds of the soul,"[40] similar to a text that keeps on writing without being written (by an autonomous mind). The monad is for him, as it is for Leibniz and Benjamin, an individual unit of microcosmic quality. It cannot be divided any further. The monad as *self* (or *soul,* as Leibniz says) folds, unfolds, *and folds again* time, matter, and space. It represents infinity in a finite way. The world must have its place in the subject so that the subject can be *for the world,* as Deleuze accentuates. The monadic subject exists as a "being-for-the-world" and is distinguished from the rest of his surroundings by his "virtuality" and his joy in creation. The engendering of virtual worlds is not one activity among other activities but it is what human liveliness for Deleuze is all about. Therefore it is of importance that the monad is "windowless," because being closed in itself and folded onto itself is the condition of perpetual new beginnings. The virtual *life as art* of the monad is an inventive behavior that brings about worlds of different facets. Common to them is the fact that they are all transitory and finite and identify themselves only through their realization. In the Baroque era however, the optimism of a Deleuzian immanence is viewed negatively as being distant from God's plenitude, because the era still lacks an Enlightenment marked by Spinozism and an extrication of the human being from the Christian-Protestant superstructure. But, as we have already mentioned, Benjamin, too, views radical immanence negatively as *distance.* This becomes obvious, for example, when in his text "Über einige Motive bei Baudelaire" (*GS* I.2:640–43; ("On Some Motifs in Baudelaire," 1939: *SW* 4:334–36) he criticizes Proust's writing as a private and restorative affair that lacks insight into the importance of salvation as a *collective* matter. This hope remains bound to Benjamin's religious belief. Otherwise his use of messianic Jewish eschatology would remain mere play.

The Fragment and the Ruin

The allegorical object is a particle, an isolated fragment. And, as Benjamin says, only "die amorphen Einzelheiten" (*GS* I.1:361; "the amorphous details," *Origin,* 185) can be understood allegorically. The allegories of the Baroque mourning play stand as fragments for *a signifying* activity, but they do not "say" what they signify in concrete terms. They are not equivalent to a *quidditas* of signification when we take into account that for Aquinas the term *quidditas* refers to a formal determination of a thing, its *essentia.* The Baroque allegories are "im Reiche der Gedanken was Ruinen im Reich der Dinge" (*GS* I.1:354; "in the realm of thoughts, what ruins are in the realm of things," *Origin,* 178). This explains the Baroque cult of the ruin. Presenting pale corpses, chopped-off heads, and tankards filled with blood, the mourning play prepares the setting for the sphere of transcendence. On the one hand, allegory has the power to save the transitory; on the other hand, it can only perform this saving act when everything vital has been decimated beforehand. The ruin is the most illustrative example for the allegorical appearance of the mourning play. It illustrates the conception of history as what Gryphius called "vergänglichkeit menschlicher sachen" (transitoriness of human things).[41] When one wrests the object that is used allegorically out of its life context, it becomes dead material. "Für das Trauerspiel des XVII. Jahrhunderts wird die Leiche oberstes emblematisches Requisit schlechthin" (*GS* I.1:392; "In the *Trauerspiel* of the seventeenth century the corpse becomes quite simply the preeminent emblematic property," *Origin,* 218).[42] The lifelessness of the body parts is indispensable, because "die Allegorisierung der Physis kann nur an der Leiche sich energisch durchsetzen" (*GS* I.1:391; "the allegorization of the physis can only be carried through in all of its vigour in respect of the corpse," *Origin,* 217). When one particularity of allegorizing is the use of objects as signs of an arbitrary signification, it requires as a prerequisite the lifelessness of these same objects.[43] The object can attain signification only when it — as "dead material" — no longer incorporates a particular content. Only then can it attain signification in conformity to what the allegorist gives it. As Albrecht Schöne shows, the Baroque stage is filled with cadavers, pictures, crowns, and scepters. But they do not refer to *specific* kings, nor do the cadavers refer to specific individuals. They are not identified. "They belong as objects of contemplation really to the decor of the stage and reveal the theatre as . . . a 'showplace of mortality'"[44] The cadaver as stage prop stands not only for the mortality of the human being but also at the same time — as Schöne confirms — for an "Erstarren zum Schaubild" (*GS* I.1:406; "petrifying transformation into an icon/emblem" *Origin*, 232) that lasts. The more futile and death-obsessed the prop is, the more important the requirement of transcendence becomes, which announces itself particularly in the "death-signs of baroque" (*GS* I.1:406; *Origin*, 232). That is why Benjamin can say: "Das barocke Kunstwerk will nichts als dauern und klammert sich mit allen Organen ans Ewige" (*GS* I.1:356; "The baroque work of art wants only to endure and clings with all its senses to the eternal," *Origin*, 181).

I would like to mention here that there is at least one German author, W. G. Sebald, who in the second half of the twentieth century takes up the *Trauerspiel* book as a source of literary inspiration, and he does so in particular in reference to the fragment and the ruin.[45] Sebald transposes the Baroque into the cosmos of postmodern thought. The characters he presents in his novels stroll like Baroque melancholics through a world that stands in the shadow of Auschwitz as if under the ethereal influence of Saturn. The rings that surround Saturn — and that give the name to Sebald's novel *Die Ringe des Saturn* (1995) — are composed of meteorites that stand figuratively for debris-like landscapes of European history, European history in general, not only of the twentieth century. In this landscape Sebald exposes his protagonists, whose lives are shaped by a loss of belief in a worldly sense. That is why these characters feel an almost pathological need for ever-repeating confirmation of some kind of stability in the fragmentary objects that they find on their journeys through debris-like landscapes. What they find may be a railway ticket that Sebald pastes into his text, or a postcard, or a photograph. These objects inspire them to reconstruct lost wholeness.[46] But like the Baroque characters they do not attain the reconstruction of a homogeneous unity. For Benjamin the achievement of allegory was that it referred to a sense of life that rejected guaranteed reference and that submitted life to an undismissable rhythm of "natural history" (*GS* I.1:358). It was in this view of life that Benjamin recognized the moment of melancholy in the Baroque allegory.[47] The objects (for example, photographs and so on) that Sebald presents in his novel *The Rings of Saturn* possess allegorical character in the same sense. But whereas Sebald presents collected objects (photos, stamps, and so on) in his novels *Austerlitz* (2001) and *Die Immigranten* (The Emigrants, 1992) like traces of individual human destinies with the aim of reconstructing individual lives, the collected objects in *The Rings of Saturn* become much more arbitrary. Moreover, Sebald is now concerned with the history of *humankind* in general and no longer with individual histories of some *emigrants*. His narrator refers us to an "experience of irremediable exposure to the violence of history, the rise and fall of empires and orders of meaning, the endless cycle of struggles for hegemony."[48] The fragments that Sebald's protagonist in *The Rings of Saturn* picks up on his way through desolate landscapes with bunkers and economically run-down cities are void of eschatology.

Sovereign and Martyr

The sovereign, along with the intriguer, is one of the main characters of the Baroque mourning play. He is the "erster Exponent der Geschichte" (*GS* I.1:243; "principle exponent of history," *Origin*, 62), almost its incarnation. In him the relation to history represents itself as *natural history*. If his real/physical body is visible, fragile, and mortal, then his symbolical body is in a way immortal. His royal "Doppelnatur,"[49] which has been analyzed by Ernst Kantorowicz in his book *The King's Two Bodies*,[50] is suffused with an ambiguous conflict that concerns his sovereignty. As a protagonist of the mourning play he holds "das historische Geschehen in der Hand wie ein Szepter" (*GS* I.1:245; "the course of history in his hand like a scepter," *Origin*, 65) but is desperately weak at the same time. Benjamin's statements follow Carl Schmitt's theory of sovereignty.[51] Schmitt has argued that the power to decide the initiation of the state of emergency defines itself.[52] Now one could imagine that the Baroque sovereign might consolidate his royalty through the power that is attributed to his sovereign decision of proclaiming the state of emergency and that — as Schmitt shows — cites an almost divine-like act of creation *ex nihilo*. But the Baroque sovereign does not. *Angst* and melancholy undermine his ability to decide. Therefore, when Benjamin writes that the sovereign holds the course of history in his hand like a scepter, this does not rule out the following statement, which we find in *Leo Armenius:* "Wo scepter, da ist furcht!" (Where there is a scepter, there is fear). This statement applies to the political situation in which the Baroque sovereign finds himself: he is surrounded by enemies and intriguers and every night "mahlt ihm . . . Durch graue bilder vor, was er bey lichte dacht" (*GS* I.1:322; "depicts for him with grey pictures what he was thinking in daylight"). This description depicts the inner condition of the sovereign. He fails through his incapacity to decide. This inability is bound to the loss of an eschatological harmony, wherein he once, as god-chosen king, saw his god-approved life. But the historical actions of counts or earls do not claim any longer "in der Flucht des Heilsprozesses zu verlaufen" (*GS* I.1:257; "to be integrated in the process of redemption," *Origin*, 78). His decisions become arbitrary and degenerate to tyrannical and despotic acts that cannot claim responsibility. The sovereign does not provoke a new and divine beginning with his decision but, as an expression of dreary contingency, his rule degenerates into tyranny. The representative of the highest god-like decision is uncovered as "Herr der Kreaturen" (*GS* I.1:264; "lord of creatures," *Origin,* 85) without overcoming the state of creature himself. He remains a creature (*GS* I.1:264; *Origin,* 85). The inability to decide shines through his ever changing decisions. So the sovereign appears as anything but a sovereign. This marks the difference between Benjamin and Schmitt,[53] but it also explains the subversive twist of the sovereign into the martyr. As a "creature" — chased by his own decisions — he cannot be made responsible for the victims of his excesses. Hence Benjamin and Schmitt agree on the fact that the decision arises out of nothing, *ex nihilo.* But while Schmitt conceives of the sovereign decision in the context of a Christian *theology of salvation,* as a force that suspends one order to establish a new one, for Benjamin this thinking is not adaptable to the Baroque concept of sovereignty. The latter is no longer part of salvation but rather the continuation of the chaos of history as *Naturgeschichte.* The decision of the sovereign in the Baroque mourning play is arbitrary, even where it tries to place and inaugurate something new. Where history is seen as natural decay of the historical, and the sovereign does not surpass the state of the *creature* (as he does, for example, on the famous frontispiece of Hobbes's *Leviathan*), he can only then be the victim, and finally the martyr, of his own actions. With this in mind, Benjamin writes that the tyrant and the martyr are "die Janushäupter des Gekrönten" (*GS* I.1:249; "the two faces of the monarch," *Origin,* 69). This becomes evident in Gryphius's play when the dying tyrant Leo Arminius embraces and kisses the Christian cross. Even the death of a brutal despot includes features of the martyr-drama (*GS* I.1:250; *Origin,* 70).

An Open Conclusion

Benjamin combines genres that normally exclude one another: critical theory and artistic prose. And if we find this liminal, two-edged diction of his also in several smaller texts, it is particularly omnipresent in his *Trauerspiel* book, with the unfortunate effect we mentioned at the beginning: that it was not seen by the first generation of readers as an innovative artistic and academic masterpiece but as a provocation that ended Benjamin's academic career abruptly. The fact that the book is nevertheless "alive" is a consolation, at least for present readers. The border-crossing diction of the book makes it possible for these readers to enter the Baroque like a mosaic field without knowing exactly where they will exit from their investigative track and what they will find in the text and its folds. This chapter has tried to illuminate some areas in this multifaceted field. But if readers find more "folds" where this essay has tried to create a plane, wrinkle-free surface . . . all the better. As Benjamin says, it is the detail that is of importance, because like the Leibnizian monad it contains the universal and has the power to reorganize the field and open up our ability to discover new and unmapped territory.

Notes

1 The citation is taken from Burkhardt Lindner, "Habilitationsakte Benjamin: Über ein 'akademisches Trauerspiel' und über ein Vorkapitel der 'Frankfurter Schule,'" *Zeitschrift für Literaturwissenschaft und Linguistik* 14 (1984): 147–65. All translations are my own, unless otherwise attributed.

2 Bernd Witte, *Benjamin: Der Intellektuelle als Kritiker* (Stuttgart: Metzler, 1976), 107.

3 Benjamin in a letter to Max Rychner: 7 Mar. 1931, in Walter Benjamin, *Briefe*, ed. Gershom Scholem and Theodor W. Adorno, 2 vols. (Frankfurt am Main: Suhrkamp, 1966),523. Further references to this work will be given in the text using the title, *Briefe*, and the page number.

4 Beatrice Hanssen compares Benjamin's *Trauerspiel* book with Warburg and Panofsky in her "Portrait of Melancholy (Benjamin, Warburg, Panofsky)," *Modern Language Notes* 114.5 (1999): 991–1013.

5 Willy Haas, "Zwei Zeitdokumente wider Willen," *Die Literarische Welt* (16.4) Jahrgang 12 (1928): 1–2; Günther Müller, "Neue Arbeiten zur deutschen Barockliteratur," *Zeitschrift für Deutsche Bildung*, Jahrgang 6 (1930): 325–33.

6 Paul de Man, *The Rhetoric of Temporality* (Minneapolis: U of Minnesota P, 1983), 35.

7 Brecht writes in his *Arbeitsjournal*: "alles mystik bei einer haltung gegen mystik" ("all mysticism with an attitude against mysticism"). Bertolt Brecht, *Arbeitsjournal, 1938–1942* (Frankfurt am Main: Suhrkamp, 1993), 14.

8 Letter to Max Rychner, 7 Mar. 1931, in *Briefe*, 523.

9 Bernd Witte, *Benjamin: Der Intellektuelle als Kritiker* (Stuttgart: Metzler, 1976), 111.

10 Winfried Menninghaus, *Walter Benjamins Theorie der Sprachmagie* (Frankfurt am Main: Suhrkamp, 1980), 81.

11 The English translations of the *Trauerspiel* book are taken from *The Origin of German Tragic Drama*, trans. John Osborne (London: Verso 2003), abbreviated in the text as *Origin*.

12 Menninghaus, *Walter Benjamins Theorie der Sprachmagie*, 85.

13 Peter Fenves, "Of Philosophical Style — from Leibniz to Benjamin," *boundary 2* 30.1 (2003): 67–87.

14 Gilles Deleuze, *Le pli — Leibniz et le baroque* (Paris: Minuit, 1988). In English, *The Fold: Leibniz and the Baroque*, trans. Tom Conley (Minneapolis: U of Minnesota P, 1993).

15 Erich Kleinschmidt, "Faltungen. monadische Konstruktivität und barocke Ausdruckskultur," *Arcadia — Zeitschrift für Literaturwissenschaft* 41 (2006): 8.

16 "Gedächtnisformierung . . . deren 'implikative' Faltungen die assoziativen Zuordnungen bestimmen. Eine humanistische, allegorisch fundierte Verweisungspoetik mit ihrer noch auf Ähnlichkeit gegründeten Signaturenlehre gewinnt im komplexer entwickelten Philosophiekontext des 17. Jahrhunderts eine kosmogonische Leitsignatur" (Kleinschmidt, "Faltungen," 7).

[17] Deleuze, *The Fold*, 15.

[18] Deleuze makes a connection between Paul Klee's art and architectural forms and René Thom's seven types of mathematical transformations. Deleuze, *Fold*, 15.

[19] Deleuze, *The Fold*, 17.

[20] Samuel Weber, "Genealogy of Modernity: History, Myth and Allegory in Benjamin's *Origin of the German Mourning Play*," *Modern Language Notes* 106.3 (1991): 465–500, esp. 469.

[21] Weber, "Genealogy of Modernity," 480.

[22] Peter Fenves, "Tragedy and Prophecy in Benjamin's *Origin of the German Mourning Play*," in Fenves, *Arresting Language: From Leibniz to Benjamin* (Stanford, CA: Stanford UP, 2001), 236.

[23] Fenves, "Tragedy and Prophecy," 235–36.

[24] Weber, "Genealogy of Modernity," 482.

[25] Weber, "Genealogy of Modernity," 482.

[26] Karl Giehlow: "Dürers Stich *Melencolia I* und der maximilianische Humanistenkreis," *Mitteilungen der Gesellschaft für vervielfältigende Kunst* (1903): 29–41; (1904): 6–18, 57–79. Erwin Panofsky and Fritz Saxl, *Dürers Melencolia I: Eine Quellen- und Typengeschichtliche Untersuchung* (Leipzig: Teubner, 1923).

[27] Michel Foucault, *Die Ordnung der Dinge* (Frankfurt am Main: Suhrkamp, 1974), 99.

[28] Bettine Menke, *Sprachfiguren: Name — Allegorie — Bild nach Walter Benjamin* (Munich: Fink, 1991).

[29] Bettine Menke, "Ursprung des deutschen Trauerspiels," in *Benjamin Handbuch: Leben — Werk — Wirkung*, ed. Burkhardt Lindner (Stuttgart: Metzler, 2006), 219.

[30] Christoph Menke, *Die Gegenwart der Tragödie* (Frankfurt am Main: Suhrkamp. 2005), 179.

31 Christoph Menke, *Die Gegenwart der Tragödie*, 180.

[32] John McCole, *Walter Benjamin and the Antinomies of Tradition* (Ithaca, NY: Cornell UP, 1993), 136.

[33] See Dominik Finkelde, *Benjamin liest Proust* (Munich: Fink, 2003), ch. 5: "Die Allegorie als inszenierter Bruch im Repräsentationsverhältnis bei Proust und Benjamin," 166–81.

[34] Heymann Steinthal, *Kleine sprachtheoretische Schriften, neu zusammengestellt und mit einer Einleitung versehen von Waltraud Bumann* (Hildesheim and New York: Olms, 1970), 424.

[35] Consequently, allegory can also be understood as a "return of a mythological ambiguity within the monotheistic tradition, that was supposed to supplant it definitively." Samuel Weber, "'Storming the Work': Walter Benjamin's Allegorical Theatre of Modernity," in Weber, *Theatricality as Medium* (New York: Fordham UP, 2004), 177.

[36] Karl Marx and Friedrich Engels, *Das kommunistische Manifest*, in Marx and Engels, *Werke*, vol. 4, Berlin: Dietz Verlag, 1974), 465.

[37] Michael Kahl, "Der Begriff der Allegorie in Benjamins Trauerspielbuch und im Werk Paul de Mans," in *Allegorie und Melancholie*, ed. Willem van Reijen (Frankfurt am Main: Suhrkamp, 1992), 293.

[38] Peter Bürger, *Theorie der Avantgarde* (Frankfurt am Main: Suhrkamp, 1984), 92.

[39] See Deleuze, *Proust and Signs* (Minneapolis: U of Minnesota P, 2004).

[40] Deleuze, *The Fold*, 23.

[41] Andreas Gryphius, Vorrede zum *Leo Armenius oder der Fürsten-Mord*, ed. Peter Rusterholz (Stuttgart: Reclam 1996), 4.

[42] Menninghaus, *Walter Benjamins Theorie der Sprachmagie*, 115–17. See also Harald Steinhagen, "Zu Walter Benjamins Begriff der Allegorie," in *Form und Funktionen der Allegorie*, ed. Walter Haug (Stuttgart: Metzler, 1979), 666–85.

[43] Kahl, "Der Begriff der Allegorie," 299.

[44] "Sie [die Leichen] gehören als Schaustücke tatsächlich zur Bühnenausstattung und geben das Theater als [. . .] *Schauplatz der Sterblichkeit* zu erkennen." Albrecht Schöne, *Emblematik und Drama im Zeitalter des Barock* (Munich: Beck, 1968), 217–18.

[45] Heiner Müller and Christa Wolf, and probably many other authors of the former German Democratic Republic, could also be mentioned. Curiously, Benjamin left no imprint on the works of West German author Peter Weiss, as might have been expected.

[46] See Dominik Finkelde, "Wunderkammer und Apokalypse: Zu W. G. Sebalds Poetik des Sammelns zwischen Barock und Moderne," *German Life and Letters* 60.4 (2007), 554–68.

[47] Eric Santner applies Benjamin's conceptualization of Baroque melancholy to the poetics of Sebald. See his *Creaturely Life: Rilke, Benjamin, Sebald* (Chicago: U of Chicago P, 2006).

[48] Santner, *Creaturely Life*, 19.

[49] Thomas Frank, Albrecht Koschorke, Susanne Lüdemann, and Ethel Matala de Mazza, *Des Kaisers neue Kleider: Über das Imaginäre politischer Herrschaft* (Frankfurt am Main: Fischer, 2002), 133.

[50] Ernst Kantorowicz, *The King's Two Bodies: A Study in Mediaeval Political Theology.* (Princeton, NJ: Princeton UP, 1957).

[51] Schmitt develops this theory in his *Political Theology: Four Chapters on the Concept of Sovereignty*, trans. George Schwab (Cambridge, MA: MIT Press, 1985).

[52] See also Samuel Weber on Benjamin's Schmitt lecture. Samuel Weber, "Taking Exception to Decision: Walter Benjamin and Carl Schmitt," *Diacritics* 22.3/4 (1992): 5–18.

[53] Giorgio Agamben emphasizes that while for Schmitt the decision of the sovereign is the binding link between sovereignty and the state of exception, for Benjamin it is not so. Benjamin disconnects sovereign power ironically from its exercise and shows that for the baroque sovereign the incapacity to decide becomes constitutive. Giorgio Agamben, *Ausnahmezustand* (Frankfurt am Main: Suhrkamp, 2004), 67–68. See also the essay by Vivian Liska in this volume.

3: Lost Orders of the Day: Benjamin's *Einbahnstraße*

Wolfgang Bock

I. People and Prospects

A Dedication

WALTER BENJAMIN'S *EINBAHNSTRASSE* (*One-Way Street*, written 1923–26, published 1928) is a collection of longer and shorter aphorisms and aperçus. It starts with a dedication that is more or less an aphorism itself:

> Diese Straße heißt
> Asja-Lacis-Straße
> Nach der die sie
> Als Ingenieur
> Im Autor durchgebrochen hat (*GS* IV.1:83)

> [This street is named
> Asja Lacis Street
> after her who
> as an engineer
> cut it through the author (*SW* 1:444)]

When Benjamin wrote this passage, it was intended as a promise for a better life. Starting in the 1920s, Benjamin developed a new interest in Marxism, which had to do with his meeting with Asja Lacis and Bertolt Brecht. Lacis was Brecht's assistant in Munich in 1923. She came from the Baltic city of Riga in Latvia, where she worked in a revolutionary children's theater. Benjamin fell in love with her on the Italian island of Capri near Naples in 1924.[1] When *Einbahnstraße* was published in January 1928, they planned to live together in Berlin, an arrangement that materialized in late 1928. But their love soon came to an end; as early as 1929 they went their own ways again. In *Einbahnstraße* Benjamin attempts to convey the impression of experience, knowledge, sensuality, and virility. He even draws attention to the contradiction between the power of his writing and a certain powerlessness in his real life, although he actually viewed this contradiction rather critically, as is shown in the pun *Für Männer* (For men): "Über-Zeugen ist unfruchtbar" (*GS* IV.1:83; "To convince is to conquer without conception," *SW* 1:446).

A Better Life

The book is one of the very rare authentically surrealistic testimonies in Germany written between the two world wars. It was published in January 1928 by Ernst Rowohlt Verlag in Hamburg. In the 1920s Benjamin tried to launch a double career as an academic and as a creative literary author; he wrote books in both fields and tried to erase the boundaries between them. In 1926 he did not succeed with his philosophical post doctorate project (*Habilitation*) at the University of Frankfurt am Main.[2] So he decided to continue as a professional freelance writer, critic, reviewer, and columnist for the *Frankfurter Zeitung* and the *Literarische Welt*, the most important *feuilleton* venues in Germany at that time. It was his later companion of the *Frankfurt School of Critical Theory*, Max Horkheimer, who did not understand his *Habilitation* thesis, *Ursprung des deutschen Trauerspiels* (The Origin of the German Mourning Play), and so the authorities of the university refused to grant Benjamin formal permission to give professorial lectures. His second academic attempt in 1929 to become a professor, at the newly founded Hebrew University of Jerusalem, did not succeed either, but that was his own doing: his friend Gershom Scholem, who had been living in Jerusalem since 1923, had tried hard to bring him into the faculty and had even sent him the money for the journey. However, Benjamin would have had to learn Hebrew, and Scholem also wanted him to agree to some of the conditions in Jewish Palestine. Benjamin hesitated for a long time — he had fallen in love with Asja and was separated from the Jewish world. So he took the travel money from Scholem but stayed in Europe and continued to work with Lacis, Brecht, and others in Berlin, Munich, and Paris.[3] When *Einbahnstraße* was published, he was at the peak of his love affair with Asja, full of hope for a new life.

A Small Book for Friends, and a Picture

In 1928 Benjamin planned a book comprising a collection of aphorisms for his personal friends, a so-called *plaquette:* "In mehreren Kapiteln, die je als einzige Überschrift den Namen eines mir Nahestehenden tragen, will ich meine Aphorismen, Scherze, Träume versammeln" (I intend to collect my aphorisms, witticisms, and dreams in several chapters, each of which will carry the name of someone close to me as its only heading), he wrote in a letter to Scholem.[4] Later on he gave each short piece a new title, which was an integral part of the work itself, and he also changed the name of the project. Before he came up with the final title, which was connected to Asja and the emphatic idea of engineering human communication in the cultural struggle, he called the book "mein Notizbuch" ("my Notebook") or "Straße gesperrt!" ("Street Closed").[5] When Benjamin tried to explain the final title to his friend Scholem, he wrote in a letter of 18 September 1926:

> Vor allem ist nun mein Buch "Einbahnstraße" fertig geworden — von dem ich Dir doch wohl schon schrieb? Es ist eine merkwürdige Organisation oder Konstruktion aus meinen "Aphorismen" geworden, eine Straße, die einen Prospekt von so jäher Tiefe — das Wort nicht metaphorisch zu verstehen! — erschließen soll, wie etwa in Vicenza das berühmte Bühnenbild Palladios: Die Straße. (*GB* 3:197)

> [The most important news is that my book *One-Way Street* [*Einbahnstraße*] is finished — I have already written you about it, haven't I? It has turned out to be a remarkable arrangement or construction of some of my "aphorisms," a street that is meant to reveal a prospect of such precipitous depth — the word is not to be understood metaphorically! — like, perhaps, Palladio's famous stage design in Vicenza, *The Street*. (*CWB*, 306)]

The inspiration for this reference to stage perspective and the hermeneutics of the surface came from a stage set of Andrea Palladio in Vicenza in 1583, which Benjamin saw at the age of twenty during an early trip to Italy.[6] In his travel diary *Meine Reise in Italien, Pfingsten 1912* (My Journey to Italy, Pentecost 1912) he described his impressions:

> Wir gehen auf das Teatro Olimpico, einem Rundbau dem Museo schräg gegenüber zu. . . . Das Theater ist in der Geschlossenheit des Raumes schön, bedeutend aber wird es, indem augenscheinlich die Möglichkeit gegeben ist, den Übergang von der Straße in das Haus auf offener Scene zu geben, indem der Schauspieler aus dem Straßenprospekt vor die sehr ausgedehnte Tor-Architektur, die als Zimmerwand betrachtet werden kann, sich begibt. Damit ist eine neue Möglichkeit für die Aufführung, ja für das Drama gegeben. (*GS* VI:276–77)[7]

> [We are approaching the Teatro Olimpico, a round edifice across the street from the Museo. . . . The theatre, in the harmonious totality of its space, is beautiful, but it becomes truly significant because it appears to allow one to see the transition from the street into the house in the middle of a scene, when the actor steps from the street to a point in front of the very expansive gate architecture, which can be viewed as the wall of a room. This makes possible a new style of performance, indeed of drama.]

Here Benjamin was using an image for the whole collection that combines a visual impression with literary and philosophical imagination. His interest is focused on the zone between the private house and the public *flânerie* or *passeggiata*. He especially likes the artificial illusions of dioramic and panoramatic theaters as proto-forms of media space in photography and film. In his description, the perspective of language is condensed in optical phenomena and vice versa. Language is always present in the visual impression itself and cannot be separated from the object. The space of the theatre stage, that of literary space, and that of reflection infiltrate each other.

This collage of different types of media is also portrayed on the cover of the book. It shows a photomontage of the Russian photographer Sasha Stone with two intersecting perspectives: a series of old German one-way-street traffic signs, with arrows, and the inside contours of a shopping mall in Berlin on the front, as well as a street scene on the back. The idea is easy to understand: connection and separation of disparate spaces at the same time. In other words, Benjamin uses *arcane* principles. Benjamin's use refers to the surrealists, but also goes back to the Renaissance philosophy of Paracelsus (*GS* I:326; *Origin,* 148–49).

Man's Self-Reflection as a Lover: References to Form and Content

An arcanum in this context is an enigmatic written picture, close to an allegory, which uses contradictions like slowness and speed in a combination of picture and text. In his anthology, Benjamin refers to that fragile and heterogeneous tradition. "Short forms" (*kleine Formen*) like the arcanum, aperçu, witty saying, aphorism, essay, or tractatus are also known from old calendars, almanacs, and moral and philosophical reflections. They are related to the idea of the *carpe diem* topos ("seize the day") and to one of the oldest popular forms of books, which intended to teach the tendencies of the day. As with a a horoscope, the reader tries to find the hidden force behind things to use them for a better life. But in modern times these hidden meanings are not so easy to find — if they ever were.

Benjamin reacts to that situation of modernity with different written reflections, which he brings into a contemporary form. Among the sixty pieces on the eighty-three pages of *Einbahnstraße* there are literary programs and manuals for writers, surrealistic associations, and reports of dreams and drug-inspired experiments, as well as short dramatic scenes of daily and moral life, love poems in prose, pedagogical reflections, comments, and travel-diary inscriptions — among them some about Riga, the hometown of his beloved Asja.

These fragments can hardly be brought into conventional categories and systems of order. But they can be explained as the historical and actual references in Benjamin's philosophical work *Ursprung des deutschen*

Trauerspiels (The Origin of the German Mourning Play). This book, written 1924–25, was also released in January of 1928 by Rowohlt, the company that had published *Einbahnstraße*. In *Einbahnstraße* Benjamin's methodological reflections on writing reach a new peak. He records his observations in metaphors that play with the optical world of the theater, photography, and the cinema. They are also close to the famous sound pictures of Chladni or to Charles Webster Leadbeater's and Annie Besant's *Thought-Forms* (1901), which tried to provide a language of esoteric, visual gestures of perception. Benjamin's notions are based on literary reflections that deal with the metaphor of the book and give the visual ideas a textual frame or *emballage:* they might be called *literary thought-figures* in reference to Gottfried Herders *Denkbilder* (thought-pictures). They stand in the tradition of arcana, impresses, emblems, and plaquettes — through a mixture of frame, picture, and comment — that Benjamin analyzes in the *Trauerspiel* book. They are also related to the Jewish concept of life as a book: this tradition suggests that we always live in the medium of the language, the written text being an invisible curtain through which we have to watch the world.

Einbahnstraße gives reports from all spheres of Benjamin's activity up until then: the youth movement, the life of students and writers, radio talks, politics, collections, philosophy, love-life and friendship, traveling, reception, and art. The collection is, as we saw, a loving gift in itself. And it contains, ironically enough, the truth about this love. In *Bogenlampe* (Arc-Lamp) the author uses a delightful picture together with a technical term as a metaphor of sadness and impotence: "Einen Menschen kennt einzig nur der, welcher ohne Hoffnung ihn liebt" (*GS* IV.1:119; "The only way of knowing a person is to love that person without hope," *SW* 1:467). That arc-lamp embraces the dialectics of melancholy — it gives out a strong light but looks downward like the head and the penis of the melancholic and ineffective lover.

II. A System of Fragments in Logical Order

A Program

The essays in *Einbahnstraße* are not just mixed together randomly; Benjamin puts them in a special order. In the first text, "Tankstelle" ("Gas Station"), he tries to define both a newly situated space of writing outside the literary institutions and the traditional separation of idealistic meaning and materialistic facts. His author, who should be seen as a producer, as he will later explain in an undelivered address that he had planned to give at the Institute for the Study of Fascism in Paris 1934, tries to be aware of the coming changes related to early revolutionary Russia — changes that would turn the position of the intellectual in society upside down. Benjamin uses a certain rhetoric: not the common book that has a distanced reader, but politically engaged papers, pamphlets, programs, and posters would be the new media upon which Benjamin tried to focus his interests.

From Dream to Awareness and Back

In his second piece, "Frühstücksstube" ("Breakfast Room"), Benjamin goes on to give rules for telling about the dreams of the night the following morning. Never do so without having eaten, he proclaims; otherwise you will miss the distance that you essentially need and you will speak as if you are still sleeping. In a nutshell it contains his later critique of psychoanalysis, which he would explain in his second article about Baudelaire.[8] Benjamin situates his interests between the traditional categories of rules of writing and advice about daily life and also with philosophical reflection, technical terms of psychoanalysis, and political agendas. He stands at a lateral axis to the bourgeois institutional separation in the area of intellect, in that he brings in new ideas but also refers to the older tradition of the arcanum, which has to be put into action and which he himself helped to found.

The Real Politician

This position implies political engagement and to this path also belongs an image of the emerging politician. In the texts "Ministerium des Innern" ("Secretary of the Interior") and "Feuermelder" ("Fire Alarm") he sketches the conflict between the anarchic-socialistic and the conservative politician and he praises the moment of *kairos,* a quality of time that one has to use or it passes by.

These texts continue a course of reflection that Benjamin started with his *Zur Kritik der Gewalt* (1919; The Critique of Violence), with "Sur Scheerbart" (his essay on the utopian novel *Lesabéndio* by Paul Scheerbart from 1920), and probably in a lost essay, "Der wahre Politiker" (The Real Politician).[9] To this context also belongs a book, *Dialectic in Daily Life,* that he later planned with Herbert Marcuse.[10] In these reflections he again cultivates a heroic intellectual attitude that differs from his practical existence. This difference allowed him to develop his lucid reflections but it also separated him from their fulfillment in reality.

Between Germany and France

As a translator of Charles Baudelaire's *Fleurs du mal,* of Marcel Proust, and of other works, Benjamin was strongly influenced by French writers and their artistic tradition.[11] This was not very common for a German intellectual of his period. The French and the Germans were at that time arch-enemies. The notion that the French were associated with the

Great Revolution and with political liberalism and parlamentarianism made them foes in the view of the average German during the time between the world wars. This was the time of the Weimar Republic, and intellectuals leaned toward an anti-democratic attitude. Together with the last item of *Einbahnstraße,* "Zum Planetarium: ("To the Planetarium"), his "Kaiserpanorama: Reise durch die deutsche Inflation" ("Imperial Panorama: A Tour through German Inflation") is the most important essay on this subject in *Einbahnstraße.* Taking a different tack from Rainer Maria Rilke, who in *Malte Laurids Brigge* described the Paris of 1910 as the city of hell, he takes a critical anthropological view of Germany itself from the outside.

Primitive rules, circumstances of life, misery, stupidity and lost irony are the criteria by which Benjamin defines the status of civilization. On that scale Germany ranked very low. In this judgment, which today is still relevant, with "no go" areas for foreigners in certain regions of East Germany and a growing aggressive nationalism in the whole country, Benjamin refers to Friedrich Hölderlin's similar verdict in his novel *Hyperion:* "So kam ich unter die Deutschen" (So I fell among the Germans).[12]

In *Ursprung des deutschen Trauerspiels* Benjamin refers to his discussion with Carl Schmitt about sovereignty and the state of emergency, which nowadays has found its foremost explicator in Giorgio Agamben.[13] In this debate Benjamin tries to get back his *attentiveness* — a term he takes from Novalis and the Romantic tradition.[14] How necessary such a presence of mind was can be seen from his prediction of destruction, which can be interpreted as anticipating the Holocaust. Benjamin's view is very dark indeed:

> IX. Die Menschen, die im Umkreise dieses Landes eingepfercht sind, haben den Blick für den Kontur der menschlichen Person verloren. Jeder Freie erscheint vor ihnen als Sonderling. Man stelle sich die Bergketten der Hochalpen vor, jedoch nicht gegen den Himmel abgesetzt, sondern gegen die Falten eines dunklen Tuches. Nur undeutlich würden die gewaltigen Formen sich abzeichnen. Ganz so hat ein schwerer Vorhang Deutschlands Himmel verhängt und wir sehen die Profilierung selbst der größten Menschen nicht mehr. (*GS* IV.1:99)

> [IX. The people cooped up in this country no longer discern the contours of human personality. Every free man appears to them as an eccentric. Let us imagine the peaks of the High Alps silhouetted not against the sky but against folds of dark drapery. The mighty forms would show up only dimly. In just this way a heavy curtain shuts off Germany's sky, and we no longer see the profiles of even the greatest men. (*SW* 1:453)]

Benjamin here uses a typical thought-picture, which is situated between the spheres of nature and the artificial background and theater curtain. Here again he follows his custom of not thinking about pure and simple dates or pictures but insisting on the a priori notion that the material in front of him is always constituted in and through language.

In the last thesis of "Kaiserpanorama" ("Imperial Panorama") Benjamin gets back to the *loss of the libation* in ancient Greece, which might be related to the spare place for a beggar or the Messiah at the table, which in the old Jewish sagas often is the same person:

> XIV. . . . Nach athenischem Brauch [der libatio] war das Auflesen der Brosamen bei der Mahlzeit untersagt, weil sie den Heroen gehören. — Ist einmal die Gesellschaft unter Not und Gier soweit entartet, daß sie die Gaben der Natur nur noch raubend empfangen kann, daß sie die Früchte, um sie günstig auf den Markt zu bringen, unreif abreißt und jede Schüssel, um nur satt zu werden, leeren muß, so wird ihre Erde verarmen und das Land schlechte Ernten bringen. (*GS* IV. 1:101)

> [XIV. . . . An Athenian custom forbade the picking up of crumbs at the table, since they belonged to the heroes. — If society has so denatured itself through necessity and greed that it can now receive the gifts of nature only rapaciously — that it snatches the fruit unripe from the trees in order to sell it most profitably, and is compelled to empty each dish in its determination to have enough — the earth will be impoverished and the land will yield bad harvests. (SW 1:455)]

This decline refers to a thought figure that Georges Bataille also used in "La notion de la dépense" ("The Notion of Expenditure").[15] Like Marcel Mauss's anthropological work on ancient forms of giving, Bataille considered an ancient form of economics, which was evident in the so-called *potlatch*. Here the goal is not simply to get the greatest profit out of a deal, but to be the most highly honored by giving the most and thus putting shame on one's opponent, or by demonstrating one's wealth by destroying property. If we do not pay attention to this universal way of exchange (gifts and wanton destruction), Bataille suggested, that force will return behind the back of the so-called actors. It will end as a gigantic exaltation in cosmic dimensions.[16]

As in a limit of cosmic law, Benjamin, by mentioning the right of *libatio* also refers to these ideas, which he might have earlier encountered in Friedrich Nietzsche's or Ludwig Klages's philosophical writings. In his last item of *Einbahnstraße*, "Zum Planetarium" (To the Planetarium) Benjamin refers to the destructive power of morally wrong behavior. He separates here an ancient mimetic or ecstatic relation between man and the stars from the visual mode in modernity. If one does not pay attention to this old connection, it takes people by surprise by itself — as was the case in the First World War and would likely be the case in Benjamin's perspective on the Second World War. In this sense the development of the technical sphere for Benjamin is not a war between humans and nature but a problem of justice and grace among human beings and in this case one of the key issues concerning coming civilizations.

With this enigmatic ending of the collection Benjamin turns back to his first item — as a program to put these ideas into action. The construction principle of his book is cyclic.

III. A Surrealist in His Own Right

Very similar to the works of Philippe Soupault, André Breton, or Louis Aragon and the idea of surrealistic pictures, but also alluding to Dada and Paul Scheerbart, Walter Benjamin in *Einbahnstraße* writes surrealistic pieces.[17] The two purest are "Polyclinic" and "Stückgut: Spedition und Verpackung" ("Mixed Cargo: Shipping and Packing"). In the first one Benjamin relates the writing process in a café to a surgical operation — connecting also the medical meaning of the operator (that is, the surgeon) to the one in the film business, that is, the cameraman. He marks a reference to Comte de Lautréamont's (a pseudonym of the author Isidor Ducasse, 1846–70, later popular with the surrealists) "beautiful as . . ." poems, among them the well known "accidental meeting of an umbrella and a sewing machine on a surgeon's table." But in this paradox, the author is patient and doctor in one person and tries to perform a kind of auto-operation.[18] In "Stückgut" ("Mixed Cargo") the pursuit of the previous thought continues, but he concentrates now on his experience with drugs: the streets of Marseille here, for example, shrink down to a book. In "Madame Ariane Zweiter Hof Links" ("Madame Ariane: Second Courtyard on the Left"), Benjamin follows the conception of his writings which allow him also to interpret the para-psychological and mystic phenomena in his literary and political program of promoting awareness.

Benjamin outwardly emphasized a rational wake-up call and an overturning of superstition to promote political action. But in another sense he also goes back to dreams and contemplation. He had his own interpretation of the sources of surrealism. In the 1920s he spent a great deal of time in France and in 1933 he again fled to Paris. His support of a progressive position brought him into contact with the French avant-garde and he became intellectually close to the surrealists. But even in the early 1930s, when he lived and worked as an immigrant in Paris, he did not have the close personal contact with them as one might assume. His intellectual closeness to them probably came from with his personal access to the body of ideas upon which the surrealists based their work.

In his *Second Manifesto of Surrealism* Breton showed a line of heterogeneous tradition that went back to the French and to cabalistic mysticism and the spiritism of the nineteenth and the twentieth centuries, the German Romantic thinkers, and, astonishingly, the early German humanists Heinrich Agrippa of Nettesheim and Paracelsus.[19] It is not known how truthful Breton was when he referred back to those writers; it is clearer that Benjamin himself gave his own, genuine version of this tradition in his writings. Benjamin wrote his dissertation on the concept and criticism of art in the early period of Romantic thinkers such as the Schlegel brothers, Novalis, and Hölderlin. In *Ursprung des deutschen Trauerspiels* he refers back to Calderón, Shakespeare's *Hamlet,* and the German humanistic tradition of allegory, sadness, and genius. This put not only Paracelsus's arcana but also Agrippa's tractatus at the center: as a pupil of the Platonic philosophers Ficino and Pico della Mirandola of Florence, Agrippa wrote a manifesto situated between magic and humanism, which the art historian Erwin Panofsky has discussed, continuing a study of Karl Giehlow. In his study, *Saturn and Melancholy,* and in another about the German renaissance artist Albrecht Dürer, Panofsky, going back to his teacher Aby Warburg, showed that the humanistic tradition of the genius and its inspirations is linked to black melancholy. The dark side of the encouragement of action in general, the opposite of acedia (hesitation), is related to the planet Saturn and the fate of the ancient god. That position of the theory of melancholy is for Benjamin related to a notion of dialectic thinking in the line of the peripatetic school of Aristotle and Theophrast. This is not systematic but fragmented (a true influence of the early Romantic period) and finds truth in monadic small pieces rather than in organic totalities; this follows the tradition of aphoristic writing as well as of the so-called *Urphänomen* of Goethe, which shows a characteristic picture of the world in a nutshell.[20] This tradition of a medium between text and image, which we earlier named the arcanum, might even be related to the German language and its internal dialectical forms. As a writer, Benjamin tries to establish a style in which he uses each word of his own language as if it were coming from a foreign idiom outside the natural movement and cadence of the phrase.[21] According to Benjamin's perspective this must be seen as a European phenomenon, because the Baroque drama itself was caught between the cultures of Spain, France, England, Denmark, Russia, Germany, and other countries. Benjamin reflected on this train of thought in the introduction to his book on the Baroque. There he preferred the literary form of the tractatus, not just because it meant he could play with forms, but also as a genre that is deeply related to his critique of wrong systematic tendencies of knowledge.[22] This seems to be Benjamin's main reason for using the aphorism as a contemporary form of knowledge, which he later described as "Dialektik im Stillstand" ("dialectics at a standstill").[23] Ornaments, letters, and calligraphic pictures here come together in a contradistinctive form. One has to look at the text as one would look at an image and vice versa and cannot consider the one without the other.

Chaque Coup Gagne: Toys and Childhood Knowledge

Benjamin's own version of what Breton called surrealism also brings in *écriture automatique*. He uses it in his pieces such as "Polyclinic," not only in recording dream stories and drug experiences, but also in texts concerning children's inspiration and their world of toys and fantasy. These works are also close to E. T. A. Hoffmann's grotesque stories such as *Der Nußknacker und der Mausekönig* (The Nutcracker and The Mouse King) from 1816. In "Spielwaren" ("Toys") Benjamin unites four such essays in the description of a mechanical cabinet of the nineteenth century that he saw in a shooting gallery at a fairground in the Tuscan town of Lucca.

But Benjamin was not only a collector of toys himself; he also had a certain interest in the holistic state of knowledge during childhood. Because he himself was an active member of the German youth and student movement of his day, he tried to anticipate a future youth, which he put into a utopian and surrealistic frame. In *Einbahnstraße* one finds some amazing pieces that he composed about the world of children, which would later be included in his works "Berliner Kindheit um neunzehnhundert" ("Berlin Childhood around 1900") and "Berliner Chronik" ("Berlin Chronicle"), which he wrote for his son Stefan. In "Vergrößerungen" ("Enlargements") Benjamin puts together a metaphoric world of books, reading children and snowflakes, school scenes, candy and early sexuality, playing hide-and-seek. His idea of a children's sphere of intuitive receptivity (which grownups have already lost), which stays fragile and is touched by linear time, is contrasted with a simple idea of progress; this status is recharged with spatial attributes and moves in circles illustrated by a simple roundabout. This idea is deeply connected to Friedrich Nietzsche's notion of the eternal recurrence of the same.

Traveling Educates!

Not only dreams and the knowledge of childhood are Benjamin's sources, but also the particular state of mind induced by traveling. This could have been a relic of the Youth movement and their *Fahrten* (excursions into "free" nature). In *Einbahnstraße* one finds a number of written traveling images, mainly from trips to Italy and France, as in the aphorisms "Papier- und Schreibwaren" (*GS* IV:1:111–12; "Stationery," *SW* 1:462), "Reisean-denken" (*GS* IV.1:122–25; "Souvenirs," *SW* 1:470–72) and "Stehbierhalle" (*GS* IV.1:144–45; "Stand-Up Beer Hall," *SW* 1:485–86).

Some of these traveling images also came from trips to Riga and Moscow, which are again connected to Asja, his love whom he visited there between 1925 and 1928, as in "Waffen und Munition" ("Ordnance"):

Ich war in Riga, um eine Freundin zu besuchen, angekommen. Ihr Haus, die Stadt, die Sprache waren mir unbekannt. Kein Mensch erwartete mich, es kannte mich niemand. Ich ging zwei Stunden einsam durch die Straßen. So habe ich sie nie wiedergesehen. Aus jedem Haustor schlug eine Stichflamme, jeder Eckstein stob Funken und jede Tram kam wie die Feuerwehr dahergefahren. Sie konnte ja aus dem Tore treten, um die Ecke biegen und in der Tram sitzen. Von beiden aber mußte ich, um jeden Preis, der erste werden, der den andern sieht. Denn hätte sie die Lunte ihres Blicks an mich gelegt — ich hätte wie ein Munitionslager auffliegen müssen. (*GS* IV.1:110)

[I had arrived in Riga to visit a woman friend. Her house, the town, the language were unfamiliar to me. Nobody was expecting me; no one knew me. For two hours I walked the streets in solitude. Never again have I seen them so. From every gate a flame darted; each cornerstone sprayed sparks, and every streetcar came toward me like a fire engine. For she might have stepped out of the gateway, around the corner, been sitting in the streetcar. But of the two of us, I had to be, at any price, the first to see the other. For had she touched me with the match of her eyes, I would have gone up like a powder keg. (*SW* 1:461)]

Here Benjamin, although in love, lapses strangely enough into a language of military images, which also proves that he grew up in the period of the German Empire. An instructive photograph presents a sad-looking nine-year-old boy in the uniform of a Prussian hussar with a saber and a lance.[24]

Lehrstücke or Teaching the Author

Benjamin's guidelines and instructions for authors reflect his moral aphorisms.[25] In "Ankleben verboten!" ("Post No Bills!") he puts together three sets of rules for the writer, which contain the number thirteen as a weak numerological reference: "Die Technik des Schriftstellers in dreizehn Thesen" ("The Writer's Technique in Thirteen Theses"), with the last precept: "Das Werk ist die Totenmaske der Konzeption" (*GS* IV.1:106–9; "The work is the death-mask of its conception," *SW* 1:458–60); "Dreizehn Thesen wider Snobisten" (*GS* IV.1:107; "Thirteen Theses against Snobs," *SW* 1:459); and "Die Technik des Kritikers in dreizehn Thesen" (*GS* IV.1:106–7; "The Writer's Technique in Thirteen Theses," *SW* 1:458–59).

These sequences correspond to the program for writers that he announced in his first section, "Tankstelle" ("Gas Station"). They are followed by another "Nummer 13" ("Number 13"), which surprisingly for the uninitiated reader combines the world of prostitution and the world of books, again with a strong masculine approach.[26] After quotations from Proust and Mallarmé he writes famous sentences like: "I. Bücher und Dirnen kann man mit ins Bett nehmen" ("I. Books and harlots can be taken to bed"); or "XIII. Bücher und Dirnen — Fußnoten sind bei den einen, was bei den anderen Geldscheine im Strumpf" (*GS* IV.1:109–10; "XIII. Books and harlots — footnotes in one are as banknotes in the stockings of the other," *SW* 1:460–61).

The Language of the Medium

Benjamin also anticipated the great influence of writing media such as pens, paper, and mechanical typewriters on the production of texts. In "Lehrmittel" ("Teaching Aids") he follows his imagination in this direction:

> Die Schreibmaschine wird dem Federhalter die Hand des Litera-ten erst dann entfremden, wenn die Genauigkeit typographischer Formungen unmittelbar in die Konzeption seiner Bücher eingeht. Vermutlich wird man dann neue Systeme mit variablerer Schriftge-staltung benötigen. Sie werden die Innervation der befehlenden Fin-ger an die Stelle der geläufigen Hand setzen. (*GS* IV.1:105)

> [The typewriter will alienate the hand of the man of letters from the pen only when the precision of typographic forms has directly entered the conception of his books. One might suppose that new systems with more variable typefaces would then be needed. They will replace the pliancy of the hand with the innervation of com-manding fingers. (*SW* 1:457)]

This seems to be a prediction of digitalization and new interfaces. It seems to anticipate the work of scholars such as Friedrich Kittler; but looked at more closely it still gives dominance to living handwrit-ing and demands a level of technique that even today is not reached.[27] A medium for Benjamin means much more than just a technical field; in his piece "Briefmarkenhandlung" ("Stamp Shop") he reflects a life inside this medium.

This text contains twelve thoughts on the language of stamps, which again are related to children's fantasies: "Marken sind die Visitenkarten, die die großen Staaten in der Kinderstube abgeben" (*GS* IV.1:137; "Stamps are the visiting-cards that the great states leave in a children's room," *SW* 1:480.) This is also a comment on and variation on a well-known surrealistic subject. He would translate parts of Aragon's *Paris Peasant* for the *Feuilleton* of the *Literarische Welt* in June 1928, where the French poet writes in the same manner as Benjamin himself does about a stamp-shop.

IV. Life-Lines, Contradictions, and Misunderstandings

Bare Life between Death and Redemption

In the category of life Benjamin once again reflects upon the contradictory possibilities that an artificial context can present. After some lucid and discreet sentences about death, the weather, and other far-placed subjects, he returns to the heart of the matter. He mentions in "Maskengarderobe" ("Costume Wardrobe") that in the tragedy of the Renaissance and the Baroque theatre the dramatic characters in the last act are often fleeing someone or something when they come onstage. This little piece may be the most topical of the collection.

> Immer wieder, bei Shakespeare, bei Calderon füllen Kämpfe den letzten Akt und Könige, Prinzen, Knappen und Gefolge "treten fliehend auf." Der Augenblick, da sie Zuschauern sichtbar werden, läßt sie einhalten. Der Flucht der dramatischen Personen gebietet die Szene halt. Ihr Eintritt in den Blickraum Unbeteiligter und wahrhaft Überlegener läßt die Preisgegebenen aufatmen und umfängt sie mit neuer Luft. Daher hat die Bühnenerscheinung der "fliehend" Auftretenden ihre verborgene Bedeutung. In das Lesen dieser Formel spielt die Erwartung von einem Orte, einem Licht oder Rampenlicht herein, in welchem auch unsere Flucht durch das Leben vor betrachtenden Fremdlingen geborgen wäre. (*GS* IV.1:143)

> [Again and again, in Shakespeare, in Calderon, battles fill the last act, and kings, princes, attendants, and followers "enter, fleeing." The moment in which they become visible to spectators brings them to a standstill. The flight of the *dramatis personae* is arrested by the stage. Their entry into the visual field of nonparticipating and truly impartial persons allows the harassed to draw breath, bathes them in new air. The appearance on stage of those who enter "fleeing" takes from this its hidden meaning. Our reading of this formula is imbued with expectation of a place, a light, a footlight glare, in which our flight through life may be likewise sheltered in the presence of onlooking strangers. (*SW* 1:484)]

Here again we have a stage, which we may imagine to be similar to the one that Palladio, with his prospect of a street, opens up in the Teatro Olimpico in Vicenza. It is this space that brings privacy into the public sphere. Benjamin shows the interruption of the action of the drama and its consequences for the ambivalence of the public view between control and freedom. For a short moment the *dramatis personae* are safe, because they become objects of reception and objects that of the watching public can view. Art here opens up a space where all other functions stop and are *aufgehoben* (cancelled and elevated to a higher synthesis) in a Hegelian sense. In the tradition of an idealist proof of the existence of God as a view from a higher position outside human experience, Benjamin here gives an allegory of the reflective space that now appears on stage. In the next step he transfers this concept and imagines our life as something to be watched over by other higher spirits or intellects, who may derive their pleasure and their art from this transformation.

This thought marks a very interesting point, because it once again demonstrates a certain crossing. Benjamin considers this conception of stage and art as a kind of redemptive moment in *Einbahnstraße*. He can rely here on his own analysis of the drama of Greek antiquity and the influence of the saga ("Sage") he develops in his *Trauerspielbuch*. There he showed that in the Greek concept of tragedy a certain combination of religious ritual, the process of justice, and aesthetic play came together in the half-circus of the antique amphitheater. In certain ritualistic proto-forms of this dramatic genre the protagonist started as a slave, victim, or fugitive who tried to escape from death — when he reached the altar he was free. Although he usually failed in the tragedy, this idea of an aesthetic sphere was related to the ancient concept of *a-sylum* at holy sites in Greece as a sphere where the normal conditions of *sylum* as a permanent fight stopped.[28]

This setting can be seen as an actualization of the ambivalent concept of bare life, which combines the beauty and the fragility of the naked body. In recent years Giorgio Agamben, the editor of Benjamin's writings in Italy, has become famous for his interpretation of the naked life in his *Homo Sacer Project*.[29] Agamben reconstructs the idea of the bare body from the concentration camp system of the National Socialists up to contemporary war and refugee camps, which can be found all over the world, but especially in the hands of the secret CIA networks. In these books Agamben tries to refer to Benjamin's concept of fugitive and naked life and reads it together with Michel Foucault's critical history of the prison.[30] In this case Agamben may be correct in describing the brutal situation of fugitives today. But it is also true to say that he once more interrupts the main trajectory of Benjamin's interests in his interpretation. Agamben brings the fragile correspondence of Benjamin's analysis to his own interest in a reversed combination. For Benjamin the sphere of artificial media is always related to the idea of potential conditions of redemption. In other words, the visual situation for him still holds something of the ancient concept of *opsis*, which always relates the spectator's view to the unity of a specific perceiving subject, a perceived object, and something concrete in between. This concept began to dissolve after 1830 with the construction of viewing apparatuses like the Panorama, which no longer aimed at a specific subject or object. It has dignity and ethical pretentions in itself, which does not occur in the situation of controlled observation.[31] The stage with the street and the line of visual perspective offers a way not only to hell but also to a utopian heaven — when it is recognized as being painted. This is not to invalidate Agamben's theory but to differentiate its entirely subjective and arbitrary interpretation of Benjamin from the latter's work itself.[32]

The End of the Critique?

It is typical of Walter Benjamin's writing that he always tries to focus on the end of his metaphorical figures. He reflects on the end of critique, the end of the book, the end of the experience of traveling, but he does so paradoxically within the very categories and media that he calls into question. This was in fact the principle of construction in the Baroque figure of the arcanum, but it has to be renewed in modernity. Peter Bürger mentions that Benjamin is the first modern author since Nietzsche who thinks "against himself" in these opposing figures of textuality and visuality.[33] In "Diese Flächen sind zu vermieten" ("This Space for Rent") Benjamin also focuses on the end of the critique: "Narren, die den Verfall der Kritik beklagen. Denn deren Stunde ist längst abgelaufen. . . . Der heute wesenhafteste, der merkantile Blick ins Herz der Dinge heißt Reklame" (*GS* IV.1:131–32; "Fools lament the decay of criticism. For its day is long past. . . . Today the most real, mercantile gaze into the heart of things is the advertisement," *SW* 1:476). In "Vereidigter Bücherrevisor" ("Attested Auditor of Books") he refocuses the end of criticism on the end of the book: "Nun deutet alles darauf hin, daß das Buch in dieser überkommenen Gestalt seinem Ende entgegengeht. . . . Und heute schon ist das Buch, wie die aktuelle wissenschaftliche Produktionsweise lehrt, eine veraltete Vermittlung zwischen zwei verschiedenen Kartothekssystemen" (*GS* IV.1:102–3; "Now everything indicates that the book in this traditional form is nearing its end. . . . And today the book is already, as the present mode of scholarly production demonstrates, an outdated mediation between two different filing systems," *SW* 1:456.). Finally, in "Stehbierhalle" he reflects on the end of the experience of travel. He himself, in contradiction to his analysis of the end, always uses written images. In this case he does not argue within a one-dimensional line of technical progress, as one might assume, but refers back to older techniques.

This little piece seems very strange and enigmatic because it again marks the difference between Benjamin's power in the writing of the text and the unhappy figure he portrayed in real life — a category he himself included in the discourse. His love of Asja kept him in Berlin instead of sending him abroad to Palestine; it also ruined him financially because he had to pay the costs of the divorce from his former wife, Dora. Dora took their son Stefan with her to London, which was also a catastrophic experience for him as a father. All his lucid inner knowledge could not help him work out a better plan of escape.

After-Life of a Fragmented Image

For a long time it was not clear whether even one of Benjamin's texts would ever find its way to a reader. Today, studies about Benjamin fill shelf after shelf in libraries and bookshops; a book entitled *Benjamins Begriffe* (Benjamin's Concepts) has been published as well as the recent *Benjamin-Handbuch* (Benjamin Handbook).[34] He is an internationally known writer, and his works have been translated into Mandarin and Brazilian Portuguese. Benjamin now is read and quoted by feminists, in contemporary postcolonial discourse, and in a host of other disciplines. At the same time he and his intellectual physiognomy are perhaps misunderstood as never before. He has never been the prophet of technological progress, as suggested by contemporary writers following Marshall McLuhan or Vilém Flusser. Benjamin held a critical view on so-called *Fortschritt*, and although his short forms might look like the dislinear writings anticipating the electronic hypertext of today, he is also very far removed from the current optimistic embrace of the new media (virtual reality, the Internet, digital communication, and so on.): In his first essay on the theory of language, "Über Sprache überhaupt und über die Sprache des Menschen," for example, he makes a connection between the will of man to use language as an instrument and medium of intentional messages and the expulsion from paradise.[35] Instead of being a technical optimist, Benjamin refers to a context of Scholasticism when he uses terms such as "information" or "communication" — a subject that he intends to be close to Heidegger and his interpretation of Duns Scotus. So his texts are still enigmatic and do not completely fit into the categories of his interpreters. He is neither a faithful follower of the Jewish cultural tradition nor a modernist — as his old friends Scholem and Adorno respectively suggest.[36] Nor is he a one-dimensional prophet of new technical progress or, on the contrary, someone who sees no possible hope in the development of the media, divergent views posited by his new friends Kittler or Agamben. Thus Kittler emphasizes Benjamin as an advocate of technical and economic progress in the history of media; for instance, he reads Benjamin's "Kunstwerk" essay more or less as a prelude to the digital optical media of today.[37] Agamben, on the other hand, tends to underestimate Benjamin's decidedly messianic faith in the progress of social history; his *Homo sacer* is a figure that ends with modernity itself in a helpless and aporistic situation, where Benjamin sees a kind of antagonistic and paradoxically helpless hope: "Nur um der Hoffnungslosen willen ist uns die Hoffnung gegeben" (*GS* I.1:201; "Only for the sake of the hopeless ones have we been given hope," *SW* 1:356) is the well known and often quoted last sentence of his *Wahlverwandtschaften* essay, which bears a close affinity to his political reflections in *Einbahnstraße*.[38] Benjamin is intellectually free enough to combine contradictions that most of his readers have never before imagined to be reconcilable. They are at the same time close to and distant from one another, and the range of his metaphorical and literal language even makes the borders of the thought-figures themselves seem to disappear. In this sense Benjamin is even nowadays a very contemporary thinker and writer. But in other cases he is a product of his time and circumstances: a German-Jewish thinker between the nineteenth and the twentieth centuries. To continue a Benjaminian mythology and a new Benjamin cult is the worse thing that could happen to him and his work.

His afterlife meandered on diverse paths. His son Stefan, who stayed in London after the war and died in the 1970s, married a Chinese woman, who was a Buddhist. And nowadays his two granddaughters, Mona Jean and Kim Yvon, are Benjamin's last close relatives. His ideas, which emerged in a distinctly German context, have now spread all over the world, and no one knows what will grow from them and where, in which culture and in which constellation we will see a new blossoming of his thoughts.

Notes

[1] See Chronology, 1924, *SW* 1:510–11. In 1925 they wrote together the text "Naples," which was published in the *Frankfurter Zeitung* the same year (*GS* IV.1:307–16; *SW* 1:414–21). See also Benjamin's "Programm eines proletarischen Kindertheaters" (1928/29; *GS* II.3:763–69; "Program for a Proletarian Children's Theater," *SW* 2:201–6).

[2] See the contribution of Dominik Finkelde in this volume.

[3] See Scholem, *Geschichte einer Freundschaft* (Frankfurt am Main: Suhrkamp, 1975), 194.

[4] Letter to Scholem, 22 Dec. 1924, *Gesammelte Briefe in 6 Bänden*, ed. Christoph Gödde and Henri Lonitz (Frankfurt am Main: Suhrkamp, 1995–2000), II:510; *The Correspondence of Walter Benjamin, 1910–1940*, ed. Gershom Scholem and Theodor W. Adorno, trans. Manfred R. Jacobson and Evelyn M. Jacobson (Chicago: U of Chicago P, 1994), 257. These works will henceforth be referred to in the text as *GB* and *CWB* respectively.

[5] Letter to Scholem, 29 May 1926, *GB* 3:161. In his review Gérard Raulet shows the early relationship of Benjamin to the Constructivists in Berlin: "One-Way Street," in *Benjamin–Handbuch: Leben — Werk — Wirkung*, ed. Burckhardt Lindner (Stuttgart: Metzler, 2006), 363.

[6] See his letter to Herbert Blumenthal, Venice, 3 Jun. 1912; *GB* 1:53–54.

[7] Palladio's design is close to Louis Aragon's description of the Passage de l'Opéra in his *Paris Peasant*, which Benjamin, in his *Passagen-Werk*, reads as a enigmatic image of heaven and hell. See Benjamin, *Das Passagen-Werk* (*AP*, h⁰, 1).

[8] See "Über einige Motive bei Baudelaire," *GS* I.2:605–54; *SW* 4:313–55. See also Wolfgang Bock, *Walter Benjamin — Die Rettung der Nacht* (Bielefeld: Aisthesis, 2000), 429–30.

[9] Cf. *GS* II.3:630–32 and 1423–25.

[10] Marcuse tried to persuade Benjamin in May 1936 to write a *Lesebuch des Materialisten* (Reading Book of the Materialist). Both had a strong interest in the proposed chapters "Die Forderung nach Glück" (The Demand of Felicity) and "Die Person des Materialisten" (The Person of the Materialist) but the project was not realized. See *GB* 5:301–4 and Max Horkheimer, *Gesammelte Schriften*, ed. Gunzelin Schmid Noerr (Frankfurt am Main: Fischer, 1995), vol 15: *Briefwechsel, 1913–1936*, 517.

[11] See *GS*, Supplement 1, *Kleine Übersetzungen*.

[12] See Friedrich Hölderlin, *Hyperion oder der Eremit in Griechenland*, in *Werke in einem Band* (Munich: Hanser, 1990), 451–54. See also Benjamin's book under the pseudonym of Detlef Holz, *Deutsche Menschen* (*GS* IV:149–234; *German Men and Women*, *SW* 3:167–235).

[13] *GS* I.1:245–48. Cf. Giorgio Agamben, *State of Exception* (Chicago: U of Chicago P, 2004); for its relation to Benjamin see ch. 1 and 4. See also the contribution by Marc de Wilde in this volume.

[14] See the other article by Bock in this volume.

[15] "The Notion of Expenditure," in *Georges Bataille: Visions of Excess — Selected Writings, 1927–1939*, trans. and ed. Allan Stoekl (Minneapolis: U of Minnesota P, 1989).

[16] See Marcel Mauss, *The Gift: The Form and Reason for Exchange in Archaic Societies* (New York: Norton, 2000) and Georges Bataille, *La part maudite, la notion de dépense* (Paris: Editions de Minuit, 1967). For a critique of this position see Wolfgang Bock, "Georges Batailles Begriff der Verausgabung und die gnostische Tradition," in *System und Erfahrung: Esoterik und Mystik in der Literatur der Moderne*, ed. Bettina Gruber (Opladen and Wiesbaden: Westdeutscher Verlag, 1997), 226–52.

[17] Concerning Benjamin and surrealism see Peter Bürger, *Theory of the Avant-Garde* (Minneapolis: U of Minnesota P, 1984), 55–82.

[18] See *GS* IV.1:131; *SW* 1:475–76.

[19] See André Breton, "Zweites Manifest des Surrealismus," in Breton, *Die Manifeste des Surrealismus* (Reinbek: Rowohlt, 1986), 90. Agrippa's first manuscript dates from 1510 and is a sophisticated and enlightened version of the subject. In 1531 the book was published in an enigmatic variant as *De occulta philosophia*.

[20] See Bock, *Walter Benjamin*, 42–52 (on Goethe), 81–87 (on monads and miniature).

[21] See Benjamin, "Notiz über ein Gespräch mit Ballasz (Ende 1929)" ("Notes on a Conversation with Béla Bálasz [End of 1929]"; *GS* VI:418; *SW* 2.1:276–77). See also my other chapter in this volume.

[22] See *Ursprung des deutschen Trauerspiels*, *GS* I.1:207–9; *Origin*, 27–29. In his philosophical manifesto *Über das Program der kommenden Philosophie* (On the Program of the Coming Philosophy; *GS* II.1:157–71; *SW* 1:100–110) of 1919, which he wrote as a critique of Kant, he himself offered more systematic remarks about the question concerning the fragment or system. But on the other hand,

it is in the logic of this question that one cannot think either with or without a systematic approach.

[23] In his *Passagen-Werk* he will come back to this form of production: "Zweideutigkeit ist die bildliche Erscheinung der Dialektik, das Gesetz der Dialektik im Stillstand. Dieser Stillstand ist Utopie und das dialektische Bild also Traumbild" ("Ambiguity is die manifest imaging of dialectic, the law of dialectics at a standstill. This standstill is utopia and the dialectical image, therefore, dream image"). Benjamin, "Paris, die Hauptstadt des XIX. Jahrhunderts" (*GS* V.1:55; Paris, the Capital of the Nineteenth Century; *AP*, 10).

[24] See Lindner, *Benjamin-Handbuch*, 689.

[25] In "Der Autor als Produzent" (The Author as Producer) he writes: "Ein Autor, der die Schriftsteller nichts lehrt, lehrt niemanden" (*GS* II.2:696; "An author who teaches writers nothing teaches no one," *SW* 2:777).

[26] For Benjamin's gender politics and language, see the contribution by Dianne Chisholm in this volume.

[27] Cf. Sonja Neef, *Abdruck und Spur: Handschrift im Zeitalter ihrer technischen Reproduzierbarkeit* (Berlin: Kadmos, 2008) and Friedrich Kittler, *Gramophone, Film, Typewriter* (Stanford, CA: Stanford UP, 1999).

[28] See Benjamin, *Ursprung des deutschen Trauerspiels*, *GS* I.1:284–89; *Origin* 106–10.

[29] See Giorgio Agamben, *Homo Sacer: Sovereign Power and Bare Life* (Stanford, CA: Stanford UP, 1998), *The State of Exception* (Chicago: U of Chicago P, 2005), and *Remnants of Auschwitz: The Witness and the Archive,* trans. Daniel Heller-Roazen (New York: Zone Books, 2002).

[30] See Michel Foucault, *Discipline and Punish: The Birth of the Prison* (New York: Random House, 1995).

[31] See David C. Lindberg, "The Science of Optics," in *Science in the Middle Ages* (Chicago: U of Chicago P, 1978), 338–68, and Katherine H. Tachau, *Vision and Certitude in the Age of Ockham: Optics, Epistemology, and the Foundations of Semantics*, 1250–1345 (Leiden, Netherlands: Brill, 1988); Jonathan Crary, *Techniques of the Observer: On Vision and Modernity in the Nineteenth Century* (Cambridge, MA: MIT Press 1992).

[32] See also Vivian Liska's contribution in this volume for further references to Agamben's actualization of Benjamin.

[33] See Peter Bürger, "Marginalia to Benjamin's One-Way Street," in *Zeitschrift für kritische Theorie* 17 (2003), 147.

[34] Michael Opitz and Ertmut Wizisla, eds., *Benjamins Begriffe* (Frankfurt am Main: Suhrkamp, 2000) and Lindner, *Benjamin-Handbuch*. One might assume that, notwithstanding the good quality of most of the articles, a kind of Benjamin encyclopedia was the last thing the author wanted to see.

[35] Cf. "Über Sprache überhaupt und über die Sprache des Menschen" (*GS* II.1:140–57; "On Language as Such and the Language of Man" *SW* 1:62–75; see also Benjamins letter to Martin Buber from Munich, 17 Jul. 1916, *GB.* 1:325–28; *CWB*, 79–81 and Samuel Weber, "Der Brief an Martin Buber vom

17. 7. 1916" in Lindner, *Benjamin-Handbuch*, 603–8. See also my other chapter in this volume.

[36] For the positions of Scholem and Adorno see Geshom Scholem, *Die jüdische Mystik in ihren Hauptströmungen* (Frankfurt am Main: Suhrkamp, 1980), vii–viii, and *Major Trends in Jewish Mysticism* (New York: Schocken Books, 1976), preface; and Theodor W. Adorno, "Charakteristik Walter Benjamins," in *Prismen: Kulturkritik und Gesellschaft,* vol. 10.1 of *Gesammelte Schriften* (Frankfurt am Main: Suhrkamp, 1977), 238–53.

[37] See Wolfgang Bock, *Medienpassagen: Bild, Schrift, Cyberspace II* (Bielefeld: Aisthesis, 2006), 76–81; Friedrich Kittler, *Eine Kulturgeschichte der Kulturwissenschaft* (Munich: Fink, 2000) and *Optische Medien* (Berlin: Merve, 2002).

[38] See the subsection "Between Germany and France" in this chapter, above, and Agamben, *Homo Sacer,* 74–78.

4: Literature as the Medium of Collective Memory: Reading Benjamin's *Einbahnstraße,* "Der Erzähler," and "Das Paris des Second Empire bei Baudelaire"

Bernd Witte

I

WALTER BENJAMIN WAS FIRST INTRODUCED to postwar Germany by Theodor W. Adorno as one of the initiators of the Frankfurt School of Social Philosophy. As an unorthodox Marxist he was later chosen by the generation of the 1968 revolts to be one of their predecessors. Alternatively, Gershom Scholem emphasized the Jewish and metaphysical roots in Benjamin's intellectual legacy. Ultimately, though, he was discovered by a large readership as the theoretical force behind a non-auratic concept of art, and this has been the basis for his international reputation. Today his fame rests on his having shaped the theoretical basis for and the historical trajectory of twentieth-century media. He is the first to have related the transformation of cultural memory to a historical revolution in communication technology. In his essay "Eduard Fuchs, der Sammler und der Historiker" he defines culture as the "Inbegriff von Gebilden" ("embodiment of creations") that are independent neither "von dem Produktionsprozeß, in dem sie entstanden" ("from the production process in which they originated") nor "von dem, in welchem sie überdauern" (*GS* II.2:477; "a production process in which they continue to survive," *SW* 3:267).

Written in 1937 during Benjamin's exile in Paris, this text expresses in theoretical terms what the author had originally sketched out in the short prose pieces in *Einbahnstraße* (*One-Way Street*, 1928) and in the literary essays of the 1920s and 1930s. The basis of his argument is the functional difference between spoken and written language, orality and literacy. Furthermore, the function that the written medium has is differentiated according to the technical and social conditions underlying its production. In Benjamin's estimation, the printed text found in novels plays a completely different role than it does in the printed matter generated by the mass press, although both forms must be considered to be the fundamental media of the nineteenth century. This distinction has engendered a popular echo in twentieth-century media theory.[1] Benjamin's analysis, however, is more than simply a consideration of language as the primordial medium, since he also integrates the influence of the newest media forms of his era — photography, film, and radio — into his theoretical considerations. This broadens the scope of his theory, giving it a prognostic value for our telematic age. In his widely read and much cited essay, "Das Kunstwerk im Zeitalter seiner technischen Reproduzierbarkeit" ("The Work of Art in the Age of Its Technological Reproducibility"), Benjamin was able to use his analysis of the cinema to demonstrate that the contents of cultural memory are dependent upon the technical formation of the media in which memory is processed and stored. This specific method links decisive impacts on the transformation of collective memory to media and, indirectly, to the development of the forms of material production. This can also serve as a point of departure for our inquiry into the transformation to which our experience, our knowledge, and our collective memory are subject in the age of electronic reproducibility. From a Benjaminian perspective, tracing the history of media helps to shed light on a highly differentiated corpus of medial forms — oral narration, written text, printed matter, mass press, photography, film, television, personal computer, text messaging — all of which complement one another and yet still maintain their individual function in today's media ensemble.

II

Walter Benjamin predates the electronic era. However, as a cultural seismographer he was able to read the early warning signs of the medial revolution to come. In an aphoristic text with the ironic title "Vereidigter Bücherrevisor" ("Attested Auditor of Books"), which appeared in the collection *Einbahnstraße,* Benjamin comments on the enormous proliferation of writing in the public areas of modern cities and points to the explicit effect that it has had on reading books:

> Die Schrift, die im gedruckten Buche ein Asyl gefunden hatte, wo sie ihr autonomes Dasein führte, wird unerbittlich von Reklamen auf die Straße hinausgezerrt und den brutalen Heteronomien des wirtschaftlichen Chaos unterstellt. Das ist der strenge Schulgang ihrer neuen Form. . . . Und ehe der Zeitgenosse dazu kommt, ein Buch aufzuschlagen, ist über seine Augen ein so dichtes Gestöber von wandelbaren, farbigen, streitenden Lettern niedergegangen, dass die Chancen seines Eindringens in die archaische Stille des Buches gering geworden sind. Heuschreckenschwärme von Schrift,

die heute schon die Sonne des vermeinten Geistes den Großstädtern
verfinstern, werden dichter mit jedem folgenden Jahr werden. (*GS*
IV.1:102–3)

[Script — having found, in the book, a refuge in which it can lead
an autonomous existence — is pitilessly dragged out into the street
by advertisements and subjected to the brutal heteronomies of economic chaos. This is the hard schooling of its new form. . . . And
before a contemporary finds his way clear to opening a book, his eyes
have been exposed to such a blizzard of changing, colorful, conflicting letters that the chances of his penetrating the archaic stillness of
the book are slight. Locust swarms of print, which already eclipse
the sun of what city dwellers take for intellect, will grow thicker with
each succeeding year. (*SW* 1:456)]

His findings, gleaned from what can only appear harmless and naïve
to the eye of the twenty-first-century subject, unveil their brutal accuracy
in the age of the computer. Words lose their consistency on the monitor
and are reduced to a "blizzard of changing, colorful, conflicting letters."
In our age, when the fruit of the tree of knowledge no longer has time to
ripen, words demonstrate their aggressiveness and a penchant for devour-
ing everything in their path, much as swarms of locusts raze vegetation as
they sweep through an area. Language has been instrumentalized for the
publicity that is peripheral to the texts that search engines ferret out, often
spilling over from the margin into the texts themselves. This method has
been perfected to the point that even the most innocuous words are no
longer able to defend themselves against the onslaught of negligible data.
    Benjamin, one of the most gifted and idiosyncratic thinkers of the
twentieth century, makes reference to yet another functional change that
written language has had to endure in the wake of modernity. He makes
the surprising observation that written and published texts that were traditionally projected into the eye of the reader horizontally "sich wieder vom
Grund heben" ("rise again from the ground"), ever since the mass press
and billboards crowding the cityscape have become one of the most popular ways of presenting the written word. "Bereits die Zeitung wird mehr in
der Senkrechten als in der Horizontalen gelesen, Film und Reklame drän-
gen die Schrift vollends in die diktatorische Vertikale" (*GS* IV.1:103; "The
newspaper is read more in the vertical than in the horizontal plane, while
film and advertisement force the printed word into the dictatorial perpen-
dicular," *SW* 1:456) This verdict is even more valid for the words projected
onto the computer screen, which materialize at the slightly-tilted vertical
angle that laptops and home computers call for. Alluding to the abundance
of urban ads, Benjamin coins the remarkable term "dictatorial vertical,"
implying that written language in the urban environment imposes a one-
dimensional, primarily economic significance on its readers. Contemplative

forms of reading comprehension that invite one to respond to what has already been written no longer appear possible.

Texts written in longhand as well as texts published in books represent a reduction of the multiple possibilities of combinations that words formed from the letters of the alphabet can ultimately configure. In order to set up something sensible, the letters have to be arranged in linear progression and then decoded according to the same sequence. A similar principle involving methods of progressive coding and decoding is valid for reading words within sentences as well as sentences within texts. The reader is required to follow the directions allocated by the lines in written or published texts. He follows these with his eyes and thoughts as he retraces the steps taken by the author. This one-dimensionality, which can be moderated in traditional texts by applying rhetorical devices, such as associations, rhyme schemes, and other formal variations, is completely abandoned in the most advanced materializations of the art of the book at the outset of modernity. Benjamin cites Stéphane Mallarmés *Coup de dés* as a prime example: "Mallarmé, wie er mitten in der kristallinischen Konstruktion seines gewiß traditionalistischen Schrifttums das Wahrbild des Kommenden sah, hat zum ersten Mal im 'Coup de dés' die graphischen Spannungen der Reklame ins Schriftbild verarbeitet" (*GS* IV.1:102; "Mallarmé, who in the crystalline structure of his manifestly traditionalist writing saw the true image of what was to come, was in the *Coup de dés* the first to incorporate the graphic tensions of advertisement in the printed page," *SW* 1:456).

What is he referring to here? In his final volume of lyrics the French symbolist author dissolves the linearity of the lines in favor of a graphical layout, which Benjamin characterizes: "Scheinbar regellos, in sehr beträchtlichen Abständen, sind Worte in wechselnden Schrifttypen über die Blätter verteilt" (*GS* IV.1:480; Seemingly without rules, generously spaced out, words are distributed in different types on the pages of the book.[2]) Because of the graphic design a space occurs around each word, giving the reader new and curious possibilities for word combinations that a continuous text could not elicit. Linear in form since their inception, the written texts in Mallarmé's book are now revealed to be two-dimensional textual pictures. The possibilities provided by an *ars combinatoria* of this type have, of course, grown exponentially since the advent of computer languages. By cutting, pasting, augmenting, and reducing texts or transforming written words into graphic images, words can now be combined freely on the surface of the monitor.

The transformation of linear script goes even further when several texts are linked together to form a hypertext. Thus they are unfolded within a three-dimensional space, which, though not discernable to sensory perception, allows specific words to be brought into correlation with each other in a multitude of combinations. Benjamin had foreseen the opportunity for writing to occupy three dimensions when in the framework of his pre-electronic study methods he first began to toy with spatial design: "Andere Erfordernisse des Geschäftslebens," Benjamin maintains, "führen weiter. Die Kartothek bringt die Eroberung der dreidimensionalen Schrift . . . Und heute schon ist das Buch, wie die aktuelle wissenschaftliche Produktionsweise lehrt, eine veraltete Vermittlung zwischen zwei verschiedenen Kartotheksystemen" (*GS* IV.1:103; "Other demands of business life lead further. The card index marks the conquest of three-dimensional writing . . . and today the book is already, as the present mode of scholarly production demonstrates, an outdated mediation between two different filing systems," *SW* 1:456) The skill of the historical materialist makes it possible to understand the current conditions of the media as well as their future by carefully observing their past. The card index, this seemingly insignificant instrument used by scientists, helps Benjamin grasp the potential of the written word that has only now been fully realized in hypertexts. Moreover, he applies these approaches to his own writing. His *Passagen-Werk* (*The Arcades Project,* 1927–40) is basically made up of a myriad of quotes and comments jotted down on index cards and arranged according to a colored filing system. The cards allow Benjamin to mix and mingle ideas, randomly joining them into singular and startling contexts. The systematic structure underlying this project still eludes us today, although research on Benjamin has grown by leaps and bounds since his work was rediscovered in the 1970s and 1980s.[3] However, Benjamin does not appear to have taken into account that hypertexts require "hyper-readers" equipped with the resources to make sense of the many implications that texts arranged in this manner can have.

III

In his 1936 essay entitled "Der Erzähler" ("The Storyteller") Benjamin compares contemporary forms of collective memory with what Pierre Nora would later term "societies of memory."[4] In these tradition is still alive and the transmission of collective experience occurs beyond the boundaries mortality has established between the generations. Memory is tied to the ritual implementation of ceremonial laws and their continuing application to one's personal life and individual historical situation. In this context, the past is experienced as a strong influence that molds the present and helps to generate identity for the individual in particular and society in general.

Relying on the naive resurgence of living memories, Nora's society of memory is nevertheless called into question when confronted by analytical reason. Similarly, the societies of craftsmen in Benjamin's "Der Erzähler" can be characterized as a reverse utopia, which derives its nostalgic seduction from the critical stance toward a deficient present. Benjamin diagnoses the present by adopting a notion borrowed from Georg Lukács's *Theory of the Novel*. In contrast to the "age of complete sinfulness," which finds its most adequate literary expression in the novel, the halcyon society of crafts-men depicted by Benjamin shines forth as an intact world, since the manual labor of the craftsmen can be associated with the traditional art of telling stories. The melancholy idealization of the past that permeates Benjamin's essay is nourished by the yearning of the lonely intellectual for a collective experience, such as he believed could be found in the Soviet Union prior to 1933. By 1936/37 and in view of the dangers posed by exile and isolation, his longing could only take refuge in a utopian view of an epoch long past.

Benjamin's starting point is a negative description of the current situa-tion, which he sees characterized by the fact that "die Erfahrung . . . im Kurse gefallen [ist]" (*GS* II.2:439; "experience has fallen in value," *SW* 3:143). This essential change in the ambient world — and that is Benjamin's innovative approach in his analysis — takes place at the same time as a change in the medial forms of expression. Thus he identifies the primordial media of the epoch as the general indicators of the transmissibility of experience. From this perspective, history shows a continual decline in the possibilities underly-ing transmissibility. Accordingly, in the eighteenth and nineteenth centuries the original epic form, the tale, is gradually superseded by the novel. Benja-min views the novel as a deficient mode in the "Formen menschlicher Mit-teilung" (*GS* II.2:443; "forms of human communication," *SW* 3:147), since the reader of novels develops into a lonely individual. His "wärmen" (*GS* II.2:457; "warming," *SW* 3:156) can only come about by triumphing over the death of the hero, whose life unfolds in the novel. That implies that wis-dom, morals, even practical advice for the reader can no longer be gleaned from the text. It only offers the questionable aesthetic consolation that the lives of all individuals find fulfillment in an immutable end and are thus structurally similar to that of the hero of the novel. The "Mitteilbarkeit aller Lebensbereiche" (*GS* II.3:1285; communicability of all forms of life) is com-pletely lost in the wake of the development of the organs of the mass press, which Benjamin judges to be the central expression of "der durchgebilde-ten Herrschaft des Bürgertums" ("the complete ascendancy of the middle class"). The press subjects the experience of human life to the domination of information, the authority of which is no longer derived from the bygone lives of the forefathers but more accurately from "der prompten Nachprüf-barkeit" (*GS* II.2:444; "prompt verifiability," *SW* 3:147). Information is no longer transferable to lived reality and finds its telos in a new value that is synonymous with actuality.

This scenario of decay has been set against the idyllic background of an almost paradisiacal society in its original state of innocence, which Benjamin exemplifies by citing an image derived from Holy Scripture: "Eine Leiter, die bis ins Erdinnere reicht und sich in den Wolken ver-liert, ist das Bild einer Kollektiverfahrung, für die selbst der tiefste

Chock jeder individuellen, der Tod, keinerlei Anstoß und Schranke darstellt" (*GS* II.2:457; "A ladder extending downward to the interior of the earth and disappearing into the clouds: this is the image for a collective experience to which even the deepest shock in every individual experience — death — constitutes no impediment or barrier," *SW* 3:157) The image of Jacob's ladder, linking heaven and earth in the hallowed world of the patriarchs, reveals that Benjamin locates the ideal world of the "vollkommenen Handwerker" ("perfect artisan"), which he associates directly with the storyteller, in a "kreatürlichen Reich" (*GS* II.2:463; "creaturely realm," *SW* 3:161) unsullied by sin. Only here is complete transmissibility possible, only here can the transmission of earlier forms of life transcend the boundaries of life and death separating generations, only here can the experience inscribed into the story be revivified and take on significance for later generations. Only the oral tale is "der Entfaltung fähig" (*GS* II.2:445–46; "capable of releasing its energy," *SW* 3:148), as Benjamin demonstrates on the basis of an episode adopted from Herodotus and derived from the biography of the Egyptian pharaoh Psammenit.

Benjamin's utopian world of the storyteller is situated in a completely ahistorical space and cannot be related to any concrete social experience. Rather, it must be understood as commentary on a literary text. The description of the halcyon world of the craftsman was inspired by the Swiss spinning rooms in Goethe's novel *Wilhelm Meisters Wanderjahre* (*Wilhelm Meister's Journeyman Years*) in which not only storytelling but also collective song plays an important role. However, Goethe's idyll was also borrowed. In the wake of the threats posed by nascent mechanization, the aging representative of German classicism turned to a social structure that even during his lifetime was no longer valid for the German territories and had been derived from the accounts in the Swiss diaries of his assistant, Heinrich Meyer. A purely oral tradition, understood as the "free art" that complements the "strict art" of the craftsmen in Goethe's view and that Benjamin sees as the art of the storyteller, had long since disappeared in Western civilization. The emergence of the alphabet nearly three millennia before and the proliferation of printed matter beginning in the fifteenth century had been responsible for the downfall of the oral narrative. In contrast to the ideal example of an active collective memory within a society poised between literacy and orality, the notion of a society of craftsmen founded on an oral tradition untainted by the negative symptoms of the written word is nothing more than the pale and abstract construction of a lonely intellectual living in exile in Paris.

IV

In March 1934 Benjamin recommenced his work on the *Passagen-Werk*, which he had begun in 1927. Originally conceived as "eine dialektische

Feerie" (*GB* 3:322; a dialectical faerie) in the style of *Einbahnstraße,* the work was "dem Prozeß einer vollkommenen Umwälzung unterworfen," "den eine aus der weit zurückliegenden Zeit meines unmittelbar meta-physischen, ja theologischen Denkens stammende Gedanken- und Bilder-masse durchmachen mußte, um mit ihrer ganzen Kraft meine gegenwärtige Verfassung zu nähren" (*GB* 5:88–89; subjected to the process of a com-plete transformation, which a mass of ideas and images stemming from the remote period of my immediate metaphysical and theological stance had to go through, in order to empower my present disposition with its full authority.) In the Bibliothèque Nationale Benjamin immersed him-self in what seemed to be an unlimited assortment of literature on Paris. When he had to interrupt his research because of the Nazi invasion of Paris in 1940, the list of primary sources he had consulted and excerpted included nearly 850 titles. According to his exposé entitled "Paris, die Hauptstadt des XIX. Jahrhunderts" ("Paris, Capital of the Nineteenth Century"), which he sketched in May 1935, the quotes gathered were to have served as the basis for six extensive investigations, of which Benjamin only began to work on the fifth, "Baudelaire oder die Straßen von Paris" ("Baudelaire, or the Streets of Paris"). The middle section of this text was completed in September 1938 and sent to New York for publication. It is certainly not by chance that the literary part of his project reached the level of completion that it did. Concentrating on the experience Charles Baudelaire, the nineteenth-century author, had had with his city, Ben-jamin pays tribute to the atomization of collective memory into private memories. By adopting a technique that he had previously developed for his analysis of Marcel Proust's *mémoire involontaire* (spontaneous mem-ory) he applies his materialistic approach to Baudelaire's private memory. His metaphorical comparison of shock as an individual sensory form and shock as part of the process of social production is a forceful attempt to construct individual experience as collective knowledge and thus make it transmissible for later generations.

In "Das Paris des Second Empire bei Baudelaire" ("The Paris of the Second Empire in Baudelaire") Benjamin develops the antithesis to his false idyll of craftsmen, the advantages of which could only be found in a traditional society strictly bound by cultural rituals. The middle section of his Baudelaire book, "Charles Baudelaire: Ein Lyriker im Zeitalter des Hochkapitalismus" (Charles Baudelaire: A Poet in the Age of High Capi-talism) planned as a miniature of the *Passagen-Werk,* but never completed, relies on historical materialism to show "wie [Baudelaire] ins neunzehnte Jahrhundert eingebettet liegt" ("how Baudelaire lies embedded in the nineteenth century," J51a,5). At the same time, Baudelaire's work is brought into contemporary perspective, that is, into a historical constel-lation reflecting the plight of European civilization, which was threatened by National Socialism in Germany, and the totalitarian socialism cultivated in the Soviet Union. Benjamin asserts: "Die historischen Erfahrungen, die Baudelaire als einer der ersten machte — er gehört nicht umsonst zur Generation von Marx, dessen Hauptwerk im Jahr seines Todes erschienen ist — sind seither nur allgemeiner und nachhaltiger geworden. . . . Um es in aller Kürze zu formulieren: es ist an dieser Dichtung noch nichts veraltet" ("The historical experiences which Baudelaire was one of the first to undergo [it is no accident that he belongs to the generation of Marx, whose principal work appeared in the year of his death] have become, in our day, only more wide-spread and persistent. . . . In a word, there is nothing yet obsolete about this poetry," J60a,1). Today, we are challenged to consider whether this assumption still holds, and, moreover, whether Benjamin's analysis of Baudelaire's universe can serve as a model for a valid method of historical investigation.

In the first chapter of his Baudelaire text, which is entitled "Die Bohème,"[5] Benjamin assumes that the proletarian movement has undergone its final defeat, which he sees symbolized in the brutal end of the Parisian Commune. "Am Ende der Kommune tastete sich das Proletariat wie ein zu Tode getroffenes Tier in seinen Bau, hinter die Barrikade zurück" (*GS* I.2:517; "After the demise of the Commune, the proletariat groped its way behind the barricades as a mortally wounded animal withdraws to its lair," *SW* 4:6). Responsible for this catastrophe are the professional conspirators, who subsequent to the debacle of the 1848 revolution and the disbanding of the organized workers were left to represent the proletariat during Louis Bonaparte's regency.[6] Blanqui, their protagonist, is characterized as "doctrinaire" and a "putschist" and — in Karl Marx's words — as the "Alchymist der Revolution" (*GS* I.2:519; "alchemist of the revolution," *SW* 4:7). In the final analysis he is described as having the "rogne" or "bitter anger," a term that was used to describe the deeply resentful politics of the Fascists during Benjamin's lifetime. Even more remarkable — and this has been overlooked until now — Benjamin recognizes the distinctive features of Lenin in the professional conspirator, especially when he says of Blanqui — once again adopting Marx's words — that he tried "dem revolutionären Entwicklungsprozeß vorzugreifen, ihn künstlich zur Krise zu treiben" (*GS* I.2:518; "to anticipate the revolutionary development process, bringing it artificially to a head," *SW* 4:6).

On the other hand, he identifies Napoleon III as the historical figure in whom the ultimate downfall of the proletariat and its revolutionary aspirations are foreshadowed. Parallels between second empire despotism and Hitler are a common theme in historical novels written during the exile period. Benjamin goes beyond these simple attempts to camouflage critical assessments of National Socialism by adopting a historical stance. More radical than his contemporaries, he believes that the sources of Fascism in the West and Socialism in the East were to be found in

the destruction of the revolutionary dynamics that the workers' movement had developed during the course of the nineteenth century. Accordingly, his Baudelaire book is as carefully candid in its dismissal of Lenin
and Stalin as it is of Hitler. In an extensive footnote he even draws an
explicit comparison between the catastrophes of nineteenth-century history and the totalitarian configurations in the 1930s: "Mit dem Ehrgeiz,
keine ihrer Unmenschlichkeiten ohne den Paragraphen zu lassen, dessen
Beobachtung in ihr zu erblicken ist, haben die totalitären Staaten einen
Keim zur Blüte gebracht, der . . . in einem früheren Stadium des Kapitalismus bereits geschlummert hat" (*GS* I.2:521, note; "With the intent
of leaving no inhumanity undocumented by the law whose observance
it indicates, the totalitarian states have fostered the flowering of a seed
which . . . was already present in an earlier stage of capitalism," *SW* 4:69
n.36). Hitler Germany and the Soviet Union are drawn together here and
characterized as political reactions to historical developments, according
to which the radical disintegration of the proletariat has been facilitated
by bureaucratic structures.

Repeatedly Benjamin's reading of Baudelaire's poetry collection *Les
fleurs du mal* (*The Flowers of Evil*) makes specific reference to the political situation during his own lifetime. In "Die Bohème" he relinquishes
all hopes that he had pinned on the Soviet Union as a political power
destined to defend the interests of the proletariat. His arguments come
close to the anti-Soviet sentiments entertained by his friends and mentors
in New York. Max Horkheimer had already expressed a thinly veiled criticism of the aberrations of socialism in the final issue of the "Journal for
Social Research" for the year 1937, in which he condemns Soviet politics
by pointing to the overt "Ökonomismus, auf den die kritische Theorie
mancherorts reduziert ist" (economism, to which critical theory has been
reduced in some parts of the world). Taking a disparaging and admoni-
tory stance, Horkheimer argues: "Der Entwicklungsgrad der wesentli-
chen Elemente der Demokratie und Assoziation gehört mit zum Inhalt
des Begriffs der Vergesellschaftung."[7] (The degree of development of the
essential elements of democracy and association are an integral part of any
concept of socialization.) In February 1938 Benjamin, deeply engrossed
in his work on the Baudelaire book, writes to Horkheimer: "Mit leiden-
schaftlicher Zustimmung lese ich, was Sie im letzten Heft publiziert
haben. Die Kritik an Rußland kann weitertragend und maßvoller schwerlich formuliert werden" (*GB* 6:23; I have read what you wrote in the
last issue with avid approval. The criticism levied against Russia could not
have been expressed more comprehensively and more moderately).

Benjamin's "tiger's leap into history" is not only limited to a dia-
tribe against socialism and Fascism. It also indicts his social group, the
intellectuals, who from the very beginning neglected to provide adequate support to the working class.[8] This also pertains to Baudelaire. A

witness to adverse political events, he responds to these by theologizing his thoughts. Benjamin interprets the satanism in *Les fleurs du mal* as a form of Gnostic religiosity, which in its blasphemy anticipates a salvation of the world from its derelict state by mobilizing the forces of Satan. In the "Doppelgesicht des Satans" (*GS* I.2:525; "dual aspect of Satan") he not only perceives "das finstere Haupt Blanquis" (*GS* I.2:524; the dark head of Blanqui) but also that of Napoleon III, implying that Satan speaks "nicht nur für die Unteren sondern auch für die Oberen" (*GS* I.2:525; "not only for the upper crust but for the lower classes as well," *SW* 4:10–11). This double portrait, which Benjamin inscribes into the figure of the devil, once again reveals the imminent threats to Europe posed by Stalin's and Hitler's totalitarianism.

Thus Baudelaire himself seems to have entrusted his fortunes to the Janus-faced devil, whom he made his guiding spirit in the guise of Satan Trismegistos in the opening poem of *Les fleurs du mal*. Benjamin points to the fact that the figure of the poet is marked by a deep ambivalence — certainly one reason why Baudelaire appears as disparaging for the true revolutionary cause as Blanqui. His work is not only a reflection of his times: it also bears the mark of Cain in its historical origin. Above all, it is marked by the blind rage of the professional conspirator. As an illustration Benjamin maintains that Baudelaire fancied himself in the "culte de la blague" (cult of bad jokes) of a Georges Sorel oder a Céline by contriving a "schöne Konspiration . . . zwecks Ausrottung der jüdischen Rasse" (*GS* I.2:516; "fine conspiracy for the purpose of exterminating the Jewish race," *SW* 4:5). Moreover, his allegorical method of writing assaults the reader with nearly the same tactics attributed to Blanqui's putschist activities; as Benjamin implies, his tropes startle the reader with unpredictable meanings and often leave him bewildered.

Benjamin accentuates the "tiefe Duplizität" ("profound duplicity") of Baudelaire's lyrics: "Sie hatte ein Ohr für die Gesänge der Revolution, aber auch ein Ohr für die 'höhere Stimme,' die aus dem Trommelwirbel der Exekutionen spricht" (*GS* I.2:527; "It had an ear for the songs of the revolution and also for the 'higher voice' which spoke from the drum roll of the executions," *SW* 4:12). In the final portion of "Die Bohème" this paradoxical condition becomes the foundation for what is a surprising analysis of literary media, especially given the context of his political intentions. According to his view, the literary market is marked by the dominance of the mass press during the second half of the nineteenth century. In contrast to the information and advertisements that are its central content, literature is only able to seek sanctuary in its *feuilleton* sections. While the increase in advertisement guarantees the possibility of better payment for the feuilletons, it is also one of the primary reasons for the corruption of the press, which Benjamin criticizes with the kind of verve that is reminiscent of the Austrian satiric writer Karl Kraus.

Referring to the confluence of "Information, Inserat und Feuilleton" ("information, advertisements, and feuilletons") he notes in the Baudelaire convolute of the *Passagen-Werk:* "Der Müßiggänger muß mit Sensationen versorgt werden, der Kaufmann mit Kunden und der kleine Mann mit einem Weltbild." ("The idler must be furnished with sensations, the merchant with customers, and the man in the street with a worldview," J90,3) In keeping with his analysis, Benjamin asserts that literature in its debased form has deteriorated to the point of becoming the source of ideology for the masses.

Therefore the conditions governing the production and publication of literature determine its content and function. As a medium of public discourse even lyrical poetry is dependent upon the general trends in economy and technology. "Um die Jahrhundertmitte veränderten sich die Bedingungen künstlerischer Produktion. Die Veränderung bestand darin, daß am Kunstwerk die Warenform, an seinem Publikum die Massenform zum ersten Mal einschneidend zur Geltung kam." ("Around the middle of the century, the conditions of artistic production underwent a change. This change consisted in the fact that for the first time the form of commodity imposed itself directly on the work of art, and the form of the masses on its public," J60,6) The poet responds to this new situation by entering the market in order to survive. This is the reason for his similarity to whores, which Benjamin underscores several times. Much as they sell their bodies, so is the product of the poet's genius the only merchandise that he can put on the market. The parallel serves to criticize the mass press in general and feuilletons as their characteristic genre in particular, showing these to be the medium of the writer under the conditions of free market economics. Like the *flâneur,* he ostensibly peruses the topography of commodities that the city has been transformed into, although in reality he is a market player with the need to find a buyer. Thus the first chapter ends with a negative summary on two counts: the literati are accused of having a false perception of themselves, while literature is revealed as being completely useless for public discourse.

V

That is the reason why the second section of the *Baudelaire* book, entitled "The Flâneur," begins with the assertion that literature has become harmless. The popular genre of the "Physiologien" (*GS* I.2:537; "physiologies," *SW* 4:18), which had their heyday in the 1840s, portrays the different types of city dwellers from the cozy perspective of the lower middle class. Benjamin's analysis aims to show that the individual, who in light of the "verschärften Konkurrenzkampf" ("intensified struggle for survival") has been transformed into the "vollkommensten aller Raubtiere" (*GS* I.2:542; "most perfect of all beasts of prey," *SW* 4:21), should be seen as a benign "fellow creature." Similar goals are served by the detective story, in which the city appears as a jungle and all traces of the individual have been lost. Benjamin correlates the genesis of this genre with the rise of a new medium and with his own experience as an emigrant: "Die Photographie ermöglicht zum ersten Mal, für die Dauer und eindeutig Spuren von einem Menschen festzuhalten. Die Detektivgeschichte entsteht in dem Augenblick, da diese einschneidendste aller Eroberungen über das Inkognito des Menschen gesichert war. Seither ist kein Ende der Bemühungen abzusehen, ihn dingfest im Reden und Tun zu machen" (*GS* I.2:550; "Photography made it possible for the first time to preserve permanent and unmistakable traces of a human being. The detective story came into being when this most decisive of all conquests of a person's incognito had been accomplished. Since that time, there has been no end to the efforts to capture a man in his speech and actions," *SW* 4:27).

With respect to this experience, the absorption of the city dweller into an anonymous mass, as practiced by the *flâneur* as the "Mann der Menge" ("man of the multitude"), proves to be phantasmagorical and illusionary. "In ihr bleibt verhüllt, was an [diesen Ansammlungen] das eigentlich Monströse ausmacht: nämlich die Massierung privater Personen als solcher durch den Zufall ihrer Privatinteressen. . . . Sie rationalisieren den Zufall der Marktwirtschaft, der sie derart zusammenführt, als 'Schicksal,' in dem sich die 'Rasse' wiederfindet" (*GS* I.2:565; "This existence conceals the really monstrous thing about [the masses]: that the concentration of private persons as such is an accident resulting from their private concerns. . . . They rationalize the accident of the market economy which brings them together in this way as 'fate' in which 'the race' is reunited," *SW* 4:36–37) The careful reader of these sentences cannot overlook that both of the terms highlighted by single quotes, which Benjamin deciphers from the self-awareness of the metropolitan mass in the nineteenth century, represent the central slogans of Fascist ideologies.

Benjamin is able to establish this association by basing his analysis of nineteenth-century society on the notion of the fetish character of merchandise, which he borrows from Karl Marx's *Das Kapital*. Forced to sell their capacity to work as a commodity, the masses find themselves determined by the capitalist order of production, which they might not have been conscious of but which clearly overshadowed their whole existence. However, the multitude, whose configuration is influenced by an "Einfühlung in die Ware" ("empathizing with commodities") also observes a delirious "Vorgefühl von ihrer eigenen Bestimmung als Klasse" (*GS*, I.2:561; "presentiment of its own determination as a class," *SW* 4:34) in it. Benjamin calls this clandestine social character "das Natürlich-Übernatürliche" (*GS* I.2:564; "the natural supernatural," *SW* 4:35), in which "isolierte Privatinteressen" (*GS* I.2:565; "isolated private concerns," *SW* 4:36) are obscured by the euphoria of social equality. If Benjamin had identified "Kapitalismus als Kultreligion" ("capitalism as a religion of pure cult")[9] at the beginning of the 1920s, he ascertains a comparable condition here in even more secular and radical form, without bringing the theological vocabulary of his earlier works into play. His diagnosis of what is truly monstrous in Baudelaire's prose poem *Les foules* as well as in Victor Hugo's exile works has its roots in the concrete social experience of the material critic. The totalitarian states give him his cue, "indem sie die Massierung ihrer Klienten permanent und verbindlich für alle Vorhaben machen" (*GS* I:565; "by making the concentration of their citizens permanent and obligatory for all their purposes," *SW* 4:36). In his readings of nineteenth-century literature Benjamin assembles the fundamental terms for his criticism of totalitarianism, terms which he not only applies to Hitler Germany and the Soviet Union under Stalin but also uses to characterize all modern societies complying with the laws of the free market economy. Hence the Baudelaire book concentrates on "die Entfaltung eines überkommenen Begriffs" ("the unfolding of a traditional term"), a goal that Benjamin alludes to when comparing *Ursprung des deutschen Trauerspiels* (The Origin of the German Mourning Play, 1928) with the *Passagen-Werk:* "War es dort der Begriff des Trauerspiels so würde es hier der des Fetischcharakters der Ware sein" (*GB* 5:83; If I dealt with the idea of mourning play there, then I would deal with the fetish character of merchandise here).

The universal context of delusion, which characterizes the constitution of societies in the age of "high capitalism," is only truly recognized in Victor Hugo's and Baudelaire's works. They represent the general exception to the universal innocuousness of literature and become a critical medium for Benjamin's own era. "Das ad plures ire der Römer war Hugos chthonischem Ingenium kein leeres Wort" (*GS* I.2:566; "To Hugo's chthonian mind, the ad plus ire of the Romans was not an empty phrase," *SW* 4:37). This sentence is Benjamin's cryptic response to the representation of the vast number of deceased in Victor Hugo's texts. What is implied can be deciphered, when one considers what he illuminates with respect to this Latin phrase in a footnote to his later essay "Über einige Motive bei Baudelaire" ("On Some Motifs in Baudelaire"): "Das Schöne ist seinem geschichtlichen Dasein nach ein Appell, zu denen sich zu versammeln, die es früher bewundert haben. Das Ergriffenwerden vom Schönen ist ein ad plures ire, wie die Römer das Sterben nannten" (*GS* I.2:638–39; "On the basis of its historical existence, beauty is an appeal to join those who admired it in an earlier age. Being moved by beauty means ad plures ire, as the Romans called dying," *SW* 4:352, n.63) These sentences allude to the condition for the possibility of the effectiveness of literature. Only when literature transports the experience of past generations and readers understand literature as a passage to the many dead present and not present in the text, and are thus willing to rewrite what has already been written, are they in a position to make use of texts as a medium of cognition for their own lives. It is self-explanatory that these requirements can be fulfilled neither by "physiologies" nor by detective stories. That Benjamin was able to glean them from Hugo's texts, inspired as they were by spiritual activities and séances, might explain the enigmatic quality of his deliberations.

Distinctive and much more precise are Benjamin's assumptions concerning Baudelaire. They introduce a category that seems to be able to destroy the phantasmagoria of the world of commodities: the shock. Benjamin's seminal interpretation of Baudelaire's sonnet "A une passante" (To a Passerby) figures as the center of his chapter "Der Flaneur" ("The Flâneur") and it is here that the cultural critic pinpoints the experience of the city dweller within the innermost experience of the individual. "In tiefer Trauer und hoheitsvollem Schmerz" ("In deep mourning and majestic pain") the woman passing by emerges from the crowd and is both thrust into the focus of the discerning subject and at the same time removed from it. For Benjamin she becomes an allegorical figure "der von der Großstadt stigmatisiert[en] Liebe" (*GS* I.2:548; "of love being stigmatized by the big city," *SW* 4:25). She confers a traumatic experience onto the poet, tearing the phantasmagorical veil asunder and revealing the true character of the masses pulsing through the city streets. Benjamin conjectures that her being has been determined by the "frosty breath of commodity economics," something that he had first experienced in the marches of the Fascist masses and the formation of the throngs in Stalin's Soviet Union. At the same time he discerns her particular form of being in the very impossibility of love in modern societies, as revealed in Baudelaire's poem. In essence, literary texts are shown to be the medium of cultural memory, the true significance of which can only be derived from the reality of recent social experience.

VI

In the third chapter of his Baudelaire book, entitled "Die Moderne" ("Modernity"), Benjamin assembles the motives that offset the fury of production in the socioeconomic sector of modernity. According to his analysis modern society is marked by an "Überforderung des Produzierenden" (*GS* I.2:574; "overtaxing of the productive person," *SW* 4:42). Since everything has been transformed into a commodity and become purchasable, the impetus to generate objects by exerting personal labor evaporates. "Die Widerstände, die die Moderne dem natürlichen produktiven Élan des Menschen entgegensetzt, stehen im Missverhältnis zu seinen Kräften. Es ist verständlich, wenn er erlahmt und in den Tod flüchtet" (*GS* I.2:578; "The resistance that modernity offers to the natural productive élan of an individual is out of all proportion to his strength.

It is understandable if a person becomes exhausted and takes refuge in death," *SW* 4:45) Conceived as a synthesis of the previous sections, this third chapter of the Baudelaire book strikes up a tableau in which the world is shown to be marked by the experience of death. At its core Benjamin resorts to an intensive reading of one of the central poems in *Les fleurs du mal*. According to Benjamin the verses in "Le cygne" (The Swan) capture the "decrepitude" of the metropolis with great clarity. He detects the same motive in another contemporary medium, in Charles Meryon's etchings, in which Paris is portrayed as a city of ruins. In this context Benjamin conceives of the rag picker and the lesbian as allegorical figures of modernity, which in view of the pervasiveness of death negate the absolute rule of commodities that liberal market economies unleash. The former culls the castaways and superfluous, making these his business in a society desperate for the innovative and novel, while the latter has renounced the productive force within the most intimate part of her body. The apotheosis of a social being anchored in death is the decisive figure of one who wants to commit suicide. Gathering data from documents in which workers were reported to have taken their own lives in response to the desperation of their own situation, Benjamin asserts that modernity stands "im Zeichen des Selbstmords" (*GS* I.2:578; "under the sign of suicide," *SW* 4:45). This emblematical characterization of the second half of the nineteenth century as well as his own period is neither founded on convincing historical evidence nor clearly expressed in Baudelaire's works. Rather, it is the product of Benjamin's own "nihilism,"[10] which propelled him to contemplate suicide on the occasion of his fortieth birthday in 1932, a resolution he did not carry out until 1940.

In one of the poems, "Petites vieilles" (Little Old Ladies) Benjamin finds an adequate image for the loneliness and poverty of the modern subject, who dwells with regret on the gardens and parks that are closed to the mass of city dwellers and thus become a focal point for their innermost yearnings (see *GS* I.2:576). Similarly, he views the modern poet as one who is excluded from society and who — in light of Baudelaire's fanciful fencing (*fantasque escrime*) — desperately tries to overcome the ruptures plaguing his existence. Like most members of the city crowd, he too is another "Depossedierter" (*GS* I.2:575; "dispossessed person," *SW* 4:43). "Wenig von dem, was zu den gegenständlichen Bedingungen geistiger Arbeit gehört, hat Baudelaire besessen: von einer Bibliothek bis zu einer Wohnung gab es nichts, worauf er im Laufe seines Daseins, das gleich unstet in wie außerhalb von Paris verlief, nicht hätte verzichten müssen" (*GS* I.2:574–75; "Baudelaire owned few of the material conditions for intellectual labor. A personal library, an apartment of his own — there was nothing he did not have to do without in the course of his life, which was equally precarious in Paris and outside the city," *SW* 4:42). Above all, he finds himself cut off from the cultural memory that could be activated to inscribe his texts into the horizon of a genuine experience: "Die Stereotypien in Baudelaires Erfahrungen, der Mangel an Vermittlung zwischen seinen Ideen, die erstarrte Unruhe in seinen Zügen deuten darauf hin, daß die Reserven, die großes Wissen und umfassender geschichtlicher Überblick dem Menschen eröffnen, ihm nicht zu Gebote standen" (*GS* I.2:574; "The stereotypes in Baudelaire's experiences, the lack of mediation among his ideas, and the frozen unrest in his features indicate that he did not possess the reserves which an individual acquires from great knowledge and a comprehensive view of history," *SW* 4:42).

Benjamin identifies the poet as the true hero of the tragedy of modernity, as one who feels the traces of the physical and cultural privation of the modern world in his own existence. Like the gladiators of antiquity he has to defend himself using tricks and deceit in order to produce his literary works. However, the heroic attitude — in keeping with that of the rag picker, of the flaneur or of the dandy — is only a mask, behind which the creative individual, all of whose artistic possibilities have been eradicated by modernity, can hide. "Denn der moderne Heros ist nicht Held — er ist Heldendarsteller" (*GS* I.2:600; "For the modern hero is no hero; he is a portrayer of heroes"). In this crisis Baudelaire resorts, as Benjamin asserts, to the same strategies as the professional conspirators: allegories become "Zentren der poetischen Strategie" (*GS* I.2:603; "loci of poetic strategy," *SW* 4:60–62).

Ultimately the historical materialist can describe Baudelaire's literary technique as putschist and thus return to the first part of his analysis. The verdict expressed there with respect to the conspirators from Blanqui to Hitler and Stalin remains valid until the final pages of the Baudelaire book. If Baudelaire is forced to set up his poems as a "Handstreich" (*GS* I.2:603; "coup de main," *SW* 4:62), in which the allegorical images grip the reader with unexpected meaning, then this is in Benjamin's estimation the sign of a catastrophic historical defeat that continues on into his own present. As is his usual practice, he ends his text with an allegorical image: "Blanquis Tat ist die Schwester von Baudelaires Traum gewesen. Beide sind ineinander verschlungen. Es sind die ineinander verschlungenen Hände auf einem Stein, unter dem Napoleon III. die Hoffnungen der Junikämpfer begraben hatte" (*GS* I.2:604; "Blanqui's action was the sister of Baudelaire's dream. The two are conjoined. They are the joined hands on the stone under which Napoleon III buried the hopes of the June fighters," *SW* 4:63). The stone that Benjamin erects before the reader's eye must be read as a monument. The "Hoffnungen der Junikämpfer" ("hopes of the June fighters") buried beneath it are the futile hopes of a revolutionary transformation of the world, such as was intended by the Parisian barricades of 1848. Karl Marx considered the uprising of the Parisian proletariat against the bourgeois republic "the most colossal event in the history of European civil wars" in his *Der achtzehnte Brumaire des Louis Bonaparte* (The Eighteenth Brumaire of Louis Bonaparte), which first appeared in 1852. According

to Marx the defeat of the insurgents by a coalition that included the bourgeois reactionary forces, the church, the farmers, and even paupers was
followed by singularly violent reprisal: "More than 3000 insurgents were
butchered after the victory, and 15,000 were deported without trial. With
this defeat the proletariat recedes into the *background* of the revolutionary stage."[11] What Marx reports with almost statistical sobriety becomes
part of a history of salvation in Benjamin's allegory. For him the proletariat
appears as the messianic savior of humankind, who takes the stage of history and whose suffering and death presage a future redemption, should
the masses be intelligent enough to join up with the "reverie" of the poet.
That Benjamin can couch his hopes in an allegorical image is telling proof
that "die großen Tendenzen der gesellschaftlichen Entwicklung . . . noch
die gleichen sind" (*GS* I.2:593; "the great tendencies of social development
are still the same," *SW* 4:55) as when Baudelaire was living and writing in
Paris. Or should Benjamin's final image be subject to a similar assumption
raised about Meryon's etchings of the city: "Das, wovon man weiß, daß
man es bald nicht mehr vor sich haben wird, das wird Bild" (*GS* I.2:590;
"When one knows that something will soon be removed from one's gaze,
that thing becomes an image," *SW* 4:53)?

That prompts two central questions: What is the close relationship
between the political and social history and the history of literature and
the media that Benjamin purports to have established? What would be
the result of contemplating jointly on these two historical spheres? Both
of these questions have been conceived from Benjamin's perspective by
taking the conditions for their material production into account. Hence
it is not a simple matter of mirroring or reflecting material circumstances,
as can easily be posited for Georg Lukács's naive Marxism. Rather, Benjamin's arguments are based on the awareness that the media themselves
have their own innate history. Not their content but their technical development is highly significant for tracing the historical past. In modernity,
both political history and the traditional media of collective memory,
literature, are the outcome of a historical catastrophe, which Benjamin
locates in a long sequence of failed revolutions extending from 1789 to
1918. This sequence, one may posit, has led to the global triumph of the
principle of the liberal market economy, which pervades all expressions of
human existence today. The distortions and aberrations of political history disclose the meaninglessness of literature and, inversely, the loss of
authenticity and functionality plaguing today's media can be read as characteristic of the deterioration in the social and political spheres.

VII

When Benjamin recommenced his work on his Baudelaire project in the
winter of 1939/40, after having been interrupted by the strong criticisms

levied by Horkheimer and Adorno against his chapters on Baudelaire, he first concentrated on the methodological basis for his philological interpretations. The crisis of transmissibility in this context is revealed in the demise of the agents of literature as an institution. Concurring with Apollinaire, he ascertains the death of the author, and in keeping with Baudelaire he recognizes the difficulties of comprehending lyric poetry, which only in rare instances conforms to the experience of its readers. Not without reason does he maintain that *Les fleurs du mal* was written for the least capable of readers, making it a classical work. These sentiments imply that lyrical poems should be seen as the canonical text of modernity, the age of individualization. Why? Because they present themselves as incomprehensible texts: they can only be read with the aid of commentary, which points to the fact that in modernity the relationship between canonic texts and commentary has been turned on its head. Whereas in the past the Holy Scriptures were made legible and accessible by commenting on them, modernity has projected the secular text into the canon by providing commentaries on it.

Initially, Benjamin secures the theoretical armature of his project by viewing, with the French philosopher Henri Bergson, the "Struktur des Gedächtnisses als entscheidend für die philosophische der Erfahrung. In der Tat ist die Erfahrung eine Sache der Tradition, im kollektiven wie im privaten Leben" (*GS* I.2:608; "structure of memory as decisive for the philosophical structure of experience. Experience is indeed a matter of tradition, in collective existence as well as private life.") That means, of course, that the data of experience tend to remain mute unless one resorts to deciphering the past human experience that has been subsumed in the texts. Going beyond the ahistorical perspective of the philosopher and referring to the categories developed in his essay on the storyteller, Benjamin concerns himself with "eine geschichtliche Determinierung der Erfahrung" (*GS* I.2:608; "a historical determination of memory," *SW* 4:314). Calling upon the *mémoire involontaire* that is prominent in Proust's works, he proves that opening a space of memory and the likelihood of individual and collective identity have been relinquished to chance in the age of the novel. Moreover, the dominance of information as evidenced in the organs of the press causes experience to dwindle away. Baudelaire's poetry responds to this historical development of the media by placing the shock that the individual is subjected to in modern society — whether as a member of the urban masses, as a drone in the mechanized production processes, or as an object of photographic reproduction — in the vortex of his poems, with regard both to their content and their structure. Therefore Benjamin is able to filter the wealth of experience in Baudelaire's poems into a single term, which he designates as "den Preis . . . , um welchen die Sensation der Moderne zu haben ist: die Zertrümmerung der Aura im Chockerlebnis" (*GS* I.2:653; "the price for which the sensation of modernity could be had: the disintegration of the aura in immediate shock experience," *SW* 4:343). That is to say: in the age of the hegemony of information, experience has been banished from its last refuge, poetry. But the shock is also inherent in the formal structure of the poem and it represents the starting point for the critic who wishes to decipher it.

The media analysis that adheres to the precepts of historic materialism that Benjamin derives from Baudelaire's texts appears to be tarnished by the false hope that the proletariat could take a messianic stance and become the savior of modernity. Although his disappointment in the Soviet Union was deeply felt, Benjamin continued to believe that the masses were the cornerstone of his historical materialism. Yet the downfall of socialism has proved that the hopes he set in the proletariat were phantasmagorical. What Benjamin was able to glean from the historical situation and the development of the media in the nineteenth century for his own present has only now become manifest. In our telematic age, the secondary orality and constantly moving images presented by television have made it the dominant medium of public discourse, especially since it derives its legitimacy and popularity from the sheer novelty of the information being disseminated. This trend is commensurate with a loss of meaning for the written word as represented in printed books. And yet humanity has developed a new and potent instrument for transmitting the written word, the computer, which is able not only to access the global archives available on the Web but also to exploit a multiplicity of textual resources as well as draw on the merging of textual and image or sound media. The goal of a media theory and communication practice based on Benjamin's principles would be to teach the kind of reading and writing that integrates all of these technological possibilities. Only then can writing remain a source from which the living can discern ethical norms or — to cite Benjamin's essay on the storyteller — bring "wisdom" to light; only then can writing retain its seminal function as an agent of cultural memory.

Notes

[1] See Walter J. Ong, *Orality and Literacy: The Technologizing of the Word*, 2nd ed. (New York: Routledge, 2002).

[2] All translations not otherwise credited are my own.

[3] Walter Benjamin Archiv, ed., *Walter Benjamins Archive: Bilder, Texte und Zeichen* (Frankfurt am Main: Suhrkamp, 2006), 199: "Unter Verwendung von Buntstiften entwickelte er einen Farbcode, ein System von Signets" (Using colored pencils [Benjamin] developed a color code, a system of signets.) See illustration on inside front cover. The construction plan of the Passagen-Werk has not been completely deciphered yet, because a large part of the material has not been made available. See Willi Bolle, "Geschichte," in *Benjamins Begriffe*, ed. Martin

Opitz und Erdmut Wizisla (Frankfurt am Main: Suhrkamp, 2000), 1:417, n. 28. The upshot is that of the 86 manuscript pages of the construction plan extant, only 16 pages, or approximately 20%, have appeared in print.

[4] Pierre Nora, *Zwischen Geschichte und Gedächtnis* (Berlin: Wagenbach, 1990), 11.

[5] This term is used by Benjamin in its negative connotation, such as it appears in Karl Marx's *The Eighteenth Brumaire of Louis Bonaparte*: "Alongside decayed roués with dubious means of subsistence and of dubious origin, alongside ruined and adventurous offshoots of the bourgeoisie, were vagabonds, discharged soldiers, discharged jailbirds, escaped galley slaves, rogues, mountebanks, lazzaroni, pickpockets, tricksters, gamblers, marquereaus, brothel keepers, porters, literati, organ-grinders, knife grinders, tinkers, beggars — in short, the whole indefinite, disintegrated mass, thrown hither and thither, which the French term la bohème" (See Karl Marx, *The Eighteenth Brumaire of Louis Bonaparte* [London: Lawrence & Wishart, 1984], 65; *Der achtzehnte Brumaire des Louis Bonaparte*, in Karl Marx, Friedrich Engels, Studienausgabe IV [Frankfurt am Main: Fischer, 1966], 77). The virtuoso play on language that Marx summons to discredit the constituents of the "Society of 10 December" is also valid for Napoleon III., whom he denounces as the "chief of the lumpenproletariat," which is a perspective that Benjamin adopted.

[6] Benjamin writes: "In ihm [Blanqui] und seinen Genossen sah Marx im Rückblick auf die Junirevolution, die 'wirklichen Führer der proletarischen Partei.' Man kann sich von dem revolutionären Prestige, das Blanqui damals besessen und bis zu seinem Tod bewahrt hat, schwerlich einen zu hohen Begriff machen" (*GS* I.2:518; "He [Blanqui] and his associates, claimed Marx in his analysis of the June Insurrection, were the 'true leaders of the proletarian party.' It is hardly possible to overestimate the revolutionary prestige which Blanqui possessed at that time and preserved up to his death," *SW* 4:6). In his essay T*he Eighteenth Brumaire of Louis Bonaparte,* to which Benjamin is referring here, Marx emphasizes the impotence of the proletarian leader: "As is known, May 15 had no other result save that of removing Blanqui and his comrades, that is, the real leaders of the proletarian party, from the public stage for the entire duration of the cycle we are considering." See Karl Marx, *The Eighteenth Brumaire of Louis Bonaparte*, 17.

[7] Max Horkheimer und Herbert Marcuse, "Philosophie und kritische Theorie," in *Zeitschrift für Sozialforschung* 6.3 (1937) :629–30.

[8] This seems to be the meaning of the cryptic motto that Benjamin derives from Pierre Ronsard's "Hymne an den Tod" ("Hymn to Death") and sets at the beginning of Convolute J dedicated to Baudelaire in the Arcades Project: "For it pleases me, all for your sake, to row / My own oars here on my own sea, / And to soar heavenward by a strange avenue, / Singing you the unsung praises of Death" (*AP* 229; see *GB* 6:125).

[9] Walter Benjamin, "Kapitalismus als Religion" (*GB* 6:100; "Capitalism as Religion," SW 1:289). See "Politik, Ökonomie und Religion im Zeitalter der Globalisierung," in *Theologie und Politik*, ed. Bernd Witte and Mauro Ponzi (Berlin: Erich Schmidt Verlag 2003), 9–19.

[10] Benjamin's use of this term can be traced back to Nietzsche, who considered suicide to be an "act of nihilism" (see *GS* I.2:578, note).

[11] Karl Marx, *The Eighteenth Brumaire of Louis Bonaparte*, 18.

5: Benjamin in the Age of New Media

Lutz Koepnick

I

UPON ENTERING THE MAIN EXHIBITION venue of the 2007 Documenta in Kassel, visitors to the Fridericianum first encountered a rather unexpected sight: Paul Klee's 1920 painting *Angelus Novus,* famous mostly of course because of Walter Benjamin's penetrating interpretation of the work as an allegorical depiction of the melancholic angel of history, trying to pay tribute to what has been smashed in the catastrophic course of modern time. Klee's painting in fact is now inextricably bound to what Benjamin wrote about it in the last months of his life. To look at it is to hear Benjamin's voice; to cast our eyes onto the painting is to access the curious mixture of the messianic and the apocalyptic that structured Benjamin's late writing. There can be little doubt that the curators of Documenta sought to draw on this association. Klee's angel, in its Benjaminian reading, here was meant to offer a road map to show how to navigate the global array of contemporary art exhibited in Kassel. In this respect the painting took on the function of a natural sign, one whose meaning was given and granted, one that spoke to the viewer with unquestionable authority. Hung as it was in the main stairwell of the Fridericianum, *Angelus Novus* served as a signifier providing its own interpretation and hence was in no need of further reading — a sign asking the viewers to subject their interpretative freedom to a set of preordained meanings similar to the way in which we allow a street map to guide us through a city without (at least initially) questioning its referential accuracy.

Any visitor, however, who stepped closer to Klee's painting and read the adjacent label was in for a surprise. For here is what the label read: "Paul Klee / Angelus Novus, 1920 / Ausstellungskopie | exhibition copy / Fotografie | Photograph: David Harris." Rather than presenting the real thing and inviting the audience to be absorbed by the originality of Klee's brushstroke, the curators openly admitted to having violated customary exhibition practices and offered a mere duplicate to the beholder's eye. While there may have been many good logistical reasons for not displaying the original, it is more than tempting to understand the curators' intervention as both a systematic and symptomatic gesture.

In his essay "Das Kunstwerk im Zeitalter seiner technischen Reproduzier-barkeit" ("The Work of Art in the Age of Its Technological Reproduc-ibility," 1935; third version, 1936–39)[1] Benjamin argues that the media of technological reproduction, such as photography and film, destroy the "aura," that is, the traditional artwork's quasi-sacred halo of original-ity and uniqueness. In so doing, Benjamin argues, film instigates a new, emancipatory way of seeing, which helps viewers to recognize the spec-tacular self-representations of Fascism, defined by Benjamin as a new and false aestheticization of politics in mass rallies, the cult of the *Führer,* and other such "auratic" effects of mass manipulation. As if bringing into play Benjamin's own valorization of mechanical reproduction over the auratic nature of the original work of art, the curators here, alluding to Benja-min's essay, seemed to empower the visiting masses "des Gegenstands aus nächster Nähe im Bild, vielmehr im Abbild, in der Reproduktion, hab-haft zu werden" (*GS* I.2:479; "to get hold of an object at close range in an image, or, better, in a facsimile, a reproduction," *SW* 4:255), at the expense of being captured by the spell of originality and uniqueness. In presenting the visitor with an exhibition copy, the curators sought to pry Klee's painting out of its auratic shell and destroy what — in Benjamin's view — would cause the viewer to submit thoughtlessly to its author-ity and vanish into the painting's commanding here and now. Instead of catering to a museological culture of staged authenticity, the makers of the Documenta thus seemed to emphasize the transitoriness and instabil-ity, the democratic appeal and anti-hierarchical language of contemporary artistic production and exhibition. In doing so, however, they of course unsettled the very rationale that informed the prominent placement of Klee's painting in the entrance's area in the first place. While Klee's angel instantly invoked Benjamin's intellectual aura and interpretative authority, the label spoke out against desires for the auratic and authoritative. While the image served as a locus of pre-stabilized meanings directly referring us to Benjamin, the label referred to Benjamin's thoughts on mechanical reproducibility, which bring into question the power of any single image to produce certain effects or references.

A curatorial oversight? A performative self-contradiction? An insider joke? This is not the place to speculate further about the intentions of Roger Buergel, the artistic director of Documenta XII, in positioning Benjamin's Klee painting as a motto at the beginning of his show. What needs to be pointed out is simply the extent to which Buergel's curatorial intervention is symptomatic of the fact that Benjamin's famous dialectic of traditional art and mechanical reproduction today no longer seems to form some kind of historical dialectic; that in our era of ubiquitous digital screens, interfaces, and technological mediations we instead have come to see the auratic and the post-auratic in an open relationship of supplementariness and coexistence, a non-climactic give-and-take structured by a logic of addition rather than one of mutual exclusion or contestation, by a conjunctive "and" rather than a combative "either/or." Though Benjamin, in "The Work of Art in the Age of Its Technological Reproducibility," had left little doubt about the fact that all art in principle is and has always been a potential object of reproduction, his decisive move was to conceptualize the media arts of photography and film as radically breaking with the representational and perceptual registers of preindustrial society and thus redefining the very nature of art and the aesthetic in modernity. The historical breakthrough of technical arts that no longer produced originals, for Benjamin did not simply change the role of certain forms of art and aesthetic experience in society but revolutionized the entire concept of art. For Benjamin, the logic of media innovation and technological change was *irresistible* and *irreversible:* the advent of newer media such as film and photography radically recalibrated the location of art and aesthetic experience in society; it completely reconfigured the structural relationships between spectator and work as much as between audience members themselves; and last but not least, it transformed the concepts and categories according to which past and present generations had evaluated the quality of art, discussed its meanings, assessed its political and social investments, and conceptualized art's effects on the beholder's body and senses. At its best, to invoke the auratic under the aegis of post-auratic culture could not but lead to a violation of the formal inventory of technological art; at its worst, it resulted in what Benjamin famously called the aestheticization of politics, that is, Fascism, understood as an attempt to satisfy the masses with symbolic spectacles of collectivity that obscure the factual fragmentation and stratification of society. The technological base of new media such as film and photography, in Benjamin's eyes, therefore, did not simply make previous artistic forms and practices look really old but instead produced conditions radically delegitimizing any attempt to bring old and new into some kind of productive conversation. Any form of art that in the age of its mechanical reproducibility aspired to the auratic was not real art at all. It instead became ideology, a mechanism masking the order of the day, a diversion from how media arts promoted distraction — a mode of viewing that does not absorb the viewer — as an antidote to the authoritarian effect of the auratic in art.

More than seventy years after its initial publication, Benjamin's essay on mechanical reproducibility has remained a key text in many debates about the role of art and the aesthetic in a society defined by advanced media. Though the technologies of artistic production and reproduction have undergone tremendous changes since the 1930s, Benjamin's conceptual matrix — the juxtaposition of the auratic and the post-auratic, of aesthetic originality and infinite reproduction, of contemplative surrender and distracted appropriation — continues to inform contemporary conversations about how electronic and digitally based new media have revolutionized the legacy of twentieth-century culture and art, including the very arts of film and photography that Benjamin himself considered as the latest turn of media innovation. However, much of what Benjamin saw in terms of a historical dialectic and logic of paradigmatic substitution in today's debates and practices emerges as a co-presence of seemingly incompatible values, notions, strategies, and intensities. Technologically mediated or produced art today may be discussed in terms of its auratic here and now as much as older forms of artistic production may be seen as having already been energized by some of the principles Benjamin associated with mechanical reproducibility. Conceptual boundaries have thus become blurry, while political effects no longer appear predetermined. Unless one wants to be seen as a conceptual die-hard, it has become virtually impossible to hang on to Benjamin's equation of auratic identification and political capitulation, as well as to his assertion that post-auratic tactics of distracted appropriation would define the royal road toward individual and collective emancipation. Though we might be surrounded by all kinds of media claiming categorical newness, contemporary cultural critics — unlike Benjamin — are far less eager to see our age of new media as a ground radically redefining the epistemological, aesthetic, ethical, and political categories according to which we should evaluate the entire history of art and cultural production.

It is one of the tasks of the pages that follow to map out a number of critical differences between contemporary discussions of new media aesthetics and Benjamin's own take on how mechanically produced art engaged the user and produced the condition that made new networks of human interaction possible. While some of these considerations warn against any uncontrolled use of Benjamin's concepts for the sake of theorizing new media today, this essay will nevertheless uphold the value and viability of Benjamin's writings for our understanding of twenty-first century media arts, not so much because of what Benjamin had to say about the political logic of technological arts, but because he offered a compelling model of how to think about the relationship between technological change, the aesthetic, and how media engage or are being engaged by the user in the first place. The focus will be on a particular, albeit highly productive, aspect of Benjamin's critical model, namely Benjamin's dual assumption, first, that media innovations deeply impact the affective registers and sensory systems of the user's body, and second, that new media, in reconfiguring our sense of seeing and touch, of bodily extension and tactility, help produce new forms of self-reflexive seeing and embodiment. My argument will proceed in two interrelated steps. I first review some basic differences between what Benjamin considered new media in the age of mechanical reproducibility and the newness of media culture in the digital age. Then I compare Benjamin's remarks about screen acting and bodily experience in classical cinema with what computer-driven animation techniques such as rotoscoping today do to the mediation of corporeality on and beyond the screen. The point of this series of reflections is not to make Benjamin's writing on new media look old but — very much in line with the operations of what we call new media today — engage this writing in an ongoing and open-ended process of remediation.

II

Though it has quickly come to displace a previous focus on terms such as "multimedia" and "cyberspace," the notion of new media — as it has occupied artists, entrepreneurs, and academics alike since the mid-1990s — has clearly raised as many questions as it has been able to answer. As Wendy Hui Kyong Chun argues, the term — unlike some of its predecessors — was not accommodating: "It portrayed other media as old or dead; it converged rather than multiplied; it did not efface itself in favor of a happy, if redundant plurality. The singular plurality of the phrase ('new media' is a plural noun treated as a singular subject) stemmed from its negative definition: it was not mass media, specifically television."[2] And yet, as unhappy as many might be with this term, it looks as if the concept has come to stay for the time being, and that — rather than lamenting its lack of clarity — we are called upon to fill it with meaningful content.

Lev Manovich's 2001 *The Language of New Media* remains perhaps the most lucid and useful attempt to define the specificity of new media,[3] in spite of the fact that many critics have developed sophisticated arguments to complicate Manovich's conceptual matrices since its publication. For Manovich, the emergence of new media cannot be exclusively explained by the rise of digitality, nor does it simply represent an intensification of the logic of mechanical reproduction as theorized by Benjamin. Instead, what makes new media new is the way in which they hybridize two distinct, albeit interrelated, technological tributaries: first, the path that led from photography to film and to the emergence of the graphical human computer interface in the 1980s, which was dedicated to the development of technology able to process, exchange, and disseminate information *in* and *across* time; and second, the trajectory that resulted in an ever more comprehensive drive to break down any information into discrete numerical data, energized by the ability of computers to encode and store any kind of input according to universal algorithmic or digital formulas. Whereas neither mechanical time-art nor digitality per se suffices to describe the media revolutions of the past two decades, it is the amalgamation of time-based representation and advanced computing power that in Manovich's view sufficiently defines what makes our own mediascapes categorically different from those of the early to mid-twentieth century.

Unlike earlier technical machines and configurations, new media combine principles such as numerical representation (each distinct element of data can be encoded in mathematical form); modularity (discrete elements can be articulated in open-ended and variable structures); automation (machines take over some of the principal tasks of recording, processing, modifying, and displaying data); variability (users can use their machines in order to infinitely change the objects produced by other users' machines); and transcoding (code is shared across perceptual or representational modalities; a sound file can be played as an image file, and so on.). And yet, even though new media bring into play an unprecedented mix of representational principles, Manovich insists that their language also bears some similarity to the communicative registers of older media, in particular those of film and photography. The historical break associated with new media is not as fundamental as the term suggests. Rather than invalidating the past, new media usher users into an era of open-ended plurality and simultaneity, an era in which both the contents and the structures of older media are mimicked, recalibrated, supplemented, or rewritten according to the technological parameters of the present. In fact, as Manovich is never shy to emphasize, in studying the representational strategies of older media products (such as Dziga Vertov's 1929 *Man with a Movie Camera*), we can learn a great deal about the structural possibilities of newer media. As Manovich shows with regard to Vertov's montage editing and modular layering of different images, the path from old to new is not a teleological one-way street. The past allows us to illuminate the present just as much as the present encourages us to discern the language of past technologies in ever-different light.

It is this emphasis on the constitutive language of new media, their ability at once to ingest and remediate the representational modalities of older ones, that simultaneously connects and differentiates Manovich's and Benjamin's understanding of the newness of new media. Like Manovich, Benjamin too was eager both to identify a particular language of film by exploring its technological make-up and to argue that film could incorporate older aesthetic forms into its specific logic: to know the hardware of a certain medium such as film was essential in order to understand and assess its software, the kind of contents it could successfully assimilate into its formal structure and disseminate to its audiences. For Benjamin, the peculiarly modern medium of film was essentially defined by the cut, that discontinuous rupture between two separate shots able to displace the viewer abruptly into unfamiliar other places and other times. The possibility of the cut, in Benjamin's perspective, situated film as a medium in which modern machines offered rudimentary forms of modularity and variability and thus situated the viewer, not as a passive recipient of a work's aura, but as an active participant in the collective process of endowing cultural objects with meaning and social relevance. Because of the disruptive and quasi-traumatic qualities of the cut, film had the inherent task of positioning the viewer as one continually prevented from empathetic identification and auratic absorption — creating a highly attentive but also profoundly distracted viewer eager to insert the filmic product into the structures of everyday life, to connect to other audience members, and thus to engage in the construction of new types of communities outside the theater. Films, on the other hand, that sought to mask the disruptive and displacing language of the cut — whether they aimed at artificially recreating aura by using film stars' images or relied on classical principles of smooth, invisible continuity editing — not only immobilized what Benjamin considered the emancipatory structures of filmic viewership, but, in a strict sense, violated the very ontology of the medium and thereby disqualified themselves from being counted as representatives of the medium in the first place. New media, for Benjamin, were new, not only because they — even when incorporating the old — broke with the representational structure of existing media, but because in so doing they also initiated the possibility of completely new cultural practices and forms of social appropriation.

While today's critical conversations about new media can certainly learn a lesson or two from Benjamin's dual emphasis on the logics of cultural technology and the social practice surrounding them, Benjamin's rather emphatic and eminently modernist notion of medium specificity renders universal applications and recyclings of his thought today problematic. Whereas Benjamin's aim was to identify a coherent, systematic, and self-contained logic of the new medium of film, such writing as Manovich's on (digital) new media emphasizes the essentially hybrid, fluid, and pluralistic character of their language. Whereas Benjamin described desired social practices as an effect of the most undistorted unfolding of a medium's inherent language, the stress on new media's hybridity in contemporary writing cautions us against any normative claims about their contents, aesthetic successes, and political missions. Even the most cutting-edge merging of time-based arts and computing power today does not allow us to make an automatic judgment about a certain work's aesthetic success or potential social usage. And even the most technophile rhetoric of innovation and progress today cannot conceal the complex logic by which various new media today borrow from and enrich the language of other (older) media — and thus ultimately efface the very assumption of categorical newness that drove Benjamin's own thought on mechanical reproduction.

III

Though Manovich's work plays an essential role in thinking through the constitutive elements of new media today and how they may differ from the culture of mechanical reproduction, other writing deserves to be mentioned here as well in order to outline the specificity of what we call new media, not least because this writing too extends and reconfigures Benjamin's own interests in the historicity of sensory perception — the aesthetic in its most emphatic sense — in light of twenty-first century media technologies. I am thinking in particular of the recent surge of inquiries emphasizing the extent to which new media, rather than dislocating users into some kind of disembodied virtual never-never land, have the ability to enable new and unprecedented forms of embodiment — experiences that highlight the extent to which sight is bound up with a viewer's entire sensory system and its sensorimotoric functions.[4] In contrast to the cyborg criticism of the 1980s and 1990s, which often delved into fantasies of an erasure of the corporeal, this newer writing on new media culture recalls certain phenomenological traditions of thought in order to conceptualize how our interactions with highly mediated environments and ubiquitous electronic interfaces today allow us to understand the role of our body as the primary medium, a membrane able to mediate different impressions of the real and situating us in ever-different perceptual positions, a mobile framing device facilitating somatic points of contact between subjective and objective worlds. Rather than extinguish the user's body in some virtual surroundings, new media allow body and world to engage in tactile exchanges and reveal the way in which our perceptual systems themselves perpetually frame and reframe, project and virtualize the phenomenal world in order to render it navigable. Whereas classical and enlightenment philosophy sought to abstract vision from the other senses, new media have the ability to show how seeing only works because it is grounded in our experiential modalities of kinesthesia (the sensation of body movement), of proprioception (the awareness of our body's position and boundaries in space), and of touch (the sensation of physical contact with objects other than our body), all three of which comprise what some critics call "tactility" (Hansen) and others the "haptic body" (Marks).[5]

It is not difficult to see that Benjamin's theory of mechanical reproduction in some respects anticipates the current turn toward exploring sensory perception and mediated forms of embodiment. Benjamin's artwork essay, by invoking both Karl Marx and art historians such as Alois Riegl and Franz Wickhoff, famously set out to argue for the historicity of the human senses, the fact that the "Art und Weise, in der die menschliche Sinneswahrnehmung sich organisiert — das Medium, in dem sie erfolgt — . . . nicht nur natürlich sondern auch geschichtlich bedingt (ist)" (GS 1.2:478; "the way in which human perception is organized — the medium in which it occurs — is conditioned not only by nature but by history," SW 3:104). Our sensory organs may produce certain perceptions of different historical realities, but different historical constellations also reshape the way in which we perceive the real in the first place, relate different modalities of perception to each other, and thus situate our bodies in the world. It is against the background of this emphasis on the historical contingencies of the human senses that Benjamin in the second half of his artwork essay comes to speculate about the psychophysical impact of cinema on the spectator: how cinema, rather than merely stimulating fantasy, subjects the viewer to a fundamental retraining of the senses. Cinema, for Benjamin, extends the perceptual challenges of both the urban environment (the overwhelming simultaneity of discontinuous visual shocks in the myriad sights in the overcrowded streets of the modern city) and of Dadaist artistic practice (the deliberate assault on the viewer by aesthetically shocking readymades such as Marcel Duchamp's urinal or the politically satiric photo-montage of John Heartfield) to the realm of modern entertainment and diversion. Because of the constitutive structure of the cut, film can hit the spectator like a bullet. Film thus assumes tactile qualities: it communicates to and defines the eye as a physiological entity and as a bodily organ, not simply as a seemingly transparent window of abstract sight. Film literally touches upon the viewer's perception because of its ballistic qualities; it is far too complex a medium to be understood in terms of pure opticality, and it recasts sight into a medium we cannot reduce to treasured assumptions of disembodied seeing.

Benjamin's interest in the physiology of cinema spectatorship, in tactile seeing, clearly has some roots in his early writing — in his recurrent preoccupation with the relationship of mind and body, with sensuous forms of experience, and with the magic of non-sensuous similarities. Unfortunately, this is not the place to trace in further detail how Benjamin's work of the 1930s recalls and reframes his own earlier research and writing on mimetic experience, empirical psychology, and the metaphysics of perception, nor to engage in a more general discussion about the intricate relationships of Benjamin's thought of the 1920s and 1930s. Suffice it to say, however, that Benjamin, in the context of his artwork essay, hoped nothing less than to move beyond the speculative and universalizing gestures of his early work and define the material conditions and historical contingencies that make particular modes of perception and embodiment possible in the first place. What is of greater interest for my argument here is instead how Benjamin's concept of embodied spectatorship can certainly also be understood as a precursor of the ideas of contemporary critics who seek to bring the body back to the realm of media theory and criticism. Often simply reduced to a theorist of the visual turn of modernity, Benjamin was very aware that the modern media of image production did not appeal to the eye alone and permitted the modern viewing subject to experience seeing in all its bodily complexity and embeddedness. And yet once again it would be a mistake to consider Benjamin's notion of tactile seeing as directly compatible with the concept of tactility and the haptic body in contemporary media aesthetics. For Benjamin's aim when stressing the ballistic aspects of cinematic spectatorship was to advocate the bursting asunder of the nineteenth-century bourgeois subject, whereas the phenomenological aspirations of contemporary media theory are profoundly dedicated to pursuing a new kind of techno-humanism, an enriched and enriching notion of the human subject self-reflexively aware of its own often quite fluid extensions and interactions, its bodily boundaries, its perceptual mechanisms, and its forms of affection and self-affection. Benjamin's fascination with tactility reflected his hope that new media would frame the legacy of bourgeois individualism and resituate the viewer within a post-bourgeois, post-individualist, and post-humanist realm of political action and emancipatory exteriority. Much of what has been written in recent years on the physiology of perception in the age of new digital media, on the other hand, aims at situating the subject as one actively seeking to frame and reframe its perceptions of the world, to develop new sensory connections and maps of its surroundings, and thus relaxing — instead of exploding — the hardened contours of subjectivity. The new medium of mechanical reproduction in Benjamin was to redeem the perceiving subject from itself and merge it into a post-aesthetic collective of at once distracted and highly attentive social players. The phenomenological turn in contemporary media aesthetics, by contrast, understands experiences with new media ensembles as a springboard for exploring the variegated processes of human perception and for embracing the aesthetic as a principal modality of maneuvering the world with our senses and assimilating this world to our contingent and aleatoric movements through space. Unlike Benjamin, contemporary media theory does not think of tactile seeing as a mere product of a subject's being subjected to ballistic attacks and destructive assaults. Instead, it wants to show how we need to explore tactility and embodiment as the inevitable source of a richer, more complex, less constrained, and fundamentally expanded notion of the human subject — its perceptions, its bodily self-identity, and its relationship to other human subjects.

IV

But what about the bodies of those not looking at the screens but standing in front of the camera and delivering their corporeality for future or real-time acts of spectatorship? How does mechanical reproduction in Benjamin's understanding affect an actor's sense of embodiment, and how does this differ from what cinema in an age of comprehensive digitization does to pro-filmic events (empirical events taking place in front of the camera) and forms of embodiment? How far can we push Benjamin's thoughts on acting in front of cinematic cameras in order

to conceptualize figurations of physicality in contemporary screen culture and how these may communicate with a viewer's desire to project
himself bodily or empathetically — at the level of the tactile and the
affective — into the action on screen?

In his artwork essay Benjamin famously maps his distinction of the
auratic and post-auratic onto the difference between acting on a theater
stage and acting in front of a camera. Theatrical performances cannot do
without a certain rhetoric of the here and now; they take place in front
of a present public and in each and every instant adjust to the physical
presence of audience members. Acting for the theater rests on principles
of temporal continuity and spatial contiguity; it invites the audience to
identify and empathize, not simply with a certain character of a play, but
with how the actor achieves unique and unrepeatable visibility during
the very act of performance. Acting for the camera, by contrast, destroys
this kind of aura. It causes the theater stage's rhetoric of authenticity and
uniqueness to vanish as the filming process replaces a living audience
with the cold gaze of a mechanical recording device. Cinema, Benjamin
insists, for the first time in history allows ordinary audience members to
appear as objects of cultural representation. Unlike the theater, it does
not require specials skills in order to be filmed for a newsreel show, situating cinema — in Benjamin's eyes — as a principally democratic and
anti-hierarchic tool of cultural exchange. Just as importantly, however,
even when relying on professional actors, cinema fundamentally changes
the way in which audience members look at and project themselves into
what is being enacted on screen. What stage actors must present as one
continuous temporal event, in a film studio can be the product of a multiplicity of discontinuous and discontiguous shots and montage effects.
Whereas in theater the audience member basically has to look at the
physical movements of the actors from a fixed and monocular viewpoint,
in the film studio an actor's movements are framed and reframed by the
movements of the camera, its ongoing repositioning, its use of special
effects, and hence its dismantling of the legacy of central perspective
and the early modern privileging of at once disembodied and distanced
sight. Benjamin summarizes:

> Die Apparatur, die die Leistung des Filmdarstellers vor das Publikum
> bringt, ist nicht gehalten, diese Leistung als Totalität zu respektie-
> ren. Sie nimmt unter Führung des Kameramannes laufend zu dieser
> Leistung Stellung. Die Folge von Stellungnahmen, die der Cutter
> aus dem ihm abgelieferten Material komponiert, bildet den fertig
> montierten Film. Er umfaßt eine gewisse Anzahl von Bewegungs-
> momenten, die als solche der Kamera erkannt werden müssen — von
> Spezialeinstellungen wie Großaufnahmen zu schweigen. So wird die
> Leistung des Darstellers einer Reihe von optischen Tests unterwor-
> fen. (*GS* I.2:488)

[The recording apparatus that brings the film actor's performance to the public need not respect the performance as an integral whole. Guided by the cameraman, the camera continually changes its position with respect to the performance. The sequence of positional views which the editor composes from the material supplied him constitutes the completed film. It comprises a certain number of movements, of various kinds and duration, which must be apprehended as such through the camera, not to mention special camera angles, close-ups, and so on. Hence, the performance of the actor is subjected to a series of optical tests. (*SW* 4:259)]

Benjamin's use of the concept of "test" in this context is at first astonishing, but the term is less puzzling if we recall that Benjamin, at various junctures of the artwork essay, sought to graft Bertolt Brecht's theory of epic theater onto his account of film, and thus to model the film studio as a modern laboratory of affects and meanings meant to obliterate the empathetic structures of identification associated with Aristotelian and bourgeois theater and art. To test, for Benjamin, means to break the spell that aura may cast on to the viewer; it disrupts the emotional glue that binds work and spectator into a self-contained unity. These Brechtian undertones of Benjamin's theory of cinematic acting become particularly clear when Benjamin continues arguing

daß der Filmdarsteller, da er nicht selbst seine Leistung dem Publikum präsentiert, die dem Bühnenschauspieler vorbehaltene Möglichkeit einbüßt, die Leistung während der Darbietung dem Publikum anzupassen. Dieses kommt dadurch in die Haltung eines durch keinerlei persönlichen Kontakt mit dem Darsteller gestörten Begutachters. *Das Publikum fühlt sich in den Darsteller nur ein, indem es sich in den Apparat einfühlt. Es übernimmt also dessen Haltung: es testet.* Das ist keine Haltung, der Kultwerte ausgesetzt werden können. (*GS* I.2:488)

[that the film actor lacks the opportunity of the stage actor to adjust to the audience during his performance, since he does not present his performance to the audience in person. This permits the audience to take the position of a critic, without experiencing any personal contact with the actor. *The audience's empathy with the actor is really an empathy with the camera. Consequently, the audience takes the position of the camera; its approach is that of testing.* This is not an approach compatible with cult value. (*SW* 4:259–60, italics in original)]

Far from merely mediating pro-filmic events to the audience and thus directing our attention and affect, in Benjamin's understanding the technical apparatus of the camera itself figures as an object of empathy and identification. And to the extent to which our act of viewing assimilates to how the camera has looked at certain events and actions, we cannot — so Benjamin's thesis — but replicate the very attitude of disaffected and laboratory-like testing, of discontinuous and constructivist looking, to which the camera subjected the actor's performance during the process of recording. It is by taking on the features of the camera, by allowing the camera to absorb and substitute the viewer's sensorimotoric operations, that we become viewers critically testing an actor's performance. It is by empathizing with and projecting affect into the medium itself that we break the spell of empathy and affect that Benjamin associates with an actor's performance in conventional theater.

There are many reasons why neither classical narrative nor even avant-garde cinema during the twentieth century really lived up to this mediation, or folding, of performative presence and spectatorial affect. While Benjamin's idea of the film studio as a laboratory — a testing ground — for fragmented performative acts is no doubt to the point, there is something quite odd about his assumption that testing cameras would automatically produce testing and critical spectators. What is more interesting to pursue in this context, however, is the fact that cinema today, to the extent to which it seeks to incorporate or emulate the language of new media in Manovich's sense, is developing all kinds of mechanisms enabling nothing more than the formation of what Benjamin would have called a critical spectator: a viewer involved in a simultaneous projection and disruption of bodily affect; a viewer at once empathizing with what he or she sees on screen and self-reflexively probing the very structures of empathy and embodiment that make such a viewing possible; a viewer assimilating to the logic of the medium in order to experience the extent to which the perceiving body itself is the primary medium and frame of experience and perception.

V

In the remainder of this essay I would like to illustrate the relevance of Benjamin's theory of mediated empathy for the present day by discussing the more recent surge of digital rotoscoping in mainstream film. An animation technique in which the hands of skillful animators trace over live action footage frame by frame, rotoscoping has of course been around ever since the early days of cinematic recording and projection. It was initially developed by the Austrian film cartoon pioneer Max Fleischer around 1915 and then extensively used in Fleischer's *Out of the Inkwell* series around 1920, in which live images of Fleischer and his brother were transformed into the figure of Koko the Clown. Benjamin himself could have seen evidence of rotoscoping techniques in Disney's *Snow White and the Seven Dwarfs* (1937) during his Paris exile. But perhaps the most significant revolution in rotoscoping techniques took place in the 1990s when computer scientists at the MIT Labs developed software and hardware solutions to move rotoscoping procedures into an all-digital arena. Though digital rotoscoping continued and continues to be troubled by what animators call boil, a certain shaking of the traces leading to a fundamental instability of the animated picture, the technique has made considerable inroads into the domains of commercial advertising, television and music video production, video game design, and, last but not least, feature-film making. Especially Richard Linklater's two films using digital rotoscoping, *Waking Life* (2001) and, even more so, *A Scanner Darkly* (2006), are of particular interest in this regard, not only because both were driven by the director's desire to elevate cinematic animation to a new level, but also because both tell stories about profound existential and perceptual confusions, about a blurring of lines between the real and the dreamlike, between the bodily and the psychic, between normality and paranoia — about a series of ontological crises that comment on the very process of mediation and transference to which rotoscoping in its most advanced form subjects the body.

This is not the place to recount the complicated saga of the making of *A Scanner Darkly*,[6] a film based on a well-known story by Philip K. Dick. Nor can I address here the film's narrative economy and the particular contributions of star actors such as Keanu Reeves, Winona Ryder, and Robert Downey Jr. to the project. What I simply would like to discuss is the very question of how digital rotoscoping alters the process of spectatorial identification and desire: on the one hand, how it — emblematic for the impact of new media on cinematic production — reconfigures our bodily relationship as viewers to both the representation of bodies on screen and the performative presence of an actor's body in front of the camera during the process of recording; and on the other hand, to what extent this reconfiguration of cinematic identification in the age of digital cinema brings us back to Benjamin's description of spectatorial testing in analog film, the curious folding of empathetic identification, as he described in his artwork essay.

There can be little doubt, first, that acting for rotoscoping largely intensifies Benjamin's understanding of the film studio as a laboratory of expressive movements and discontinuous performative gestures. Because the recording's digital footage will later be intensely reworked on the computer anyway, there is no need to get things absolutely right during the filming; nor is there much need to act in a most detailed architectural setting, since rotoscoping will largely strip set designs of their texture and particularity. Similar to what actors experience during a blue-screen take, individual moves and bodily gestures must be enacted in relative isolation from their spatial surroundings, the focus being much more on the mechanics of certain actions than on how they might respond to, inhabit, or shape distinct spatial surroundings. The prospect of rotoscoping, for the actor, deflates the thick materiality of space; it subtracts space from place, space here being understood in Michel de Certeau's sense as practiced place — that is, as something infused with, appropriated, and hence brought to life by the movements, trajectories, itineraries, and vectors of its users.[7] To act for digital rotoscoping is thus to act in a profound bubble; to abstract the body's language from how this body fills, structures, and vibrates within a given space; to transform this body self-reflexively and experimentally, as it were, into a seemingly autonomous, albeit fundamentally heterogeneous, apparatus producing usable gestures and expressions. Whether this type of intensified, albeit highly self-enclosed, acting requires greater or lesser skill than conventional stage acting is not for me to decide. What is important to note, however, is that rotoscoping requires the actor to understand his bodily work as merely one component within a much larger and ongoing process of visual transformation and recoding. The heightened intensity and laboratory-like autonomy of rotoscopic acting goes hand in hand with a profound decrease in what one might call thespian commitment, or in recourse to Benjamin's vocabulary: the auratic here and now of acting. To act here does not only mean to subject oneself to a sequence of visual tests. It is to offer the body to a series of mediations that morph and reinterpret this body's expressions long before they ever become visible on screen.

Second, what happens to the actor's body at the level of representation, once it has been rotoscoped and projected onto a screen, is nothing less than what could be described in phenomenological terms as an ongoing probing of the gray area between body image and body schema. Because of their stress on the tracing of bodily boundaries in motion, rotoscopic procedures produce conceptual images of the body that are different from the ones brought forth by both conventional cinematography and ordinary animation processes. For rotoscoping does not capture the human body as a mere image entailing all its physical operations and symptomatic signs of inner states; nor does it picture this body as a more or less predictable container of flesh, skin, and soul. Instead, because of its constitutive strategy of tracing and retracing bodily contact areas, rotoscoping interprets the phenomenal body as a mobile surface or negotiable threshold — an osmotic membrane, as it were — energized by this body's very movements across time and space. In doing so, it highlights not simply the points of contact between body and world, but the pre-existential potentiality of establishing such a contact to begin with. Rotoscoping represents the body as an open framework constantly engaged in testing its proprioceptive faculties, its ability to determine its extensions in space, and its ever-shifting boundaries produced by actual or projective movements. In this process, the technique recasts the body image into what recent media theorists, scientists, and philosophers have come to discuss as the body schema. As Shaun Gallagher and Jonathan Cole write:

The body schema consists of certain functions that operate across various parts of a complex system responsible for maintaining posture and governing movement. The first set involves the input and processing of new information about posture and movement that is constantly provided by a number of sources, including proprioception. A second set involves motor habits, learned movement patterns ("motor schemas" or programs). The final set of functions consists of certain intermodal abilities that allow for communication between proprioceptive information and perceptual awareness, and in integration of sensory information and movement.[8]

Rotoscoping represents the human body as a body schema constantly involved in integrating actual or virtual movements with the ontological need to define (or liquefy) proprioceptive certainties. Like the work of new media artists such as Rafael Lozano-Hemmer or Jeffrey Shaw, rotoscoping has the potential to represent the human body as a fundamentally unstable frame or medium that provides primary access to the world to the extent that it is included in this very world. Precisely by tracing over the movements of actual bodies frame by frame and hence stressing the vicissitudes of bodily contours, rotoscoping — to return once again to Benjamin's notion of film making as a laboratory — constantly probes the extent to which the performer's body does not simply inhabit the world as image but at once constitutes and mediates its physical and perceptual relationships.

It is not difficult to see that rotoscoping brings about fundamental oppositions between what happens in front of the camera and what we may see on screen: whereas during the act of filming the actor needs to understand how to abstract her body from the materiality of its surrounding space, the process of digital tracing produces images in which this body at once appears curiously embedded in space and serves as a mobile frame warranting the possibility of spatial relationships in the first place. Such disjunctures between the act of filming and its representation on screen, thirdly, tend to place the viewers in a position of ongoing incredulity and uncertainty, constantly probing and suspicious of the ontological reliability of what they see on screen. Unlike mainstream narrative cinema, in which the use of film stars' images contains Benjamin's paradoxical hope for Brechtian alienation, digital rotoscoping urges the viewer indeed to become a certain kind of highly attentive but also profoundly distracted (that is, non-absorbed) observer. Rotoscopy operates like a critical lens refracting our view of the bodies on display; we simultaneously look at it and seek to look through it, thus seeing ourselves seeing our very act of seeing. As viewers follow the contours of Bob Arctor or Donna Hawthorne traversing the paranoid mindscapes of *A Scanner Darkly*, they seek to relate what they see on screen to both a less schematic world of body images as it presented itself to the camera and of course to their knowledge about the star personae of Reeves and Ryder as they exist outside the world of this film. Rotoscoping urges us not simply to identify with the output of digital production procedures, but in doing so to perform an ongoing process of spectatorial triangulation, of mapping different ontological orders and forms of embodiments on top of each other, and thus to constantly probe our own acts and objects of affective investment. In contrast to the identificatory mechanisms of analog cinema, it is precisely the digital transformation of the image of the star into body schemata that invites the viewer to become what Benjamin's theory of film had envisioned for analog cinema, namely to assume the role of a critic who remains fully aware of cinema's mediation of affect, whose gaze subjects the world on screen to a series of optical tests, and whose act of viewing triggers a process of exploring the very nature of embodied viewing and the tactile, proprioceptive, and kinesthetic dimensions of perceptual awareness.

VI

A product of the analog film's attempt to absorb new media technologies, post-cinema today is routinely understood as a step into a realm beyond verifiable reference, authenticity, realism, and bodily grounding. And yet, as I have argued in the preceding pages, such a view of the impact of new media on contemporary cinema not only underestimates the extent to which new media themselves inherit certain features of the cinematic, but it also crudely overlooks the way in which new media's hybridization of time-art technologies and computing power can produce intensified forms of embodiment and sensory perception in Benjamin's sense. We are in fact far from misguided when we argue that some of Benjamin's often quite counterfactual hopes for the medium of film have only come to full fruition in our own age of new media. Benjamin's emphasis on tactile viewing is finding relevance today as new media technologies stress the interplay of touch, the proprioceptive, and the kinesthetic — the lodging of sight in the experiential modalities of the moving body and its affects. Benjamin's vision of film as a laboratory of expressive gestures is being realized today as post-cinema stimulates actors to abstract their bodily registers from their surroundings and critically explore these registers' expressive dimensions. And Benjamin's wish for what he called a critical spectator clearly has a correlative in the ability of new-media users today to deal with the vicissitudes of multiple mediation and to invest identification and empathy into the very machines that produce our many second lives on screen.

Benjamin's broader assumptions about the emancipatory politics of film and technical reproduction have often proved to be dead wrong; new media and post-cinema today testify to the fact that the mechanical and the auratic, reproducibility and a heightened sense of the here and now, can go hand in hand and in fact mutually reinforce each other. There are good reasons, however, not to relegate Benjamin's keen insights about the coupling of body and sight, of spectatorship and embodiment, of mediation and empathy, to the dustbins of modernist intellectual history. There has perhaps never been a greater need to learn how to see and sense ourselves seeing than today, and whether we think of Klee's *Angelus Novus* at Documenta, of Linklater's *A Scanner Darkly*, or of the interventions of various contemporary artists working at the boundary between art, engineering, and entertainment, new media technologies today can go a long way to foster this sense of intensified seeing and critical embodiment and thus reclaim what in Benjamin's own age cinema was able to achieve only to a small degree.

Notes

[1] All subsequent citations from this essay will be from the third version (*GS* I.2:471–508; *SW* 4:251–83).

[2] Wendy Hui Kyong Chun, "Introduction: Did Somebody Say New Media?," in *New Media Old Media: A History and Theory Reader*, ed. Wendy Hui Kyong Chun and Thomas Keenan (New York: Routledge, 2006), 1.

[3] Lev Manovich, *The Language of New Media* (Cambridge, MA: MIT Press, 2001).

[4] See, for instance, Vivian Sobchack, *Carnal Thoughts: Embodiment and Moving Image Culture* (Berkeley: U of California P, 2004); Laura U. Marks, *Touch: Sensuous Theory and Multisensory Media* (Minneapolis: U of Minnesota P, 2002); Mark B. N. Hansen, *New Philosophy for New Media* (Cambridge, MA: MIT Press, 2004) and *Bodies in Code: Interfaces with Digital Media* (New York: Routledge, 2006); Caroline A. Jones, ed., *Sensorium: Embodied Experience, Technology, and Contemporary Art* (Cambridge, MA: MIT Press, 2006); Anna Munster, *Materializing New Media: Embodiment in Information Aesthetics* (Hanover, CT: Dartmouth College P., 2006); and Bernadette Wegenstein, *Getting Under the Skin: Body and Media Theory* (Cambridge, MA: MIT Press, 2006).

[5] Hansen, *New Philosophy*, and Marks, *Touch*.

[6] For more, see Robert La Franco, "Trouble in Toontown," *Wired* 14.03 (Mar. 2006), http://www.wired.com/wired/archive/14.03/scanner.html (accessed 2 Jan. 2008).

[7] Michel de Certeau, *The Practice of Everyday Life* (Berkeley: U of California P, 1984).

[8] Shaun Gallagher and Jonathan Cole, "Body Image and Body Schema in a Deafferented Subject," *The Journal of Mind and Behavior* 16.4 (Autumn 1995): 376; qtd. in Hansen, *Bodies in Code*, 42.

6: One Little Rule: On Benjamin, Autobiography, and Never Using the Word "I"

Eric Jarosinski

> *In our childhood we know a lot about hands since*
> *they live and hover at the level of our stature.*
> — Vladimir Nabokov, *Speak, Memory*

To READ WALTER BENJAMIN'S autobiographical writings is to engage with much more, and much less, than the story of his life. What they might lack in coherent detail, especially in regard to Benjamin's adult life, is an absence indicative of the many questions they articulate about the identity of the self, the nature of experience, and the possibility of giving expression to both within modernity. While the figure of Benjamin has assumed numerous guises in the now nearly seventy years since his death in 1940 — among them, the Marxist critic, the Jewish mystic, the "last European" — the image he presents of himself in his own writings is too variegated to allow for any single designation to be adequate. The task confronting the reader is to engage with the image Benjamin constructs of himself as carefully and critically as when approaching one of his own enigmatic constellations or "thought-images." This is a challenge complicated by what is perhaps an ironic twist in the course of Benjamin's reception, as his image has become imbued with a certain cult value in recent decades, at times generating an overly reverent aura around the same thinker who famously diagnosed its demise.

How then to picture Benjamin today? His autobiographical writings seem a good place to start. First, however, it is important to realize that in sketching Benjamin, or for that matter sketching Benjamin sketching Benjamin, we are also portraying ourselves at a given moment: our critical categories, theoretical assumptions, and modes of representation. It should probably come as no surprise that, in addition to an ever-growing literature on Benjamin's life and work, with each study showing traces of its own intellectual, disciplinary or political agenda, there are now Benjamin pages on Facebook and MySpace, lending such Web sites dubious confirmation as one of the most prominent stages for our own acts of early twenty-first-century "self"-portraiture. ("Orientation: straight. Religion: atheist. Education: post grad. Status: married. 1,024 friends."[1]) However we might assess Benjamin's image and "status" today, it would be wise to remain mindful of the ominous dictum about the reciprocal relations between subject and object issued by the painter of the infamous portrait of Oscar Wilde's Dorian Gray: "It is not he who is revealed by the painter; it is rather the painter who, on the coloured canvas, reveals himself."[2] Likewise, to engage meaningfully with the figure of Benjamin is also to confront our own critical practices, as the desire to reveal is apt to be frustrated and confounded by his texts' self-conscious resistance to static notions of fixed identities and stable presences.

In introducing Benjamin's own acts of self-portraiture, I will take as my starting point one of his most unusually programmatic, yet characteristically diminutive assertions: "Wenn ich ein besseres Deutsch schreibe als die meisten Schriftsteller meiner Generation," he writes in 1932 in "Berliner Chronik" ("A Berlin Chronicle"), the fragmentary first version of his childhood memoirs, "so verdanke ich das zum guten Teil der zwanzigjährigen Beobachtung einer einzigen kleinen Regel. Sie lautet: das Wort 'ich' nie zu gebrauchen, außer in den Briefen" (*GS* VI:475; "If I write better German than most writers of my generation, it is thanks largely to twenty years' observance of one little rule: never use the word 'I' except in letters," *SW* 2:603). By no means "self-explanatory," this "little rule" appears to have significant reach in pointing out the affinities and tensions between the collective and the individual, language and identity, subject and object, which mark much of Benjamin's work. It suggests numerous avenues of investigation, prompting readers to ponder the simultaneous absence and presence of the subject throughout his writings and its consequences, not only for Benjamin's "self," but for the very possibility of the self as such in modernity.

Indeed, though Benjamin's recollections might putatively trace the life of an individual, they are also various inscriptions and readings of what he would call "the signatures of our age," offering prolonged meditations on the complex relations and ruptures marking his own historical moment, and extending well into the future in his consideration of their consequences. As Bernd Witte has observed, we see Benjamin "installing the perspective of the materialist historian of 1932 already in the unconscious sensations of childhood" in his account of his boyhood in Berlin; at the same time, this installation is also an unsettling of perspective, in which the past and the present come into contact, generating a productive friction of meaning, at times tempered by a touch of dreamlike, melancholic nostalgia.[3] Benjamin's recollections leave their own distinctive stamp, as individual as his own infamously intricate and nearly indecipherable handwriting, on the tradition of autobiography. In introducing his own figure and rhetorical figures into a literary space typically defined by narratives of development and completion, it becomes the scene of dispersal and fragmentation as much as, if not more than, construction. Such acts of interpolation are integral to a critical maneuver that characterizes much of his work, as Benjamin's writing here and elsewhere takes hold of its object as much as its means of representation, leaving its imprint on both. As his childhood friend Gerhard (Gershom) Scholem recalls: "Er packte jede Sache von einem gänzlich originellen und unerwarteten Gesichtspunkt aus an und tastete sich an die Dinge heran" (He approached all things from an entirely original and unexpected point of view and felt his way toward things).[4] While indebted to previous studies of language, vision, and the body, whose main strands will also be traced here, the reading I propose will focus on this very tactile element in introducing Benjamin's autobiographical texts.

Taking the writing of his life into his own hands, Benjamin confronts many of the complex theoretical issues he formulates elsewhere about the nature of experience in modernity and its implications for the subject. Specifically, he is concerned with the ability to read the present as a complex text that has much in common with its root, the Latin *textum,* which as Benjamin reminds us, means "web." A multi-layered network characterized by connections as well as ruptures, it is spun by memory, which, as he writes in "Zum Bilde Prousts" ("On the Image of Proust"), "hier die strenge Webevorschrift gibt. Einheit des Textes nämlich ist allein der actus purus des Erinnerns selber. Nicht die Person des Autors, geschweige die Handlung" (*GS* II.1:312; "issues strict regulations for weaving. Only the *actus purus* of remembrance itself, not the author or the plot, constitutes the unity of the text," *SW* 2:238). While waiting in a Parisian café, Benjamin once quickly sketched a diagram of his life, which he was greatly distressed at later losing; when he interrogated his past, "die Antworten zeichneten sich wie von selber," yielding the image of "einer Reihe von Stammbäumen" or a labyrinth (*GS* VI:491; "the answers were inscribed, as if of their own accord," "a series of family trees," *SW* 2:614). We can as little reproduce the diagram here as Benjamin could retrieve it, yet its structure does illuminate the challenge Benjamin poses to any simple conception of a unified subject or self-assured position of the "I." Benjamin's "little rule" reflects this, yet not simply in the name of writing "better German," of course. Much more, it seeks to lend expression, if possible, to a modernity in which, as he notes in the essay "Erfahrung und Armut" ("Experience and Poverty"), "die Erfahrung ist im Kurse gefallen" (*GS* II.1:214; "experience has fallen in value," *SW* 2:731) and "Festhalten ist heut Sache der wenigen Mächtigen geworden, die weiß Gott nicht menschlicher sind als die vielen" (*GS* II.1:219; "holding on to things has become the monopoly of a few powerful people, who, God knows, are no more human than the many," *SW* 2:735). Like so much in Benjamin's work, the "little" is apt to unfold into something much larger and var-iegated; he would not have us read its flattened image, however, but its folds, site of a furtive and sometimes unruly but never fully consummated touch. These are the moments of an at times erotically charged, "eigen-sinnig-wollüstiges Verharren auf der Schwelle, ein Zögern" (*GS* VI:472; "obstinate and voluptuous hovering on the brink, a hesitation," *SW* 2:600) that Benjamin describes in the many thresholds he encounters, but does not always cross, during his childhood in Berlin.[5]

Benjamin's conception of autobiography records the degree to which the writing of a life and the life itself diverge, fail to fully touch, such as in Marcel Proust's *In Search of Lost Time,* which he greatly admired and par-tially translated. Calling it "der höchste physiognomische Ausdruck, den die unaufhaltsam wachsende Diskrepanz von Poesie und Leben gewin-nen konnte" (*GS* II.1:311; "the highest physiognomic expression which the irresistibly growing discrepancy between literature and life was able to assume," *SW* 2:237), Benjamin found its author to possess an extraordi-nary power to make things visible, and clearly took it as a model for his own autobiographical writings. He ascribes this to the work of Proust's "weisender Finger" (*GS* II.1:321; "pointing finger," *SW* 2:245), which Benjamin is careful to distinguish from physical contact. "Diese Geste ist keinem fremder als Proust," he writes. "Er kann auch seinen Leser nicht anrühren, könnte es um nichts in der Welt" (*GS* II.1:321; "To no one is this gesture more alien than to Proust. He cannot touch his reader, either; he couldn't do this for anything in the world," *SW* 2:245). With touch foreign or out of touch with itself, Proust's work is deictic, indicating the location but not invoking the experience of touch itself.

Touch of Experience

In recollecting his childhood, memories recalled at the age of forty from the distance of what would later become permanent exile, Benjamin pon-ders to what degree he made his mark on Berlin, and it on him. He sets about reading the traces of his own childhood in Berlin at a time in which he finds it harder, and in exile forbidden, to leave new ones; this explains some of the melancholy of his recollections, but also their exploration of new difficulties facing the reading and writing of experience. If Benjamin's writing of the city gives voice to anything, it is to these very complexities, reflected in his friends' own experience of Benjamin himself. While Scho-lem speaks of Benjamin's highly tactile mode of thought, Theodor W. Adorno once referred to him as possessing a "strangely objectified and untouchable quality," conjecturing that Benjamin owed his productivity to the sense that "something objective and historical had been precipi-tated in his touchy, subjective form of response, something that rendered him capable of turning himself into an organ of objectivity."[6] A productive estrangement, not only in the context of the urban, is perhaps the most characteristic aspect of Benjamin's own identity, whose cracks and fissures are both traced and performed in his work, yet at a distance.

In his autobiographical writings he is certainly stepping back as well, viewing his life primarily through the eyes of a child, even if he once was that same boy in Berlin. Readers of Benjamin will recognize the significance of the child throughout his work — in his collection and study of toys and children's books, for instance — as a figure of fascination, change, and a fragile hope for a new way of seeing and thinking. In *Einbahnstraße* (*One-Way Street,* 1928), the image of a child reading (a child who will reappear in "Berliner Chronik" as none other than the young Benjamin himself) demonstrates a means of engaging with the world and its representation that is lost in adulthood. The child is more deeply touched by what he reads, and the tactile element of reading is highlighted throughout, as books are handed out to pupils, some of whom see their desired book land in someone else's hands, and when reading, they always have one hand on the page (*GS* IV.1:113; *SW* 1:463). In this childhood world of experience, as Anja Lemke has observed in her study of psychoanalysis, memory, and the self in Benjamin's boyhood recollections, every thing can become a sign, and every sign a thing.[7] Indeed, such childlike transformations and fluidity of categories are central to one of the most famous thought-images of *Einbahnstraße,* "Baustelle" ("Construction Site"), in which children are drawn to refuse and joyfully set to work combining it "in eine neue, sprunghafte Beziehung" (*GS* IV.1:93; "in a new, intuitive relationship," *SW* 1:450). Benjamin develops such nuance and fluidity of experience into what Heinz Brüggemann has recently discerned as a conscious literary strategy aimed at discovering elementary forms of reading as perception and appropriation.[8] Of the various hints of this strategy's emergence in the years prior to his major autobiographical texts, none is more touching than the way Benjamin's scholarly and fatherly interests converge in his careful transcription of words spoken (and created anew) by his son Stefan from 1921 to 1932 in a small archive he titled "Opinions et pensées." In a list headed "Worte ~~und Sätze~~ vor dem 27. November 1921" (Words ~~and Sentences~~ prior to November 27, 1921), he catalogues the new relationships between words his son established and made his own in such neologisms as "Fromesser" for "Professor," "Tascheschule" for "Schulmappe," and "Gratophoph" for "Photograph."[9] That "sentences" was written and then crossed out might indicate a proud father's impatience, or the seemingly complex syntax emerging from their little ironic and comedic illuminations. Stefan was most certainly making full sentences by the time of Benjamin's last entry in 1932, however; this was the same year his father returned to the scene of his own childhood, where he would recall his own misunderstandings and neologisms and weave them into the lines and vignettes of "Berliner Chronik."

"Berliner Chronik": "Like a Man Digging"

While I have been using the term autobiography for Benjamin's recollections of his childhood, he explicitly states in "Berliner Chronik" that the text resists this designation — at least as conventionally understood:

> Erinnerungen, selbst wenn sie ins Breite gehen, stellen nicht immer eine Autobiographie dar. Und dieses hier ist ganz gewiß keine, auch nicht für die berliner Jahre, von denen hier ja einzig die Rede ist. Denn die Autobiographie hat es mit der Zeit, dem Ablauf und mit dem zu tun, was den stetigen Fluß des Lebens ausmacht. Hier aber ist von einem Raum, von Augenblicken und vom Unstetigen die Rede. Denn wenn auch Monate und Jahre hier auftauchen, so ist es in der Gestalt, die sie im Augenblick des Eingedenkens haben. Diese seltsame Gestalt — man mag sie flüchtig oder ewig nennen — in keinem Falle ist der Stoff, aus welchem sie gemacht wird, der des Lebens. (*GS* VI:488)

> [Reminiscences, even extensive ones, do not always amount to an autobiography. And these quite certainly do not, even for the Berlin years that I am exclusively concerned with here. For autobiography has to do with time, with sequence and what makes up the continuous flow of life. Here, I am talking of space, of moments and discontinuities. For even if months and years appear here, it is in the form they have at the moment of commemoration. This strange form — it may be called fleeting or eternal — is in neither case the stuff that life is made of. (*SW* 2:612)]

Here, as in numerous self-conscious comments on the text's own status, what appears to be something of a disclaimer is, in fact, the work's very project. To talk of one's life in terms of "space, of moments and discontinuities" does indeed yield a "strange form," yet one that bears the imprint of the very strangeness of the self in modernity that Benjamin outlines here and elsewhere. In portraying his childhood he frequently separates himself from those exuding an air of self-satisfaction or self-assurance; the closest he comes to leading a "self-contained" existence is with a small group of friends with whom he was active in the youth movement, itself not free of divisions, who sought educational and social reform. The same applies to Benjamin's relationship to Berlin. Even though he is introducing his readers to his own home town, he emphasizes the importance of his guides in the form of nursemaids, his mother, friends, even his later experience of another city, Paris, which taught him "Vorbehalt" (*GS* VI:467; "caution," *SW* 2:597).

These hesitancies and displacements all appear to be signs of what Benjamin refers to as "die Vorkehrung des Subjekts, das von seinem 'ich' vertreten, nicht verkauft zu werden fordern darf" (*GS* VI:476; "the precaution of the subject represented by the 'I,' which is entitled not to be sold cheap," *SW* 2:603). In a recent study Eric Downing has sought to position Benjamin's writing of his childhood within the tradition of the German *Bildungsgeschichte,* a story of the education, maturation, and development of a young man. While significant strands of this tradition are clearly discernible, he argues, one of the main reasons that "Berliner Chronik" both is and *is not* such a tale hinges on the contingency of the subject Benjamin creates in disfiguring the process of literal "formation" implied, along with education and culture, by the German term *Bildung.* The young Benjamin's resistance to the order established by the Berlin upper-middle-class, to which his parents belonged, is also an offensive against reigning notions of the self: "To destroy the bourgeois order," Downing observes, "means to attack not only its schools and parental homes but its 'Ich' as well."[10]

As various critics have noted, this "smashing" of authority is performed in "Berliner Chronik" as something more akin to a painstaking excavation in keeping with the trope of the archaeological throughout. At the same time, however, this "strange form" of autobiography turns away from its own trope to the degree that it operates according to an equally strange notion of archaeology, with the search as significant as what is found, and the site of discovery even more meaningful than the artifacts themselves. To follow Benjamin's notion, only in this way can a trope, as something other than itself, remain true to itself. It is announced in an oft-quoted allegory of memory:

> Die Sprache hat es unmißverständlich bedeutet, daß das Gedächtnis nicht ein Instrument zur Erkundung der Vergangenheit ist sondern deren Schauplatz. Es ist das Medium des Erlebten wie das Erdreich das Medium ist, in dem die toten Städte verschüttet liegen. Wer sich der eigenen verschütteten Vergangenheit zu nähern trachtet, muß sich verhalten wie ein Mann, der gräbt. . . . Denn Sachverhalte sind nur Lagerungen, Schichten, die erst der sorgsamsten Durchforschung das ausliefern, was die wahren Werte die im Erdinnern stecken, ausmacht: die Bilder, die aus allen früheren Zusammenhängen losgebrochen als Kostbarkeiten in den nüchternen Gemächern unserer späten Einsicht — wie Trümmer oder Torsi in der Galerie des Sammlers — stehen. Und gewiß bedarf es, Grabungen mit Erfolg zu unternehmen, eines Plans. Doch ebenso ist unerläßlich der behutsame, tastende Spatenstich ins dunkle Erdreich und der betrügt sich selber um das Beste, der nur das Inventar der Funde und nicht auch dies dunkle Glück von Ort und Stelle des Findens selbst in seiner Niederschrift bewahrt. (*GS* VI:486–87)

> [Language has unmistakably made plain that memory is not an instrument for exploring the past but its theater. It is the medium of

past experience, just as the earth is the medium in which dead cities lie buried. He who seeks to approach his own buried past must conduct himself like a man digging. . . . For the matter itself is merely a deposit, a stratum, which yields only to the most meticulous examination of what constitutes the real treasure hidden within the earth: the images, severed from all earlier associations, that stand — like precious fragments or torsos in a collector's gallery — in the sober rooms of our later insights. True, for successful excavation a plan is needed. Yet no less indispensable is the cautious probing of the spade in the dark loam, and it is to cheat oneself of the richest prize to preserve as a record merely the inventory of one's discoveries, and not this dark joy of the place of the finding as well. (*SW* 2:611)]

Much could be, and has been, said about this extremely rich passage. Its tropes are known to numerous traditions, though none could ever fully subsume the allegory as a whole. Within the constraints of the excavation here, most important are the extremely tactile motifs of digging itself, of "turning the soil," "scattering," "meticulous examination," "cautious probing." In a letter to Scholem, Benjamin refers to the text as expeditions into the various depths and layers of memory; the plural is significant, as we see him returning not once but repeatedly to various scenes and images of his youth.[11] Like any successful archeologist, Benjamin too has a plan, the recording agenda of a chronicle, though its temporal structure does not dictate the work of memory in the text. Instead, we find him with his hands dirty, more in the "dark joy" of digging than the sober insight of inventorying. "Berliner Chronik" itself remained a fragment, a figure that held a privileged position within Benjamin's critical concepts, as he found its very lack of completion indicative of the dynamics of the whole. In Benjamin's writing of the city in "Berliner Chronik," he seeks to mobilize the fragmentary in countering the same structuring myth of urban totality and transparency that Fascism would later use to its advantage in depictions of Berlin's supposedly clear, orderly, hygienic countenance under Hitler. In doing so, he deploys a strategy similar to that in *Einbahnstraße*, which incorporates montage in order to make visible the fragmentation of modernity, which, in turn, has fueled the desire for myths of totality. Although a much more personal text, "Berliner Chronik" stages a similar position, mobilizing numerous tropes to point to the complex, multi-layered experience of urban life. We see Benjamin, who, as his friends remember, tended to shroud many aspects of his personal life in mystery, writing about his life as mediated by his own theories of mediation and rupture, experiencing them first-hand.

Benjamin's spade often returns to the excavation site, turning and scattering its soil throughout much of the text, especially in a particularly telling vignette: his memory of visiting an aunt in the Berlin suburb of Steglitz and examining her toy mineworks. A cross-section of an excavation is placed before him on the table, but it is of quite a different order than that invoked in the passage cited above. The scene it depicts is marked by motion as uniform as the geometry of the glass cube in which it is housed, and in which "kleine Männer Karren führten, mit der Spitzhacke schufteten, mit Laternen in die Stollen leuchteten, in den Förderkörben aufwärts und abwärts stets in Bewegung waren" (*GS* VI:472; "little men pushed wheelbarrows, labored with pickaxes, and shone lanterns into the shafts in which buckets were perpetually winched up and down," *SW* 2:601). Swept away from Benjamin's own excavation site is the dark loam, so too the lone digger and the careful turning and probing of the soil in ever new places. With its glass walls marking clear boundaries between inside and outside, we already know just how far these little men can dig, and what, if anything, they can hope to find. Not its soil but its tools take center stage; these wheelbarrows, pickaxes, lanterns, and winches are all instruments more suited for the sober task of collecting and inventorying. Indeed, this excavation is itself an object on display, and in direct contrast to the images of sandpits in the Tiergarten of Benjamin's childhood, it is to be seen and not touched.

If we were to read the aunt's mineworks as a miniature Benjaminian allegory of one of his own allegories — not a "man digging" but "little men" digging — this would seem to be an excavation site that loses its illuminating potential once it is controlled, made present, reproduced, and proudly displayed as domesticated. While the excavation site positions memory as the theater of the past, such an instrumentalization in the mineworks would seem to make it, not unlike the aunt's district itself in the years of inflation, a "Schauplatz der niederträchtigsten Zerstreuungen" (*GS* VI:472; "a theater of the most squalid diversions," *SW* 2:601). With the area's prostitutes, "Hüterinnen des Vergangnen" ("guardians of the past") having since taken up residence in backrooms or hidden away in attics, only the aunt remains on display, always at her bay window, which unlike the loggias so important in the text as figures of an interpenetration of interior and exterior, is very much enclosed (*GS* VI:472; *SW* 2:601). Yet the mineworks do yield a certain treasure, for the young Benjamin and perhaps for his readers, as the toy casts the aunt and the allegory of excavation in a new light. While introduced as a sovereign enthroned in her bay window, from which the street was ruled, the strict limitations and confines embodied in the mineworks give rise to a new image: Benjamin's Aunt Lehmann as a bird held in a cage. Her street, Steglitzer Straße, could henceforth only be associated with a *Stieglitz*, a goldfinch.

What I have been positing here as an allegory of the excavation allegory points to the movement of the trope, not just in this instance but throughout. In the image of an absurd substantiation or instrumentalization of an allegory, making it verifiable and predictable, we see it evade our grasp. Now contained within a glass rhombus, the mineworks reminds us that the allegorical excavation site, with all its dirt and digging, is and must remain an allegory, an untouchable figure, which we can follow but never fully possess. Its various incarnations throughout the text are echoes, yet as something other; any truly allegorical echo (perhaps suggested by the excavation site's rhetoric of "genuine reminiscences" and "real treasure") would have to be deformed in each iteration to remain the real treasure: images, cut off from past associations, still to be discovered.

If the dirt of the allegorical excavation site is not in the toy mineworks, where is it? And how are we to read its dispersal? "Berliner Chronik" is certainly thick with earth, dirt, and debris. It settles, among other places, on the dirty cushions of a taxi, a schoolyard monument coated in soot, and the dust-covered trees of summer. Each serves as a more telling, grittier instance of Benjamin's complex notion of engaging with the past than that encased in the mineworks, as they lead an unsheltered existence, subject to material conditions, reminding us amid Benjamin's recollections that much is also forgotten or neglected. But remembering the work of allegory, perhaps it would be wiser to look for those slightly more deformed echoes of the excavation site: Benjamin's mother's impatient search through her basket of keys for something hidden at the bottom; the graves of his childhood friends; the snug hollows of the café; the "subterranean layers" of the Youth Movement; the sandy playground of the Tiergarten; or the underground passageways of Benjamin's boyhood books. Clearly the grime raised in digging has been widely dispersed, then touched upon in these memories, as evidenced by the text's dirty hands. They appear on a prostitute, whose hands, certainly not the cleanest, Benjamin recalls, released him from entanglement in the city streets. His own hands show signs of grime when his mother takes Benjamin and his brother shopping at a clothing store and their hands hang from their suits, as he remembers, like soiled price tags. And as a child of the upper-middle class, Benjamin recollects that his first encounter with poverty came in the scene of a humiliated man trying to pass out flyers to passersby, who avoided his untouchable handbills.

"Berliner Chronik" is also marked by moments of contact and friction, however, to which Benjamin is acutely attuned. In drawing our attention to the excavation site of memory, he points not only to preservation but also to the most scrutinizing perceptions of the wearing away of the past. These images range from the hundreds of feet scuffing their way up the school stairs to the sound of his mother's knife as she (seemingly imperceptibly) scrapes off excess butter while making his father's lunch. Such keen perception is matched only by Benjamin's memory that his father, who was a partner in an auction house, had developed the ability to determine the quality of a carpet just by using the ball of his foot if his shoes had thin soles. Such tactile acuity would seem necessary in light of Benjamin's images of a grand erosion, erasing contours and making things harder to read, if not illegible and invisible. He comments, for instance, that while many of the same façades still stand in Berlin, he cannot see them as he did as a child, because they have been worn away by the brush of his gaze. Memories themselves are subject to a similar tactile deterioration, with the sharpest being those that have been isolated and preserved by shock and kept from rubbing against the others.

In reworking "Berliner Chronik" into "Berliner Kindheit um 1900" ("A Berlin Childhood Around 1900"), the text changes drastically, losing some of the former's rough edges and grating frictions. Reflecting a not uncommon view, Scholem, editor of "Berliner Chronik," considers the latter text a "literary metamorphosis," in which Benjamin's class-conscious politics have almost disappeared in the "milder," "even more forgiving" light he casts on his childhood.[12] While he is correct in pointing to the near-absence of any mention of Benjamin's evolving political investments, often characterized as an "unorthodox Marxism" or "dialectical materialism," critics such as Gerhard Richter have pointed to the way in which Benjamin enacts rather than illustrates his positions in his autobiographical texts, challenging the reader to rethink the political by way of "thought-images" rather than providing more programmatic examples.[13] Certainly the final version of 1938 employs a rich and rigorous style that is the culmination of numerous acts of writing and rewriting of what was originally conceived as a series of short texts for a newspaper. Benjamin began writing what would become "Berliner Chronik" in Berlin in January 1932, then continued work on the Balearic island of Ibiza throughout the spring. He then drew on this material to write "Berliner Kindheit" throughout the fall, completing an early version in 1934, finalized four years later while he was in Paris. Despite numerous efforts to secure a publisher, much of "Berliner Kindheit" never made it into print in Benjamin's lifetime.[14] Though on its surface it does in fact seem less political and more literary than "Berliner Chronik" — it is certainly more "polished" — the carefully constructed rhetorical quality Scholem detects can also be seen to stage some of Benjamin's most pressing political concerns, particularly those arising from new technologies of representation. At the time of Benjamin's childhood, he knew for instance that photography, like the railway station, was already becoming out of date, giving way to the cinema. This is expressed in the downward movement critics have traced in "Berliner Chronik," a digging and sinking into the depths of the past. Though not free of the dust and dirt of "Berliner Chronik," "Berliner Kindheit" is marked by a gentler touch, if not a state of suspension. The digging hand of the archaeologist remains, but it is also brought into contact with the hovering eye not unlike that of a movie camera, as Benjamin's reworking of his childhood memories also suggests a necessary though enigmatic reconfiguration of critical capacities in modernity.

"Eine Berliner Kindheit um 1900": "to get hold of the images"

The epigraph with which Benjamin begins the final version of "Berliner Kindheit" is also an image (or to unfold this "little" epigraph more fully, the image of an image in memory) of the *Siegessäule* (Victory Column) in Berlin's Tiergarten. We have seen it before, buried in the depths of dust and dirt of the latter half of the "Berliner Chronik." Or have we? Something curious has happened in its unearthing. In the "Berliner Chronik" it is rendered as follows:

"Motto: O braungebackne Siegessäule
Mit Kinderzucker aus den Wintertagen." (*GS* VI:488)

["Epigraph: O brown-baked column of victory
With children's sugar from the winter days." (*SW* 2:612)]

In "Berliner Kindheit," however, it now appears as:

"O braungebackne Siegessäule
mit Winterzucker aus den Kindertagen." (*GS* VII.1:385)

["O brown-baked column of victory,
With winter sugar of childhood days." (*SW* 3:344)]

In rising to the surface of the text, the "children's sugar" (*Kinderzucker*) of "Berliner Chronik" has now become "winter sugar" (*Winterzucker*); its "winter days" [*Wintertage*] are now "childhood days" (*Kindertage*). Suddenly, the archaeologist of the "Berliner Chronik" takes on a different task: just as these words are transposed, and the verses more heavily dusted with metaphor, the reader's position also changes, drawn from the depths to the surface, from a focus on a fragment to a disfigurement, and the archaeology of the "Berliner Chronik" becomes a characteristically Benjaminian archaeology of the present. He imagined just such a moment in "Zentralpark" ("Central Park"), unpublished notes he made on Baudelaire and allegory from 1938 to 1939, writing: "Der Grübler, dessen Blick, aufgeschreckt, auf das Bruchstück in seiner Hand fällt, wird zum Allegoriker" (*GS* I.2:676; "The brooder whose startled gaze falls on the fragment in his hand becomes an allegorist," *SW* 4:179). This would also seem to be the reader's position in interpreting Benjamin's "Berliner Kindheit," as reading itself becomes disfigured: As Werner Hamacher has observed of the text, "Reading is not the gathering of disparate things, but rather that dispersion in which gathering alone is possible."[15] Although Benjamin rearranged, dropped, and added a great deal in his revisions of "Berliner Chronik," the epigraph's reemergence is as telling as its transformation. Benjamin brings to the surface not only this textual artifact but also the possibility of the otherness and legibility of the surface itself, even if its reading in this new position is only to serve as a placeholder for its next incarnation in a new displacement.

If the "Berliner Chronik" gives rise to a "strange form" of autobiography, "Berliner Kindheit" signals a "längeren, vielleicht einen dauernden Abschied" (*GS* VII.1:385; "long, perhaps lasting farewell," *SW* 3:344) as Benjamin calls it in the opening lines, not only from a genre and from Berlin, but from a moment that has clearly passed. In this final version Benjamin bids farewell to his childhood, while also bidding the reader to say goodbye to a mode of reading that does not take full account of the formation and de-formation of images in an age increasingly shaped by the visual, by fragmentation, and by a threat to critical distance. Indeed, many objects recede in the "Kindheit" at the same time that they come into reach: the image in "Berliner Chronik" of *der Neue See* (New Lake), with its slippery ice encrusted over the great depths below, appears as "derselbe See, der mich, gerahmt, im dunklen Speisezimmer bei meiner Großmutter erwartete" (*GS* VII.1:429; "the very same lake that, enclosed in a frame, awaited me in my grandmother's darkened dining room," *SW* 3:384); likewise, the dark shadows of "Berliner Chronik," which Benjamin finds filling the city as the name of the deceased resides in a tombstone, appear in "Berliner Kindheit" as shadow puppets, and the skirts of the market women, with their earthy undersides, appear as a simulation, an apparition of a woven band and curly frill cast upon the rim of bedside basins in the moonlight. While such images cannot be tangibly grasped, Benjamin argues in his essays on photography and film that they can, in fact, be manipulated and instrumentalized to great aesthetic and political effect as the reproductions and reproducibility of technology have come to shape the human perceptual apparatus.

Traced in theoretical essays such as "Das Kunstwerk im Zeitalter seiner technischen Reproduzierbarkeit" ("The Work of Art in the Age of Its Technological Reproducibility"), these developments are also inscribed into and by the images the "Berliner Kindheit" itself constructs; significantly, they are largely moving images.[16] Following its archaeological trope, "Berliner Chronik" is the site of an excavation, whose finds "[man] mag flüchtig oder ewig nennen" (*GS* VI:488; "may be called fleeting or eternal," *SW* 2:612) depending on the contingencies of reading, be it by the collector, the gallery curator, the sober inventory-keeper, or the rhapsodic digger. At the same time, it is also the scene of photographic portraiture, a snapshot that *must* be called both "flüchtig" *and* "ewig," as a passing, irretrievable moment is frozen in a flash. In "Berliner Kindheit" we see how the movement of the filmic image — which changes the position of the terms, while also erasing their conjunction — is also performed as what we might call the "ewig flüchtig" ("eternally fleeting"). Considering such new modalities of representation, the challenge Benjamin poses himself at the outset of the text is considerable: "Dagegen habe ich mich bemüht, der *Bilder* habhaft zu werden, in denen die Erfahrung der Großstadt in einem Kinde der Bürgerklasse sich niederschlägt" (*GS* VII.1:385; "I have made an effort to get hold of the *images* in which the experience of the big city is precipitated in a child of the middle class," *SW* 3:344). Benjamin draws our attention to the *images,* of course, yet his italics seem to be occasioned by what follows: "habhaft," literally, have-able, tangible. That his effort is also indicative of a desire, one that may never be fulfilled, is enacted in what is akin to a filmic "second take" in the vignette headed "Zwei Blechkapellen" ("Two Brass Bands"), in which he remembers Berliners' first awkward amorous encounters in strolling the path between the cafés of the Berlin zoo: in "Berliner Chronik" there was "keine höhere Schule des Flirts" "no higher school of flirtation"; here, the gaze of a young man first "[fiel] auf eine Vorübergehende" (*GS* VI:484; "fell . . . on a passing girl," *SW* 2:609); in "Berliner Kindheit," however, this school of flirtation has turned to love, and the gaze now "[suchte] einer Vorübergehenden sich anzudrängen" (*GS* VII.1:428; "sought to fasten on a girl passing by," *SW* 3:383).

How then to "take hold" of such images, especially those on the move, passing by? While it would seem to contradict his insistence on distance, Benjamin will seek to make images "habhaft" by allowing them to take possession of him, as the "Kindheit" fully embraces the allegorical mode, not as a tool or instrument for exploring the past, but as the earth of the excavation site of "Berliner Chronik," the medium without which the site of discovery cannot exist; now the very air of the text — and clouds, as Hamacher has famously argued — have become fully permeated by the allegorical, something other than itself. This mode was not completely foreign to "Berliner Chronik," of course, yet its appearance, for instance in the aunt's mineworks, represents an insertion of Benjamin's archeological fragment into the world of images, an *initiation.* In "Berliner Kindheit" we also detect its corollary, from the outside in, in the figure of *inoculation* with which Benjamin introduces the text.

Inoculation, the insertion under the skin of something similar to the illness — a germ of the whole, in miniature — transforms illness into a protection. It does so by recognizing, and destroying, the intrusion of that which it resembles but is no longer. As an eminently allegorical infusion, yet one that seems to have potentially fatal consequences, the inoculation announces the same critical intention Benjamin found in Baudelaire: "Die barocke Allegorie sieht die Leiche nur von außen," he writes in "Zentralpark"; "Baudelaire sieht sie auch von innen" (*GS* I:2; "Baroque allegory sees the corpse only from the outside. Baudelaire sees it also from within," *SW* 4:186). The Baroque allegory was the subject of Benjamin's (rejected) *Habilitation* thesis, *Ursprung des deutschen Trauerspiels* (The Origin of the German Mourning Play); here it is put into motion.[17] As

Susan Buck-Morss has pointed out, this "allows Benjamin to make visibly palpable the experience of a world in fragments, in which the passing of time means not progress but disintegration."[18] In the strictest sense, "visibly palpable" would seem to be a contradiction, but only if the image is taken as semblance; for Benjamin, however, the image is the only accessible and retrievable form of the historically concrete.

Indeed, though the famous excavation site of "Berliner Chronik" has disappeared in "Berliner Kindheit," the archaeological has not entirely faded, as much of its dirt and grime still clings to the text. Even in this "polished" form, dust still covers the trees of the Tiergarten and soot coats long forgotten statues. Yet the focus of our labors has shifted, away from three-dimensional fragments and toward two-dimensional images — thus the work of interpretation has to assume a new dimension while the fragments of the excavation site appear to lose one. This shift is performed in the very structure of the text, and the rising to the surface we saw in the epigraph. Now subheads hover above the body of each vignette ("Der Strumpf" ["The Sock"], "Das Telefon" ["The Telephone"], "Das Fieber" ["The Fever"], and so on), offering some clue of its content, but not of the way in which it will be set into motion, figured as a figure, in saying something other than, or in excess of, the object itself. Akin to the fragments, or even the "inventory," invoked in the excavation site of "Berliner Chronik," these headings present the reader with an object, yet the real treasure will be found not only in exploring their "resting place" in the texts below but in stirring them up, activating their relation between depth and surface.

This brings us back to Aunt Lehmann's mineworks, which in "Berliner Chronik" I suggested was an allegory of the allegory of the excavation site, an image of how bringing closer can also mean further remove, and how a true allegory will always appear as something other, evading our grasp. The mineworks appears again in "Berliner Kindheit" as one of several related yet dispersed allegorical echoes of the excavation site, including the young Benjamin's courtyard, in which "das nackte Erdreich" ("bare earth") and the "schwarz[e] Kute" ("black pit") of a tree's soil are now fenced in and enclosed under iron bars (*GS* VII.1:386; *SW* 3:345); or in the basement apartments, with ventilation shafts covered by grating, that Benjamin could peer down into and then steal away from with their images in his clutches. Despite the reappearance of certain vignettes, the scale has clearly shifted in "Berliner Kindheit," and the echoes have increased. The aunt, ruler of the street into which she no longer sets foot, now becomes a stand-in for such a figure in every childhood, one of numerous "Feen, die ein ganzes Tal durchwalteten . . . ohne jemals in ihnen zu erscheinen . . . , die immer . . . auf uns gewartet hatten" (*GS* VII.1:398–99; "fairies who cast their spell over an entire valley without once descending into it . . . , who always . . . had been expecting us," *SW* 3:358). Such multiplication and magnification is often evident in the text, as the close-up photos of the "Berliner Chronik" are combined with the kinetic, wide-angle panning shots more characteristic of "Berliner Kindheit." As Benjamin states in the introduction, his task is not simply to trace the "zufällige biographische" ("contingent biographical") but the "notwendige gesellschaftliche" ("necessary social") irretrievability of the past (*GS* VII.1:385; *SW* 3:344). Just as Benjamin's childhood bed becomes a public space when he becomes sick, the interior of the apartment and its allegorical treasures would also seem to extend well beyond its walls. Indeed, while the hermeticism and fortifications of the apartment have increased — from the now double seal of the bay window to the bulkier maidservants, offering the protection necessary for places "die so Kostbares in sich zu bergen hatten" (*GS* VII.1:400; "called on to shelter such precious things," *SW* 3:359) — a greater social and political relevance leaks into, and out of, the mineworks. Now the glass-encased view of a workplace and machines is further instrumentalized, with the mine giving a demonstration of the value of an honest day's work. Yet it also reveals its treasures, and the "Silberblick . . . an den das Biedermeier sich verloren hatte" (*GS* VII.1:400; "gleam of silver in its veins which had . . . dazzled the Biedermeier," *SW* 3:359). This "ganzes, lebendiges" ("complete working") mine, for all its contrivance, appears significantly more intact, and human, than the aunt with her "brüchige und spröde . . . Stimme" (*GS* VII.1:399; "voice . . . fragile and brittle as glass," *SW* 3:358).[19] While she again appears in the image of a bird in a cage, Aunt Lehmann is now a "talking" bird, who sings her own "sich verloren sein," or loss of herself, in the "gleam of silver" she has tried to possess, encase, and display, but which has instead possessed her.[20]

While we might think of the caged bird as the new medium of this mine, again without dirt, it is only part of a larger apparatus represented by the mineworks itself, which both is and is not a toy. Now ruled by an apparatus (just as the school bell of "Berliner Chronik" now echoes in the ringing telephone), its movements function "pünktlich im Takte eines Uhrwerks," and are overseen by little mine inspectors (*GS* VII.1:399; "precisely in time to a clockwork," *SW* 3:359). The appearance of the apparatus, the works dictating the work of the mineworks, is by no means incidental. While in "Berliner Chronik" the past was the medium of memory, in his recollection of the telephone Benjamin asks if the fact that he hears phone conversations echo differently now "mag am Bau der Apparate oder der Erinnerung liegen" (*GS* VII.1:390; "because of the structure of the apparatus or because of the structure in memory," *SW* 3:350). Looking at it this way, one might venture an interpretation of this strangely inhuman aunt as an allegory of just such an apparatus, the camera. Fixed in her aperture-like doubly secured window alcove, always awaiting us, her gaze rules over a space she herself has never materialized in; she appears under a black bonnet, not unlike the hood of early cameras; her voice, like photographic plates, is made of a sensitive glass, similarly fine-tuned; and her maidservants imitate her perfectly and represent her with dignity, almost photographically, without words.

Indeed, Benjamin's reading of this camera's representation — the glass mineworks shown to him as soon as he arrives — is more a reading of the apparatus from which it has sprung: the aunt's position in the window, the mechanics of her gaze, her dark and gloomy housing. He is not dazzled by the mineworks but admiring of the mimicry of the servants, a second-hand representation of the aunt that reveals her status as an apparatus. The result is a lifting of the veil surrounding the name "Steglitz," an uncovering that emerges from reading, rather than lifting, coverings themselves. As such, the insight is reflective of the increased attention Benjamin pays to the same discovery he recalls making as a child in inserting his hand into a sock, forming a small pocket, then reflecting on its disappearance as the hand emerged: "Er lehrte mich, daß Form und Inhalt, Hülle und Verhülltes dasselbe sind. Er leitete mich an, die Wahrheit so behutsam aus der Dichtung hervorzuziehen wie die Kinderhand den Strumpf aus 'der Tasche' holte" (*GS* VII.1:417; "It taught me that form and content, veil and what is veiled, are the same. It led me to draw truths from works of literature as warily as the child's hand retrieved the sock from 'the pocket,'" *SW* 3:374). If form and content are in fact the same, there is no longer an inside to be uncovered, a façade to be seen through. Like a photograph, there is nothing deeper within that will yield to touch without destroying the surface that makes it legible. Desire is still very much present, but it is to be held in check. An image is not unlike the spools of thread that tempt the young Benjamin. When he can, he tries to resist puncturing the paper bearing a brand name that covers the core within; poking his finger through the paper destroys the legibility of the label, while granting him access to its core — yet he already knows it to be hollow.

Nowhere is this more the case than with film, which requires a mode of reading different from that of Benjamin's childhood books, which entangled him in their frayed bindings, stood ready for repeated readings, and registered his fingerprints. Both, however, appear in the allegory of reading in a storm. In winter, Benjamin recalls standing by his window, as a blizzard tells him stories as much as his books: "Was es erzählte, hatte ich zwar nie genau erfassen können, denn zu dicht und unablässig drängte zwischen dem Altbekannten Neues sich heran" (*GS* VII.1:396; "What it told, to be sure, I could never quite grasp, for always something new and unremittingly dense was breaking through the familiar," *SW* 3:356). With the distant lands of his stories melding like the snowflakes, the young Benjamin is reading like an allegorist, just as the grown Benjamin, inoculated with the allegorical, is now remembering and writing. He notes that "die Ferne, wenn es schneit, nicht mehr ins Weite sondern ins Innere führt" (*GS* VII.1:396; "distance, when it snows, leads no longer out into the world, but within," *SW* 3:356), and indeed, the storm has come to him, mixing with the text. The whirling flakes permeating and permeated by the distant cities of Benjamin's books not only appear here as the snow dusting the shoulders of the reading child of *Einbahnstraße;* they also become that of both versions of the epigraph, its transposition of terms made permeable, as both "children's sugar" *and* "winter sugar" on days that are both "winter days" *and* "childhood days."

Yet a storm is also raging somewhere else in this vignette, not yet from paradise as in Benjamin's later "Über den Begriff der Geschichte" ("On the Concept of History"), but in other books, held in a cabinet, forbidden, which he only encountered once, in a dream, and which he could never find again. They do not stand but lie flat, like frames; yet they are anything but static, filled by a raging storm, as "ein wechselnder und trüber Text sich wölkte, der von Farben schwanger war" (*GS* VII.1:397; "a brooding, changeable text — a text pregnant with colors — formed a cloud," *SW* 3:356). The image of this kinetic, colorful, tempestuous birth is illuminated by a death, as these hues, though brilliant and fleeting, were also shaded by "einem Violett, das aus dem Innern eines Schlachttiers zu stammen schienen" (*GS* VII.1:397; "a violet that seemed to come from the entrails of a slaughtered animal," *SW* 3:356). The child's attempt at an allegorical reading of the snowstorm appears again here in the struggle to decipher titles that flash up from these frames, each both stranger and more familiar than the last (*GS* VII.1:397; *SW* 3:356–57). As irretrievable as Benjamin's lost diagram of his life, the books disappear along with their dream image when he wakes, before they can be fully understood, grasped. The dream is both the form and the content of these books, which must disappear with the end of sleep, as irretrievable as the past itself.

The stormy movement of the images springing from flat books would have us think of film, a nascent medium arising from the death, if not ritual slaughter, of photography. This medium in decline takes shape in another figure Benjamin sees in his dreams, one that looks back at him: "das bucklichte Männlein" ("the little hunchback"), Benjamin's "grau[er] Vogt" ("gray assessor"), who was pushed off the stage long ago, even though his aunt, "dazzled" by the *Silberblick* of photography's magnesium flash, might refuse to follow, anchoring herself in the bay window of her ever-more fortified apartment, struck silent while also singing her demise like a canary (*GS* VII.1:430; *SW* 3:385). The violet light illuminating these scenes, setting them in motion, is familiar. A similar luminescence faintly glows in "Berliner Chronik," where it is the only light illuminating a café amphitheater Benjamin dubbed "die Anatomie" ("The Anatomy School"), a space resembling a theater after its time and a cinema before its own, "ein verlaßner, ungefähr kreisförmiger, mit violettem Tuche ausgespannter und violett beleuchteter Raum" (*GS* VI:483–84; "a forlorn, approximately circular chamber in the upper story, hung with violet drapery and illuminated with a violet glow," *SW* 2:609). It is here, Benjamin writes in "Berliner Chronik," that years later, to the beat of a jazz band, he would later discreetly write his *Habilitation* on Baroque allegory.

If "Berliner Chronik" is more a record, even if a strange and strangely individual record, of Benjamin's early years, the scene of his study of allegory, "Berliner Kindheit" might best be called its activation, which, as has been noted, is at once its radicalization. Not only has Benjamin placed the writing of his life within the realm of the allegorical; in the inoculation he has inserted the allegorical mode into himself. This is a critical maneuver that also seems to be a violation of Benjamin's taboo of contact that he expresses in his insistence on distance, and as we see in the allegory of the child chasing a butterfly (the "man digging" of "Berliner Kindheit"), indeed it is. He wishes "in Luft und Licht mich aufzulösen, nur um ungemerkt der Beute mich zu nähern und sie überwältigen zu können" (*GS* VII.1:392; "to be dissolved into light and air, merely in order to approach my prey unnoticed and subdue it," *SW* 3:351). Yet, as with the butterfly hunter, the transformation is fleeting: "Je falterhafter ich im Innern wurde, desto mehr nahm dieser Schmetterling in Tun und Lassen die Farbe menschlicher Entschließung an und endlich war es, als ob sein Fang der Preis sei, um den einzig ich meines Menschendaseins wieder habhaft werden könne" (*GS* VII.1:392; "the more butterfly-like I became in heart and soul — the more this butterfly itself, in everything it did, took on the color of human volition; and in the end, it was as if its capture was the price I had to pay to regain my human existence," *SW* 3:351). Yet it was never truly lost, we see, as Benjamin's "pointing finger" leads to the trampled grass and flowers of the scene of the hunt. This is the image of the same "erstarrt[e] Unruhe" ("petrified unrest") Benjamin finds in allegory, a simultaneous shattering and conservation, as allegory "hält an den Trümmern fest" (*GS* I.2:666; "holds fast to the ruins," *SW* 4:169). A taboo against contact has indeed been broken, overcome by what in *Einbahnstraße* Benjamin calls an "überschießend[e] Geberde" (*GS* IV.1:91; drastic gesture that overleaps its mark) yet the prohibition remains, as "die Zone der feinsten epidermalen Berührung tabu bleibt" (*GS* IV.1:91; "the zone of finest epidermal contact remains taboo," *SW* 1:448). The writer inhabited, inoculated, by the allegorical mode itself, "heftig verschlungen" (*GS* IV.1:91; "violently engulfed, eaten," *SW* 1:448) in fact, may have overstepped the line in finding a means to "take hold" of images, yet they crumble in his grasp; moreover, he cannot take these fragments into his own hand but must wait for his figures to be activated — in reading — where they will again flutter like Benjamin's butterfly, evading capture.

Conclusion: Collecting and Unpacking the Self

If as a child Benjamin would become entangled and pulled into his books, as an adult he would in fact hunt them like butterflies, netting some of his most cherished quarry while himself a transient, discovering cities while in pursuit of books. In his 1931 essay "Ich packe meine Bibliothek aus" ("Unpacking my Library"), he comments on two figures, the child and the collector, who offer a pair of the most illuminating, and touching, images of acquisition that also mark a loss. If we were to follow Adorno's observation that Benjamin was "hardly a person at all but rather an arena for the movement of the content that forced its way to expression through him," this essay might best bear the Benjaminian stamp of the autobiographical.[21] Strangely, it is also one of the few texts in which Benjamin speaks to us so directly, not only violating his "little rule" by saying "I," but also addressing us as "you." The intimacy established with the reader, alone with Benjamin as he unpacks his final boxes late at night, is akin to that of the relationship he seeks to illuminate, the ties between a collector and his possessions. He does so by giving insight into something "Unverhüllteres, Handgreiflicheres" (*GS* IV.1:388; "something less obscure, something more palpable," *SW* 2:486) than the usefulness or history of his books, instead illuminating the act of collecting itself rather than providing an inventory of a collection.

The "man digging" of "Berliner Chronik" is here a "man collecting," now recollecting, as his books become a stage for images in memory of their former resting places (*GS* IV.1:388; *SW* 2:487). For all of its apparent melancholy, however, Benjamin tells us the scene is not marked by the elegiac but by anticipation; the collector, like the child, allows for the "Wiedergeburt" ("rebirth") of his possessions, the "Erneuerung des Daseins" ("renewal of existence") through an activation of the collector's "taktischem Instinkt" ("tactile instinct"): "Man hat nur einen Sammler zu beobachten, wie er die Gegenstände seiner Vitrine handhabt. Kaum hält er sie in Händen, so scheint er inspiriert durch sie hindurch, in ihre Ferne zu schauen" (*GS* IV.1:389–90; "One has only to watch a collector handle the objects in his glass case. As he holds them in his hands, he seems to be seeing through them into their distant past, as though inspired," *SW* 2:487, 489). Though authenticity is always subject to scrutiny in Benjamin's work, his insistence that such renewal is only possible in the hands of the genuine collector, the collector as he ought to be, is striking, yet not contradictory (*GS* IV.1:396; *SW* 2:492). A "man digging" continually turns and scatters the soil, just as the "man collecting" recognizes that it is the incompletion of the collection that gives collecting meaning. The true collector would seem to be one whose collection consists not of objects but of irretrievable moments of collecting. "Das Phänomen der Sammlung verliert, indem es sein Subjekt verliert, seinen

Sinn" (*GS* IV.1:395; "the phenomenon of collecting loses its meaning when it loses its subject," *SW* 2:491), Benjamin cautions; that is, when collecting becomes a tangible, yet fixed collection — perhaps one on display in the gallery or sober room of contemplation invoked in "Berliner Chronik" — the collection can no longer be transformed and must await a renewed dispersal at the hands of yet another collector.

While Benjamin cherishes his objects and feels responsible for their care, it is not the loss of his collection that he fears most, but of collecting itself. Indeed, he would have to forsake his own library in Berlin in order to collect material in the Bibliothèque Nationale in Paris for his massive, and incomplete, *Passagen-Werk* (*The Arcades Project*). Written less than two years before going into exile, Benjamin's meditation on collecting comes at a time when this activity's end is on the horizon, a demise that allows Benjamin to fully grasp its significance for the first time: "Erst im Aussterben wird der Sammler begriffen" (*GS* IV.1:395; "Only in extinction is the collector comprehended," *SW* 3:492). Indeed, continually drawn to outmoded objects or practices, Benjamin found things most legible when they disintegrated, just as the frayed pages of his childhood books reveal their woven strands, the web or *textum* that is the material, yet forgotten, metaphorical, text in the reader's hands.

As a collector, Benjamin has invited us into his study as if fellow collectors, which as *Leser*, or gatherers, we literally are; he wants to talk to us about collecting, but also about reading. Even if threatened by those stormy volumes of the cinematic *Wunderkabinett* of his dream, Benjamin would cling to the book — and a fixation on paper, bindings, and writing implements fine enough to render his miniscule handwriting — in attempting to make his own memories, words, and images *habhaft*. Yet no matter how palpable, this *haben* (having) always anticipates its escape from *Haft* (arrest); Benjamin challenges the readers to activate the figures of his text, setting *Haft* in motion as *haften*, as they themselves "cling to" or "adhere" to the something else of allegory, with its "petrified unrest" taking shape as a momentary suffix appended to another potential activation.

Haften, of course, also means "to be liable." Certainly the attempt to follow the motion of Benjamin's tropes in this essay has much to answer for, as do all readings and rereadings of his texts, no less for what they latch onto as for what they lay aside. Still, it is remarkable that for all of their handling in past decades, Benjamin's writings are anything but threadbare. If I have unraveled anything here, I hope to have also added something to this resiliency. We will now leave Benjamin where he leaves us, in his study, well past midnight, with the last crate of books broken open but not yet fully unpacked. Books do not come alive in the collector, Benjamin tells us in bidding farewell, but he who takes up residence in them does. This essay is another of the dwellings that Benjamin has erected out of books and "nun verschwindet er drinnen, wie recht und billig" (*GS*

IV.1:396; "now he is going to disappear inside, as is only fitting," *SW* 3:492). We can read Benjamin's disappearance as a loss — one exceeded only by a life cut short in 1940 while fleeing from the Nazis — but we will remember that this is not an elegy. Rather, I would suggest that it is an invitation, and moreover a challenge, to search for Benjamin within his pages even without any assurance that we will ever truly find him there.

Notes

1 http://profile.myspace.com/index.cfm?fuseaction=user.viewprofile&friendid= 45978899, accessed 15 Mar. 2008.

2 Oscar Wilde, *The Picture of Dorian Gray*, in *The Best Known Works of Oscar Wilde* (New York: Wise, n.d.), 107.

3 Bernd Witte, *Walter Benjamin: An Intellectual Biography*, trans. James Rolleston (Detroit, MI: Wayne State UP, 1997), 11.

4 Gershom Scholem, *Walter Benjamin und sein Engel* (Frankfurt am Main: Suhrkamp, 1983), 163. All translations are my own unless otherwise noted.

5. For a highly influential reading of myth and thresholds, see Winfried Menninghaus, *Schwellenkunde: Walter Benjamins Passage des Mythos* (Frankfurt am Main: Suhrkamp, 1986).

6 Theodor W. Adorno, *Notes to Literature*, ed. Rolf Tiedemann, trans. Shierry Weber Nicholsen (New York: Columbia, 1992), 2:238, 234. Translation of *Noten zur Literatur. Gesammelte Schriften*, Vol. 11 (Frankfurt am Main: Suhrkamp, 1974), 589, 583.

7 Anja Lemke, *Gedächtnisräume des Selbst: Walter Benjamins "Berliner Kindheit um neunzehnhundert"* (Würzburg: Königshausen & Neumann, 2005), 13.

8 Heinz Brüggemann, *Walter Benjamin über Spiel, Farbe und Phantasie* (Würzburg: Königshausen & Neumann, 2007), 270.

9 Walter Benjamin Archiv, ed., *Walter Benjamins Archive* (Frankfurt am Main: Suhrkamp, 2006), 77.

10 Eric Downing, *After Images: Photography, Archaeology, and Psychoanalysis and the Tradition of Bildung* (Detroit, MI: Wayne State UP, 2006), 187.

11 Walter Benjamin, letter to Gershom Scholem, 26 Sept. 1932, in Gershom Scholem, *Walter Benjamin: The Story of a Friendship* (New York: Schockem, 1988), 190. Translation of *Die Geschichte einer Freundschaft* (Frankfurt am Main: Suhrkamp, 1975).

12 Gershom Scholem, *Walter Benjamin und sein Engel*, 174.

13 See Gerhard Richter, *Walter Benjamin and the Corpus of Autobiography* (Detroit, MI: Wayne State UP, 2000).

14 See Chronology for publication dates in vols. 2 and 3 of *Selected Writings*.

15 Werner Hamacher, "The Word Wolke — If It Is One," in *Benjamin's Ground: New Readings of Walter Benjamin*, ed. Rainer Nägele (Detroit, MI: Wayne State UP, 1988), 175.

[16] Here Benjamin introduces a particularly enigmatic notion of "tactile appropriation." For an insightful reading of the hand in the essay, see Eva Geulen, "Under Construction: Walter Benjamin's 'The Work of Art in the Age of Mechanical Reproduction,'" in *Benjamin's Ghosts*, ed. Gerhard Richter (Stanford, CA: Stanford UP, 2002).

[17] See Dominik Finkelde's contribution in this volume.

[18] Susan Buck-Morss, *The Dialectics of Seeing: Walter Benjamin and the Arcades Project* (Cambridge, MA: MIT Press, 1989), 18.

[19] The English translation in *SW* loses the description of the mine as literally "complete" and "lively."

[20] Carol Jacobs has meticulously traced the many sonorous echoes of *Steglitz* and *Stieglitz* in her highly illuminating reading of the scene. See "Walter Benjamin: Topographically Speaking," in *Walter Benjamin: Theoretical Questions*, ed. David S. Ferris (Stanford, CA: Stanford UP, 1996), 94–117.

[21] Theodor W. Adorno, *Notes to Literature*, ed. Rolf Tiedemann, trans. Shierry Weber Nicholsen (New York: Columbia, 1992), 2:233. Translation of *Noten zur Literatur. Gesammelte Schriften*, Bd. II (Frankfurt am Main: Suhrkamp, 1974), 583.

7: The *Passagen-Werk* Revisited: The Dialectics of Fragmentation and Reconfiguration in Urban Modernity

Karl Ivan Solibakke

I

SINCE ITS PUBLICATION IN 1982 Walter Benjamin's *Passagen-Werk* (*The Arcades Project*) has become an essential compendium of nineteenth-century modernism in European intellectual history and an exhaustive though fragmentary inquiry into the emergence of bourgeois urban culture between the Revolution of 1830 and the Paris Commune in 1871. Compiled in the years between 1927 and the Nazi invasion of France in 1940, the material the German-Jewish cultural critic drew together laid the groundwork for what was to have been a definitive monograph on Paris during the central decades of the nineteenth century. Transforming geographic space into a matrix of text, Benjamin explores the reconfiguration of early contemporary cityscapes and maps out an allegorical blueprint for bourgeois cultural memory. True to the encyclopedic spirit of his analysis, the doctrine of historical materialism he championed, and his passion for accruing written artifacts like shards at an archaeological dig, Benjamin noted: "Geschichte schreiben heißt, Jahreszahlen ihre Physiognomie zu geben. ("to write history means giving dates their physiognomy," N11,2) or, more simply, writing history is citing history. "Ihre Theorie," Benjamin observes, "hängt aufs engste mit der Montage zusammen" ("its theory is intimately related to that of montage," N1,10). Interweaving excerpts from 850 secondary sources with original commentaries, observations, and glosses, the author substantiates how changes to urban existence were mirrored in the surfaces, façades, and contours of a rapidly evolving metropolis. In particular, new technologies impacted communal sites, and these came to embody collective memory and public visions in Paris, "the capital of the nineteenth century." "Es ist das Eigentümliche der technischen Gestaltungsformen (im Gegensatz zu den Kunstformen)," he asserts, "daß ihr Fortschritt und ihr Gelingen der Durchsichtigkeit ihres gesellschaftlichen Inhalts proportional sind" ("It is the peculiarity of *technological* forms of production — as opposed to art forms — that their progress and their success are proportionate to the *transparency* of their social content," N4,6). The arcades, glass-covered shopping and bourgeois recreation areas, became testimonies for a discernible moment in the continuum of European cultural history. Their decline or disappearance at the time that Benjamin began to chronicle their significance not only points to a historical index but also heralds the passing of nineteenth-century collective memory as the twentieth century began to encroach on the cityscape.

From his vantage point in the 1920s and 1930s Benjamin struck a pose as disquieting as that of his renowned angel of history in "Über den Begriff der Geschichte" ("On the Concept of History"), peering out over the ruins of the nineteenth century as Fascism in Western Europe and Stalinism in the East were jeopardizing the future of European intellectual ideas, and artistic movements such as aestheticism, surrealism, and decadence were subject to spurious assessments of their degeneracy. Resembling the debris left behind by natural or man-made catastrophes, Benjamin's textual fragments aspire to catalog the emblems and signs of an era condemned to extinction. With regard to this historical objective, his dialectical method blends the imagistic and the textual into the presence of the now. For in resuscitating both the topographical and topological traces embedded in cultural artifacts Benjamin exposes his present to rigorous scrutiny. Above all, he envisions a gap in time that superimposes past and present upon one another. The historical layers within that interstice mirror the vulnerability of metropolitan experience, pitting ephemeral revelations against linear notions of collective advancement. Turning his back on the notion of optimism in nineteenth-century history, Benjamin's historiography is transitory, even impulsive in character and resists any alliance with the grand narratives that commemorate social progress. Cultural practices are parsed down to their barest semiotic constituents and can be read as part of the "book of nature"; "so soll es hier mit der Wirklichkeit des neunzehnten Jahrhunderts gehalten werden," Benjamin asserts. "Wir schlagen das Buch des Geschehenen auf" ("that is how the reality of the nineteenth century will be treated. We open the book of what happened," N4,2). When navigating the scores of pages in the *Arcades* the reader retraces Benjamin's footsteps, perusing the city with the eye of the *flâneur,* and only in hindsight does much of the semiotic data take on relevance. That is why coming to terms with the fragment requires a synchronic and diachronic methodology, in which the empirical and ideal facets of individual cultural factors merge with the chronological and phenomenological insights provided by historical materialism.

Confronted with Benjamin's textual montages, the reader is also obliged to sort through the debris that once made the arcades models of bourgeois cultural recollection and reconstruct the semiotic web that helped spawn Parisian urbanity. While the process of reading fragments also implies writing them anew, and this appeal to the reader's creativity is one of the project's incentives, it also represents its principal flaw. It is easy to become confused by the wealth of detail, feel overwhelmed by Benjamin's epistemological range, or even imagine going astray in the labyrinth of a virtual metropolis. Ultimately, the failure to limit his data may have been Benjamin's recognition of the project's shortcomings. Like the collector in the biographical sketch "Ich packe meine Bibliothek aus ("Unpacking My Library," 1931) and in the socio-cultural cameo "Eduard Fuchs, der Sammler und der Historiker" ("Eduard Fuchs, Collector and Historian," 1937), Benjamin, the inveterate collector of textual fragments, became obsessed with the spoils of his research. His obsession eventually subverted any hope of producing a body of coherent text and thus bringing the project to a close. Indeed, it has even been conjectured that the *Passagen-Werk* is a failure, given that Benjamin was only able to elaborate on some of the many pieces of data he had collected on Charles Baudelaire.[1] While his volume on the French poet foreshadows the vibrant literary, social, and cultural observations the Parisian project might have ultimately developed, the technological, architectural, economic, and socio-psychological facets at the center of the *Passagen-Werk* never reached the same level of fruition. Also a torso, the book on Baudelaire remains an eloquent tribute to the prerogatives of literary expression, since Benjamin saw in Baudelaire's lyrics a seismographic mirror of the ruptures and shocks that both beset and stimulated nineteenth-century urban imagination.

Besides the notes on Baudelaire, ample portions of the material gathered for the *Passagen-Werk* found their way into other seminal texts written or published during the late 1920s and 1930s. These include Benjamin's most widely-read essay, "Das Kunstwerk im Zeitalter seiner technischen Reproduzierbarkeit" ("The Work of Art in the Age of Its Technological Reproducibility," 1935–39), as well as his pieces "Der Sürrealismus: Die letzte Momentaufnahme der europäischen Intelligenz" ("Surrealism: the Last Snapshot of the European Intelligentsia," 1929), "Kleine Geschichte der Photographie" ("Little History of Photography," 1931), the essay "Eduard Fuchs, der Sammler und der Historiker" ("Eduard Fuchs, Collector and Historian," 1937) and the succinct theses "Über den Begriff der Geschichte" ("On the Concept of History, 1940). Common to all of them is Benjamin's awareness that as a universal phenomenon and in all of its expressions modernity entails a complicated process of self-referential inscriptions. These reconfigure the materiality of cultural signs, whether they are manifest in the artifacts deposited in museums and archives or dependent upon auxiliary media to make them reproducible for a larger audience. Benjamin detected that contemporary cultural semiotics was no longer accessible to traditional norms of denotation and connotation but had to compete against the forces of entropy that erode collective identity and invalidate conventions of collective memory. As one of the pioneers of a visual turn in twentieth-century culture, largely stimulated by the early proliferation of photography and film, he nevertheless demonstrated a steadfast devotion to the written word as the primary archive of cultural historiography, one that could preserve memory from the ravages of time, the imperfection of recollection, and the inevitability of human mortality.

The remainder of this chapter aims to consider the *Passagen-Werk* from synchronic and diachronic perspectives. Sections II and III provide insights into the basic structure and scope of the fragment, spotlighting the significance of commodities and focusing on their role in Benjamin's version of historical materialism. Part IV is devoted to Benjamin's philosophy of history and its practical application in the *Passagen-Werk*. Pursuant to surveying the vast fragment on a synchronic level, sections V and VI contrast two concepts of urbanity, one which predates Benjamin's by eighty years, while the other comes into view nearly half a century after his death. Adopting a diachronic perspective, the contention is that the *Passagen-Werk* should be perceived as the historical link between Heinrich Heine's contemporary configurations of the Parisian metropolis as it crosses the threshold into modernity and Paul Virilio's postmodern rendition of the cyber city after the dawn of telematic global design. Heine, Benjamin, and Virilio are unanimous in their appreciation of the cybernetic forces that persistently work to redesign collective urban codes by subverting and supplanting sensations of how time and space are interfaced in municipal models. As communication technologies come to support ever more sophisticated channels of interaction, literal, visual, virtual, and multi-dimensional data are accessed and processed by media providers at ever faster rates of transmission. Echoing Heine and Benjamin, Virilio reveals that the last vestiges of city surfaces have been launched onto today's digital highways and that these global thoroughfares have usurped the arcades and passages once found in Walter Benjamin's "capital of the nineteenth century."

II

During his lifetime Benjamin collated the material designated for the *Passagen-Werk,* the quotations culled from a variety of sources and his glosses, into thirty-six folders, which he designated as "convolutes." Initially accumulated between 1927 and 1929/1930 and then after a long hiatus once again during his years in exile in France, these were catalogued while Benjamin was doing research at the *Bibliothèque Nationale* in Paris, located at that time adjacent to the Passage Vivienne in the heart of the metropolis. The compilations were color-coded and given labels, such as "Mode" ("Fashion"), "Eisenkonstruktion" ("Iron Construction"), "Baudelaire," "Der Flaneur" ("The Flâneur"), "Die Straßen von Paris" ("The Streets of Paris"), "Fourier," "die Photographie" ("Photography"), or "die Börse Wirtschaftsgeschichte" ("The Stock Exchange Economic History"). These serve as headings, under which an abundance of material is inventoried. Of these Convolute K, entitled "Traumstadt und Traumhaus, Zukunfts-träume, anthropolog(ischer) Nihilism(us), Jung" ("Dream City and Dream House, Dreams of the Future, Anthropological Nihilism, Jung"), and Convolute N, with the rubric "Erkenntnistheoretisches, Theorie des Fortschritts" ("On the Theory of Knowledge, Theory of Progress"), have been singled out by Benjamin scholars, since both provide insight into Benjamin's methodological considerations and epistemic strategies. In addition to the folders there are two exposés, one in German, dated 1935, and another, in French, that was penned as a grant proposal for The-odor W. Adorno's and Max Horkheimer's Institute for Social Research in 1939. The material in the six sections of the exposés has been arranged along dual premises, that is, by linking historical personages with archi-tectural or topographical topoi: "Fourier oder die Passagen" (Fourier, or the Arcades), "Daguerre oder die Panoramen" (Daguerre, or the Panora-mas), "Grandville oder die Weltausstellungen" (Grandville, or the World Exhibitions), "Louis Philippe oder das Interieur" (Louis Philippe, or the Interior), "Baudelaire oder die Straßen von Paris" ("Baudelaire, or the Streets of Paris"), and "Hausmann oder die Barrikaden" (Haussmann, or the Barricades). Although beneficial for assessing the scale of the final work, they can only be compared to "girders" or scaffolding, since the range of details encompassed in the individual convolutes exceeds the factors spelled out in the exposés. It has been surmised that the wealth of material collated includes fundamental perspectives that Benjamin might well have incorporated into the final monograph. Among these are a reconsideration of the ideological significance that Karl Marx had for nineteenth-century capitalist paradigms; a reassessment of Victor Hugo's importance for the history of French architecture; and possibly observa-tions about the effects lights and artificial illumination have on the optical aesthetics of municipal spaces as theaters of modernity.[2]

The entries in the first convolute, "Arcades, Magasins de Nouveau-tés, Sales Clerks," ponder the deeper meaning of the architectural marvels that enjoyed their heyday in the period between 1822 and 1840. Seeing them as allegories or monads of cultural memory, Benjamin imbues the arcades with temporal significance, calling them the "locus classicus für die Darstellung der Passagen, denn aus ihr entspinnen sich nicht allein die divagations über den Flaneur und das Wetter, sondern auch was über die Bauweise der Passagen in wirtschaftlicher und architektonischer Hinsicht zu sagen ist, könnte hier seine Stelle finden" ("locus classicus for the pre-sentation of the arcades; for not only do the divagations on the flâneur and the weather develop out of it, but also what there is to be said about the construction of the passages, in an economical and architectural vein, would have a place here," A1,1, translation modified). Erected at the height of *flânerie* and during the adolescent years of bourgeois capitalism, the Parisian arcades stimulated a new dogma of aggressive merchandising and the first intimations of the voracious appetite for consumer goods that characterizes today's affluent societies. Nestled under glass roofs illuminated by gaslights at night, they offered respite from the bustling traffic and the vagaries of Parisian weather. The effortless transition from street to covered passage kindled a heightened sensitivity for collective space, all the more so since the constructions were neither completely indoors nor fully outdoors, neither entirely interior nor exterior in character. Rather, as interstitial spaces they conjured up liminal areas, in which people and objects, nature and culture converged to form "eine Stadt, eine Welt im kleinen" (*GS* V.1:45; "a city, a world in miniature," *AP,* 3).

The enigmatic and captivating ambience of the arcades reflects three developments that are central to Benjamin's theory of cultural design at the outset of the modern urban experience. As living quarters and public spaces began to emulate one another, leaving one's dwelling only meant substituting the cosiness of the private for the diversion of urban topographies, all the more mesmerizing in view of their marble backdrops and stylish promenades. Blending civilization with natural environments, the passages not only simulate bourgeois economic aspirations but also illustrate the inclination to transform city surroundings into prosceniums for collective representation. Benjamin writes:

> Das Interieur trat nach außen. Es ist als wäre der Bürger seines gefesteten Wohlstands so sicher, daß er die Fassade verschmäht, um zu erklären: mein Haus, wo immer ihr den Schnitt hindurch legen mögt, ist Fassade. . . . Die Straße wird Zimmer und das Zimmer wird Straße. Der betrachtende Passant steht gleichsam im Erker.

> [The domestic interior moved outside. It is as though the bourgeois were so sure of his prosperity that he is careless of façade, and can exclaim: My house, no matter where you choose to cut into it, is façade. . . . The street becomes room and the room becomes street. The passerby who stops to look at the house stands, as it were, in the alcove. (L1,5)]

Just how dynamic this spatial ambivalence is can be deduced by replacing the "passer-by" in the text cited with the *flâneur,* that agent of metropolitan observation and interface, with his aptitude for scouting out liminal spaces and scrutinizing them in their aggregate configurations. What is more, the amalgamation of interiors and exteriors could only come about as innovations in steel and glass were applied to municipal design. In this respect, Convolutes E, F, G, P, and Q contain significant contemplations on the early years of urban renewal and the technological revolution initiated by linking vistas, panoramas, and visionary cityscapes to nineteenth-century advancements in engineering. *The Ring of Saturn or Some Remarks on Iron Construction* (*AP*, 885–87), originally filed under Convolute G and among the drafts forming the early sketches for the *Passagen-Werk*, is Benjamin's remarkably cogent appraisal of the unlimited opportunities for iron construction.[3]

Second, as prototypes of department stores or latter-day shopping malls, the arcades were lined with textile stores and elegant shops that tantalized the eye, whetted consumer appetite, and aroused the yearning to acquire. In a society rapidly giving way to pecuniary temptation and fiscal fervor, they become socio-cultural signatures sanctioned by sacred implications. Benjamin reaffirms Heinrich Heine's commentaries on the inviolability of bourgeois prosperity when he sees the arcades forming one of the sources for the "ivresse religieuse des grandes villes" ("religious intoxication of great cities"), triggering Baudelaire's observation that "die Warenhäuser sind die diesem Rausch geweihten Tempel" ("the department stores are temples consecrated to the intoxication of the masses," A13). Undeniably, the concept of an all-pervading commercialism rooted in the lure of the object had begun to permeate the psychosocial underpinnings of modern bourgeois societies; however, these objects of desire are "wish images," which have signifiers conveying latent layers of historical subtexts reminiscent of a righteous and classless society. Their contribution to cultural memory was to elicit "das nachdrückliche Streben . . . , sich gegen das Veraltete — das heißt aber: gegen das Jüngstvergangene — abzusetzen. Diese Tendenzen weisen die Bildphantasie, die von dem Neuen ihren Anstoß erhielt, an das Urvergangene zurück" (*GS* V.1:47; "the resolute effort to distance oneself from all that is antiquated — that is, however, the recent past. These tendencies deflect the imagination (which is given impetus by the new) back upon the primal past," *AP*, 4, translation modified). Seeking out sociocultural origins or plumbing the depths of collective semiotics required "reading" forgotten traces of time, even within the newest articles of production. Located at the focal point of this practice of exhuming cultural artifacts from uncharted repositories of collective memory is the written word, which as an archive is flexible enough to resonate with the past even as the act of writing transforms the present into an enduring form of temporal suspension.

Third, the spatiotemporal liminality evoked by the arcades becomes a factor in Benjamin's evaluation of modern individuals and their dependence upon the sanctuary provided by private and public interiors as well as the scores of objects gathered or exhibited there. These "wish images" are instilled with deep-seated, mythical connotations, implying that they offer consolation and respite from the pressing challenges of social commerce. In view of that, the reign of Louis Philippe between 1830 and 1848 is generally recognized as a turning point in sociocultural history, when individuals as collectors begin to accumulate vast repositories of objects within their private domains. In both his 1935 and 1939 exposés to the *Arcades* Benjamin lingers on this trend:

> Unter Louis-Philippe betritt der Privatmann den geschichtlichen Schauplatz. . . . Der Privatmann, der im Kontor der Realität Rechnung trägt, verlangt vom Interieur in seinen Illusionen unterhalten zu werden. . . . Diese Notwendigkeit ist umso dringlicher, als er seine geschäftlichen Überlegungen nicht zu gesellschaftlichen zu erweitern gedenkt. In der Gestaltung seiner privaten Umwelt verdrängt er beide. Dem entspringen die Phantasmagorien des Interieurs. Es stellt für den Privatmann das Universum dar. In ihm versammelt er die Ferne und die Vergangenheit. Sein Salon ist eine Loge im Welttheater. (*GS* V.1:52)

> [Under the reign of Louis Philippe, the private individual makes his entry into history. . . . The private individual, who in the office has to deal with reality, needs the domestic interior to sustain him in his illusions. This necessity is all the more pressing since he has no intention of allowing his commercial considerations to impinge on social ones. In the formation of his private environment, both are kept out. From this derive the phatasmagorias of the interior — which, for the private man, represents the universe. In the interior, he brings together the far away and the long ago. His living room is a box in the theater of the world. (*AP* 8–9)]

Transforming private space into a theater of illusions, the individual hoards articles that are divested of their commodity character and invested with the devotional value more appropriate to cultural or religious icons. Icons induce reminiscences of a utopian world spatially and temporally removed from the chaotic forces governing urban reality. They also transmit hidden expanses of history within an artificial and finite space, one that has for all intents and purposes been compressed to the dimensions of a box. An allegory for the apprehensions and vulnerabilities posed by capitalism, life in the city banishes individuals into museum-like cubicles filled with props and accoutrements, all of which have intuitive value. Given that they encapsulate the spoils of human remembrance, these spaces are as much monads as they are phantasmagorias, that is, architectural and other urban manifestations of collective illusions or dreams, capable of evoking bygone eras and nostalgia for the primordial as well as invalidating the logic of spatiotemporal distances. According to Benjamin, the objects even detach themselves from any claim to biographical or utilitarian significance. Instead, they come to materialize the dialectical images and receptacles of communal remembrance, even though the memories they call to mind are more apt than not to be subverted when confronted by reality. Given the elasticity of the phantasmagorical, the question as to what influences modern urban subjects comes into focus, especially when so much emphasis is placed upon the epistemological and cultural meaning invested in the commodities on hand. After all, these too can only acquiesce to the readings that their contemporary iterations provoke. Hence modernity materializes as a distorted mirror comprising dialectical images that continuously surge back and forth between object and subject or vice versa without specifying where the true origins of the relationship might lie.

In the long run, a random collection of objects or, for that matter, a mixture of textual fragments, is a playing field for the dialectics of modern cultural aesthetics. Left adrift within the semiotics of the social order, individuals are expected to mold the memory texture in which to embed their particular "wish images." No longer tempered by norms and traditions, amorphous zones of communicative, social, und cultural memory are generated, which also give rise to the abstract signatures of modernity. Capitalizing on Benjamin's iconic and material dialectics, the *Passagen-Werk* succeeds in demonstrating how text and image relinquish their medial boundaries and coalesce in liminal spaces or spatiotemporal "force fields." When text and image enter into an optical synthesis and thus stimulate the most elusive forms of edification, then the boundaries between individual, collective, and cultural remembrance defer identity, making modernity a game of deception; "jeder dialektisch dargestellte historische Sachverhalt polarisiert sich und wird zu einem Kraftfeld, in dem die Auseinandersetzung zwischen Vorgeschichte und Nachgeschichte sich abspielt" ("every dialectically presented historical circumstance polarizes itself and becomes a force field in which the confrontation between its fore-history and after-history is played out," N7a,1). At this juncture the relationship between the signifier and the signified becomes intimidating, ghostly, even terrifying. "Entscheidend ist weiterhin," Benjamin observes, "daß der Dialektiker die Geschichte nicht anders denn als seine Gefahrenkonstellation betrachten kann, die er, denkend ihrer Entwicklung folgend, abzuwenden jederzeit auf dem Sprung ist" ("What is even more decisive is that the dialectician cannot look on history as anything other than a constellation of dangers which he is always, as he follows its development in his thought, on the point of averting," N7,2) This "'constellation of dangers" is Benjamin's lasting contribution to a dialectical method of reconfiguring and recoding urban life, in which emblematic, semiotic, and imagistic components are telescoped down to the surface of the written word.

III

In the context of Benjamin's theory of historical materialism, commodities form the substance of collective dreams. The fantasies in which objects assume an essential role give rise to the psycho-sociological magma out of which secular utopias ultimately materialize. At first sub-liminal, these illusions mirror the objectives of a bourgeois class bent on transforming daydreams and reveries into the tangibles of urban sophis-tication. On one level Benjamin exposes the blind folly of the bour-geoisie by mounting "die Traumstadt Paris als ein Gebilde aus all den Plänen von Bauten oder Entwürfen von Straßenzügen, den Anlagepro-jekten, den Systemen von Straßennamen, die nie durchgedrungen sind, in die wirkliche Stadt Paris" ("within the actual city of Paris, Paris the dream city — as an aggregate of all the building plans, street layouts, park projects, and the street-name systems that were never developed," L2a,6). Resembling the caricaturist Grandville's *Les ponts des planètes* (The Bridges of the Planets), a futuristic vision of the cosmos that could easily have come from a Jules Verne novel, the city dissociates itself here from its geographical reality as a discrete distribution of space. Linear space is transformed into network design, in which the focal points and peripheral zones are reduced to nothing more than aphorisms, paragraphs, and convolutes, symbolizing Benjamin's "Traumhäuser des Kollektivs: Passagen, Wintergärten, Panoramen, Fabriken, Wachs-figurenkabinette, Kasinos, Bahnhöfe" ("dream houses of the collective: arcades, winter gardens, panoramas, factories, wax museums, casinos, railroad systems," L1,3). Like Grandville's futuristic formations, gram-mar and syntax develop into the micrological labyrinth for dream cities that amalgamates the empirical with the ideal and transforms physical sensations into virtual imagery. Semiotic networks engulf the physical features of the metropolis, revealing it to the mind's eye as surreal, frag-mented, and intangible. Beatrice Hanssen has shown how intimately the abstract process of contextualizing the city can be linked to the trauma of surrealistic visions, which enable "the release of a flood of images, rushing across the threshold between sleep and awakening" and trigger "a new synaesthetic experience in which sound and image merged."[4] More decisive than the upsurge of heterogeneity in urban aestheticism, surrealism intrudes on the politics of topographical and corporeal space, redefining the relationship of subjects to their environment and trans-figuring spatial representations of the human body.

On another level, Benjamin's bourgeois utopias — made all the more tangible by the dream-like arcades and passages imitating bour-geois interiors — are but one example of the intricate role that dreams play in Benjamin's cultural commentary. They also stand at the cross-roads of his interest in Marxist theories of fetishism and the subcon-scious desires enmeshed in the commodities of production, his incisive examination of Proust's *mémoire involontaire* in the Baudelaire book, his appropriation of Sigmund Freud's concepts of the individual and collec-tive unconscious, and the allusions to Nietzsche's "Eternal Return" that he finds prefigured in the writings of Louis-Auguste Blanqui (1805–81), the French revolutionary mystic (*GS* V1:75–77; *AP*, 25–26). While Benjamin's historical materialism aims to distance itself from teleological notions in the individual sphere, his collective ambitions are not entirely divorced from the meaning that time and the temporal have for human happiness. The nineteenth century materializes as a grand hallucination, the outcome of a dream vision, and Benjamin argues that the era should be perceived as a "dreamtime," albeit one in which the individual consciousness anchors itself in reflection at the same time that the collective consciousness "in immer tieferem Schlafe versinkt" ("sinks into ever deeper sleep," K1,4). The delusions of the Parisian bourgeoisie, its inclination to sink into a dreamlike stupor during the formative years of the capitalist social order, had catastrophic consequences for the twentieth century, made manifest by two world wars within the space of a generation as well as the ecological ravages wrought by rampant industrialization and the squandering of finite natural resources. Yet, as the purveyor of translucent images rooted in the fading texture of an urban era on the brink of extinction, Benjamin did endorse one antidote for the decay that collective reverie sowed. His "kopernikanische Wendung in der geschichtlichen Anschauung" ("Copernican revolution in historical perception") boldly predicts that an "Einfall des erwachten Bewußtseins" ("flash of awakened consciousness," K1,2) would herald a turnaround both perceptive and vigorous enough to come to terms with the nineteenth century's culpability for the tragedy of the first half of the twentieth century. "Politik erhält den Primat über die Geschichte" ("politics attains primacy over history," K1,2) as collective forces awaken from their trancelike stupor and undergo a Copernican "Wendung des Eingedenkens" ("turn of remembrance," K1,3), making Benjamin's brand of historical philosophy an agenda for redeeming the remnants of the past, immediately prior to their erasure from the slate of cultural memory.

The principles of memory that Benjamin spent most of his life developing are assessed in the last text that he was able to complete before his suicide, the theses he expounded in "Über den Begriff der Geschichte." In this work he not only sums up the methodology behind his historical materialism and fortifies the theoretical groundwork for what he identifies as "weak messianic" forces to offset the havoc wrought by centuries of cultural manipulation but also stresses that political and historical catastrophes are closely linked to the question of whether the tragedies leading to a permanent "state of emergency" in the sociocultural domain are not representative of human fate in general and of delusions about what might be the best of all possible worlds. His pessimistic observations disclose the nature of urban space as a theater for human forgetfulness and cultural exploitation. And yet, as catastrophic as the century had appeared to Benjamin at the time of his suicide in 1940, it would be a misrepresentation of the metaphysical undercurrent in his intellectual legacy to give no credence to the "messianic" forces his mnemonic goals project into the past in order to redeem the future in the "Jetzt einer bestimmten Erkennbarkeit" ("now of a particular recognizability," N3,1).[5] In its immediacy, the *Passagen-Werk* is tantamount to remembrance, reconstruction, and revival all in one.

IV

The *Passagen-Werk* joins a select group of texts about European cities — Marseille, Naples, Moscow and Berlin — that Benjamin drafted during his extensive travels and show him to be a master of topographical writing. The fascination these texts radiate is linked not only to his talent for showing how urban experience influences cultural representation but also to his realization that the convergence of past and present in city spaces generates the imagery for new collective identities. Having considered the *Passagen-Werk* from a synchronic perspective and before attempting to situate it within the diachronics of urban theory from Heinrich Heine in the nineteenth century to Paul Virilio in the twenty-first, it would be beneficial to reflect on some of the basic tenets underlying Benjamin's philosophy of history and historical materialism as documented within the vast fragment.

> Zur Elementarlehre des historischen Materialismus. 1) Gegenstand der Geschichte ist dasjenige, an dem die Erkenntnis als dessen Rettung vollzogen wird. 2) Geschichte zerfällt in Bilder, nicht in Geschichten. 3) Wo ein dialektischer Prozeß sich vollzieht, da haben wir es mit einer Monade zu tun. 4) Die materialistische Geschichtsdarstellung führt eine immanente Kritik am Begriff des Fortschritts mit sich. 5) Der historische Materialismus stützt sein Verfahren auf die Erfahrung, den gesunden Menschenverstand, die Geistesgegenwart und die Dialektik.

> [On the elementary doctrine of historical materialism. (1) An object of history is that through which knowledge is constituted as the object's rescue. (2) History decays into images, not into stories. (3) Wherever a dialectical process is realized, we are dealing with a monad. (4) The materialist presentation of history carries along with it an immanent critique of the concept of progress. (5) Historical materialism bases its procedures on long experience, common sense, presence of mind, and dialectics. (N11,4)]

Embedded in Convolute N, this passage provides unusually coherent parameters for appraising the project, since the guiding principles behind Benjamin's reconfiguration of municipal modernity are encapsulated here: the idea that historical data and time are condensed and reclaimed in the object; the idea that modern history is imagistic and not epic; the idea that monads signify modern allegories for dialectical processes; the idea that historical materialism precludes the notion of linear progress; and finally the idea that historical materialism is structured logically and within easy reach of language, the most precise and supple instrument for cultural analysis. Placing objects in the vortex of cultural design and dialectics may not have been entirely new, since dialectical materialism is fundamental to the economic theories advocated in Friedrich Engel's and Karl Marx's philosophy of social progress. Nevertheless, Benjamin's emphasis on "reading" the object as a medium of transformation exploits commodity fetishism, which he did not locate in the articles of production, as Marx did, but in the items for consumption, such as those on display in the arcades or in bourgeois living rooms. When we hone in on the imprint that commodities make on the collective psyche, it becomes evident that they are meaningful as dialectical images or symbols of cultural equivalence, especially when they form the basic components for semiotic codes. They hark back to a "paradisiacal pre-history," even while heralding "utopian expectations" of a liberated society.[6] Phantasmagorical in nature, objects interrupt the continuum of time to suggest images in the collective consciousness in which the old and the new interpenetrate. In fact, the discerning eye identifies material objects, ciphers, and even events as clusters of closely related elements. That is also why the dialectics of time and place allude to palimpsests, in which the literal and figurative essence of commodities embraces several layers of historical experience. Linked to the reciprocity of time and place, these phantasmagorias are indexed with regard to the "presence of the now." Compressed into the passage work of cultural imagery at the point of their concurrence, they come to a momentary standstill, and it is here that they are decipherable for the fraction of an instant.

> Nicht so ist es, daß das Vergangene sein Licht auf das Gegenwärtige oder das Gegenwärtige sein Licht auf das Vergangene wirft, sondern Bild ist dasjenige, worin das Gewesene mit dem Jetzt blitzhaft zu einer Konstellation zusammentritt. Mit anderen Worten: Bild ist die Dialektik im Stillstand.

> [It is not that what is past casts its light on what is present, or what is present its light on what is past; rather, image is that wherein what has been comes together in a flash with the now to form a constellation. In other words: image is dialectics at a standstill. (N3,1)]

The fissure dividing the temporal modes impacts the meanings derived from "reading" the entities embedded in each constellation. The past surfaces as discrete or shattered flashes of wakefulness no longer bound to schematic principles. These flashes disclose ruptured epiphanies and sustain textual montages lacking spatiotemporal continuity. Benjamin's epistemological stance — at once deconstructionist and phenomenological in spirit — can be equated to the isolated, sporadic elements of experience called for in a perception of the present that explodes the continuum of history. Exploding temporal continuity is equivalent to imploding the chronological formations that are a staple of idealistic historiographies, since Benjamin sacrifices the logic of time for an inchoate mass of semiotic fragments. These, then, form textual constellations by reconfiguring past and present into dialectical images. Like the shards in the *Passagen-Werk*, they can be harvested for random, even explicitly aleatoric, readings. If, as a consequence, historiography loses its grip on what was once the telos of social and cultural progress, then the "Fortschrittsbegriff mußte [. . .] der kritischen Theorie zuwiderlaufen ("the concept of progress had to run counter to the critical theory of history") and was then only viable for something immeasurable: "die Spannung zwischen einem legendären Anfang und einem legendärem Ende der Geschichte" ("the span between a legendary inception and a legendary end of history," N13,1). When we look at it this way, we can see that Benjamin aims to deconstruct spatiotemporal myths and legends by denying a notion of progress in both religious as well as nineteenth-century secular views of history and by applying his phenomenological version of "profane illumination" to the demographic and socioeconomic upheavals that the European continent had weathered in the first half of the nineteenth century. However, he also sees mythological and theological principles reinstated even after they had been superseded by the secular pragmatism that is the backbone of materialist historicism; this is indeed one of the many anomalies that the *Passagen-Werk* brings to light.

Coupled with an appreciation for the potential of imagery, Benjamin's dialectical approach to temporality must be seen as a historical turn; all the more so, since time and space are subsumed into a monad of cultural and historical design. Rooted in Gottfried Wilhelm Leibniz's notion of an ideal nucleus, monads symbolize the totality of world being, abbreviating and condensing infinitude into a single virtual entity. Not only do they embrace all of the temporal conditions pertinent to a virtual model of the universe, but they also encompass all the dimensions of cosmic space. Without doubt, this model — Benjamin likens its aptitude for recognizing comprehensive representations of space and time as an "ursprüngliches Vernehmen" (*GS* I:217) or "primordial mode of apprehending" (*Origin*, 37) — also figures as the prototype for Benjamin's lasting contribution to twentieth-century philosophy, his dialectical image. In an explanation that has become indispensable for any contemplation of the philosophical, cultural, and mnemonic magnitude of the dialectical image, Benjamin singles out the visual focus in his concept and affirms that its legitimacy only becomes evident in language: "nur dialektische Bilder sind echte . . . Bilder; und der Ort, an dem man sie antrifft, ist Sprache" ("only dialectical images are genuine images . . . ; and the place where one encounters them is language," N2a,3). Consequently, the transition from ideal constellations to tangible configurations of empirical elements occurs as a continual process of virtual representation and textual assimilation, both of which surface briefly and disperse before the next cluster of textual imagery flashes into view. The effect is not dissimilar to that of a succession of film scenes, which are not continuous and flowing but sporadic and irregular, as though they were being projected through a strobe light, an invention used to photograph objects in slow motion that can be traced back to the year 1931.

Obviously, the observer learns to synchronize multiple series of configurations, reading them as a virtual language in which the last vestiges of the experiential are anchored and the intangible is prefigured. Seen within the context of Benjamin's dialectic of "fore- and after-history" (*GS* I:226), these configurations not only devolve from primordial perceptions but are also propelled by an intellectual awakening, "leading back to the origin of history by way of 'bracketing' in which all positions of consciousness, all positings of political orders, and all dikes of culture burst asunder, it is at the same time, against the flow of time, a miniaturization of the ruptured world — and therefore its image."[7] Since the images have been inscribed into the written word, texts or configurations of words are the medium in which the ideal and empirical come together to generate the most comprehensive form of modern symbolization. Accessed as nuggets of semiotic material, the textual fragments in the *Passagen-Werk* supersede the dimensions that physical space once had, foreshadowing the spatiotemporal abstractions underlying contemporary cultural design. The crux of Benjamin's concept revolves around his observation that modern urban psyches have been forced to surrender themselves to the supremacy of the "optical unconscious." As he explains in the artwork essay, photography and film do not merely record external reality mimetically, but by applying techniques such as close-ups and slow motion they also disclose hidden layers of the visible not accessible to the naked eye. Consequently, these media open up a realm of the optical unconscious analogous to the Freudian unconscious of the human psyche (*GS* I.2:500; *SW* 4:265–66). On the one hand, this analogy rests on the presupposition that the spectrum of human understanding and its stimulation call for visual modes to synthesize textual, imagistic, and iconic fragmentation. On the other, it is essential to recognize, as Benjamin did in a report from Paris penned in the final months of 1936 (*SW* 3:236–48), that the photographic medium instrumental in establishing pictorial as opposed to textual forms of cultural design began its extraordinary progress during the epoch of the *juste milieu* (the period of Louis Philippe's regency).

V

Drawing attention to Baudelaire's clairvoyance for comprehending the broken imagery that imposed itself on modern urban spaces, Benjamin alleges that modernity adopts an allegorical mode of cultural representation. With its advent, symbolic forms once founded on sacred connotations were projected into secular allegories, which according to Benjamin the Baroque dramatists regarded as the hieroglyphics or iconology of historical decline and decay. Temporal in nature, allegories conjure up primordial landscapes by eliciting apparitions of death and fragmentation. Benjamin explains this concept in his *Trauerspiel* book (*Ursprung des deutschen Trauerspiels;* Origin of the German Mourning Play, 1928): "Während im Symbol mit der Verklärung des Untergangs das transfigurierte Antlitz der Natur im Lichte der Erlösung flüchtig sich offenbart, liegt in der Allegorie die *facies hippocratica* der Geschichte als erstarrte Urlandschaft dem Betrachter vor Augen" (*GS* I.1:343 "Whereas in the symbol destruction is idealized and the transfigured face of nature is fleetingly revealed in the light of redemption, in allegory the observer is confronted with the *facies hippocratica* of history as a petrified, primordial landscape," *Origin,* 166). Because they are able to detect temporal extremes and marshal visions of the past in the now, allegories mix reality with the mystification of the primeval. Accordingly, dialectical approaches to cultural semiotics combine allegories with the intentions of the clairvoyant artist, who while cognizant of his vision of the future is also acutely aware that he has been deprived of the assurance of divine signification.

The index realigning the relationship between images and cultural signs is characteristic of Benjamin's approach to language as an allegorical medium and a cornerstone of the dialectical image codified in the *Passagen-Werk.* Not unlike Baudelaire, Benjamin seeks out flash-like correlations between the present and citations of past fragments that are wrenched out of their original contexts and suffused into the horizon of the modern materialist. In essence, however, he reinforces an ongoing process of fragmentation and symbolization that was not unfamiliar to nineteenth-century cultural commentary. Despite paying tribute to the social theorist Charles Fourier (1772–1837) and the photographic inventor Louis Jacques Daguerre (1787–1851), as well as to Grandville, Baudelaire, and the urban modernizer Baron Georges Eugène Haussmann (1809–91) for the technical and intellectual contributions that made modern cityscapes possible, the *Passagen-Werk* makes little or no reference to two of the most innovative and provocative depictions of Parisian urbanity in German intellectual history, *Französische Zustände* (French Conditions) and *Lutezia* by Heinrich Heine (1797–1856).[8] Why Benjamin chose not to allude to Heine remains a conundrum, although he does mention reading Heine's prose on Paris in a letter to Werner Kraft in 1936

(*GB* 5:237). The peculiarity of this situation is even more noteworthy if one considers that Benjamin was distantly related to Heine; both his father and mother were descended from the same lineage as the great nineteenth-century poet. While he was apparently aware of his illustrious heritage, Benjamin provides little evidence of having based his cultural commentary on Heine's, only briefly citing Charles Benoist's observation that *Lutezia* vividly depicts the powerful influence of Communism on the workers in the Parisian suburbs (V5a,1).

Originally penned as editorials for the *Allgemeine Zeitung* in Augsburg, Heine's Parisian commentaries are precise and complex readings of the changes impacting metropolitan culture during the reign of Louis Philippe between 1830 and 1848. Particularly germane for Benjamin's dialectical and materialistic method is Heine's reconfiguration of contemporary semiotic systems, which undergo a marked process of atomization in the twenty years between *Französische Zustände* in 1834 and *Lutezia* in 1854. Whereas the earlier work is comprised of nine chapters, in which Parisian topographies are recognizable, the later work condenses the cityscape and its cultural manifestations to a system of textual fragments. Its fifty articles unfold seemingly irreconcilable zones of discourse that transcend traditional styles of cultural commentary and serve to chart urban dissolution. In anticipation of the visual turn in the twentieth century, Heine also transforms geopolitical realities into ciphers commensurate with new and unfamiliar readings of metropolitan experience. Elusive, perplexing, and uncanny, urban fragmentation casts an eye from the city center to its margins and peripheries, at the same time that seemingly irrelevant fringe elements — Heine's masses and Benjamin's ragpickers illustrate this rupture — supplant sociocultural norms. As a result, Heine transforms the growing abstraction of metropolitan experience into a virtual network of philosophical, political, and sociocultural imagery consistent with allegories of cultural erosion. He specifically invokes a broad range of collective expressions and blends music, the visual arts, theater, dance, and architecture with politics or folkloristic elements, so that the multifaceted textures of his Paris prefigure the semiotic micrology and complex iconology found in Benjamin's *Passagen-Werk*. Unquestionably, the dominance of time over space in Heine's urban commentary can be seen as paving the way for three concepts that have become cornerstones of Benjamin's cultural theory: the notions of the phantasmagorical as a historical cipher, of the "time of the now" (*Jetztzeit*) as the amalgamation of the past into the immediate present, and of the dialectical image as the true insignia of modernity.

Any appreciation of Heine's and Benjamin's aptitude as topographical theorists also has to have high esteem for their skill at codifying modern signatures of cultural memory. This talent may have been predicated by the increased flow of semiotics over European borders, as more and more commodities were designated for international markets, and national economies endorsed colonial expansion. Exposure to cultural discrepancies on the one hand and mass communication media on the other made both of them sensitive to a rapidly changing fascination for secular beliefs, unfettered by classical, ideological, or religious traditions. After the bourgeoisie came to power in 1830, the semiotic codes espousing modern cultural design were no longer anchored to homogeneous ideologies, given that mnemonic repositories and cultural symbols were among the first to be decoupled from religious dogma or philosophical convictions. Yet Heine and Benjamin, both of whom were well acquainted with Marx's philosophy of economic progress, but who had chosen to adopt different positions, do provide convincing evidence that economic beliefs, the cult of capitalism, replaced the theological and metaphysical principles once forming the framework of sociocultural remembrance.[9] During the reign of Louis Philippe urban experience succumbed to the exigencies of rampant commodification, implying that the tokens feeding the circulation of secular symbols were indicative of the material objectives championed by bourgeois cultural memory.

Nestled in a web of icons and images, the constituents of urban society had to be unearthed level by level and scrutinized using new methods of observation and imaginative epistemologies of memory. In keeping with this archaeological or stratified disposition, urbanity succumbs to cybernetics, the idea that perpetual movement — bustling traffic, masses of pedestrians, rapidly fluctuating visual sensations, and the incessant flow of goods — is vital to the dynamics of the temporal and counters the intransigence of the spatial. What is more significant is that Heine's reconfiguration of the conventions governing time and space anticipates the proliferation of data in today's telematic and telecommunications network, in which "near" and "far" have been almost completely decoupled from the spatial impact they once had. Long before Benjamin's notion of profane illumination, the jarringly uncanny imagery posed by surrealistic approaches to spatial representation, recast collective memory to match the politics of "image-space and body-space," Heine raised the specter of the death of material space within the epistemological strongholds of modern cityscapes. In response to economic expansion between 1830 and 1840, the railway network radiating out from the French capital revolutionized demographic mobility and accelerated industrial growth. Hence the flow of time superseded the durability of space as the primary factor in urban experience, heralding the historical index Benjamin integrates into his dialectical images. He refers to the close analogies between the *Passagen-Werk* and the *Trauerspiel* book in a letter to Adorno in May of 1935, asserting that his insights had undergone a pattern of resolution during which these ideas, though originally derived from metaphysical sources, had achieved a cumulative stage in which the dialectical image seemed strong enough to withstand any opposition raised by random traces of metaphysical thought (*GB* 5:95–100; *SW* 3:50–52).

Having repositioned his theories and addressed the fundamental question of the historical image central to the orthodox Marxist debate, Benjamin maintains that the pre-eminence time took on implied spatial sensations could no longer be trusted, thus inviting the question of the *difference* between virtual and physical space. In line with the unpredictability of dreams, individuals saw themselves beleaguered, even victimized, by the spatiotemporal consequences of "modernity, which are expressed, in encoded form, in a thousand inadvertent, overlooked, or otherwise worthless cultural forms."[10] Benjamin's approach to modern fragmentation picks up the threads of Heine's process of symbolization by weaving them into historical materialism and its reification of the objects the bourgeoisie transforms into collective icons. These, then, become the new symbols or nodules that tie together the many fibers in Benjamin's fabric of contemporary urbanity. Today, the configurations offsetting the effects of cultural fragmentation are no longer symbolic, as they were for Heine, or linked to commodities, as they are in Benjamin's historical materialism, but entrenched in the electronic circuitry that the Internet age has stimulated.

VI

In 1984 the French cultural theorist, urbanist, and cartographer Paul Virilio published an essay reevaluating the contemporary metropolis, *La Ville Surexposée* (*The Overexposed City*), which documents postmodernist concerns about the atomization and disintegration of urban spaces, while projecting the spirit of Heine's and Benjamin's observations onto early modern interpretations of the city into the twenty-first century.[11] Whereas Heine adapted metropolitan fragmentation to a micrology of semiotic commentary and Benjamin exploded the city out of the continuum of linear history by imagining a constellation of material images, Virilio condenses the cityscape into binary zones that render it compatible to electronic circuitry and Internet topologies. Distinctly spatial, the first of these zones exhibits architectonic and political parameters, while the second is grounded on the temporal dominance underlying the virtual flow found in telematic networks. "From here on," Virilio argues, "constructed space occurs within an electronic topology where the framing of perspective and the gridwork weft of numerical images renovate the division of urban property" (87). The first zone brings material resources together, derived from what were once physical properties: walls, thresholds and gradations, all situated within a sociopsychological map. The second zone constitutes "a synthetic space-time" (98), in which the representations, images, and codes are dissociated from defined reference points, including the notions of locale or spatial permanence.

As Virilio sees it, communication technology revolutionizes current approaches to knowledge and memory, given that the "geodesic capacity to define a unity of time and place for all actions now enters into direct conflict with the structural capacities of means of mass communication" (98). Abridged from three dimensions to two and stimulated by "info-graphic technologies" (98), the grid-work of municipal topographies has been reduced to the factor of time required for split-second conveyance from one surface to the next. Thanks to an exponential increase in transmission speeds, these dynamics develop into vectors of transitory and incandescent revelations, even though the increased vulnerability of data flow exposes it to easy manipulation as well as to being proved invalid. The effects on intellectual and cognitive autonomy are vital, since "the man/machine interface replaces the facades of buildings as the surfaces of property allotments" (88). Much as Heine and Benjamin saw the impact economic and demographic acceleration had on urban environments, Virilio asserts that the instantaneity of postmodern communication deployment has inaugurated "trans-historical temporality" (96), which is not measured in units of "chronological and historical time, time that passes" but in "time that exposes itself instantaneously" (86). People find themselves in a time warp in which durable space and geometric patterns sustaining direct mandates for sensory perceptions have all but evaporated. Confronted with "transportation and transmission time" (88), sensory perceptions yield to the user codes set up to access network links, at the same time that data highways circumnavigate the globe and fictitious identities are engineered for chat rooms and virtual games.

Conversely, urban inhabitants wrestle with a progressive suspension of material surfaces. The multi-layered inscriptions that once connected streets, buildings, and pedestrian walkways to grid-works and city blocks and divided suburban and ethnic neighborhoods from city centers, at one time podiums for representative edifices and monuments, indeed all of these intramural and extramural effects in traditional cityscapes, have been condensed to data interfaces that surface on screens almost as quickly as they can be deleted by a mouse click. Virilio speculates that the rectangular display at home, at work, and in Internet cafés has superseded the city square as the hub of municipal activities. To the extent that E-mail replaces traditional forms of communal discourse, monitors have been instituted as "the crossroads of all mass media" (97). Exhibiting cognitive and interactive dimensions, television, computer, and cellular screens counterbalance the loss of physical and psychosocial human contact.

Besides the construction possibilities that today's communication networks provide, a variety of spatial and temporal mutations is constantly redefining everyday experience and visual representations of contemporary life. For Virilio these engender constructed space, which goes beyond the question of how urban landscapes are perceived and also revise deep-seated perceptions about movement and location. He writes: "Constructed space is more than simply the concrete and material substance of constructed structures, the permanence of elements and the architectonics of urbanistic details. It also exists as the sudden proliferation and the incessant multiplication of special effects which, along with the consciousness of time and of distances, affect the perception of the environment" (94). On a material level, the architectonic surfaces of the city, the constituents of geodesic representation, and the continuum of time and space have become increasingly indiscernible. Uniformity has made the world's metropolises from Paris to Mexico City and Berlin to Shanghai starkly homogeneous. Distinctive signatures the cities once boasted can now be accessed as "special effects" on the Internet, where, depending upon the sophistication of the technology, larger-than-life apertures can be engineered for the viewer. According to Virilio spatial construction is now cinematographically contrived, and the desire to construct virtual worlds finds confirmation within the framework of postmodern urbanistic interfacing. Interfacing, in turn, necessitates a never-ending series of fissured images resembling the discrete fragments of film scenes. This only serves to corroborate Heine's and Benjamin's assumptions about dialectical methods for gathering, storing, and retrieving cultural memory. In our telematic age objects and events no longer fluctuate as they once did; rather, "without necessarily leaving, everything arrives" (88) That is essential for the "the rites of passage of a technical culture" (87), one premised, as Benjamin might have argued, on its own technological reproducibility. Digital cameras, cellular phones, and miniature video players have superseded discursive forms of cultural observation, reconfiguring the frontiers of visions and dreams in global textures.[12] Consistent with Benjamin's approach to the optical unconscious, Virilio's assessment of constructed space revolves around the notion that technological imagery governs contemporary peripheral environments. This omnipresence of imagery bears close resemblance to Benjamin's speculations about the dominance of the optical in modern cities and also ties into the idea of the optical unconscious within the substratum of the collective psyche. Initiated, as has been shown, by the triumphant rise of the photographic medium in the third decade of the nineteenth century, the optical unconscious evokes new "Bildwelten, welche im Kleinsten wohnen, deutbar und verborgen genug, um in Wachträumen Unterschlupf gefunden zu haben, nun aber, groß und formulierbar wie sie geworden sind, die Differenz von Technik und Magie als durch und durch historische Variable ersichtlich zu machen" (*GS* II.1:371; "image worlds, which dwell in the smallest things — meaningful yet covert enough to find a hiding place in waking dreams, but which, enlarged and capable of formulation, make the difference between technology and magic visible as a thoroughly historical variable," *SW* 2:512). In a nutshell, the optical unconscious distinguishes the point at which Heine, Benjamin, and Virilio converge, since it is the medium of the kind of virtual cultural memory that Heine envisaged in 1850, Benjamin documented in his *Passagen-Werk,* and Virilio foretold for the global communication network in the twenty-first century.

Ultimately, the megalopolis of the twenty-first century no longer has demarcations, a "localized and axial estate" (84), for which verification according to spatial determinants is possible. Having forsaken boundaries and margins, the allotments of intramural and extramural space have been supplanted by a "single urban mass" (86) that folds subdivisions and fringes of municipal areas into a geodesic void. In other words, metropolitan design opens up a new "technological space-time," which even more radically than in Heine's and Benjamin's reading of urbanity eradicates the spatial difference between "near" and "far" and the temporal divergences applicable to "now" and "then." These developments represent the most recent stages in the diachronics of fragmentation and reconfiguration in the cultural sphere that began with Heine's symbolic forms in the nineteenth and progressed to Benjamin's historical materialism in the twentieth century. It appears that Virilio's technological interfaces embrace what little remains of our spatiotemporal reality, transforming it into the arcades of telematic semiotics. However, the starting point for what he outlines as the cybercity, today's trans-representational episteme, is already prefigured in the fragmentation and reconstruction of the ambient world in Heine's *Lutezia* and Benjamin's *Passagen-Werk.*

VII

Reading the *Passagen-Werk* from cover to cover poses a challenge for even the most enthusiastic bibliophile, and it has been posited that the countless permutations in Benjamin's montages are portents of today's Internet-surfing techniques. The suggestion is that the textual fragments are the predecessors of digitalized hypertexts, a rudimentary storage facility with which nineteenth-century culture is "decomposed/composed" for "transport and transmigration networks whose immaterial configuration reiterates the cadastral organization and the building of monuments" (V, 94) as digitally formatted memory banks. Within the tangle of hypertexts the semiotic pieces are hardly recognizable on a comprehensive level, meaning that investigating the *Passagen-Werk* rests on two vectors of analysis. Either it can be approached in its entirety or smaller segments can be selected and amalgamated on a discretionary basis, possibly in keeping with aleatoric principles.

Choosing the one vector, the reader would adopt a strictly scientific stance toward Benjamin's project, study the exposés in detail, speculate on how the series of convolutes might interact with one another and then painstakingly assess each textual fragment to determine its location in the mosaic of nineteenth-century urban memory. Opting for the other, the reader would drift from "flotsam to jetsam," stopping indiscriminately to decipher one of Benjamin's glosses, take in a quote, or simply compare and contrast the flow of the entries filed under the topic headings. These labels tend to evidence the same kind of "hit or miss" quality attributed to the terms employed in Internet search engines, activating as they do an inadvertent and bewildering number of "links" as arbitrary as their latter-day descendants. On a virtual level, the reader perambulates inside the interstitial spaces afforded by hypertexts, much as the French bourgeoisie did in the Parisian arcades some 180 years ago. Both approaches to Benjamin's *Passagen-Werk* are highly recommended, especially in view of the fact that any synchronic and diachronic appraisal of Benjamin's textual imagery requires applying the same fissured cybernetics he enlisted while compiling his notes. Apart from putting the fragments on the Web, where they would be as "self-operative" as Virilio's overexposed city, reading the *Passagen-Werk* is an exercise in "dialectics at a standstill," that is, in discerning pithy moments when past and present converge into sparks of historical exactitude. The scope of the dialectical image can best be admired within the panoptic of Benjamin's convolutes, arcades within the *Arcades,* which weave the phantasmagorias of commodities and spatiotemporal scenery into the complex texture of early modern urbanity. Virilio's verdict that "the grand narratives of theoretical causality were displaced by the petty narratives of practical opportunity and, finally, by the micro narratives of autonomy" (96) might certainly have been endorsed by Benjamin, had he lived to witness the dawn of our telematic era and its cybernetic stratagems for cultural semiotics. Unquestionably, though, he would have deeply lamented the "constellation of dangers" jeopardizing the written word in our postmodern age, since he regarded it as the most accessible, resilient, and mimetically accurate medium for chronicling and storing the artifacts of cultural remembrance.

Notes

1 See Bernd Witte, "'Dans une situation sans issue . . . ' Exil und Tod des Schriftstellers Walter Benjamin," in *Gehetzt: Südfrankreich, 1940; Deutsche Literaten im Exil,* ed. Ruth Werfel (Zurich: Verlag Neue Zürcher Zeitung, 2007), 191–216.

2 See Margaret Cohen, "Benjamin's Phantasmagoria: The *Arcades Project,*" in *The Cambridge Companion to Walter Benjamin,* ed. David Ferris (Cambridge: Cambridge UP, 2004), 199–220.

3 For a description of the various work phases see Timo Skrandies, "Unterwegs in den Passagen-Konvoluten," in *Benjamin Handbuch,* ed. Burkhardt Lindner (Stuttgart and Weimar: Metzler, 2006), 274–84.

4 Beatrice Hanssen: "Introduction: Physiognomy of a Flâneur," in *Walter Benjamin and the Arcades Project,* ed. Beatrice Hanssen (London and New York: Continuum, 2006), 6.

[5] See also Marc de Wilde's and Vivian Liska's contributions in this volume.

[6] Max Pensky, "Method and Time: Benjamin's Dialectical Image," in Ferris, *The Cambridge Companion to Walter Benjamin*, 184–85.

[7] Peter Fenves, "Of Philosophical Style — from Leibniz to Benjamin," in *boundary 2* 30:1 (2003): 86.

[8] Among the sporadic references to Heine in the *Passagen-Werk*, Benjamin also cites two stanzas from Heine's Hebraic epos *Jehuda ben Halevy* (A7a,2) and a passage from his essay on the February Revolution (a14a,2).

[9] See Burkhardt Lindner, "Was ist das Passagen-Werk?" in *Urgeschichte des 20. Jahrhunderts*, ed. Peter Rautmann and Nicolas Schatz (Bremen: Hauschild, 2006), 77–94.

[10] Max Pensky, "Method and Time," 183.

[11] Paul Virilio, "The Overexposed City," in *The Paul Virilio Reader*, ed. Steve Redhead (New York: Columbia UP, 2004), 83–99. Further references to this work will be given in the text, using page numbers alone, or V and the page number, as necessary.)

[12] See Rolf J. Goebel, "Europäische Großstadttopographie und globale Erinnerungskultur: Benjamins *Passagen-Werk* heute," in *Topographie der Erinnerungen*, ed. Bernd Witte (Würzburg: Königshausen & Neumann, 2008), 73–78.

8: Benjamin's Politics of Remembrance: A Reading of "Über den Begriff der Geschichte"

Marc de Wilde

Introduction

T HE TASK OF ACTUALIZING Walter Benjamin's political thought confronts us with a problem: many of the positions that he himself, writing in the 1920s and 1930s, regarded as necessary and critical must seem to us, reading him in the twenty-first century, to have become outdated and unacceptable. What are we to think, for example, of his admiration for the revolution's law-destroying violence, his eulogy of the sacrifice, and his attack on parliamentary democracy? And, more fundamentally, what are we to think of his defense of Communism, and his plea for a political messianism? Even some of Benjamin's most generous readers have had difficulties in coming to terms with these positions. They have applied various reading strategies to save Benjamin from himself, arguing, for example, that his Communism was merely a period phenomenon, not affecting his more original, critical positions, and that his messianism should not be taken literally.[1] In the end, however, such readings have remained unsatisfying, for they have tended either to historicize Benjamin's notion of politics, making it irrelevant to the present, or to correct it, thus downplaying aspects of it that he himself considered important.

I believe there is another, more promising, way to engage with Benjamin's political thought. It takes as its point of departure not a historicization or a correction of his illusions but rather an *experience of disillusion*. At the end of his life Benjamin became disillusioned with some of his deepest political convictions, most notably, his "belief" in Communism. I want to argue that this experience of disillusion is precisely what makes his political thought still valuable and relevant for us today, for it led him, among other things, to formulate a critique of totalitarian ideologies that, to this date, has remained unsurpassed in philosophical depth and rigor. Its tenor was that the totalitarian ideologies were entangled in a cycle of violence, caused by their tendency to forget — or to mythologize — the past for the sake of creating a supposedly perfect society. In an attempt to counter these totalitarian ideologies, Benjamin set out to design a radically different kind of politics that, instead of instrumentalizing the past for present purposes, understood itself to be in the service of preceding generations. It was based not only on the pragmatic view that a present politics would remain self-critical as long as it reflected on mistakes made in the past but also on a deeper, theological conviction: the task of a present politics was to "save" or redeem the past from oblivion.

In the mid-1920s Benjamin considered joining the German Communist Party (KPD). He believed it was the only political movement capable of defeating Fascism. More particularly, he thought it could counter the Fascist tendency to aestheticize politics. In the course of the 1930s, however, news of the Moscow trials prompted him to express doubts concerning Communism's political reality in a letter to Max Horkheimer: "Ich verfolge die Ereignisse in Rußland natürlich sehr aufmerksam. Und mir scheint, ich bin nicht der einzige, der mit seinem Latein zuende ist" (Naturally I am following the events in Russia very closely. And it seems to me I am not the only one who has run out of answers).[2] At first Benjamin seemed unwilling to give up the hope he had invested in Communism; as late as 1938 he could still see "die Sowjetunion . . . als Agentin unserer Interessen in einem künftigen Kriege wie in der Verzögerung dieses Krieges" (GB 5:148; the Soviet Union as the agent of our interests in a future war or in the postponement of such a war). But that same year the continuous flow of reports on the Stalinist purges forced him to reconsider his earlier appraisal of Communism, reflecting on its possible affinity with National Socialism instead. He thus came to believe that "die schlechtesten Elemente der KP mit den skrupellosesten des Nationalsozialismus kommunizierten" ("the worst elements of the Communist Party resonated with the most unscrupulous ones of National-Socialism"), the worst being the sadism present in the "Expropriierung der Expropriateure" ("expropriation of the expropriators"), which was not unlike the sadism Hitler applied to the Jews (GS VI:540; SW 4:159).

On 19 August 1939, the Soviet Union entered into a trade agreement with the Third Reich, followed five days later by a non-aggression pact to which a secret appendix on the partition of Eastern Europe was added. To Benjamin the news came as a shock, the echo of which can be heard in his most famous work, "Über den Begriff der Geschichte" ("On the Concept of History"), put in writing a few months later, in the winter of 1939–40. Reading the theses to his fellow refugee, the Jewish author Soma Morgenstern, Benjamin claimed he had written them as an "Antwort auf diesen Pakt" ("answer to this pact").[3] According to the tenth thesis, they sought, "in einem Augenblick, da die Politiker, auf die die Gegner des Faschismus gehofft hatten, am Boden liegen und ihre Niederlage mit dem Verrat an der eigenen Sache bekräftigen, das politische

Weltkind aus den Netzen zu lösen, mit denen sie es umgarnt hatten" (*GS* I.2:698; "at a moment when the politicians in whom the opponents of Fascism had placed their hopes are prostrate, and confirm their defeat by betraying their own cause, . . . to extricate the political worldlings from the snares in which the traitors have entangled them," *SW* 4:393). It was his disappointment with Communism that led Benjamin to write the theses. His main motive was to understand why Communism had betrayed its cause by siding with Fascism instead of opposing it.

In what follows, I will engage in a close reading of Benjamin's "Über den Begriff der Geschichte" in order to clarify his (late) understanding of politics. I will argue that Benjamin, in the theses, sketches the outlines of what I propose to call a *politics of remembrance,* originating from a theologically understood responsibility toward the past. He conceived of this politics, I believe, as an antidote to National Socialism and Communism, in which he recognized the forces of a mythical forgetting. Characteristic of these ideologies was a rhetoric of progress, in light of which the committed violence acquired an appearance of necessity. Their spokesmen were thus unwilling to accept the violence for what it was, and were, rather, speaking — in terms of what we may call a secularized eschatology — of a "purification," an "expiation," or a "final solution." As Benjamin suggested, these totalitarian ideologies could be defeated only when the underlying conceptions of history from which they derived their legitimacy could be refuted. Communism, he believed, was thus based on a "vulgar" notion of Marxism, which sought to justify violence as a necessary means of realizing a classless society. In its turn, Fascism would be grounded in a dogmatic form of "historicism," which represented the existing power relations as the only possible outcome of history, as its "fate" and "destiny." In the theses, Benjamin polemically — and thus politically — turned against these conceptions of history in order to delegitimize the totalitarian regimes they supported.

The Dwarf in the Chess Machine: Theology, Politics, Remembrance

Benjamin begins his essay with a famous metaphor, meant to clarify the relation between his dialectical understanding of history, which he calls "historical materialism," and theology:

> Bekanntlich soll es einen Automaten gegeben haben, der so konstruiert gewesen sei, daß er jeden Zug eines Schachspielers mit einem Gegenzuge erwidert habe, der ihm den Gewinn der Partie sicherte. Eine Puppe in türkischer Tracht, eine Wasserpfeife im Munde, saß vor dem Brett, das auf einem geräumigen Tisch aufruhte. Durch ein System von Spiegeln wurde die Illusion erweckt, dieser Tisch sei

von allen Seiten durchsichtig. In Wahrheit saß ein bucklichter Zwerg darin, der ein Meister im Schachspiel war und die Hand der Puppe an Schnüren lenkte. Zu diesem Apparat kann man sich ein Gegenstück in der Philosophie vorstellen. Gewinnen soll immer die Puppe, die man "historischen Materialismus" nennt. Sie kann es ohne weiteres mit jedem aufnehmen, wenn sie die Theologie in ihren Dienst nimmt, die heute bekanntlich klein und häßlich ist und sich ohnehin nicht darf blicken lassen. (*GS* I.2:693)

[There was once, we know, an automaton constructed in such a way that it could respond to every move by a chess player with a countermove that would ensure the winning of the game. A puppet wearing Turkish attire and with a hookah in its mouth sat before the chessboard placed on a large table. A system of mirrors created the illusion that this table was transparent on all sides. Actually, a hunchbacked dwarf — a master at chess — sat inside and guided the puppet's hand by means of strings. One can imagine a philosophic counterpart to this apparatus. The puppet, called "historical materialism," is to win all the time. It can easily be a match for anyone if it enlists the services of theology, which today, as we know, is small and ugly and has to keep out of sight. (*SW* 4:393)]

Considering the many interpretations that have been proposed, Benjamin's image of the dwarf in the chess machine has proved to be a source of confusion rather than of clarity. Although the image itself suggests that the dwarf (or theology) pulls the strings, guiding the moves of the puppet (or historical materialism), Benjamin in his explanation of the metaphor proposes the opposite: theology is merely in the "service" of historical materialism. This leads to the following question: who is *really* in charge, the dwarf of theology or the puppet of historical materialism?

The metaphor of the dwarf in the chess machine, which identifies the relation between historical materialism and theology as among the main philosophical stakes of Benjamin's theses, has prompted a debate between, on the one hand, scholars inspired by Marxism who, in the wake of Bertolt Brecht's observation that "the small work is clear and illuminating (despite its metaphors and Judaisms)," emphasize the importance of historical materialism at the expense of theology, and, on the other hand, cultural theorists who, following in the footsteps of Gershom Scholem, emphasize the work's "deep connection with theology," claiming that "[often] nothing remains of historical materialism but the word."[4] Among the former critics, Rolf Tiedemann is the most outspoken, answering the question raised in the title of his essay "Historical Materialism or Political Messianism?" in favor of historical materialism. In the theses, he argues, Benjamin "does not assign the task of redemption to a redeemer who is to intervene in history from the outside. Instead, it is 'our' task:

as Marx maintained, "humanity makes its own history.'"[5] According to Tiedemann, even explicitly theological concepts in Benjamin's theses, such as "the Messiah, redemption, the angel, and the Antichrist," are thus merely to be taken as "images, analogies, and parables, and not in their real form."[6] On Tiedemann's reading, then, theology is subservient to historical materialism.

Cultural theorists, by contrast, tend to emphasize the importance of theological motifs in Benjamin's theses despite their materialist phrasing. Irving Wohlfarth, for example, characterizes the messianic structure of Benjamin's last reflections as "triadic": they would be dependent upon the belief that paradise was lost, and that man, exiled in time, has to await the second coming of the Messiah, who will restore the ruins of history and eternity itself.[7] Until that moment, Wohlfarth argues, it would be impossible to have a definitive — or even adequate — understanding of history. Therefore the image of the past as described by the historical materialist has to remain fragmented and dialectical, bearing witness to contradictions that cannot be solved in a meaningful narrative, a "universal history," until the Messiah has come. "Only when redemption is complete," Wohlfarth writes, "will the local quotations that have been exploded out of their historical context be reinserted within it."[8] Contrary to Tiedemann's interpretation, Wohlfarth suggests that for Benjamin materialism is subservient to theology; it would need theology to produce a true image of history, "saving" the fragments of the past. In Wohlfarth's view, then, it is theology that pulls the strings, even if it has to remain hidden in a materialist language until the Messiah has arrived.

I believe that these interpretations, though not untrue, are one-sided. More particularly, I want to argue that the puzzling "reversal" in Benjamin's metaphor of the dwarf in the chess machine — at first, in the metaphor itself, theology seems to pull the strings, but in the end, in Benjamin's explanation, it turns out to be merely in the "service" of historical materialism — does not designate the precedence of one of these concepts over the other but rather points at their interdependence. Thus in Benjamin's view theology is at work in historical materialism as the critical element that prevents the truth from being appropriated prematurely, forcing the image of history, which always threatens to fossilize as a dogma, to open itself up to new experiences. Yet this phrase is already too schematic, in that it indicates only the negative, critical function of theology, whereas Benjamin also recognizes its positive function; he thus suggests that the historical materialist's task is to "save" and redeem the past by giving it a new topicality in the heart of the present.[9] Benjamin's metaphor of the dwarf in the chess machine should be read accordingly: only if historical materialism becomes aware of its theological origins will it be able to unfold its truth, that is, to grasp the true image of the past which suddenly — in a flash — becomes recognizable.

Yet ultimately it is the figure of the "hunchbacked dwarf" who holds the key to the metaphor. He belongs to a family of little men who populate many of Benjamin's writings. In order to lay bare the meaning of this figure it is necessary to examine the other contexts in which it appears. The first is in Benjamin's autobiographical essay "Berliner Kindheit um neunzehnhundert" ("Berlin Childhood around 1900"). Here the figure of the "hunchbacked dwarf" refers to the way the past is experienced in memory: in it, Benjamin suggests, the world appears on a reduced scale in which things and places seem to have shrunk. The world as it is remembered is thus a world of little men and dwarfs.

> Wo [das bucklicht Männlein] erschien, da hatte ich das Nachsehn. Ein Nachsehn, dem die Dinge sich entzogen, bis aus dem Garten übers Jahr ein Gärtlein, ein Kämmerlein aus meiner Kammer und ein Bänklein aus der Bank geworden war. Sie schrumpften, und es war, als wüchse ihnen ein Buckel, der sie selber nun der Welt des Männleins für sehr lange einverleibte. (*GS* IV.1:303)

> Where the hunchback appeared, I could only look on uselessly. It was a look from which things receded — until, in a year's time, the garden had become a little garden, my room a little room, and the bench a little bench. They shrank, and it was as if they grew a hump, which made them the little man's own. (*SW* 3:385)

In this passage the figure of the "little hunchback" stands for the experience of a *Verschränkung* ("folding") that characterizes the image of the past as it appears in memory. According to Benjamin, memory produces a shortened picture of the world, a "monad." In it, things and places that at the time seemed unrelated suddenly seem to coincide. The figure of the "little hunchback" thus triggers a vision of eternity, not as a timeless truth, but as time infinitely shortened in memory.

The figure of the "little hunchback" resurfaces in Benjamin's essay on Franz Kafka. Here it serves to elucidate the theological meaning of remembrance. Its image is prompted by those characters in Kafka's novels who are forced to go through life bent forward because doorposts are too narrow or ceilings too low. On Benjamin's reading, these characters, who in their gesture of bending forward seem to express a certain humbleness, testify to a theological truth: that man will not feel at home in this world until the Messiah has come. The figure of the "little hunchback" turns out to be the *Urbild* of a life that, because of the passing of time, has been wrenched out of joint. It refers to the theological insight that redemption, which promises to restore what has been distorted, has not yet taken place. "Dies Männlein," Benjamin writes, "ist der Insasse des entstellten Lebens; es wird verschwinden, wenn der Messias kommt, von dem ein großer Rabbi gesagt hat, daß er nicht mit Gewalt die Welt verändern wolle, sondern nur um ein Geringes sie zurechtstellen werde" (*GS* II.2:432; "This little man is at home in distorted life; he will disappear with the coming of the Messiah, who (a great rabbi once said) will not wish to change the world by force but will merely make a slight adjustment in it," *SW* 2:811). I want to argue that in this passage Benjamin alludes to a kind of "minimal redemption," suggesting that the Messiah will not create a new world but merely restore the existing world in its original state. He will, more particularly, repair the damage done by the passing of time, done by the forces of oblivion. In the figure of the "little man" we can therefore recognize the motif of a minimal redemption as the critical and saving potential of remembrance.

Understanding the "hunchbacked dwarf" of Benjamin's first thesis in light of the "little men" and "hunchbacks" in his other writings has enabled us to uncover the practice — or, rather, imperative — of remembrance as an important yet hidden motif in the theses. In this thesis Benjamin envisages the task of the historical materialist as describing a dialectical image of history that does justice to the memory of preceding generations. This task, he suggest, is "theological" because it is modeled after a certain image of eternity as the sudden resurgence of the past as *Jetztzeit* ("now-time," *GS* I.2:703; *SW* 4:396). It is "political" because it makes the past into a "scandal for the present,"[10] questioning the legitimacy of the existing order in the name of those who have been forgotten. It thus seeks to counter the forces of oblivion that are at work in the totalitarian regimes. By founding his "concept of history" on the imperative of remembrance, Benjamin criticizes those regimes, and the conceptions of history by which they are supported, that have suppressed the past for the sake of what they consider to be "progress."

The Politics of Forgetting: Historicism and "Vulgar Marxism"

In historicism and "Vulgärmarxismus" (*GS* I.2:699; "vulgar Marxism," *SW* 4:393), Benjamin recognizes the forces of oblivion that, in the twentieth century, would decisively contribute to the legitimization of the totalitarian regimes. While Benjamin accuses "vulgar Marxism" of having forgotten the suffering of the *past* for the sake of a supposedly better future, he blames historicism for having forgotten the suffering of the *present* for the sake of a supposedly more truthful image of the past. What these two have in common is a belief in progress, and, more particularly, a belief that, while advocating a classless society and writing a universal history respectively, they are in fact contributing to an illusory completion of history itself. Yet it is this very belief that has led them to obscure the suffering in the present and past, giving it the appearance of being rational and necessary instead.

Although Benjamin sympathizes with Marx's materialism, which, he claims, is able to counter the "narcotic effect" of Hegelian idealism, he regrets that Marx based his philosophy on a belief in progress, which has fatally undermined its critical potential. According to Benjamin, this belief, first of all, testifies to a confusion of technological with moral progress: "Er will nur die Fortschritte der Naturbeherrschung, nicht die Rückschritte der Gesellschaft wahr haben" (GS I.2:699; "It recognizes only the progress in mastering nature, not the retrogression of society," SW 4:393). Thus it led, not only to a "technocratic" mentality compatible to that of Fascism, transforming the relations between human beings into reified and instrumental reflexes, but also to an "ominous" concept of nature, justifying the unlimited exploitation of nature for the sake of socioeconomic advancement. Furthermore, being based on the supposition that history is slowly moving in the direction of a classless society, it led the working class to accept its continuing oppression as a temporary yet inevitable circumstance, while being aware that redemption will not fall to its lot except in the distant future. Finally, it resulted in the illusion that progress is in fact unstoppable and that capitalism will in the end, because of its own contradictions, collapse of its own accord, so that the working class has only to wait, passively, for a classless society to arrive.

Initially Benjamin's critique seems to be aimed not at Marx himself but rather at his heirs, the "vulgar Marxists" and "social-democrats" (GS I.2:699; SW 4:393). But in the relative intimacy of his private notes Benjamin leaves little room for doubt as to whom he is ultimately addressing: "Marx sagt, die Revolutionen sind die Lokomotive der Weltgeschichte. Aber vielleicht ist dem gänzlich anders. Vielleicht sind die Revolutionen der Griff des in diesem Zuge reisenden Menschengeschlechts nach der Notbremse" (GS I.3:1232; "Marx says that revolutions are the locomotive of world history. But perhaps it is quite otherwise. Perhaps revolutions are an attempt by the passengers on this train — namely, the human race — to activate the emergency brake," SW 4:402). Contrary to Marx, Benjamin suggests that revolutions are not the carriers of an unstoppable progress, but rather of its interruption, that is, moments in which history is suddenly brought to a standstill, and "the truly new" announces itself. In the final analysis, this critique originates from a theologico-political understanding of Marxist thought: with the concept of a classless society, Benjamin argues, Marx had, in fact, secularized a notion of messianic time. The problem was not this secularisation as such but rather Marx's particular understanding of messianic time, according to which redemption, that is, a classless society, would not be realized until the end of history. As a result the disciples of Marx would situate a classless society in the far future, and with the emergence of social democracy would even try to redefine it as an "ideal" or an "endless task." The working class would thereby abandon its original messianic intention, its impatience to create a classless society here and now, satisfying itself with the illusion of liberating its grandchildren instead.

In one of his preparatory notes to the theses, Benjamin summarizes this theologico-political critique of Marxism: "Dem Begriff der klassenlosen Gesellschaft muß sein echtes messianisches Gesicht wiedergegeben werden, und zwar im Interesse der revolutionären Politik des Proletariats selbst" (*GS* I.3:1232; "A genuinely messianic face must be restored to the concept of classless society and, to be sure, in the interest of furthering the revolutionary politics of the proletariat itself," *SW* 4:403). This would imply, first, that the concept of a classless society is grounded in a radically different notion of time, for it should no longer be understood as history's end or culmination point but rather as its "oft mißglückte, endlich bewerkstelligte Unterbrechung" (*GS* I.3:1231; "frequently miscarried, ultimately achieved interruption," *SW* 4:402). It would mean, second, that something other than the belief in progress must be driving the revolutionary movements to realize redemption in the present. This driving force, Benjamin suggests, is "das Bild der geknechteten Vorfahren" ("the image of the enslaved ancestors"); it is the source of their "best[e] Kraft ("best strength"), their "Haß" ("hatred") and their "Opferwillen" (*GS* I.2:700; "spirit of sacrifice," *SW* 4:394). What Benjamin describes here as "the image of the enslaved ancestors" can, I believe, have but one meaning: it is an image of the past produced in the practice of remembrance. It is, in other words, the *memory* of their suffering ancestors that urges the working class to strive for a radical break with the "given," which amounts to a redemption of humanity that is no longer postponed. I consider this to be Benjamin's decisive correction of Marxism: what drives the revolutionaries is not, as Marx and his followers claimed, their belief in progress but rather a practice of remembrance, grounded in a particular responsibility toward the past.

At first sight Benjamin's intention to do justice to the singular, nonreducible quality of every historical moment seems to correspond with the aim of historicism to describe the past — as its leading figure, Leopold von Ranke, famously put it — "wie es eigentlich gewesen [ist]" (the way it actually was). Yet upon closer consideration Benjamin turns out to reject the Rankean criterion, arguing that the historian is always forced to select images of the past in view of the present. There is, first of all, a practical reason for this, for if the historian failed to make a distinction between those images of the past that are relevant and meaningful to the present and those that are not, then his narrative would become incomprehensible, a mere arbitrary enumeration of "facts." But Benjamin mentions another reason as well: a truly "universal history," doing justice to the singular quality of every moment of time, would remain premature as long as humankind has not entered the state of redemption. Consequently, the historical materialist has to engage with the finite historical situation in which he finds himself. According to Benjamin, the historical materialist cannot grasp history in its totality, since he belongs to a humankind that is not yet redeemed. Instead he is forced to select incomplete and fragmented images of the past. Here we perceive the outline of a particular kind of responsibility that Benjamin ascribes to the historian: he has to do justice to the past in its qualitative singularity, while remaining aware that a decision, reducing its singularity to a concept, is inevitable. It is, therefore, impossible for Benjamin's historical materialist to describe history — in accordance with Ranke's criterion — "wie es eigentlich gewesen [ist]."

Benjamin's theological critique of historicism has a political background as well: "Vergangenes historisch artikulieren heißt nicht, es erkennen 'wie es denn eigentlich gewesen ist.' Es heißt, sich einer Erinnerung bemächtigen, wie sie im Augenblick einer Gefahr aufblitzt" (*GS* I.2:695; "Articulating the past historically does not mean recognizing it 'the way it was.' It means appropriating a memory as it flashes up in a moment of danger," *SW* 4:391). This danger is primarily of a political nature, for Ranke's advice to forget the present while approaching the past causes the historian to ignore the political interests underlying the prevailing image of history. In this context, Benjamin finds it particularly significant that Ranke's method of "empathizing" with the past goes hand in hand with a certain melancholia: "Sein Ursprung ist die Trägheit des Herzens, die *acedia*, welche daran verzagt, des echten historischen Bildes sich zu bemächtigen, das flüchtig aufblitzt" (*GS* I.2:696; "Its origin is indolence of heart, that *acedia* which despairs of appropriating the genuine historical image as it briefly flashes up," *SW* 4:391). This melancholia, Benjamin suggests, is, on the one hand, the source of all true historical understanding, for it testifies to the awareness that the truth — here: history in its qualitative singularity — lies beyond the realm of certain knowledge. But it can, on the other hand, become the source of a fatal illusion as well: emphasizing the ultimate elusiveness of the past, it causes apathy, which is not without political risks: "Die Natur dieser Traurigkeit wird deutlicher, wenn man die Frage aufwirft, in wen sich denn der Geschichtsschreiber des Historismus eigentlich einfühlt. Die Antwort lautet unweigerlich in den Sieger" (*GS* I.2:696; "The nature of this sadness becomes clearer if we ask: With whom does historicism actually sympathize? The answer is inevitable: with the victor," *SW* 4:391).

Emphasizing the "Gefahrenkonstellation" ("constellation of danger") underlying the image of the past, Benjamin seeks to bring to light a political moment in the historicist rhetoric of objectivity: the claim of historicism that it is describing history "the way it was," is in fact serving the ruling classes. The historical materialist should be aware of this; he should realize that the image of the past, as it is constructed and read in the present, is always also implicated in a certain configuration of power. Yet this does not mean that the image of the past is merely political, nor that it is fatally dependent on the interests of the present. It is, by contrast, based on what Benjamin describes as "eine geheime Verabredung zwischen den gewesenen Geschlechtern und unserem" (*GS* I.2:694; "a secret agreement between past generations and the present one," *SW* 4:390), according to which the latter, instead of freely inventing the image of the past, is *obliged to respond* to the (utopian) claims of the former. This figure of "a secret agreement" is, I believe, meant as a metaphor of the particular *responsibility* from which the practice of remembrance originates, that is, the moral and political *responsiveness* toward the past that is demanded from those who remember, and without which their image of the past cannot be truthful. Although Benjamin's historical materialist thus actively construes the image of the past, he does not do so arbitrarily, for in it he seeks to respect the memory of preceding generations.

The Politics of Remembrance: The Dialectical Image as the Image of Memory

It is impossible to understand Benjamin's concept of history without taking into consideration his attempt, in *Das Passagen-Werk* (*The Arcades Project*, 1927–40), to concretize and apply it to the history of nineteenth-century Paris. Here Benjamin defines what in his theses he calls the "wahre Bild der Vergangenheit" (*GS* I.2:695; "true image of the past," *SW* 4:390) as a dialectical image bringing together the demands of both the present and the past. The dialectical image emerges in what he calls "das Jetzt einer bestimmten Erkennbarkeit" ("the now of a particular recognizability," N3,1), when the present suddenly recognizes itself in the past, identifying with the suffering of preceding generations and responding to their (utopian) claims. The image is dialectical in that it not only testifies to an affinity, but also to a discrepancy or an "entstellte Ähnlichkeit" (*GS* II.1:314; "displaced similarity," *SW* 2:240 [trans. modified]) between the past and the present.[11] More specifically, the image shows how the utopian dreams of preceding generations have remained unfulfilled, or have even transformed into outright nightmares in the present. The dialectical image, for example, reveals how the nineteenth-century dream of technology's making the inexhaustible sources of nature available for human consumption has, a century later, turned into the nightmare of a war machine consuming humanity instead. In Benjamin's view, this later betrayal of technology forms part of the objective image of the past. The dialectical image thus juxtaposes different moments of history that, because of an displaced similarity, together form a critical constellation that calls into question the prevailing conceptions of history and the totalitarian politics they support.

In her groundbreaking study of the *Passagen-Werk*, Susan Buck-Morss argues that the notion of the dialectical image can be understood only against the background of a "materialist pedagogy."[12] This pedagogy would amount to the attempt to "educate the image-creating medium" within the reader, that is, the ability to confront the image of the past with the "fleeting images of his or her lived experience" (292). Considered on their own, the fragments of the past that Benjamin presents in his *Passagen-Werk* seem to be cited uncritically, lacking, as Theodor W. Adorno suggested,[13] the necessary theoretical explanation. However, as Buck-Morss shows, they are, in fact, selected according to a strict principle: because of the utopian promise they embodied in the eyes of the people of their own time, they represent the exact antithesis to the historical situation in which Benjamin's readers find themselves, that is, the 1930s, in which Fascism and Communism had betrayed that utopian promise. Thus, while Benjamin seems to sketch the dream worlds of the past uncritically, he is actually expecting the reader to add to these the images of his or her own situation, which gives them a critical potential. If we want to unravel the true political meaning of the dialectical image we should, therefore, as Buck-Morss argues, "make visible the invisible text of present events that underlies it" (290).

Buck-Morss suggests that Benjamin's pedagogic intention not only presupposes a historical contextualization — making visible the invisible text in the image — but also an *Aktualisierung* (a making-present): "in the service of truth, Benjamin's own text must be 'ripped out of context,' sometimes, indeed, with a 'seemingly brutal grasp'" (340). On this point Buck-Morss agrees with Irving Wohlfarth, who as early as 1986, just after the *Passagen-Werk* had been published, argued that the work demanded a "'firm and brutal grasp' on our own historical conjuncture."[14] The dialectical image would, more particularly, stand for a practice of critical citation, prompted by a messianic intention to preserve the past from falling into oblivion. Doing justice to Benjamin's aim would thus entail learning "how to *utilize* his work, to recast its recasting, to cite it differently — neither piously nor indiscriminately" (23). In other words, the challenge would be to project Benjamin's images into the present, thereby simultaneously articulating their meaning and elucidating our own historical situation. Only thus, by *actualizing* these images, "making them present," would we be able to attain a "weakened but practical version of his messianic theory and practice of citation" (24).

Although actualization is, indeed, necessary, there are limits to it as well. Most importantly, as I have argued, Benjamin's dialectical image is embedded in a particular responsibility toward the past. Although it can — and should — be grasped out of its context, it cannot be projected arbitrarily onto any other context instead, for it only becomes "readable" — and thus citable in a meaningful, critical way — in a particular present, that is, in the "now" to which it corresponds because of a "displaced similarity." "Jede Gegenwart," Benjamin argues in the *Passagen-Werk*, "ist durch diejenigen

Bilder bestimmt, die mit ihr synchronistisch sind: Jedes Jetzt ist das Jetzt einer bestimmten Erkennbarkeit" ("Every present is determined by the images which are synchronic with it: each 'now' is the now of a particular recognizability," N3,1). This constellation of past and present made visible in the dialectical image is far from arbitrary; rather, it appears *involuntarily* at a particular moment in time, namely the moment at which the tension between past and present, between the utopian promises of the past and their betrayal in the present, becomes greatest, such that the memory of the suffering ancestors becomes unbearable. At this particular moment in time the past suddenly, in a flash, flows together with the present, forming a critical constellation that calls into question the existing regimes of historical truth as well as the economies of power from which they stem (see *Passagen-Werk*, N10,3; N10a,1; N10a, 2; N10a 3).

Understanding the dialectical image as a medium of remembrance, grasping the image of the past where it suddenly appears involuntarily, Benjamin seems to have modeled it after what Marcel Proust famously described as a "mémoire involontaire" (involuntary memory): it eludes subjective intention; it flashes up in an instant; it is fragmented and isolated from its original context; it suggests the presence of the past, yet infinitely shortened and condensed into an image. There are, however, important differences. Unlike Proust's involuntary memory, Benjamin's dialectical image does not restore the past in its original state, with its limits and illusions, but rather juxtaposes it with the present, seeking to activate its critical potential. This means that in the dialectical image a "translation" is necessary: the utopian hope of preceding generations should be presented in such a way that it becomes readable in — and thereby has an impact on — the present. In the dialectical image, the historical materialist thus actively engages with the past, responding to its silent call for justice; he seeks to do justice to its memory by translating it into a present political experience. Bringing to light the wish images of preceding generations, he does not prove — with a gesture of cynicism — their naiveté, but rather seeks to make good on promises inscribed in these images that have been broken throughout the course of history.

Here we approach the core of Benjamin's argument: serving as a medium of remembrance, the dialectical image is grounded in a *theological* responsibility to save the past from the forces of forgetting — and, ultimately, to save it from history itself — by giving it a new life in the present. In dialogue with Max Horkheimer, Benjamin makes his most explicit remarks on the theological function and meaning of the dialectical image. Answering Benjamin's suggestion that the dialectical image can give a new life to the past, Horkheimer wrote in a letter of 16 March 1937: "Die Feststellung der Unabgeschlossenheit ist idealistisch, wenn die Abgeschlossenheit nicht in ihr aufgenommen ist. Das vergangene Unrecht ist geschehen und abgeschlossen. Die Erschlagenen sind wirklich erschlagen . . . Nimmt man die Unabgeschlossenheit ganz ernst, so muß man an das jüngste Gericht glauben" (quoted in *Passagen-Werk*; "The determination of incompleteness is idealistic if completeness is not comprised within it. Past injustice has occurred and is completed. The slain are really slain . . . If one takes the lack of closure entirely seriously, one must believe in the Last Judgment," N8,1). Quoting Horkheimer's letter in the *Passagen-Werk*, Benjamin adds the following comments:

> Das Korrektiv dieser Gedankengang liegt in der Überlegung, daß die Geschichte nicht allein eine Wissenschaft sondern nicht minder eine Form des Eingedenkens ist. Was die Wissenschaft "festgestellt" hat, kann das Eingedenken modifizieren. Das Eingedenken kann das Unabgeschlossene (das Glück) zu einem Abgeschlossenen und das Abgeschlossene (das Leid) zu einem Unabgeschlossenen machen. Das ist Theologie; aber im Eingedenken machen wir eine Erfahrung, die uns verbietet, die Geschichte grundsätzlich atheologisch zu begreifen, so wenig wir sie in unmittelbar theologischen Begriffen zu schreiben versuchen dürfen.

> [The corrective to this line of thinking may be found in the consideration that history is not simply a science but also and not least a form of remembrance. What science has "determined," remembrance can modify. Such mindfulness can make the incomplete (happiness) into something complete, and the complete (suffering) into something incomplete. That is theology; but in remembrance we have an experience that forbids us to conceive of history as fundamentally atheological, little as it may be granted us to try to write it with immediately theological concepts. (N 8,1).]

Elsewhere Benjamin had already explained why we may not write history with immediately theological concepts: it is impossible for us, as finite human beings, to relate directly to the messianic (*GS* II.1:203; *SW* 4:305). Consequently, Benjamin nowhere claims that the historical materialist is capable of anticipating the real, messianic arrest of time, which will redeem humanity, ending its history of suffering. What he does claim is that the historical materialist, by seeking to give new life to the past in a practice of remembrance, may in the heart of the present produce an elusive vision of eternity. This image is as ungraspable as involuntary memory itself; it has already passed as soon as it is consciously perceived. It is revealed in the midst of the transitory moment, not as a timeless truth but as time infinitely shortened to the "now of recognizability." Although the historical materialist cannot relate directly to the messianic, an indirect relation is hereby granted to him. He only has to follow a detour, via the (image of) the past, via the claims to redemption — the claims to happiness, to an ending of suffering — of preceding generations, and to do justice to their memory in the present. In this sense remembrance can indeed "modify" history, for it can renew the (utopian) claims of the past, seeking to accomplish now what before was ignored and has remained unaccomplished.[15]

Epilogue: The Politics of Remembrance Now

If doing justice to Benjamin's theoretical endeavor means that we have to rip his text out of its original context, projecting it onto ours instead, we should reflect on the possibilities for a politics of remembrance in our time. To that end I want to consider briefly — without pretending to treat the subject exhaustively — what might be one of the most interesting recent examples of such a politics: the impact of the imperative "nie wieder Auschwitz" (never again Auschwitz) on German foreign policy after the reunification. I have chosen to discuss this particular case because of its origin, that is, the attempt to do justice to the memory of the Shoah, and its result, that is, the justification of military violence in the present, both of which, to me, seem particularly important. I believe this example might serve to illustrate the critical potential as well as the limits of a politics of remembrance in our time.

The legacy of the National Socialist atrocities has played an important role in postwar German foreign policy. In the German Federal Republic the prevailing idea was that Germany, because of the violence it had caused in the past, had a particular responsibility to prevent violence in the present. Politicians on the left argued that this responsibility entailed a policy of peace and pacifism, implying, among other things, that the German army would only have a defensive function and would never again participate in military actions abroad. They summarized their position with the imperative "nie wieder Krieg" ("never again war"), meant to serve as a guideline for German foreign policy. This imperative led some, particularly among "Die Grünen" (the Green Party), to conclude that, even in cases of serious violations of human rights and genocide, Germany had to abstain from military intervention, using other means, such as diplomatic and economic sanctions, to end the violence instead.

In the course of the 1990s, the meaning of the National Socialist legacy for German foreign policy was reinterpreted. After fierce debates within his party, the Greens, the German Minister of Foreign Affairs, Joschka Fischer, declared, on 7 April 1999: "Ich habe nicht nur gelernt: nie wieder Krieg. Ich habe auch gelernt: nie wieder Auschwitz" (I have not only learned: never again war. I have also learned: never again Auschwitz).[16] Changing the imperative "nie wieder Krieg" to include a reference to Auschwitz, Fischer made possible what just a few years earlier had seemed unthinkable: the first out-of-area deployment of German soldiers in a non-defensive armed conflict since the Second World War, that is, their participation in KFOR, the NATO-led intervention force in Kosovo. Although Fischer's plea for military intervention was, in fact, highly controversial, bringing him to the verge of his downfall as a political leader of the Green Party, it proved to be effective in that the decision to deploy German troops to Kosovo was eventually supported by a majority in parliament.

This controversy raises the question whether the impact of the imperative "nie wieder Auschwitz" on German foreign policy satisfies the demands of Benjamin's politics of remembrance. I believe it does not. In this context, Fischer's redefinition of the imperative is particularly revealing: Auschwitz is cited in order to make Germany's participation in KFOR acceptable to the German public and, more particularly, to the Green Party's electorate. Benjamin's politics of remembrance, by contrast, focuses on an image of the past that resists instrumentalization for present political purposes. It is therefore useless to ideological modes of thinking. To put it more precisely: the memory image guiding Benjamin's politics of remembrance cannot serve to justify present political positions but rather serves to disrupt them. It is an "unsettling image" not only in that it literally "unsettles" us, as we cannot come to terms with it, unable to appropriate and instrumentalize it in a concept, but also in that it challenges our "settled" opinions about history and politics.

Interestingly, the image of Auschwitz to which Fischer appeals is potentially precisely such an unsettling image — it is, perhaps, even the unsettling image *par excellence*. But the way it is cited in this instance, isolated from its original context and inserted into a political program, it has lost its capacity to unsettle. Fischer's Auschwitz is a monumentalized Auschwitz. It is a reified image of suffering, in which suffering has acquired a universal significance, such that a distinction between the Albanian minority in Kosovo and the Jews in the concentration camps can no longer be made. Yet, here as well, memory has resisted its instrumentalization. This becomes clear in light of the protests voiced by survivors of the Shoah and relatives of the victims against what they see as Fischer's "misuse of the dead of Auschwitz" to justify Germany's involvement in the bombings of Serbia.[17] Here Auschwitz has once again become an unsettling image, calling into question the way in which present political positions are legitimized.

Although one certainly does not need to call on Benjamin's theories in order to criticize Fischer, the confrontation between the two might help us to distinguish between different ways of engaging with the past. More particularly, I propose to distinguish between two divergent positions: on the one hand, there is a Benjaminian "politics of remembrance," which focuses on images of the past that can be neither appropriated, nor translated into a political program, but that remain unsettling and disrupt political positions wherever they threaten to become dogmatic. And, on the other hand, there is what we might call a "politics of commemoration," which tends to reify the past, producing official and monumental images of it that are ultimately meant to justify partisan political interests in the present. Whereas Fischer's appeal to Auschwitz is an example of the latter position, the objections raised against it are an example of the former. The images of the past on which the politics of remembrance is orientated are "dialectical" in that they cannot serve as a stable ground for politics; rather, they reveal the groundlessness of the political as such: they open up a space of critique and contestability. It is this space that the politics of commemoration has sought to bring to a closure: it has monumentalized the past, producing fixed and instrumentalized images of it that are no longer contestable. These images are not disruptive but affirmative: they are the self-congratulatory images of a present that has forgotten how to listen and respond to the claims of the past — claims that, as Benjamin already observed in his second thesis, cannot be settled cheaply (*GS* I.2:694; *SW* 4:390).

Notes

[1] Rolf Tiedemann, "Historical Materialism or Political Messianism," in *Walter Benjamin: Critical Evaluations in Cultural Theory*, vol. 1, ed. Peter Osborne (1983; repr., London: Routledge, 2005), 149.

[2] Letter from Walter Benjamin to Max Horkheimer, 31 Aug. 1936, in Walter Benjamin, *Gesammelte Briefe*, ed. Christoph Gödde and Henri Lonitz (Frankfurt am Main: Suhrkamp, 1998), 5:373. Further references to this work are made using the abbreviation *GB* and the page number.

[3] Gershom Scholem, *Walter Benjamin: Die Geschichte einer Freundschaft* (Frankfurt am Main: Suhrkamp, 1997), 275.

[4] Bertolt Brecht, *Arbeitsjournal: Erster Band, 1938 bis 1942*, ed. Werner Hecht (Frankfurt am Main: Suhrkamp, 1973), 294, and Gershom Scholem, "Walter Benjamin und sein Engel," in *Zur Aktualität Walter Benjamins*, ed. Siegfried Unseld (Frankfurt am Main: Suhrkamp, 1972), 87 and 131.

[5] Rolf Tiedemann, "Historical Materialism or Political Messianism," in *Critical Evaluations*, 1:145.

[6] Tiedemann, "Historical Materialism," 149.

[7] Irving Wohlfarth, "On the Messianic Structure of Walter Benjamin's Last Reflections," in *Critical Evaluations*, 1:169 and 192. (Originally published in 1978.)

[8] Wohlfarth, "Messianic Structure," 193.

[9] Cf. Stéphane Mosès, *L'ange de l'histoire: Rosenzweig, Benjamin, Scholem* (Paris: Seuil, 1992), 152.

[10] Norbert Bolz, "Aesthetics? Philosophy of History? Theology!" in *Benjamin's Ghosts: Interventions in Contemporary Literary and Cultural Theory*, ed. Gerhard Richter (Stanford, CA: Stanford UP, 2002), 230.

[11] For this concept, see also Sigrid Weigel, *Entstellte Ähnlichkeit: Walter Benjamins theoretische Schreibweise* (Frankfurt am Main: Fischer Taschenbuch, 1997).

[12] Susan Buck-Morss, *The Dialectics of Seeing: Walter Benjamin and the Arcades Project* (Cambridge, MA, and London: MIT Press, 1999), 287–330.

[13] Letter from Theodor W. Adorno to Gershom Scholem, dated 9 May 1949, quoted in *GS* V.2:1072.

[14] Irving Wohlfarth, "Re-fusing Theology: Some First Responses to Walter Benjamin's Arcades Project," in *New German Critique* 39 (1986): 16.

[15] Stéphane Mosès, "Eingedenken und Jetztzeit: Geschichtliches Bewußtsein im Spätwerk Walter Benjamins," in *Vergessen und Erinnern*, ed. Anselm Haverkamp, Renate Lachmann, and Reinhart Herzog (Munich: Fink, 1993), 389–90.

[16] Nico Fried, "Ich habe gelernt: nie wieder Auschwitz; Die Erinnerung an das Vernichtungslager gehört zu den Leitlinien von Außenminister Joschka Fischer," in *Süddeutsche Zeitung*, 23 Jan. 2005.

[17] Esther Bejarano, Kurt Goldstein, and Peter Gingold (1999), "Offener Brief an die Minister Fischer und Scharping," in *Frankfurter Rundschau*, 23 Apr. 1999.

9: The Legacy of Benjamin's Messianism: Giorgio Agamben and Other Contenders

Vivian Liska

IN THE OPENING LINES OF HIS SEMINAL ESSAY "Bewußtmachende oder ret-tende Kritik,"[1] published in 1973 on the occasion of Benjamin's eightieth birthday, Jürgen Habermas locates the relevance of Benjamin's work in the conflicts it continues to raise among those who consider themselves close to his philosophical and political vision. Habermas recognizes a direct continuity between the battle lines defining the reception of Benjamin's writings since their publication in the fifties and sixties and the divergent political positions that had an impact on him in his lifetime. These positions were, for Habermas, embodied by Benjamin's friends Gershom Scholem, Theodor W. Adorno, and Bertolt Brecht and, to a lesser extent, by the school reformer Gustav Wyneken and the surrealist artists. Habermas assigns to each of these figures a set of heirs — among them Hannah Arendt, but also the rebellious students of 1968 — each taking up one of what can summarily be defined as the Jewish-mystical, the leftist modernist, the orthodox Marxist, the neoconservative, and the anarchic dimensions of Benjamin's legacy.

More than three decades, a millennial turn, and generations of Benjamin scholars later, the contemporary relevance of his work can still be assessed in terms of its power to generate disagreement, but the lineage is no longer as clear cut as in Habermas's scheme. The main controversies among the various figures summoned by Habermas focus on the question of whether theology or Marxism predominates in Benjamin's thinking. While the academic reception, which Habermas calls "a corrective" but "not an alternative," and which has grown immeasurably since the publication of his article, generally turned away from these former debates to less contentious areas, the most original representatives among today's readers of Benjamin return to these early conflicts and probe the unresolved issues of yesterday's debates in the light of situations and problems of the present. Benjamin's messianism, the element of his work where theology and politics are most indissolubly intertwined, lies at the center of their attention.

Faced with urgent concerns at the turn of the twenty-first century — the fate and status of democracy, the embattled legacy of Marx and the renewed impact of religion in both the theoretical and political realms — Jacques Derrida and Giorgio Agamben turn to Benjamin's messianism in elaborating their own positions. Derrida, though repeatedly invoking Benjamin's messianism in his political writings of the nineties, explicitly distances himself from Benjamin's views, which he deems "too messianico-marxist or archeo-eschatological."[2] By contrast Agamben, a leading figure in contemporary Continental thought, who from 1979 to 1994 served as editor of the Italian edition of Benjamin's collected works, fully embraces Benjamin's legacy and performs the most radical recovery of his messianic thinking to date. In his references to Benjamin, which permeate his work from his early theoretical studies on aesthetics and language to his latest juridical and political texts, he forcefully wrenches Benjamin away from the views of his former *milieu*, especially those of Scholem and Adorno, as well as from his later readers, foremost among them Derrida. For Agamben, the constitutive inability of Derridean deconstruction to reach closure partakes in perpetuating the prevailing dismal condition of humanity through an attitude that he terms "a petrified or paralyzed messianism."[3] An exploration of these new battle lines reveals the challenges and risks of an actualization of Benjamin's messianism today.

Agamben's recovery of Benjamin's messianism occurs as an often implicit but occasionally overt critique of some of the major interpretations of Benjamin's thought developed both in his lifetime and after. His earliest references to Benjamin can be found in dialogue with Hannah Arendt, whose view of Benjamin is, in accordance with her own political thinking, situated at the furthest remove from theologically inspired ideas of redemption. Agamben takes up important elements from her writings about Benjamin but, without ever explicitly refuting them, shifts them in a direction that reintroduces Benjamin's most theological ideas. Agamben's disagreement with Scholem unfolds in a more direct mode: He overtly develops his Pauline vision of Benjamin's messianism against Scholem's insistence on its mostly Jewish roots and, more particularly, argues against Scholem's notion of a "life in deferral and delay" (*P*, 166) that derives from messianic expectations in the Jewish tradition.[4] In a similar vein, Agamben also takes to task Adorno's hypothetical understanding of messianic redemption as nothing more than a virtual or fictional vantage point to be adopted for the sole purpose of assessing the bleak state of the world.[5] Most explicitly, Agamben rejects Derrida's "messianicity without messianism," his exhortation of an endless "anticipation without anticipation" and his definition of the messianic as an existential structure of infinite deferral and radical openness toward an incalculable, unpredictable future.[6] Against Derrida, Agamben recovers aspects of Benjamin's messianic thinking that foreground the urgency to terminate deferral and to grasp the messianic potential of every moment in the present.

Benjamin's messianism is structured according to a triadic scheme of paradise, fall, and redemption. Directed against the determinism prevalent in an idealist philosophy of history and the belief in progress inherent in historicism, Benjamin's messianic triad does not proceed as a teleological evolution. Instead it is marked by discontinuities that disrupt a linear chronology and open up a different relationship to the past. Rather than conceiving of a temporal continuum leading to an eschatological goal, Benjamin reveals "splinters" (*SW* 4:397) and "sparks" (*SW* 4:391) that interrupt the "homogenous empty time" (*SW* 4:261) and prefigure a redemption that is yet to come. These manifestations of discontinuity form the point of departure and main focus of Giorgio Agamben's own thinking, inspiring his revision of some key aspects of Benjamin's messianism: the discontinuity of time and tradition, the end of history, the fate of language, and the interruption of the reign of an oppressive law based on mythical authority rather than justice. A close reading of Agamben's treatment of these aspects of Benjamin's messianism in dialogue and dispute with other contenders of his legacy confirms the validity of Habermas's insight into the source of Benjamin's continuous relevance and brings the conflicts and controversies raised by his thinking *à l'ordre du jour.*

The Gap in Time

In Habermas's scheme, Hannah Arendt represents the most conservative of Benjamin's heirs. Habermas calls her "an intelligent and undaunted apologist" of a "neo-conservative Benjamin" whom she defends against the ideological claims of his friends.[7] It is surprising, therefore, that Agamben, this most radical of Benjamin's inheritors today, seems to have been introduced to his thought by way of Arendt's writings. In a 1970 letter to Arendt, Agamben writes: "I am a young writer and essayist for whom discovering your books last year has represented a decisive experience. May I express here my gratitude to you, and that of those who, along with me, in the gap between past and future, feel all the urgency of working in the direction you pointed out?"[8] In this letter, Agamben, twenty-six years old, assures Arendt of his intention of continuing to work in the direction she has shown and situates himself in a "gap between past and future." He is clearly referring to Arendt's foreword to her book of essays *Between Past and Future,* whose original title, "The Gap between Past and Future,"[9] gives notice of the space of thought that the following "exercises in political thinking" occupy. In this foreword Arendt describes the conditions of the handing down of an inheritance in modernity when transmissibility itself has become problematic. Arendt's "gap in time" designates a break in the linear chronological flow as an intermediate period, as an interval, "which is altogether determined by things that are no longer and by things that are not yet" and which, Arendt continues, has repeatedly been shown to contain "the moment of truth" (*BPF*, 9). "The moment of truth" about Agamben's relationship to Arendt's thinking can be read from his own remarks written at this time on the passing on of a legacy in periods of a break in tradition. The legacy that is at stake here is also Benjamin's.

In the same year as Agamben's letter to Arendt his essay "L'angelo malinconico," which also provides the conclusion to the book *L'uomo senza contenuto,* and which was published in English in 1999 under the title "The Melancholy Angel," appeared in the periodical *Nuovi argomenti*.[10] This essay can be read as a dialogue with Arendt's preface to *Between Past and Future* and, above all, with her essay on Walter Benjamin.[11] The first pages of Agamben's "The Melancholy Angel" provide an insight into the dynamic of the small but decisive shifts Agamben makes in the midst of virtually word-for-word appropriations of her text. The opening quotation, the wording, and the order of the initial paragraphs of Agamben's piece repeat almost verbatim the beginning of the third part of Arendt's, in which she comments on Benjamin's reflections about the function of quotation and the meaning of collecting. Like Arendt, Agamben introduces his essay with a reference to Benjamin's theory of quotation. According to Benjamin's theory, quotation does not, as is usually assumed, serve the reliving and passing on of what is past, but alienates this past by tearing the quotation out of its original setting, thereby breaking up the original context in which it occurs. Agamben quotes Benjamin's description of the power of quotations, which "arises not from their ability to transmit the past and allow the reader to relive it, but, on the contrary, from their capacity to 'make a clean sweep, to expel from the context, to destroy'" (*MA*, 104).[12] In her essay on Benjamin, Arendt quotes these same words, adding the qualification that the "discoverers and lovers of this destructive power originally were inspired by an entirely different intention, the intention to preserve" (*WB*, 193). By contrast, the Benjamin quote in Agamben's essay is followed by considerations of the "aggressive force" of quotations, and the explanation that Benjamin had understood "that the authority invoked by the quotation is founded precisely on the destruction of the authority that is attributed to a certain text by a certain culture" (*MA*, 104). Whereas in the following pages Arendt stresses Benjamin's "*duality* of wanting to preserve and wanting to destroy" (*WB*, 196; my emphasis), Agamben intensifies Benjamin's *dialectic* of a saving destruction. The divergence of their views becomes especially obvious when Arendt acquits Benjamin of the "dialectical subtleties of his Marxist friends" (*WB*, 200), which in another text she disparages as a trick "where one thing always reverses into its other and produces it" ("bei dem immer das Eine in das Andere umschlägt und es erzeugt"),[13] and instead situates Benjamin in the vicinity of Franz Kafka as a poetic thinker (*WB*, 205).

Similar discrepancies exist between Arendt's and Agamben's comments about Benjamin's reflections on collecting. The figure of the collector, Arendt writes,

> could assume such eminently modern features in Benjamin because history itself — that is, the break in tradition which took place at the beginning of this century — had already relieved him of this task of destruction and he only needed to bend down, as it were, to select his precious fragments from the pile of debris. (*WB*, 200)

Arendt compares the recovery and preservation of these treasures to that of pearls und corals. This hardly sounds like a revolutionary vocabulary, even if these historical fragments are the treasures of revolutions und the moments of freedom. While it is doubtful whether Arendt's emphasis on preservation and appreciation does justice to the destructive aspect of Benjamin's attitude, such a doubt also holds true for Agamben's contrary reading, which, though undoubtedly closer to Benjamin, addresses exclusively the destructive impulse of his understanding of tradition and focuses primarily on the moment of disruption itself. Significant in this connection is Agamben's comment on Benjamin's imperative "to shake off the treasures that are piled up on humanity's back . . . so as to get its hands on them" (*P*, 138–59, 153). Here, Agamben comments, "tradition does not aim to perpetuate and repeat the past but to lead to its decline" (*P*, 153). However, even in Benjamin's image of breaking fragments out of the continuum of the past, something still remains literally "at hand." Agamben does grant Benjamin's relation to the past an aspect of "taking possession" of what has been, yet, for him, what is to be cherished of the past is precisely "what has *never happened*" and therefore remains a potential that is yet to be fulfilled and can only be completed in a religiously and politically redeemed world. The messianic realm revealed here could not be more alien to Arendt.

Arendt's and Agamben's treatment of Benjamin's approach to the past illustrates the discrepancies between their processes of thinking. Antitheses that Arendt leaves in juxtaposition or in succession consistently reverse into one another in Agamben: The view that the new can appear *only* in the destruction of the old, indeed, that it occurs out of this destruction, contrasts with Arendt's ideas of a new beginning. Hence in the final chapter of *On Revolution* she emphasizes that "the end of the old is not necessarily the beginning of the new" and that "freedom is not the automatic result of liberation, no more than the new beginning is the automatic consequence of the end."[14] It can only be achieved with the constitution of a new political order. For Arendt, the interval between the "no longer" and the "not yet," which she calls the "hiatus" between old and new orders, interrupts the "omnipotent continuum of time" and opens up the space in which thought, politics, and freedom can occur. For Agamben there is no space in the interface between old and new: "The continuum of linear time is interrupted, but does not create an opening beyond itself" (*MA*, 113). Where Arendt creates a space, Agamben sees a break; where she opens up a path, he encounters a point of reversal; where she assesses the possibilities of human intervention in history, he performs a turnaround that seems to catapult him out of the continuum of time altogether. For Arendt the interruption of the omnipotent continuum of time takes place thanks to the intervention of man. For Agamben, no man stands at the point where past and future meet.

For him this point is occupied by two angels standing back to back. These figures are adopted from Benjamin's writings. In the force of the past pressing forward Agamben sees the storm against which Benjamin's backward-facing "Angel of History"[15] is struggling, while the angel in Dürer's "Melencolia I," discussed by Benjamin in *Ursprung des deutschen Trauerspiels* (Origin of the German Mourning Play), surrounded by now useless objects, gazes forward without moving.[16] Agamben calls the melancholy angel, who cannot continue his flight into the future, that is, can no longer transmit anything, the angel of art. Both angels freeze at the place where past and future meet. While the angel of history strives in vain to return to paradise in the face of the storm of progress, the angel of art has, according to Agamben, fallen into a state of "messianic arrest" (*MA*, 110). The past before the angel of history, which can no longer be gathered up, read, and interpreted, becomes intransmissible in the eyes of the angel of art. Yet out of the defamiliarizing gaze observing this split, a new truth emerges. In this estrangement there then also lies the new truth of art: it is the remnant that alone can save humankind from the predicament of being caught between past and future, by making the impossibility of transmission, of tradition, its content: "By destroying the transmissibility of the past, aesthetics recuperates it negatively and makes intransmissibility a value in itself in the image of aesthetic beauty, in this way opening up for man a space between past and future, in which he can found his action and his knowledge" (*MA*, 110). While Arendt's space of thought implies a freedom of movement and regards the possibility of a new beginning *sui generis,* guaranteed by the simple fact of being born, there remains for Agamben, who preserves only the spaceless rupture itself, no other possibility of moving than the dialectic reversal on the spot itself. To perceive and register this rupture is, for him, the task of the present and a precondition for messianic redemption. It consists neither in creating a space of freedom *in* history nor in leaping out of it, but in the necessity and possibility of thinking its end. Echoing Benjamin, Agamben insists that this possibility stands open in every "interval in time," that is, in every "now-time" (*Jetztzeit*), as a gate, one might add with Benjamin, through which the Messiah can enter at any moment (*GS* I.2:704). However, what this possibility entails for the fate of history differs significantly from Benjamin's idea of a redeemed world. In a variation on Benjamin's dictum that history in its totality will only become readable to redeemed mankind (*GS*, I.3:1239), Agamben, on the last pages of his essay, liberates humankind from the burden of history, but the result would probably make not only Arendt but also Benjamin shudder: "When man could appropriate his historical condition . . . he could exit his paradoxical situation" and "at the same time gain access to the total knowledge capable of giving life to a new cosmogony and to turn history into myth" (*MA*, 114). With this dream of a transformation of history into myth, Agamben's early appropriation of Benjamin indicates the risk of conjuring up an interruption of time as a messianic end of history. This danger may be precisely what less radical fellow travelers and followers of Benjamin have tried to avert.

The Idea of Prose

Agamben's emphasis on a redemptive reversal occurring at an empty spatial and temporal spot where beginning and end fall together is accompanied by a critique of different traditions of thought that rest on the structure of an infinite deferral. This critique becomes most concrete in his essay entitled "Language and History: Linguistic Categories and Historical Categories in Benjamin's Thought."[17] In this essay Agamben addresses Benjamin's messianic concepts of a universal history and the universal language that corresponds to it. In the course of his argumentation he rejects various possible interpretations of these concepts, ranging from Ludwig Zamenhof's artificially constructed universal language, Esperanto, to Hans-Georg Gadamer's hermeneutics and from Scholem's interpretation of the Cabala to Jacques Derrida's deconstruction. At first sight these thinkers have little in common, but it becomes clear that it is their common appeal to an "infinite task" (Kant's *unendliche Aufgabe*) that motivates Agamben to consider them as opponents to Benjamin's messianic thinking.

Agamben's "Language and History" interprets a single passage from Benjamin's paralipomena to his "On the Concept of History." It focuses on the link Benjamin establishes between "pure language" and "universal history" and retraces the correspondences that exist for Benjamin between genres of narration, history, and redemption. These correspondences arise out of a revision of Hegel's theory of aesthetics. In the traditional triadic scheme developed by Hegel, the epic, in which human experience is grasped in its unity and totality, stands at the beginning. The epic, the most ancient account of history, told in the form of heroic song, was later sublated into poetry, which was in turn sublated into disenchanted and no longer integral prose. In Hegel's progressive scheme, prose aims at regaining the original totality corresponding to the ancient epic, the genre in which universal history is to be told. For Benjamin, the conception of a constantly progressing and developing history, which in the end comes to itself in pure self-recognition, is just as much in crisis as continuous narration. His messianic thought is also modeled on the triad of paradise, fall, and still pending redemption, but it is marked by discontinuities, which also characterize his theory of narration. But in modern times the genre of a continuously flowing, all encompassing narrative has lost its validity. From now on narration must either signal the impossibility of its own continuity or mark its status as a mere model for the historiography of a messianic age that is yet to come.

Benjamin gave no clear answer to the question "in welcher Verfassung sich die 'erlöste Menschheit' befindet, welchen Bedingungen das Eintreten dieser Verfassung unterworfen ist und wann man mit ihm rechnen kann" (*GS* I.3:1232; "what the situation of a 'redeemed humanity' might actually be, what conditions are required for the development of such a situation, and when this development can be expected to occur," *SW* 4:402). Instead he recovers scattered messianic fragments that point to anticipatory forms of this future state. These can be found in Benjamin's work in various experiences and figures: from Proust's *mémoire involontaire* to a *leibhaftige Geistesgegenwart* (embodied presence of mind), from the *flâneur* to the collector, from the translator to the materialist historian, from Kafka's seemingly insignificant assistants to the righteous man. This heterogeneous group includes the chronicler and his secularized alter ego, the storyteller. Benjamin's essay "Der Erzähler" ("The Storyteller")[18] contains few messianic echoes, but the note written in preparation for his "Über den Begriff der Geschichte" provides clues about the condition of redeemed mankind that also concern the question of narration in a messianic world:

> Die messianische Welt ist die Welt allseitiger und integraler Aktualität. Erst in ihr gibt es eine Universalgeschichte. Was sich heute so bezeichnet, kann immer nur eine Sorte von Esperanto sein. Es kann ihr nichts entsprechen, eh die Verwirrung, die vom Turmbau zu Babel herrührt, geschlichtet ist. Sie setzt die Sprache voraus, in die jeder Text einer lebenden oder toten ungeschmälert zu übersetzen ist. Oder besser, sie ist diese Sprache selbst. Aber nicht als geschriebene, sondern vielmehr als die festlich begangene. Dieses Fest ist gereinigt von jeder Feier. Es kennt keine Festgesänge. Seine Sprache ist integrale Prosa, die die Fesseln der Schrift gesprengt hat und von allen Menschen verstanden wird wie die Sprache der Vögel von Sonntagskindern. (*GS* I.3:1239)

> [The messianic world is the world of total and integral actuality. In it alone is there universal history. What goes by the name of universal

history today can only be a kind of Esperanto. Nothing can correspond to it as long as the confusion originating in the Tower of Babel is not smoothed out. It presupposes the language into which every text of a living or dead language must be translated in full. Or rather, it is itself this language. Not though, as written, but as festively celebrated. This celebration is purified of every ceremony; it knows no celebratory songs. Its language is the idea of prose itself, which is understood by all men as is the language of birds by Sunday's children. (*P,* 48)]

Other versions of this fragment in Benjamin's paralipomena to "Über den Begriff der Geschichte" end with the following remark: "Die Idee der Prosa fällt mit der messianischen Idee der Universalgeschichte zusammen (siehe auch Erzähleraufsatz)" (*GS* I.3:1235 "The idea of prose coincides with the messianic idea of universal history. [Compare the passage in 'The Storyteller']," *SW* 4:404.) The most extensive variant of the note contains an additional reference to "die Arten der Kunstprosa als das Spektrum der universalhistorischen — im 'Erzähler'" (*GS* I.3:1238; "the types of artistic prose as the spectrum of universal historical types [in 'The Storyteller']," *SW* 4:406).[19] It may not be an exaggeration to see in Benjamin's note a prismatic spectrum that brings together all the messianic sparks relating to history, language, and narration that are scattered in his work.

Benjamin's fragment projects the condition of redeemed humankind as a comprehensive, fulfilled presence of language and history. Only in a messianic world, only at the end of time and from its end can history be recounted in its entirety. Benjamin is here criticizing the narrating historicism of the nineteenth century, which deludes itself in claiming that it can still tell history in an epic form.[20] For Benjamin, this conception of history creates the illusion of an intact world, sides with the victors, and does not take account of the oppression of humankind. The prerequisite of a rightful and just universal history, which only falls to redeemed humankind, is the healing of the confusion of tongues through a universal language "understood by all men," which is reminiscent of Benjamin's early essays "Über Sprache überhaupt und über die Sprache des Menschen" (*GS* II.1:140–57; "On Language As Such and On the Language of Man," *SW* 1:62–74) and "Die Aufgabe des Übersetzers" (*GS* IV.1:9–21; "The Task of the Translator," *SW* 1:253–66). Integral actuality — fulfilled concurrence of all events — is expressed in a language freed of mediation and difference, of writing and signs, a language of immediacy that will eventually deliver nature from its dumb sorrow and reconcile it with humankind. With the concept of the "idea of prose," which refers to Benjamin's doctoral thesis, *Der Begriff der Kunstkritik in der deutschen Romantik* (*GS* I.2:7–123; *The Concept of Criticism in German Romanticism, SW* 1:116–200) and the reference to the storyteller essay, this passage, in addition to the essays on language, takes up two early texts that are less about language than about epic forms. But how can the messianic hope for immediacy and "integral actuality" go together with narrative, which always also presumes tension, difference, deferral, and mediation?

Benjamin's addendum to the note, which after mentioning the messianic "idea of prose" refers to the "Arten der Kunstprosa als das Spektrum der universalhistorischen — im 'Erzähler'" (*GS* I.3:1238; "the types of artistic prose as the spectrum of universal historical types — in the 'Storyteller,'" *SW* 4:406), suggests a passage in the storyteller essay, in which Benjamin presents history as "die schöpferische Indifferenz zwischen allen Formen der Epik" (*GS* II.2:451; "the creative indifference between all forms of the epic," *SW* 3:152, translation modified). Then, Benjamin continues, "würde sich die geschriebene Geschichte zu den epischen Formen verhalten wie das weiße Licht zu den Spektralfarben" (*GS* II.2:451; "written history would bear the same relationship to the epic forms as white light bears to the colors of the spectrum," *SW* 3:152). The concept of "creative indifference" — the possibility of creatively reconciling polarities and contrasts — signifies in Benjamin an alternative, romantically inflected, form of sublation, which evades Hegel's idea of progress and avoids its dialectical loss of the concrete. The white light of history-writing, in which all epic forms are inherent just as all poetic forms are inherent in prose, would only seemingly be uniform. The purity of this light would not be an emptiness, not an absence of colors, but instead an absolute fullness. Benjamin elucidates this figure of thought, echoing Hegel's definition of types:

> Wenn nämlich . . . die Geschichtsschreibung die schöpferische Indifferenz der verschiedenen epischen Formen darstellt (wie die große Prosa die schöpferische Indifferenz zwischen verschiedenen Maßen des Verses), so schließt deren älteste Form, das Epos, kraft einer Art von Indifferenz die Erzählung und den Roman ein. (*GS* II.2:453)

> [For if . . . the writing of history constitutes the creative matrix [in the original: *schöpferische Indifferenz*] of the various epic forms (just as great prose the creative matrix of the various metrical forms), its oldest form, the epic, by virtue of being a kind of common denominator [in the original: *eine Art von Indifferenz*], includes the story and the novel. (*SW* 3:154)]

In this vertical stratification, in contrast to Hegel, all the lower forms are preserved without loss in the higher ones. For Benjamin, the epic contains both the novel and the story, but in his distinction between story and novel it is clearly the story that, as the secularized form of the chronicle, points forward to a messianic "full" prose. The "idea of prose," which Benjamin introduces in his note as a form of universal history writing

(*Geschichtsschreibung*), appears as the last in this series of sublations. It is not reached through a Hegelian teleological advance but in messianic fulfillment. In the "idea of prose" the potentials of all the forms absorbed in it continue to have an effect. Accordingly, in the all-encompassing light of the messianic idea of universal history, which coincides with the "idea of prose," the story is also preserved as one of the colors of its spectrum.

The metaphor of the white light and the spectrum, of the invisible fullness of colors it contains, corresponds to Benjamin's definition of the Romantic "idea of art" as "absolute medium of reflection" (*Reflexionsmedium, GS* I.1:87) in his dissertation *Der Begriff der Kunstkritik in der deutschen Romantik* (The Concept of Criticism in German Romanticism). There, prose is called "die Idee der Poesie" (*GS* I.1:101; "the idea of poetry," *SW* 1:174). For the Romantics it represents the highest form of poetry, containing all its possibilities and liberating poetry from its codifications. In prose "gehen sämtliche gebundenen Rhythmen ineinander über" und "verbinden sich zu einer neuen Einheit" (*GS* I.2:102; "all metrical rhythms pass over into one another" and "combine in a new unity," *SW* 1:174) This is characterized by "sobriety" (*Nüchternheit*) and corresponds to a successful disenchantment of the epic and its festive songs. If in Benjamin's dissertation prose is the "idea of poetry," in which all poetic forms are liberated, then the messianic "idea of prose" — corresponding to this model of "creative indifference" — is its highest stage: It is "universal history," which contains all varieties of art prose within itself, just as the "white light" of "written history" contains the spectral colors of all the epic forms. It encompasses everything that has ever occurred and frees it from its codified bonds, indeed from its own artificiality. This messianic feast of freedom contains no festive songs, therefore, and does not return unchanged to the heroic songs of the epic: it is sober and "general," like the prose described in the dissertation. This "idea of prose" encompasses all other forms of art and, as universal narrative, takes in and preserves all the experience of creation.

In the storyteller essay, to which the addendum to Benjamin's note refers, two opposing figures vouch for storytelling. One is taken from literature: Sheherazade. She is the one who thinks of a new story whenever her tale comes to a stop, and who resides, in one form or another, in each storyteller. The second, opposite figure is taken from life: the dying man. In Benjamin's exposition, both figures take on a messianic dimension, which brings them into line with the idea of a universal history at the end of time. Sheherazade, while embodying that "unmessianic" movement of narrative that defers the end, is for Benjamin also the guardian of epic memory, who creates the web that all stories form together in the end. The narrative of the dying man, on the other hand, comes into being as retrospection. The stuff his stories are made of, Benjamin writes, are "his lived life" (*gelebtes Leben*). The gift of the storyteller, like that of the dying man, is the ability "sein gan-zes Leben erzählen zu können" (*GS* II.2:464; "to relate his *entire* life," *SW* 3:162). Universal history is the collective analogy to that narrative: it relates the *entire* history of all creatures on earth from its messianic end point. As with the dying man, even if he is "the poorest wretch," the storyteller recovers the past in its totality and all hierarchical differ-ences are dissolved. Sheherazade and the dying man together embody messianic figures who preserve in the spectrum of the "idea of prose" the double movement of deferral and retrospection, infinity and closure, "hope and memory."[21] The concept of the "idea of prose" contains not only the pure, perfect, and in itself complete *idea*, but also *prose* as the general, manifold, and worldly story of all creation. In Benjamin's messianic world, the *restitutio in integrum* of the past is fulfilled in the shape of a web of stories spun from the matter of "lived life." At the conclusion of the storyteller essay Benjamin defines the storyteller as the "advocate of all creation" on the day of the Last Judgment. The integral prose he uses has the task of preserving the particularity of each individual phenomenon in its entirety and of doing justice to all crea-tures. It would be a language of names to the extent that it no longer denotes arbitrarily but evokes and vivifies authentically what it names: Benjamin's messianic ethics of narration is founded in the desire for a complete narrativity, which, with this highest form of attentiveness, calls things by their name.

An initial insight into the difference between the two writers' "idea of prose" is provided by Agamben's text of the same name in his volume of poetic-philosophical short texts that likewise bears this title.[22] Like Ben-jamin in his early study of art criticism in the Romantic period, in this short text Agamben, too, develops the essence of prose from its relation to poetry. But whereas Benjamin, in line with Schlegel, calls prose the "idea of poetry" and with the metaphor of the white light sees contained in it "all the possibilities and forms of poetry," Agamben situates the relationship of prose and poetry at the interface *between* them. Agamben describes the specificity of poetry as the divergence between rhythm and meaning. The location of this divergence is the enjambment, the con-tinuation of a syntactic unit from one line or couplet of a poem to the next with no pause, which Agamben calls "the distinguishing character-istic of poetic discourse" (*IP*, 39). It is the point where poetry and prose are at the same time most radically different and yet united to an almost indistinguishable degree. In the enjambment, verse introduces the syntax of prose and, paradoxically, becomes poetry at the very point where it disavows the metrical language of poetry. It is also at this point that the "idea of language," which is "neither poetry nor prose, but their middle term" (*IP*, 41), occurs. Unlike Benjamin's metaphor of the white light which, even if invisible, contains the fullness of all spectral colors, this middle — a mere interruption in the flow of the poetic sentence, a blank space on the page — is empty. In other words, for Agamben, the relationship between prose and poetry occurs between them: the enjambment is the end of the verse in mid-sentence, which creates an interruption, a literally empty spot.

Agamben elucidates the relationship between language and history in terms of the discrepancy between the original language of names and the historically mediated language of communication between human beings, which has always been already transmitted and is hence inauthentic. According to Agamben's explication of Benjamin's note, names always already precede all speech as original sign and cannot be grasped or circumvented. Thought without presuppositions is not possible in a language of signs. The mediation to which names are subject through history determines an endless chain of presuppositions, which place thought and human beings under a ban. Agamben transfers this conception of language as an imaginary prison to Benjamin's philosophy of history. Because history came into being at the same time as the fall of language from its original unmediated state, the end of history coincides with the end of the communicative language of signs and with the restitution of the Adamic language of names. To Agamben, Benjamin's "idea of prose" aims at the messianic end of a history understood as fate and therefore as unfreedom. This corresponds in many respects to the understanding of history in Benjamin's note. Since, however, Agamben does not take into consideration the reference to the storyteller essay and the significance of prose as epic form and identifies the "idea of prose" entirely with the "idea of language," his conception of the term leads to an aesthetic of emptiness and an ethics of disconnectedness, to which Benjamin would hardly have subscribed. This can be shown in exemplary fashion by way of the difference between the conceptions of the "expressionless" (*das Ausdruckslose*) in Agamben and in Benjamin.

In his essay on Goethe's *Die Wahlverwandtschaften* (*Elective Affinities*), Benjamin links the "expressionless" — a feature of language that has no meaning in itself but interrupts a falsely harmonious continuity — to Friedrich Hölderlin's concept of the "caesura." For Hölderlin this hesitation in the poetic meter produces a "counter-rhythmical interruption" (*gegenrhythmische Unterbrechung, GS* I.1:181), a resistance to the flowing rhythm of hymns. While Benjamin insists on the function of this interruption as a rupture of the illusion of wholeness, Agamben considers it as the event itself. In "Idea of the Caesura," another short text in his *Idea of Prose,* Agamben refers to the same Hölderlin passage about the caesura as Benjamin and comments: "What does the interruption of the rhythmic transport in the poem reveal? . . . The rhythmic transport, which bears the momentum of the poem, is empty and bears only itself. It is the caesura, which as *pure* word, thinks this emptiness — for a while . . . The poet . . . awakes and for a moment studies the inspiration which bears him; he thinks only of his voice" (*IP*, 44, translation modified). This reading of the Hölderlin quotation, which flows into an awareness of the voice, bears the traces of Agamben's earlier book *Language and Death,* the starting point of which is Heidegger's *Zum Wesen der Sprache* (On the Essence of Language).[23] In Agamben's book the voice plays a crucial role that reveals the origins of his own ethics implied in his understanding of the "idea of prose": "The Voice, as we know, says nothing; it does not mean or want to say any significant proposition. Rather, it indicates and means the pure taking place of language and it is as such a purely *logical* dimension . . ." In this sense, Agamben continues, language as Voice is "the original ethical dimension in which man pronounces his 'yes' to language." And it is this affirmation of language that "opens up to man the possibility for the marvel of being and the terror of nothingness."[24] This ethics also determines Agamben's later interpretation of Benjamin's "idea of prose." There, pure "saying" is not only the task of the philosopher but becomes the ethical task as such: "It is . . . the actual construction of this relation and this region [of pure language] that constitutes the true task of the philosopher and the translator, the historian and the critic, and, in the final analysis, the ethical engagement of every speaking being" (*P,* 59).

Agamben's "idea of prose" calls for an integral actuality, that is, of a fulfilled now-time without tension, displacement, and deferral. While Benjamin's "Jetztzeit" contains worldly splinters pointing to a messianic fulfillment, Agamben's "now" can be understood as an attempt to think a "pure" interruption, free of all mediation, conception, and precondition, uninfected by a world that presents itself as one continuous catastrophe. The urgency, however, that is constantly conjured up in Agamben's thinking, stands in curious contrast to the emptiness that is simultaneously appealed to. At its center stands the absence of a word that is very much present in the sphere of Benjamin's "Concept of History": the revolution as true, "lived" interruption of catastrophe. Contrary to Benjamin's revolutionary thrust, Agamben's hypostatization and, one might say, the "de-functionalization" of the interruption itself creates a break in the bridge between Agamben's linguistic philosophy and his political thought. There is no path here that leads from "the marvel of being and the terror of nothingness" to an ethics and politics of justice. That impasse lies in the nature of a thinking that is concerned not with paths but with cuts, thresholds, and empty spaces, which no longer stand in any relation to what they interrupt. Ultimately it becomes a matter of the theoretical enthronement of discontinuity itself.

The messianic forces that, for Benjamin, interrupt the time continuum and point toward a redeemed world are for Agamben rendered absolute and empty to the point where they are no longer redeeming bearers of hope and signals for the cessation of a false continuity. Instead, interruption becomes an end in itself, eliding the experiential content and the worldly bearings of Benjamin's messianic figures. His sparks and splinters, poetic metaphors of a profane illumination, whose luster indicates the path of redemption, become abstract locations of discontinuity: the threshold, the limit point, the interface, "the in-between" as such. Perhaps in an increasingly complex post-revolutionary age their emptiness can be perceived as the only possible form of saving the radicalism of Benjamin's political-theological legacy, but what is in danger of being lost is the very thing that is to be saved: lived, worldly life itself.

Studying the Law

It is in his politico-theological essays of the eighties and nineties such as *Homo Sacer* and *The Time That Remains*,[25] that Agamben most consistently and substantially invokes Benjamin's messianic thought. In *The Time That Remains,* his reading of Paul's "Letter to the Romans" inspired by Jakob Taubes,[26] Agamben conflates Benjamin's criticism of the law, most explicitly developed in his *Critique of Violence,* with an antinomian messianism that he finds prefigured in Paul's suspension of the law. This liberating redemption from the law once more occurs at an empty point of disruption on which Agamben's entire structure of the messianic rests. This structure is defined by a "point of indistinction" that lies outside the field of oppositions and undoes the division between them, which Agamben calls "the very principle of the law." At this point the reversal from oppression to redemption can take place. It is on this spot that a potentially oppressive de-limitation of the law — a state in which the law itself steps beyond its boundaries — turns into a redemptive one in which the law's oppressive power is undone. This figure, which is based on the belief that all divisions will eventually disappear, underlies Agamben's entire structure of the messianic. It delineates his theory of what he calls, with Benjamin, "the 'state of emergency' in which we live."[27] Designed to thwart the perpetuation of the dismal state of the world and the continuation of a "bad infinity," Agamben's philosophy proposes a figure of thought that would interrupt the eternal deferral of the end and the unbounded reign of the law. He invokes the apostle Paul and Walter Benjamin as his leading figures and, in a Jewish reading of Paul[28] and a Paulinian reading of Benjamin,[29] conflates their visions.

"From a political-juridical perspective," Agamben writes in *Homo Sacer,* "messianism is . . . a theory of the state of exception — except for the fact that in messianism there is no authority in force to proclaim the state of exception; instead there is the Messiah to subvert its power."[30] In keeping with the antinomies of messianic precepts, Agamben equates the conditions of redemption with the structures governing the decline: both rely on the self-suspension of the law. Agamben echoes Benjamin's imperative expressed in the eighth Thesis on the Philosophy of History: "Dann wird uns als unsere Aufgabe die Herbeiführung des wirklichen Ausnahmezustands vor Augen stehen" (*GS* I.2:697; "Then we will clearly see that it is our task to bring about the true state of exception," *SW* 4:392) While the negative state of exception proclaimed by the sovereign spills over into every aspect of life and puts the entire planet under the ban of an oppressive law, the "true," messianic state of exception suspends the validity of the law and releases bare life from its ban into a new freedom. Only when life has absorbed the law to the point of suspending it, instead of letting the law rule over life, will the ban be abolished and humanity redeemed. In this redeemed world, not only the law will be undone, but along with it, the medium that supports and transports it — the written word. Among the unexpected commonalities between Paul and Benjamin suggested by Agamben is their similar attitude to writing. Agamben conflates Paul's injunction to suspend the written commandments of the Torah with Benjamin's messianic idea of a history that will no longer be written but will be "festively performed." Against Derrida's theory of Grammatology, in which the medium of writing is potentially subversive of the codified and controlling order, Agamben assimilates the letter with the law and imagines redemption as the demise of both.

In "Idea of Study," a short text from *Idea of Prose* (*IP*, 63–65), Agamben recalls how after the destruction of the temple the study of the Scriptures became, in the Jewish tradition, a surrogate for the sacrificial rituals. In contradistinction to rabbinic commentators like Maimonides, who imagine messianic times in terms of a reconstruction of the temple and a reinvigoration of the Torah and its commands, Agamben echoes cabbalistic speculations about the eventual demise of all commentaries and conflates the deposing of today's hermeneutic temple keepers with a messianic anticipation of the end of all study. In the course of his argument, Agamben takes up, but radicalizes and slightly shifts, Benjamin's reflections about the messianic mission carried out by the scribes and students of the Scriptures in Kafka's writings. These reflections, which make up the last pages of Benjamin's Kafka essay, develop the thought that "das Recht, das nicht mehr praktiziert, sondern nur noch studiert wird, das ist die Pforte der Gerechtigkeit" (*GS* II.2:437; "the law which is studied and not practiced any longer is the gate to justice," *SW* 2:815). In keeping with Benjamin's interpretation, Agamben considers the study of the law a beneficial replacement for its practice and a subversive assault on the power of the lawmakers, but in Agamben's messianic design, study itself is only an intermediary stage. Eventually, it should lead to a renunciation of the very desire for a messianic reconstruction of the temple and, in the end, to its vanishing from human memory. For Benjamin, however, Kafka's students are the forebears of the Messiah because they are the ones who watch that "the best" not be forgotten, "denn es betrifft die Möglichkeit der

Erlösung" (*GS* II.2:434; "for it involves the possibility of redemption," *SW* 2:813). Studying becomes, for Benjamin, tantamount to a redeeming resistance against progressing time and forgetting the past. Benjamin describes the messianic task of Kafka's students as a journey backwards, a flight toward the past. Citing Kafka's aphoristic text "Wunsch, Indianer zu werden" (The Wish to Be an Indian), Benjamin illustrates the ecstatic vision of such a ride. He likens the equestrian flight "over the smoothly mown heath, with the horse's neck and head already gone" to the fulfillment of the "fantasy about the blessed rider" who gallops toward the past in a "leerer, fröhlicher Reise" (*GS* II.2:436; "empty, happy journey," *SW* 2:814, trans. modified) in order to redeem what has been forgotten. In the penultimate paragraph of his essay Benjamin once again takes up the comparison between studying and the "fantasy about the blessed rider." However, Benjamin's assessment of this rapturous ride changes after his remark that Kafka's students are "pupils who are no longer in possession of the Holy Writ." Now, Benjamin writes, there is nothing to support them on their "leeren, fröhlichen Fahrt" (*GS* II.2:437; "empty, happy journey," *SW* 2:815, translation modified). This ecstatic flight without "the horse's neck and head," without weight, without law and reality, might be happy, but, Benjamin seems to be saying, it is also empty, a mere fantasy, an idealist abstraction. Accordingly, Benjamin indeed distinguishes the path taken by Kafka from the one taken by the students who have lost the Scriptures. Unlike them, Benjamin writes, Kafka "hat das Gesetz [seiner Fahrt] gefunden" (*GS* II.2:437; "has found the law of his own journey," *SW* 2:815, translation modified). Benjamin finds Kafka's "law" most powerfully expressed in the little story entitled "Die Wahrheit über Sancho Pansa" (The Truth of Sancho Panza).[31] Benjamin calls this story, which he quotes in its entirety at the end of his essay, a "Niederschrift . . . , die nicht nur darum seine vollendetste wurde, weil sie eine Auslegung ist" (*GS* II.2:437; "a little prose piece which is his most perfect creation — and not only because it is an interpretation," *SW* 2:815). Could this most perfect of Kafka's creations be, after all, about a law?

According to Agamben, the messianic task of Kafka's students no longer lies in practicing or observing the law but in studying it, in order to deactivate it and ultimately let it disappear into oblivion. This last step is absent in Benjamin's reflections. To him also, Kafka's writings, like the Haggadah, the transmission of the scriptural law in stories, do not simply lie at the feet of this law, the Halacha, but instead raise "eine gewichtige Pranke," a weighty paw" against it (*SW* 3:326).[32] However, Benjamin does not go as far as Agamben. For Benjamin, Kafka does not set out on an empty, happy journey void of the law and the written word, but instead, in his recasting of Cervantes' tale, pays tribute to an older text in reinterpreting it. Kafka reconfigures Cervantes' idealistic knight, Don Quixote, as the product of Sancho Panza's imagination, his practical and responsible companion:

Sancho Pansa, der sich übrigens dessen nie gerühmt hat, gelang es im Laufe der Jahre, durch Beistellung einer Menge Ritter- und Räuberromane in den Abend- und Nachtstunden seinen Teufel, dem er später den Namen Don Quixote gab, derart von sich abzulenken, daß dieser dann haltlos die verrücktesten Taten aufführte, die aber mangels eines vorbestimmten Gegenstandes, der eben Sancho Pansa hätte sein sollen, niemandem schadeten. Sancho Pansa, ein freier Mann, folgte gleichmütig, vielleicht aus einem gewissen Verantwortlichkeitsgefühl dem Don Quixote auf seinen Zügen und hatte davon eine große und nützliche Unterhaltung bis an sein Ende. (*GS* II.2:438)

[Without ever boasting of it Sancho Panza succeeded in the course of years, by supplying a lot of romances of chivalry and adventure for the evening and night hours, in so diverting from him his demon, whom he later called Don Quixote, that this demon thereupon freely performed the maddest exploits, which, however, for the lack of a preordained object, which Sancho Panza himself was supposed to have been, did no one any harm. A free man, Sancho Panza philosophically followed Don Quixote on his crusades, perhaps out of a sense of responsibility, and thus enjoyed a great and profitable entertainment to the end of his days. (*SW* 2:815–16)]

In this story, Don Quixote is Sancho Panza's own demon. Desiring to save the world and thus losing any sense of reality, Don Quixote is then seconded by Sancho Panza, who has decided to trail the crusading knight. Fearing the knight's destructive fantasies and follies, he follows him everywhere and watches over his actions. Thus, he also provides himself — and we might add us as well — with a "great and edifying entertainment." In a letter to Scholem of 11 August 1934 Benjamin underscores his deep appreciation for Kafka's Sancho Panza with the following words: "Sancho Pansas Dasein ist musterhaft, weil es eigentlich im Nachlesen des eignen, wenn auch närrischen und donquichotesken besteht" (Sancho Panza's existence is exemplary, because it consists in Kafka's rereading of his own foolish und donquixotic side).[33] Kafka's "law" and the perfection of his writing, which Benjamin discovers in "Sancho Panza," does not lie in the fantasy world of Don Quixote riding off into the void — a void resembling Agamben's — but in his servant's vigilant wisdom and his concern for the concrete. In Kafka's exegesis of Cervantes's figures, Sancho Panza reins in his own destructive demon and lightens the burden of the world by providing it with wondrous stories about knights and their adventures. In his letter to Scholem, Benjamin explains why he refrains from addressing the topic of the law in Kafka's writings, calling it his "blind spot." The law that Benjamin unearths in Kafka's story is indeed of a very different nature.

The wisdom of Sancho Panza's "great and profitable entertainment" may indeed have the power to undo the oppression of the law, but the place of this reversal is neither a spot, nor a threshold or a gap as Agamben would have it. Instead, this place, in Benjamin, rather uncannily resembles the space of literature, its fullness and worldliness, its power to save the past and its commitment to the concrete particulars of the ordinary world.

Habermas, who otherwise calls for a strict distinction between literature and philosophy, introduces into his essay "Bewußtmachende oder rettende Kritik," quoted at the beginning of this essay, a brief literary intermezzo when he draws what he calls a "surrealistic scene" in which he imagines "Scholem, Adorno and Brecht gathered together for a peaceful symposium around a table, under which Breton and Aragon are squatting, while Wyneken stands at the door."[34] In spite of all the reservations that can be voiced against Agamben's reading of Benjamin — his utterly un-Benjaminian rehabilitation of myth at the expense of history, his Heideggerian emphasis on ethos over ethics, his Paulinian messianism devoid of political revolution, and above all his depletion of Benjamin's concrete wordliness — the Italian philosopher would undoubtedly be a major participant at this table if a similar scene were to be imagined today. Habermas's image of a table around which Benjamin's legacy is reclaimed for the present evokes one of Arendt's most famous political metaphors: In *The Human Condition* she imagines a table "located between those who sit around it."[35] The "in-between" created by Arendt's table, would, however, be very different from Agamben's. In Arendt's scene, this table, surrounded by those who share a common concern for what both separates and relates them, is not an empty spot but the world itself.

Notes

1 Jürgen Habermas, "Bewußtmachende oder rettende Kritik: Die Aktualität Walter Benjamins," in *Zur Aktualität Walter Benjamins: Aus Anlaß des 80. Geburtstags von Walter Benjamin*, ed. Siegfried Unseld (Frankfurt am Main: Suhrkamp, 1972), 173–223; "Consciousness-Raising or Redemptive Criticism: The Contemporaneity of Walter Benjamin," *New German Critique* 17 (Spring, 1979): 30–59.

2 Jacques Derrida, "Force of Law: The Mystical Foundation of Authority," *Cardozo Law Review* 11.919 (1992): 1045.

3 Giorgio Agamben, *Potentialities: Collected Essays in Philosophy* (Stanford, CA: Stanford UP, 1999), 171. Further references to this work are cited in the text using the abbreviation *P* and the page number.

4 Scholem writes: "Thus in Judaism the Messianic idea has compelled a *life lived in deferment*, in which nothing can be done definitively, nothing can be irrevocably accomplished" (emphasis by Scholem). Gershom Scholem, *The Messianic Idea in Judaism* (New York: Schocken Books, 1995), 35.

[5] For Agamben's critique of Adorno's approach to messianism, see Giorgio Agamben, *The Time That Remains: A Commentary on the Letter to the Romans*, trans. Patricia Dailey (Stanford, CA: Stanford UP, 2005), 35–37.

[6] Derrida develops these reflections on messianism in Jacques Derrida, *Specters of Marx, the State of the Debt, the Work of Mourning & the New International*, trans. Peggy Kamuf (New York and London: Routledge, 1994); and more explicitly in Jacques Derrida, "Marx & Sons," in *Ghostly Demarcations: A Symposium on Jacques Derrida's Specters of Marx*, ed. Michael Sprinker (London and New York: Verso, 1999), 213–69.

[7] Habermas, "Consciousness-Raising or Redemptive Criticism," 31.

[8] Arendt Archive, Manuscript Division Library of Congress, letter of 21 Feb. 1970 from Agamben to Arendt. Quoted in Mira Siegelberg, "Arendt's Legacy Usurped: In Defense of the (Limited) Nation State," *Columbia Current* (Dec. 2005): 33–41, here 38.

[9] Hannah Arendt, "The Gap between Past and Future," in *Between Past and Future* (New York: Viking P, 1968), 3–15, here 3. Further references to this work are cited in the text using the abbreviation *BPF* and the page number.

[10] Giorgio Agamben, "The Melancholy Angel," in *The Man without Content*, trans. Georgia Albert (Stanford, CA: Stanford UP, 1999), 104–15. Further references to this work are cited in the text using the abbreviation *MA* and the page number.

[11] Hannah Arendt, "Walter Benjamin, 1892–1940" in *Men in Dark Times* (San Diego, New York, and London: Harcourt Brace, 1995), 153–206. Further references to this work are cited in the text using the abbreviation *WB* and the page number.

[12] Agamben quotes from Arendt's Benjamin essay (*WB*, 193).

[13] Hannah Arendt, *Zwischen Vergangenheit und Zukunft: Übungen im politischen Denken I* (Munich: Piper, 2000), 33. This reference is to the German edition of *Between Past and Future*, in which this sentence differs from the English version. The German text was written or translated by Arendt herself. See the afterword in this edition, 373–74.

[14] Hannah Arendt, *On Revolution* (London: Penguin, 1991), 205.

[15] See "Über den Begriff der Geschichte" (*GS* I.2:697; "On the Concept of History," *SW* 4:392). See also Marc de Wilde's contribution in this volume.

[16] *GS* I.1:319. See also Dominik Finkelde's contribution in this volume.

[17] Giorgio Agamben, *Walter Benjamin: tempo storia linguaggio*, ed. Lucio Belloi and Lorenzina Lotti (Roma: Reuniti, 1983), 65–82. Quoted here from "Language and History: Linguistic and Historical Categories in Benjamin's Thought," in Agamben, *Potentialities*, 48–62.

[18] Walter Benjamin, "Der Erzähler" (*GS* II.2:438–65) and "The Storyteller" (*SW* 3:143–66.). See also Bernd Witte's contribution to this volume.

[19] For further versions see *GS* I.3:1234 and 1235.

[20] Cf. Irving Wohlfarth,"Krise der Erzählung, Krise der Erzähltheorie: Überlegungen zu Lukács, Benjamin und Jauss," in *Erzählung und Erzählforschung im*

20. Jahrhundert, ed. R. Klopfer and G. Janetzke-Dillner (Stuttgart: Kohlhammer, 1981), 278.

[21] In the storyteller essay Benjamin quotes these terms from Georg Lukács's *Theory of the Novel* (*GS* II.2:454).

[22] Giorgio Agamben, *Idea della prosa* (Milano: Giangiacomo Feltrinelli, 1985). In English, "Idea of Prose," in *Idea of Prose*, trans. Michael Sullivan and Sam Whitsitt (New York: SUNY P, 1995), 39–41. Further references to this work are cited in the text using the abbreviation *IP* and the page number.

[23] Giorgio Agamben, *Il linguaggio e la morte* (Turin: Einaudi, 1982). In English, *Language and Death*, trans. Karen Pinkus (Minneapolis and London: U of Minnesota P, 1991).

[24] Agamben, *Language and Death*, 86.

[25] Giorgio Agamben, *Il tempo che resta* (Torino: Bollati Boringhieri, 2000). In English, *The Time That Remains: A Commentary on the Letter to the Romans*, trans. Patricia Dailey (Stanford, CA: Stanford UP, 2005). Further references to this work are cited in the text using the abbreviation *TTR* and the page number.

[26] Jacob Taubes, *Die Politische Theologie des Paulus* (Munich: Wilhelm Fink, 1993). In English, *The Political Theology of Paul*, trans. Dana Hollander (Stanford, CA: Stanford UP, 2003).

[27] Agamben borrows this term from Benjamin's "On the Concept of History" (*SW* 4:392).

[28] Referring to Taubes, *The Political Theology of Paul*, Agamben deems Paul's message to be among "the oldest and most demanding messianic texts of the Jewish tradition" (*TTR*, 3).

[29] The final part of Agamben's *The Time That Remains* is devoted to this argument. (See *TTR*, 138–45).

[30] Giorgio Agamben, *Homo sacer. Il potere sovrano e la nuda vita* (Torino: Einaudi, 1995). In English, *Homo Sacer: Sovereign Power and Bare Life*, trans. Daniel Heller-Roazen (Stanford: Stanford UP, 1998), 57–58. Further references to this work are cited in the text using the abbreviation *HS* and the page number.

[31] Franz Kafka, *Nachgelassene Schriften und Fragmente II* (Frankfurt am Main: Fischer, 2002), 38.

[32] Benjamin, *Briefe 2*, ed. Gershom Scholem und Theodor W. Adorno (Frankfurt am Main.: Suhrkamp, 1978), 763.

[33] Walter Benjamin, *Briefe 2*, 618.

[34] Habermas, "Consciousness-Raising or Redemptive Criticism," 32.

[35] Hannah Arendt, *The Human Condition* (Chicago: U of Chicago P, 1958), 48.

10: Paris on the Amazon? Postcolonial Interrogations of Benjamin's European Modernism

Willi Bolle

I. Introduction

THE FIRST PUBLICATION OF Walter Benjamin's *Passagen-Werk* (*The Arcades Project; GS* V.1 and V.2)[1] in Latin America — the Brazilian edition, launched in 2006 under the title *Passagens*[2] — promises, together with the Spanish version published in 2005 in Barcelona, to inaugurate a new phase of reception on this continent. In this context I wish to inquire into the usefulness and significance of Benjamin's study on the European metropolis of Paris for a better understanding of huge cities on the "periphery" of the world, such as Rio de Janeiro, Buenos Aires, Ciudad de Mexico, and São Paulo. To what degree, one may ask, are the categories of the *Passagen-Werk* transferable and operational with regard to these new metropolitan centers; what kind of complementary categories should perhaps be created to take account of the difference between these cities and the traditional European metropolis, such as Benjamin's Paris of the nineteenth century; and, last but not least, what may the "hegemonic centers" learn from the specific historical experience of peripheral cultures?

I propose to study these questions from the perspective of "histoire croisée" or "entangled history." Elaborated in recent years by scholars such as Michael Werner and Bénédicte Zimmermann,[3] this method tries to overcome the concepts of unilateral "cultural transference" and "asymmetric comparison," which frequently continue to be tributaries to the idea of a cultural "mission" of hegemonic countries intent on imposing their cultural values on the rest of the world. Major components of the "histoire croisée" are the interaction between colonial powers and colonized countries, the crossing and reversibility of points of view, the inclusion of the voices of the excluded, the historicity and "constructedness" of cultural patterns, the entanglement of perspectives, and the hybridity of cultures. Together they reflect the influence of four decades of postcolonial studies, such as those of Frantz Fanon;[4]

Edward W. Said;[5] Bill Ashcroft, Gareth Griffiths, and Helen Tiffin;[6] and Homi Bhabha,[7] among others. In the field of Benjamin studies, I have tried to "actualize" (cf. N2,2) Benjamin's portraits of European cities by testing their applicability to the knowledge of a Third World mega-lopolis such as São Paulo, establishing for this purpose intertextual relations with Brazilian writers.[8] Continuing this methodological trajectory, in his book *Benjamin heute* Rolf Goebel explores the intercultural significance of Benjamin's figure of the *flâneur* in the literary and critical discourses on the interaction between the modern European metropolis and (post)colonial spaces, taking as references scholars such as Homi Bhabha and Rey Chow.[9]

Paris, which Benjamin calls "die Hauptstadt des XIX. Jahrhunderts" (*GS* V.1:45; "the capital of the nineteenth century," *AP*, 3), will in this essay basically figure as the center of a colonial empire. We have to consider Benjamin's "Jetzt der Erkennbarkeit" ("now of recognizability"; Q°,21; N3,1; N3a,3; N9,7; N18,2, and so on) as the historiographic perspective of his project, elaborated between 1927 and 1940. Generally indicating the belated significance of a moment of the past in the present, this term for my purposes will be applied specifically to the epoch between the First and Second World Wars. The crucial experience of Benjamin's generation — which he intended to express in his work on Charles Baudelaire, the model-book of the *Passagen-Werk* — was being sent to the battlefields twice, in 1914 and in 1939, by the German government. Even more catastrophically, this call to arms coincided with the deportation to the concentration camps of Jews and other victims of National Socialist terror. As the historian Fritz Fischer explains in his book *Griff nach der Weltmacht* (Grab for World Power, 1961),[10] the aim of imperial Germany in the First World War was to become a world power, and Hitler's plans in the Second World War were quite similar: to make Germany the center of a colonial empire. Thus, when Benjamin entitles the central part of his model-book "Das Paris des Second Empire bei Baudelaire" (*GS* I.2:511–604; "The Paris of the Second Empire in Baudelaire," *SW* 4:3–94), we should bear in mind that an important underlying motivation was the reflection on the experience of the Second Reich and the Third Reich in his own country.

The issue of "colonial imperialism" is explicitly mentioned in one passage of the first sketch of the *Passagen-Werk*, which was used again in the second phase of the work. The Place du Maroc in the neighborhood of Belleville (a district of Paris) is considered by Benjamin a "Monument des Kolonialimperialismus" ("monument of colonial imperialism," L°,25 and P1a,2). This topic appears also in a number of other fragments, spread over different convolutes. Thus Benjamin was well aware of the problems of colonialism, but there is no evidence that he intended to dedicate to them a special convolute. For the purpose of this essay, it will be interesting to assemble all (or almost all) the fragments about colonialism, so as to capture Benjamin's view on this subject. The *leitmotif* of this constellation could be an unpublished résumé of fragment J54a,7 made by Benjamin: "Blick [der Metropole] auf das koloniale Imperium" ("View of the colonial empire [from the metropolis]");[11] it will be completed by fragments which also show the reverse view, looking at the metropolis from the colonial empire. This assemblage of passages (in section II) will be the core of this essay.

Benjamin's choice of fragments about the relations between the European metropolis and its periphery is a kind of last instantaneous snapshot of colonialism at the threshold of postcolonial times. While concepts such as "Kolonialpoesie" and "Kolonialpolitik" ("colonial poetry,"[12] and "colonial politics"[13]) already express a critical position toward "colonial imperialism," his use of the everyday-word "Kolonialwaren" ("products from the colonies," A6a,1), very common in Germany in the 1930s, reveals him to be still embedded in the generalized colonialist mentality. The ambiguity of this threshold position makes Benjamin's work particularly interesting for postcolonial writers and scholars. Learning from his study of the Second Empire from the perspective of the period between the First and Second World Wars, we have to consider the difference between Benjamin's epoch and our own era of globalization. Under the sign of the "now of recognizability" it is important to read his work in light of the historical transformations that have occurred since the composition of the *Passagen-Werk:* from the movements of decolonization, such as the Algerian War, to the migration of "dark masses" from the periphery of the world to the most advanced centers such as, for instance, Paris, the "city of light," in whose suburbs conflicts of ethnic violence between economically disenfranchised youths and the government exploded in September 2005.

As to the conception and method of postcolonial studies adopted in this essay, I would like to make it clear in advance that I do not intend to apply a determined theoretical frame to Benjamin's and other writers' work. Rather, my text has been written in the opposite direction: from the inside of concrete literary facticity toward the elucidation of some specific problems. Perhaps this is a way of experimenting with Benjamin's formula: "Konstruktion aus Fakten. Konstruktion unter vollständiger Eliminierung der Theorie" ("Construction out of facts. Construction with the complete elimination of theory"; O°,73). Applying Benjamin's dictum to the intersection of German and Brazilian studies, I intend to extract theoretical potential from literary texts themselves. In fact, who could be a more legitimate voice of postcolonialism if not the writers of countries with a colonial past?

After a synthetic review of the relations between the metropolis and its periphery it will be interesting to analyze a few fragments in detail, in order to get a more concrete vision of some social and cultural problems that already existed in the "capital of the nineteenth century" and that reappear in our days in the megacities of the Third World, cities that can be understood as gigantic and monstrous reproductions of the model of the "civilized European metropolis." From the perspective of an intercultural dialogue, I propose to investigate Benjamin's concepts of "madness" (section III) and "hell" (section IV), confronting them with the vision of Latin-American authors. Our postcolonial interrogations on Benjamin's European Modernism will then be completed by posing a final question, "Paris on the Amazon?" (section V), which deals with the problem of cultural identity.

Before starting our analysis, just one more observation. Among Benjamin's works we will focus on the *Passagen-Werk*, with its three phases: the first sketch with 405 fragments; the Big Archive, as I propose to call the 36 convolutes containing 4,234 fragments of "Aufzeichnungen und Materialien"; and the unfinished model-book, the "Baudelaire," for which Benjamin used 1,745 of these fragments.

For our kind of investigation it has been more instructive to work with the *Passagen-Werk* as a big archive rather than as a book. The thousands of materials assembled by Benjamin make it a research device that is not finished and complete but constitutes an open repertoire, always in movement, expressing and stimulating the spirit of experimentation and invention. Let us remember that Benjamin, in his early work *Einbahnstraße* (*One-Way Street*, 1923/28), argued in favor of direct communication between the "Zettelkasten" (card box) of the researcher who organized it (in this case, himself) and the researcher who studies in it (*GS* IV.1:103; *SW* 1:456). Let us also remember another passage, which has received little attention from critics, where Benjamin compares "de[n] Menschen" ("the human being") to a "Schaltbrett, an dem tausende von Birnen sind; bald erlöschen die einen, bald wieder [die] andern, [und] entzünden sich neu" ("an instrument panel on which are thousands of electric bulbs. Some of them go out at one moment, some at another, [and] come back on again," M°,12). This comparison contains an exact description of the *Passagen-Werk*. It is a hypertext with thousands of fragments.[14] If we organize a selection of those fragments into constellations and combine these constellations with an attempt to reveal a "noch-nicht-bewußtes Wissen" ("not-yet-conscious knowledge," K1,2) of concrete "Ausdruck[sformen] der Wirtschaft in ihrer Kultur" ("[forms of] expression of the economy in its culture," N1a6), then we will obtain — in the sense of Benjamin's dialectical historiography — an ideal device for the study of the phenomenon of the modern metropolis and its relations with peripheral countries, in literary texts as well as under the open sky of history.

II. The View of the Colonial Empire from the Metropolis — and the Reverse View

In his unpublished résumé of fragment J54a,7, quoted above, Benjamin focuses on the relation between the metropolis ("the capital") and its colonies. Here is the complete text:

> Baudelaire erfaßte, indem er der schwindsüchtigen Negerin in der Hauptstadt entgegenging einen sehr viel wahreren Aspekt des kolonialen Imperiums von Frankreich als Dumas, der im Auftrage von Salvandy ein Schiff nach Tunis bestieg.

> [When he went to meet the consumptive Negress who lived in the city [in the capital], Baudelaire saw a much truer aspect of the French colonial empire than did Dumas when he took a boat to Tunis on commission from [the minister of Colonization] Salvandy.]

Benjamin compares the ways in which two French writers of the Second Empire, Charles Baudelaire and Alexandre Dumas, viewed this relation. While the best-seller author Dumas planned to write a book which "donnerait bien à 50 ou 60.000 [français] le goût de colonizer" ("would give some fifty or sixty thousand [Frenchmen] a taste for colonialism," d4,1), intending to make a profitable deal with the French government, Baudelaire maintained his independence from colonial politics. Moreover, having in his youth spent several months in the French colony La Réunion in the Indian Ocean, he recognized the physiognomy of the colonies in the capital itself, concretely inscribed in the figure of the poverty-stricken black woman affected by tuberculosis. It is worth noting that Benjamin's use of the word "negress" indicates an unreflective use of typical colonial language, considered offensive from a postcolonial point of view.

Starting from this programmatic text J54a,7, let us now assemble a whole constellation of fragments from the *Passagen-Werk*, in order to get a more complete idea of Benjamin's vision of the relations between the European metropolis and its colonies. As already pointed out, I am trying to show these relations from the perspective of entangled history. Despite the fact that Benjamin, unlike Baudelaire, never traveled beyond Europe, he may be considered a precursor of the advocates of "histoire croisée." The distance and irony in his comments on several quotations from colonial authors constitute critiques of Eurocentrism; as an alternative he also tries to obtain a reverse view of the metropolis from the colonial periphery. With the following constellation of fragments I intend to document this interchange of points of view in its historic dimension.

The topic of the view of the colonial empire from the metropolis may be found emblematically represented by Grandville (the caricaturist and illustrator Jean-Ignace-Isidore Gérard, 1803–47) in his design "The Bridge of Planets," which is a part of his book *Un autre monde* (Another World, 1844), on which Benjamin comments in fragments M°,2 and F1,7. It shows bourgeois citizens contemplating the universe from the panoramic platform of the Saturn balcony or promenading in the midst of the planets as if they were crossing a bridge on the river Seine. This image illustrates how the European bourgeoisie was projecting its dream of global expansion.

The first technological system that materialized the dream of global power, the telegraphic system, is presented in fragment T3,1, with a quotation from Jacques Fabien's *Paris en songe* (1863). Instead of reproducing the central part of this text in a conventional way, I propose to cut it into five pieces and comment on them by means of an imaginary voyage around four continents of our planet.[15] First quote:

> Nos gros bonnets de la finance, de l'industrie, du haut négoce, ont trouvé bon . . . de faire . . . le tour du globe à leur pensée, eux restant au repos . . .
>
> [Our great heads of finance, industry, big business have seen fit . . . to send . . . their thoughts around the world, while they themselves remain at rest . . .]

To illustrate this quote, let us start our *tour du monde* in South America, for example, in the city of São Paulo, whose ancient status as a colonial foundation is still present in such downtown buildings as the Pátio do Colégio. From this typically peripheral metropolis we may fly to the "authentic" metropolis of Paris. The second quote —

> Pour cela, chacun d'eux a cloué, dans son cabinet de travail, sur un coin du bureau, les fils électriques . . .
>
> [To this end, each of them has nailed up, in a corner of his office, electric wires . . .]

— may be supplemented by a trip from Paris to Calcutta. In this city on the Ganges River we focus on a building from colonial times: Government House. While we read the third quotation —

> . . . les fils életriques, qui rattachent sa caisse avec nos colonies d'Afrique, d'Asie, d'Amérique.
>
> [. . . electric wires connecting his executive desk with our colonies in Africa, Asia, and the Americas.]

— we continue our trip to the matrix of the ancient colony, to London, choosing the place where formerly stood the palace of the East India

Company, from where Great Britain administered its most lucrative colony. Fourth quote:

> Commodément assis devant la table, il a fait bavarder sous ses doigts les lointains correspondants . . .

> [Comfortably seated before his schedules and account books, he can communicate directly over tremendous distances; . . .]

From London we fly to Cairo in Egypt, contemplating not only the pyramids but also the strategic Suez Channel. Our voyage through several ancient European colonies ends with one more trip to Paris, while we read this final quotation:

> . . . les lointains correspondants de ses comptoirs semés sur la surface du globe.

> [. . . at a touch of the finger, he can receive reports from all his far-flung agents on a startling variety of matters.]

With this example of a voyage through the continents I have tried to translate into concrete topographical visualization the network of power that extends over the whole planet and through which only electric impulses are travelling.

In Paris, of course, we would land on top of the Eiffel Tower. Inaugurated at the World Exhibition of 1889, this 300-meter-high building — at its time the highest in the world — is the ancestral symbol of worldwide power in modern history, followed in the twentieth century by the Empire State Building and by the former Twin Towers of the World Trade Center in New York City. The role of the Eiffel Tower is sometimes remembered in terms of "étude de la télégraphie sans fil" ("research on wireless telegraphy," F4a,4) and other times considered from the pragmatic aspect of world trade: "Quand un navire arrivera en Chine, la T.S.F. en transmettra la nouvelle à la Tour Eiffel ou à Londres" ("When a ship arrives in China, the T.S.F. will transmit the news to the Eiffel Tower or to London," W9a,3). Let us also observe that this construction, made of 12,000 metal fittings and 2 ½ million rivets, is for Benjamin a paradigm of the "Stahlgerüst der materialistischen Geschichtsschreibung" ("steel structure of materialistic historiography"; his résumé of N1a,1), that is, of the construction of the *Passagen-Werk* in form of a network-like montage of fragments (cf. N1,10).

Once on the Eiffel Tower, we could complement our intercontinental incursions by a skywalk over Paris; preferably in a typical balloon of the nineteenth century, such as that of the photographer Nadar (Félix Tournachon, 1820–1910), portrayed by Honoré Daumier in a famous lithograph (see *AP*, 682). Through this aerial *flânerie* over the

European metropolis we can perceive it as an accumulation of monuments and cultural treasures. From the Eiffel Tower we fly over the river Seine to the Place de l'Étoile, where the Arc de Triomphe stands. Quoting verses of Victor Hugo — "Arche! alors tu seras éternelle et complète, / Quand tout ce que la Seine en son onde reflète / Aura fui pour jamais . . ." ("Arch, you will loom eternal and intact / When all that the Seine now mirrors in its surface / Will have vanished forever . . . ," C6; C6a,1) — Benjamin shows the metropolis under the sign of transitoriness and perishability.

Let us continue along the Avenue des Champs Élysées. We arrive then at another place of memory: the Place de la Concorde, formerly the Place de la Révolution, where the obelisk brought from Luxor, Egypt, was erected in 1836. This obelisk inspired one of Benjamin's most notable thought figures in *Einbahnstraße:* "Papier- und Schreibwaren: Briefbeschwerer" (*GS* IV.1:111–12; "Stationers: Paperweight," *SW* 1:462). His observation, in that text, that those who grew up in cultures using the alphabet are unable to read the hieroglyphs has an allegorical meaning. The citizens of the twentieth century do not know the fundamentals of writing, while in our era of radical transformations of digital media there is an urgent necessity to relearn reading and writing. In addition, the obelisk is an example of how intensely the insignia of the colonial period — especially from Egypt — are present in the European metropolis.

From the Concorde we continue our aerial walk over the Tuileries, the gardens of the Louvre, the ancient palace of the kings of France, now a museum. Above its contemporary entrance by the Chinese-American architect I. M. Pei, which has the form of a pyramid (another Egyptian occurrence), let us drive northward. We have then before us one of the most beautiful perspectives created by Baron Haussmann's nineteenth-century urbanization: the avenue that leads to the glamorous opera house. Nearby, at the junction of Boulevard des Italiens with Boulevard Haussmann, there is the archeological site of the Passage de l'Opéra (see *AP,* 49), the classic shopping arcade whose description by Louis Aragon — just before its demolition in 1924 — was the major stimulus for Benjamin's *Passagen-Werk.* We finish our aerial tour over Paris following the *grands boulevards* — Haussmann, Montmartre, Poissonnière — and we land on the Boulevard Bonne-Nouvelle, joining there the passersby in order to get a closer view of the city.

This boulevard is a central point for our study of the entangled history of the metropolis and the periphery. The section that lies "hinter dem théâtre des Variétés . . . und von den Flaneurs nicht frequentiert wurde" ("behind the Théâtre des Variétés, and that was not much frequented by flâneurs"), the part of the city "jenseits der Grenzen des Boulevards" ("beyond the boulevards") was named by Alfred de Musset "les grand[e]s

Indes," "Groß-Indien" ("the East Indies"; cf. M5,5 and M11a,3). This designation evokes an abandoned *hinterland*, a *banlieue* — literally, the territory of approximately one mile around the city over which a ban was extended, home to the excluded "dunkle Massen" ("obscure [or dark] masses"; cf. E6a,1), who have no place on the stage of the capital of the empire. In other words: at a small distance from the area of the social life and the bourgeoisie's pretentious displays meant to impress others, at the periphery of Paris, the periphery of the world begins.

Imperialism, "der sich breit und hohl ausspannt wie dieses sein Bild [that is, die Krinoline]" ("spreads out and puffs up exactly like [a crinoline]," B2a,7), observes the German critic Friedrich Theodor Vischer in 1861. The lithograph (1855) by Honoré Daumier, showing fashionable courtesans wearing crinolines (see *AP,* 67), also gives us an idea of the importance of caricature in Benjamin's imagistic (*bildhaft*) historiography. As the most spectacular creation of nineteenth-century fashion, the crinoline, which was used by ladies of the upper class as well as by the cocottes of the *demi-monde,* symbolized a power that "[sich] wie eine Glocke über Gutes und Schlimmes, Berechtigtes und Unberechtigtes der Revolution [von 1848] gestürzt hat" ("settle[d] its dominion like a hoop skirt over all aspects, good and bad, justified and unjustified, of the revolution," B2a,7). The pompousness of the crinoline is used here as a symbol for political arrogance combined with ostentatious accumulation. In the capitals of the empires — as we saw during our walk through Paris — as nowhere else, the most precious cultural goods are accumulated, as, for example, in the famous collection of president Adolphe Thiers, which represents "un abrégé de l'univers" ("a miniature of the universe," H3,1).

From Paris, a short trip to London. We come upon another compact image of the world in the era of empires: the banker Nathan Rothschild, portrayed by Karl Gutzkow in his book *Öffentliche Charaktere* (Public Personages,1835),

> [Er] zeigt Euch, wenn Ihr ihn besucht, ein Kästchen, das aus Brasilien mit ganz frischen, eben aufgefischten Diamanten angekommen ist, um damit die Zinsen der brasilischen laufenden Schuld zu dekken. Ist dis [*sic*] nicht interessant?

> [[He] will show you, if you pay him a visit, a casket just arrived from Brazil with freshly mined diamonds intended to cover the interest on the current Brazilian debt. Isn't that interesting? (U1,5)]

Brazil is thus one of the pieces of the gigantic puzzle of quotations by which Benjamin seeks to present a miniature of the global network of power, centered in the nineteenth century in the two metropolises London and Paris. The quotation above illustrates well the kind of historiography intended by the author of the *Passagen-Werk:* instead of an "abstrakte Konfiguration der Geschichte in den 'Epochen'" ("abstract configuration of history in its 'epochs'"), he seeks concreteness and a "Pathos der Nähe" ("pathos of nearness," S1a,3), which allows us to perceive the physiognomy of objects and people. Thus we are transported to the places where diamonds are mined by slaves, as in the district of Diamantina (Tijuco), minutely described by travelers such as Johann B. von Spix and Carl Friedrich von Martius in *Travels in Brazil in the Years 1817–1820* and by Wilhelm Ludwig von Eschwege in his book *Pluto Brasiliensis* (1833).

Still in London, the Crystal Palace (see the photographs in *AP,* 159 and 185) is the major symbol of the world exhibitions, which started there in 1851 and were realized then alternately in the French and the British capitals. It is worth noting that in the name "Crystal Palace" there is a superposition of the spheres of mythology and of political-economic history, whose imbrications Benjamin proposes to decipher: on the one hand, the palace entirely made of quartz glass suggested a world of fairy tales and fairyland (cf. F5,4; G6/G6a,1); on the other, that colossal building served the practical purpose of exhibiting a wide range of commodities for the world market.

The world expositions, as "Wallfahrtsstätten zum Fetisch Ware" (*GS* V.1:50; "places of pilgrimage to the commodity fetish," *AP,* 7), presupposed the existence of a world market, which began to constitute itself half a century before. After Napoleon's return from the Egyptian campaign (1798–99) — a milestone of French colonial expansion — the Passage du Caire was constructed (A10,1). In a watercolor of another passage constructed in the same period — the Passage des Panoramas around 1810 (*AP,* 36) — we observe people wearing Napoleonic hats walking through a profusion of commodities that evokes an oriental bazaar. Is this not a dialectical image: the oriental market under western domination?

French colonial expansion is quite well documented in the *Passagen-Werk.* First it is reflected by fragments that speak of the appeal of commodities. One example is the fashion of shawls: "Die ersten Shawls tauchen in Frankreich im Gefolge des ägyptischen Feldzugs auf" ("The first shawls appear in France in the wake of the Egyptian campaign," O9,5). Since the beginning of the nineteenth century, the arcades of Paris make evident a political project that was given impetus by the world exhibitions since the middle of the century. As the journalist and novelist Karl Gutzkow reports, their salons were "voll orientalischer Szenen, die für Algier begeistern sollen" ("full of oriental scenes calculated to arouse enthusiasm for [the colonization of] Algiers," I2,2).

Reinforcing these economic enterprises, several journals launched direct political appeals for colonialism. An example is the poem of F. Maynard, "À l'Orient," published in 1835 in the periodical *Foi Nouvelle:*

Notre drapeau n'a plus assez du ciel de France,
Aux minarets d'Égypte il faut qu'il se balance,
. . .
Alors ils nous verront, en travailleurs agiles,
Avec nos lanières de fer
Dompter les sables du desert;
Et comme des palmiers, croîtront partout des villes.

[Our flag has lost patience with the sky of France;
Over the minarets of Egypt it now must wave.
. . . . .
Then will they see us, workers adept,
With our ribbons of iron
Subduing the desert sands;
Cities, like palms, will spring up everywhere. (a12,4)]

The colonial project of the metropolis is presented here as a mix of arrogant political power and civilizing mission. An important part of this colonial ideology was the travel literature: "C'est la France qui la pre-mière . . . a renforcé ses armées d'une brigade de géographes, de naturalis-tes, d'archéologues" ("It is France that first . . . reinforced its armies with a brigade of geographers, naturalists, and archaeologists," d9,2), Charles Louandre informs us in 1847. From a methodological point of view, this quotation and the next one are examples of how Benjamin uses succinct literary documents as textual monads to express the larger workings of political and social history.

In this sense, the already mentioned Algerian affair of Alexandre Dumas is typical of the involvement of bestselling authors in both litera-ture and politics:

En septembre 1846, le ministre Salvandy lui proposa de partir pour l'Algérie et d'écrire un livre sur la colonie . . . Dumas . . . donnerait bien à 50 ou 60.000 d'entre eux le goût de colonizer . . . Salvandy offrait 10.000 francs pour solder les frais de voyage; Alexandre exi-gea en outre . . . un vaisseau de l'État . . . Les parlementaires . . . s'emparèrent de l'incident.

[In September 1846, Minister Salvandy proposed to him that he travel to Algeria and write a book about the colony. . . . Dumas . . . would give some fifty or sixty thousand [Frenchmen] a taste for colonialism. . . . Salvandy offered 10.000 francs to cover the cost of the voyage; Alexandre demanded, in addition to this, . . . a state ves-sel. . . . Members of Parliament seized on the incident. (d4,1)]

The suspicion that this was a case of corrupt use of public money pro-voked a parliamentary inquiry and resulted in public scandal.

Military aspects of colonial expansion also figure prominently in several fragments. In the utopia of the social theorist and reform activist Charles Fourier (1772–1837) one finds a "messianische Zeittafel" ("messianic timetable") whose last stage would be the "Ausschwärmen der Kolonialstaffeln" ("dispatching of colonial squadrons," W11a,6). The belligerent intention is still more explicit in the "untätige Offiziere . . . [die in den Panoramen] passende Schlachtfelder für ihre phantastischen Kolonialkriege suchen" ("inactive officers . . . searching [in the panoramas] about for suitable battlefields to wage their imaginary colonial wars," Q1,5). These quotations illustrate the imaginative, indeed the imaginary and phantasmagoric aspects of the colonial enterprise whose material realities they tend to legitimate. And finally there is a passage written in 1855 by Maxime du Camp (1822–94), which may be read as a presage of the *clash of civilizations* of our present time:

> Dans deux cents ans, bien avant peut-être, de grandes armées parties d'Angleterre, de France et d'Amérique . . . descendront dans la vieille Asie sous la conduite de leurs généraux; leurs armes seront des pioches, leurs chevaux des locomotives. Ils s'abattront en chantant sur ces terres incultes et inutilisées . . . Ce sera peut-être ainsi que la guerre se fera plus tard contre toutes les nations improductives.

> [In two hundred years — well before, perhaps — great armies from England, France, and America . . . will descend upon old Asia under the leadership of their generals. Their weapons will consist of pickaxes, and their horses will be locomotives. Singing, they will fall upon these uncultivated, unused lands . . . It is thus, perhaps, that war will be waged, in the future, against all unproductive nations. d3,3]

There is a relation between wars of the hegemonic powers against peripheral countries or between themselves and, on the other hand, conflicts that occur in the heart of the metropolis. Sometimes wars against "foreign enemies" were means used by governments to divert attention away from internal social problems. This was the case of the government of Napoleon III, which declared war against Prussia in 1870. The military defeat of France was followed, in March 1871, by the insurrection of the Commune, with barricades in the streets of Paris (see the photograph in *AP*, 794). The crushing of the Commune by the French army, after the armistice concluded by the republican provisional government with the external enemy, sealed the end of revolutions in Western Europe.

According to Eric Hobsbawn, the era of revolutions was already over in 1848, with the defeat of proletarian forces by the bourgeoisie.[16] In the Chamber of Deputies in Paris a debate then occurred on the question of where to send the vanquished insurgents. As in ancient Rome, the holders of power considered that the most appropriate places for deportation would be the colonies. The deputy Jacques Arago, brother of the great physicist, argued in favor of Patagonia. The benefits resulting from this operation, for the French state as well as for those deported, were exposed in these arguments:

> Ces femmes, dont les plus jeunes sont fort appétissantes après une heure de natation . . . Ces antilopes, ces oiseaux, ces poissons, ces eaux phosphorescentes, ce ciel tout leopardé de nuages courant çà et là comme un troupeau de biches errantes . . . tout cela c'est la Patagonie, tout cela c'est une terre vierge, riche, indépendante. . . . [C]itoyens, . . . transportez en Patagonie les hommes que vos lois ont frappés; puis vienne le jour de la lutte, et ceux-là meme que vous avez exilés seront aux avant-postes, debout, implacables, barricades solides et mouvantes.

> [These women, of whom the youngest are so alluring after an hour's swim . . . These antelopes, these birds, these fish, these phosphorescent waters, this sky alive with clouds coursing to and fro like a flock of wandering hinds . . . all this is Patagonia, all this a virgin land rich and independent. . . . Citizens, . . . transport to Patagonia the men whom your laws have smitten. When the day of battle [against England] arrives, those you have exiled will have become staunch mobile barricades, standing implacable at the outposts. (a12,5)]

With this quotation, in which the text of the *Passagen-Werk* literally takes us to South America, we conclude this constellation of fragments showing the entangled history of the metropolis and the peripheral countries.

III. Madness — to Be Fought with the "whetted axe of reason"?

The phenomenon of madness, a major ingredient of life in the modern metropolis, is commented on by Benjamin in the first sketch of the *Passagen-Werk* in these terms:[17]

> Gebiete urbar zu machen, auf denen bisher nur der Wahnsinn wuchert. Vordringen mit der geschliffnen Axt der Vernunft und ohne rechts noch links zu sehen, um nicht dem Grauen anheimzufallen, das aus der Tiefe des Urwalds lockt. Aber aller Boden mußte einmal von der Vernunft untergemischt, vom Gestrüpp des Wahns und des Mythos gereinigt werden. Dies soll für den des 19ten Jahrhunderts hier geleistet werden.

> [To cultivate fields where, until now, only madness has reigned. Forge ahead with the whetted axe of reason, looking neither right nor left so as not to succumb to the horror that beckons from deep

in the primeval forest. But every ground must at some point have been turned over by reason, must have been cleared of the undergrowth of delusion and myth. This is to be accomplished here for the terrain of the nineteenth century. (G,13)[18]]

Benjamin considered this fragment to be one of the programmatic texts of his "neue, . . . dialektische Methode der Historik" ("new, . . . dialectical method of doing history," F°,6), as its transcription to convolute N ("Erkenntnistheoretisches, Theorie des Fortschritts"; "On the Theory of Knowledge, Theory of Progress") shows. The cause he advocates — reason fighting madness, delusion, and myth — expresses a common sense and a general emancipatory interest, so that everybody can agree with it. However, what makes the argument problematic is the kind of metaphors used by Benjamin. In this fragment — which contains, as far as I can see, no signal of conscious irony or self-irony — there is something surprising: it does not seem dialectical at all. The underlying idea of the text is that of a mission, in the spirit of *Aufklärung*, against madness, delusion, and myth. The means of that mission is the "axe of reason." This oxymoron certainly is not the most appropriate expression for the task of a philosopher. Reason with the blade in hand!? Reason, which should oppose unreason and abuse of power, using for this end a means of violence? Forging ahead "looking neither right or left" — why this staring gaze, which dispenses of the full capacity of vision and, per extension, of the other senses? Should the alternative to madness be a reason out of its mind? As *locus horribilis* Benjamin presents us the "Urwald" ("primeval forest"). Is not the horror of modern times located also in civilized countries? Let us think, for instance, of the battlefields of the First World War. The philosopher seems to have forgotten the insight of Goya that the sleep (or dream) of reason bears monsters. Faced with the "Urwald," Benjamin sees himself in the role of an "urbar Macher" (bearer of reason, who "makes [the ground] arable"), "clearing the undergrowth of delusion and myth." Thus, he is the "cultivator" who transforms the wilderness into a place of "culture" (see the Latin *colo = I cultivate*, and its derivations *cult, culture*). This comes to be exactly the role that according to history the "civilized" Europeans have accomplished for the "savages" they colonized. In a strange manner, Benjamin falls back into the typical missionary attitude of the colonizers, who usually are the object of his critique. In short: the fragment above seems to be a blind passage in the *Passagen-Werk*, contradicting the otherwise dialectical and emancipatory intentions of the author. There is still a lack of critical insight concerning the oxymoron of the "axe of reason."

It will be instructive to investigate comparatively how the problem of dealing with madness in the modern metropolis — posed by Benjamin, but badly resolved by him — has been treated by a Brazilian writer, his

contemporary Mário de Andrade (1893–1945), who along with Oswald
de Andrade (1890–1954) is the main representative of Brazilian modernism. Significantly, this movement did not take place in the capital Rio de
Janeiro, but in São Paulo, the emergent industrial and economic center
of the country, with immigrants from all over the world. The modernists
broke with two patterns of the self-image of Brazil cultivated by the traditional literary elite, which both were forms of alienations, because they
internalized the European way of seeing Brazil and obstructed the search
for Brazil's own identity: on the one hand, picturesque exotism and, on
the other, the inclination of cities like Rio, Manaus, or even São Paulo to
consider themselves a kind of Paris in the Americas. Mário de Andrade
turns this impasse into a matter for critical reflection. In the verses "São
Paulo . . . / Gallicism to cry in the deserts of America"[19] he articulates
the status of the city as that of a dependent, peripheral metropolis and
also the necessity to incorporate reflection on this *conditio periférica* in
the search for identity. This posture goes hand in hand in de Andrade
with assimilating and elaborating poetic techniques that can be universally
relevant. In this context is situated the *desvairismo*, as he calls his representation of madness and his dialogue with it.

The poem cycle *Paulicéia desvairada* (*Hallucinated City of São Paulo*
or *São Paulo, City of Madness*), published in 1922, after the Week of Modern Art that took place in São Paulo, is Mário de Andrade's most significant work, along with his novel *Macunaíma* (1928). The conclusive part
of *Paulicéia* (*PD*, 103–15) is a "profane oratorio," offering an allegorical
representation of that programmatic event, which occurred on the cen-
tennial of Brazil's independence. Almost all the city's three-quarters of
a million inhabitants are shown on the stage in four choruses of people:
first, the "Trembling Senilities," that is, the millionaires and the grand
bourgeoisie; second, the "Conventional Orientalisms," or artists at the
service of the holders of power; third, the "Green-and-Golden Youth,"
rebels full of hope, having in their middle the poet accompanied by "My
Madness"; and fourth, the Indifferent Masses of the Poor. The struggle
between these forces results in victory of the Green-and-Golden Youth,
but they are exhausted and fall asleep. My Madness sings them a lullaby.
Like an expressionist woodcut, this polyphonic spectacle evokes the arch-
image of madness: nobody wants to listen any more, and nobody can stop
to cry any more.

Unlike Walter Benjamin, who wants to fight madness with the axe of
reason, Mário de Andrade aims toward a constructive dialogue with the
state of madness (*desvario*) by means of what he calls *desvairismo* (*PD*,
59), which is a major component of his poetics. In the form of elliptical
sentences or "vibrations" — as in the verse "São Paulo! Shock experience
of my life . . ." (*PD*, 83) — the voice of madness, mixed with sensations of
pain, hallucination, and trance, reverberates through the verses of *Paulicéia*

desvairada from the beginning to the end. Through his poetic forms de Andrade tries to master the state of madness provoked by the big city. The allegorical figure of My Madness, with which the poet converses, represents the collective feeling as well as a major component of the poetic task. Madness and delusion (Benjamin's *Wahnsinn* and *Wahn*) are for de Andrade the basis of poetic production, insofar as they are linked to the lyrical impulses of the soul; these are explicitly designated as "a sublime affective state — near to sublime madness" (*PD*, 72). This state, called *lirismo* by de Andrade, is for him the primitive state per excellence.

Primitivism is an important component of the poet's dialogue with modern technological civilization, and it is crucial for the question of how to deal with the non-rational element (represented by Benjamin as the "Urwald") when it is detected in urban civilization. On the scale of the dialogue with "primitive thinking," in the twentieth century, Benjamin's position is closer to that of Lucien Lévy-Bruhl's colonialist vision of the thinking of "inferior societies"[20] than to Claude Lévi-Strauss's valorization of the "savage mind,"[21] of which Mário de Andrade may be considered a precursor. The poet's characterization, in 1922, of the lyric impulse as a "cry of the unconscious" (*PD*, 59), is on his part an assimilation of Sigmund Freud's finding, in 1913, that "den Inhalt des *Ubw* kann man einer psychischen Urbevölkerung vergleichen" ("the content of the unconscious may be compared to a psychological primal population").[22] Hence both authors, Freud and de Andrade, overcome the biased vision of primitivism, recognizing it as a not-to-be-exorcized part of modern urban humankind. One may regret, in this context, that Benjamin — who created a suggestive philosophical constellation with concepts such as "Ursprung" (origin, source), "Urphänomen" (primordial phenomenon), "Urpflanze" (primordial plant), "Urbild" (archetype), "Urgeschichte" (primal history) — did not integrate in it the terms "Urwald" (primeval forest) and "Urbs"/"Urban" (city, urban), which could be understood as dialectical poles (via "urbar machen" and "urban machen") in the spirit of his new historiography.

For the author of *Paulicéia desvairada*, poetry has an aesthetic function in the sense of structuring the new kind of perception imposed by the rhythm of the modern metropolis. The poet transforms himself into a test subject. With his work he aims to register the shocks that are hitting the nervous system of the city's inhabitants. Here de Andrade takes up again the topos of the "experience of shock" that originated with Baudelaire in the Paris of the nineteenth century and anticipates Benjamin's description, who understands it, moreover, as a major symptom for the decline of the aura.[23] The big modern city is indeed the place where the uninterrupted flow of sensations — "shocks and ever more shocks"[24] — becomes the normal condition. The prophecy cited in the *Passagen-Werk* that "die Menschen . . . von dem Tempo der Nachrichtenübermittlung wahnsinnig werden würden" ("people will have been . . . maddened by the tempo of news reporting," B2,1) seems to have turned into reality in the "hallucinated" city of São Paulo. For Mário de Andrade, in contrast to Benjamin, shock and madness have both a negative and a positive connotation; to make them curable, one has to become familiar with them.

A remedy against excessive demands of consciousness and traumatic shocks consists for Mário de Andrade in the construction of a poem as "a shock-producing machine" (*ENI*, 258). Shocks are created in the poem as in a laboratory, so that they can be worked out psychologically and socially. In order to express the "unrestrained furor of the elements" (*PD*, 66) of the monster city, the poet mobilizes techniques of elliptic syntax, snapshots, superposition, and polyphony. His antitheses reveal social dissonances. By means of linguistic montage, the apparent cosmopolitanism is disenchanted and shown as a combination of interests of multinational capitalism. At this point, de Andrade's diagnosis is consistent with that of Benjamin.

Instead of picturesque Brazilian local color the reader of *Paulicéia desvairada* encounters the working rhythm of the city. As a major marketplace for coffee the peripheral metropolis São Paulo is very sensitive to the "English shouts" of the stock values on the world market. Mário de Andrade does not show directly the working collective; it is, like a hidden figure, a "dull rumor" under the "golden chorus of the coffee sacks" (*PD*, 102). It also appears at night, when the inhabitants of a neighborhood of the city are taken over by the rhythm of a party, in a "delirium of flesh of light" (*PD*, 96). Last but not least, the multitude of the big city is integrated in de Andrade's work as a "furor of the masses" (*PD*, 67), which is a metaphor he uses to speak of his lyrical impulse. The physiognomy of the modern metropolis has been captured by him in the form of a snapshot showing his own face from the inside:

> There, in front of you . . . — Mário, take the mask!
> — That's reasonable, my Madness, that's reasonable. (*PD*, 99)

The second verse is an emblematic self-portrait of the Brazilian modernist. He is possessed and protected by Madness, at the same time Reason is on his left and on his right. This oxymoron is — in the early 1920s — the anticipated answer and alternative position of the poet of the hallucinated city to Benjamin's strategy of facing madness and delusion with the "axe of reason."

While madness in Benjamin's fragment seems to be something that exists in a history and in the world exterior to the author, Mário de Andrade, self-critically, localizes madness not only in society but also in himself. As I suggested above: the "URwald" of the irrational is a constitutive part of the civilized inhabitant of the "URbs." De Andrade identifies madness and delusion as elements of the lyrical impulses, without which neither poetic reflection nor the cognition of madness and delusion is possible. These, as well as the dialogue with the references to "primeval forest" and "horror" are incorporated into poetic labor. Thus de Andrade's poetics of *desvairismo* does not have recourse to an understanding of *Aufklärung* that succumbs to the attraction of violence, but reactivates the conception of Art as a "heilkundige Zauberin" ("enchantress capable of healing"), as Friedrich Nietzsche called it in his interpretation of antique tragedy.[25]

IV. Hell — a Metaphysical Speculation or a Place of the Excluded?

In the *Passagen-Werk,* Benjamin aims to portray modernity, or more exactly "the modern," as "the time of hell":

> Das "Moderne" die Zeit der Hölle. Die Höllenstrafen sind jeweils das Neueste, was es auf diesem Gebiete gibt. Es handelt sich nicht darum, daß "immer wieder dasselbe" geschieht, geschweige daß hier von der ewigen Wiederkunft die Rede wäre. Es handelt sich vielmehr darum, daß das Gesicht der Welt gerade in dem, was das Neueste ist, sich nie verändert, daß dies Neueste in allen Stücken immer das Nämliche bleibt. — Das konstituiert die Ewigkeit der Hölle. Die Totalität der Züge zu bestimmen, in denen das "Moderne" sich ausprägt, hieße die Hölle darstellen.

> [The "modern," the time of hell. The punishments of hell are always the newest thing going in this domain. What is at issue is not that "the same thing happens over and over," and even less would it be a question here of eternal return. It is rather that precisely in that which is newest the face of the world never alters, that this newest remains, in every respect, the same. — This constitutes the eternity of hell. To determine the totality of traits by which the "modern" is defined would be to represent hell. (S1,5; cf. G°,17)]

Benjamin's conception of the modern and his plan to represent it with infernal elements are based on a theological perspective and on theological are concepts: "time of hell," "punishments of hell," "eternity of hell." He explains this theological armature with the secularized elements of commodity capitalism, where the *mise-en-scène* of "the newest" — through novelty, fashion, and advertising — always has the same results. For his project of determining the traits of the modern under the sign of hell — or to elaborate a "physiognomy of hell,"as he entitled one of the thirty categories of his model book of the *Passagen-Werk* — Benjamin assembles a considerable number of fragments with literary representations of hell, from Dante to Kafka, as well as some philosophical, mythological, and topographical observations.

The topography of subterranean Paris, with its caverns and metro system, underground galleries and catacombs (see especially convolute C), where "jeder haust hier einzeln, die Hölle sein Hofstaat" ("each name dwells alone; hell [being] its demesne"), is compared by Benjamin to mythological places in ancient Greece, "an denen es in die Unterwelt hinabging" ("where the way led down into the underworld," C1a,2). The Middle Ages are remembered, too, when some clever persons, "gegen hohe Bezahlung und Schweigegelübde [sich erbötig machten,] ihren Mitbürgern dort unten den Teufel in seiner höllischen Majestät zu zeigen" ("after exacting a considerable sum and a vow of silence, undertook to guide their fellow citizens underground and show them the Devil in his infernal majesty," C2,1). Commenting on a phrase from Karl Marx about "die verborgene Stätte der Produktion, an deren Schwelle zu lesen steht: 'Unbefugten ist der Zutritt verboten'" ("the hidden haunts of production, on whose threshold we are faced with the inscription: 'No admittance except on business,'" X7a,3), Benjamin compares this inscription to that of Dante on the Gates of Hell: "Lasciate ogne speranza, voi ch'intrate" ("Leave ye all hope behind who enter here"[26]). This topos of the loss of any hope is taken up by Franz Kafka, as Benjamin points out in his essay of 1934 on the writer; but the *Passagen-Werk* focuses on another aspect of Kafka's work: the motif of the ever-repeated heathscapes in the paintings of the artist Titorelli in *Der Proceß* (The Trial) — a simile of the "Zeit der Hölle" ("time of hell"), where "das Neue . . . immer [das] ewig Selbe [ist]" ("the new . . . is always the eternally selfsame," S2a,3).

For Benjamin this is the main characteristic of hell, summarized by the categories of "boredom" and "eternal return" (convolute D). Switching from literature to the condition of the first specialized factory workers around 1840, he quotes the historian Jules Michelet (1798–1874): "Voici 'l'enfer de l'ennui' dans les tissages: 'Toujours, toujours, toujours, c'est le mot invariable que tonne à notre oreille le roulement automatique dont tremblent les planches. Jamais l'on ne s'y habitue'" ("There were 'true hells of boredom' in the spinning and weaving mills: '*Ever, ever, ever*, is the unvarying word thundering in your ears from the automatic equipment which shakes even the floor. One can never get used to it,'" D4,5). This observation of a representative historical fact is amplified by Benjamin into a general philosophical characterization of "modernity" as a time "[qui] n'a pas su répondre aux nouvelles virtualités techniques par un ordre social nouveau" ("incapable of responding to the new technological possibilities with a new social order," GS V.1:76; *AP*, 26). In Auguste Blanqui's *L'éternité par les astres* (1872) he discovers a testimony that stimulates him to make this general judgment. The text of the French revolutionary, written during his forty years in prison, is a "kosmologische Spekulation" ("a cosmological speculation"): "Die kosmische Weltansicht, die Blanqui darin entwirft, indem er der mechanistischen Naturwissenschaft der bürgerlichen Gesellschaft seine Daten entnimmt, ist eine infernalische" ("The cosmic vision of the world which Blanqui lays out, taking his data from the mechanistic natural science of bourgeois society, is an infernal vision," D5a,6). It is infernal insofar as, according to Blanqui, the universe on Earth "se répète sans fin" ("repeats itself endlessly") on other stars, "jou[ant] imperturbablement . . . les mêmes représentations" ("perform[ing] — imperturbably — the same routines," D7; D7a). What we call "progress," explains Benjamin, is just a phantasmagoria; it is not possible for humans to change their destiny by making history. Thus, "résignation sans espoir, c'est le dernier mot du grand révolutionnaire" ("resignation without hope is the last word of the great revolutionary," GS V.1:76; AP, 26). Although it seems that Benjamin here somehow comes close to Blanqui's position and to Nietzsche's idea of "eternal return," he finally opposes them in the name of a "dialektische[r] Begriff der historischen Zeit" ("dialectical conception of historical time," D10a,5). According to Benjamin, the course of history is not predetermined but may be changed by humans.

Charles Baudelaire's representations of hell are also important here. "*Les fleurs du mal* sont l'*enfer* du XIXe siècle" ("*Les fleurs du mal* is the *Inferno* of the nineteenth century," J11,4) writes André Suarès in 1933, also alluding to Dante. Comparing Baudelaire to Victor Hugo, Alcide Dusolier (1864) places the former, who "écroua *réellement* dans la prison d'enfer l'homme moderne, l'homme du dix-neuvième siècle" ("*actually* incarcerated modern man — the man of the nineteenth century — in the prison of hell"), highly above the latter, who "avait fait de la 'diablerie' un décor fantastique à quelques légendes anciennes" ("made *la diablerie* a fantastic setting for some ancient legends," J42,1). On the other hand, a deprecating observation of Baudelaire on Musset, on his "impudence d'enfant gâté qui invoque le ciel et l'enfer pour des aventures de table d'hôte" ("spoiled-child's impudence, invoking heaven and hell in tales of dinner-table conversations"), is refuted by a quotation of Brunetière's referring to Baudelaire: "Ce n'est qu'un Satan d'hôtel garni, un Belzébuth de table d'hôte" ("He is just a Satan with a furnished apartment, a Beelzebub of the dinner table," J13a,5).

This is a point that makes us pay more attention to the strong literary stylization and high degree of abstraction in Baudelaire's and other authors' representations of hell. In Baudelaire's famous tale "Le joueur généreux," where the poet meets with Satan in his subterranean dwelling, an ambience of high comfort and luxury, the poor are completely eclipsed. The metropolis of the excluded, on the other hand, appears in a poem of Shelley's, of whom Benjamin says that "[er] beherrscht die Allegorie, Baudelaire wird von ihr beherrscht" ("[he] rules over the allegory, whereas Baudelaire is ruled by it," J81,6). The first stanza of Shelley's "Peter Bell the Third, Part the Third: Hell" (written in 1819, published in 1839) reads:

Hell is a city much like London —
A populous and a smoky city;
There are all sorts of people undone,
And there is little or no fun done;
Small justice shown, and still less pity. (M18)

"Hell is a city much like São Paulo" — this is what we could echo back, taking up Shelley's portrait of a European metropolis from the perspective of a megacity of the Third World in postcolonial times. We are now at a turning point: a switch should be made from Benjamin's assemblage of literary representations of hell and metaphysical speculations to other kinds of documents, which deal with hell not so much as "was uns bevorstünde" ("something that awaits us"), but which, as Strindberg says, is "dieses Leben hier" ("this life here and now," N9a,1). As a complement to Benjamin's vision, which offers a theological armature for a better understanding of the secularized "always the same" in everyday life, let us now hear some voices from the "periphery," which make us perceive — as did Frantz Fanon in the 1960s with his book *The Damned of the Earth* — what "hell" means concretely in terms of the living conditions of the marginalized and the excluded in our time.

So we go, once again, to São Paulo, the *city of madness,* whose number of inhabitants in its metropolitan area grew from three-quarters of a million in 1922, when Mário de Andrade portrayed it, to 20 million on the threshold of the twenty-first century, turning it into the third largest city in the world and the largest in the Southern Hemisphere. São Paulo is a place where we can study the intersection of an (imitated) European metropolis with a Third World megalopolis. Around its core, constituted by a widespread business area and a good number of fine residential neighborhoods, extends *the periphery,* a mixture of modest dwelling zones and hundreds of slums or *favelas,* places of poverty and misery. From there arise the voices of RAP (Rhythm and Poetry) and Black Music. Initially these constituted marginal phenomena, but in recent years they have been accepted more and more also by middle-class youth. Let us look at two texts of a well known RAP band of São Paulo: the Racionais MC's, the "Rational Masters of Ceremonies." Their CDs, especially *Sobrevivendo no Inferno* (2002, Surviving in Hell),[27] give an insight into our contemporary cities that complements and at the same time is quite different from that of Benjamin.

The song *Fim de Semana no Parque* (Weekend in the Park)[28] presents a theme that makes us remember a passage by Baudelaire, quoted in Benjamin's essay "Die Moderne," which is a part of his model book for the *Passagen-Werk:*

Es ist unmöglich, nicht von dem Schauspiel dieser kränklichen Bevölkerung ergriffen zu werden, die den Staub der Fabriken schluckt, Baumwollpartikeln einatmet, ihre Gewebe von Bleiweiß und von allen Giften durchdringen läßt. . . . Diese Bevölkerung verzehrt sich nach den Wundern, auf die ihr doch die Erde ein Anrecht gibt; . . . sie wirft einen langen von Trauer beschwerten Blick auf das Sonnenlicht und die Schatten in den großen Parks. (*GS* I.2:576–77)

[It is impossible not to be gripped by the spectacle of this sickly population, which swallows the dust of the factories, breathes in particles of cotton, and lets its tissues be permeated by white lead, mercury, and all the poisons . . . ; this languishing and pining population to whom the earth owes its wonders, . . . and who cast a long, sorrowful look at the sunlight and shadows of the great parks. (*SW* 4:44)]

The RAP song *Weekend in the Park* is a South-American counterpart to Baudelaire's text, insofar as it presents the story of a boy from a *favela,* who takes a weekend stroll through one of the few parks in the city. In the *favelas,* even when they have resounding names such as Angela Garden or Ipê Park, there are no green areas; these are a privilege of the fine residential neighborhoods. From the outside, through the wall, the boy views a club of rich people:

Look at that club, which is up-to-date
Look at that tennis court and that soccer field
Look, how many people
There is an ice-cream lounge, a cinema, a warm swimming pool
Look how many fine boys, how many pretty girls
There is a cart race to watch
Exactly as I saw yesterday on TV
Look at that club
Which is so up-to-date.

All this the black youth sees "from the outside"; "he is dreaming through the wall. . . ." The text presents in miniature an example of the entangled history of the metropolis and its periphery: the view of the excluded and marginalized people, the "dunkle Massen" ("obscure [or dark] masses"), toward the place of the "blendenden Massen" ("brilliant masses"; cf. E6a,1) as representatives of the metropolitan center and its privileges.

What the youth sees is an extract of the glamorous world of wealth and of commodities, already presented by the *Passagen-Werk* in the windows of the arcades — and, currently, of the shopping malls — this "Urlandschaft der Konsumption" ("primordial landscape of consumption"; A°,5) with its promise of happiness. Happiness, formerly seen from a religious viewpoint, is secularized and synthetically reproduced for consumers by advertising arrangements in the "Tempel[n] des Warenka-pitals" ("temples of commodity capital," A2,2) and by the entertainment industry at world exhibitions, which are "Wallfahrtsstätten zum Fetisch Ware" ("places of pilgrimage to the commodity fetish," *AP*, 7). As heard in songs of the Racionais MC's, those brilliant things are videogames for children; for youth, brand new tennis shoes; and for adult men Rolex watches, fancy clothes, the thunderous motorbike or the car of the year, and the fashionable (blond) girl. Those who have all this are considered outstanding persons.

But how can the excluded actually get these commodities? This is the question for those who grew up in extreme poverty, experiencing hunger, lack of education, and disturbed family life, which expose them to dis-dain and humiliation. As a way out of this situation, some youth consider crime as an option:

> Looking for my dream of consumption:
> To be a criminal is here the most practical
> It's rapid, sadistic, and fairly tactical.
> (*A Vida é Desafio* [Life is a Challenge])[29]

Instead of getting a formal education, these youth enter the school of crime: watching out for the police, distributing drugs, committing rob-beries, first small and then big ones. Their idols are the much admired and much feared "big-time" gangsters. With guns in hand, the disdained and humiliated *favela* youth are respected.

The price for choosing crime is, as all statistics demonstrate, a prema-ture and violent death or, in other words, "the way to hell." The diaboli-cal thing, however, is that the alternative of an honest lifelong existence in misery is also hell. This dilemma represents the main issue of the songs of the Rational Masters of Ceremonies, who choose their name very con-sciously. They act "rationally," in opposition to the phantasmagorias of a whole capitalist system of consumerist seduction and delusion. The group is engaged in social pedagogy: its music and texts express the everyday experiences of *favela* inhabitants; mostly through role-playing, they make youth consider that the option for what seems to be the "the most practi-cal" way to get "the newest" will probably throw them into a situation which is worse than the "always the same" of their everyday life.

The song *Tô Ouvindo Alguém me Chamar* (I Hear Somebody Call-ing Me)[30] is a significant example of this program. A young man from the periphery — the voice of the text — has been shot down in the street; the text describes the agony he is feeling. The unfolding of one's whole life before death is, as we remember, also a motif of Benjamin's presentation of the metropolis (cf. F°,15). The song begins with the words the young man heard just before the shots: "Hey, brother, this is what Guina is send-ing you." Guina was the gangster who introduced the protagonist to the world of crime. He always admired Guina: "Thunderous motorbike . . . , fashionable girls . . . , brand new clothes . . ." In flashes the song evokes the most important moments of the protagonist's life.

Flashback 1: Assault on a bank, when he killed one of the guards. At that time he felt a sensation of power never known before: "For the first time I saw the system at my feet." Now he feels a strong pain in his completely dried-out throat, and he swears: "If I get out of here, I'll change my life." Then the refrain: "I Hear Somebody Calling Me."

Flashback 2: Assault on a mansion, followed by murder. And a flashback in the flashback: remembering Guina's childhood. "A mixture of hate, frustration, and pain." His father was an alcoholic, completely ruined; his way to school was an everyday humiliation. So he entered the school of crime. Admission exam: assault on a bus; final exam: assault on a bank. Now he is no longer an underdog. "He had a certain ability to command, / intelligence, and personality, / skills for occupying a good position / perhaps in a multinational company." Flashback to the speaker's present: "What am I doing here?" Lately he had nightmares and hallucinations, and he got the message that somebody wanted to kill him. He no longer feels his arms and abdomen. Breathing difficulty. Refrain: "I Hear Somebody Calling Me."

Flashback 3: The protagonist was then 17 years old, and he had to "survive in hell." Six years ago, his first crime: assault on a gas station, when he shot someone. Now he wants to quit. But there is the rumor that he has squealed on Guina, who is in prison, and the paranoia that his accomplices will take revenge. For a moment this fear is overcome by joy because of the birth of his nephew: "He shall study! / As to me, the Devil guides my destiny." It was hot tonight. Let's hop to the bar, buy some cigarettes. "It will be quick, no need to take my gun." Two youth come toward him: "Hey, brother, this is what Guina is sending you." Four shots. He hits the ground, the bloody clothes stick to the body. "If I get out of here, I'll change my life." And the refrain: "I Hear Somebody Calling Me." The sound of the electrocardiograph, which was heard in the background during the whole time, disappears.

This analysis has meant to show what the meaning of "hell" is in postcolonial times for inhabitants of the periphery of Third World megacities. As we saw in Benjamin's texts, madness, delusion, and hell are components inherent to the historical project of the bourgeoisie. Whereas Benjamin shows them basically from the outside and often confines himself to *denounce* them, we have heard some voices from the South-American periphery who make us perceive madness, delusion, and hell from the inside. As such states are located also in ourselves, we should learn to engage in a *dialogue* with them, including in this dialogue the inhabitants of the periphery, as shown in the songs of the Rational Masters of Ceremonies. It cannot be the "rational" historical project of middle classes to create conditions that transform the youth of our "planet of slums"[31] into criminals who will choose these very classes as targets.

V. Paris on the Amazon?

In the final part of this essay let us return to the issue of transferability of European cultural patterns to Latin America. What has been the importance of Paris as a model imitated and incorporated by Brazilian cities since the last decades of the nineteenth century — even to the point that some of them regard themselves as "Paris in America"? This was not only the case of the former capital Rio de Janeiro and the economic center São Paulo, but especially of Belém and Manaus, which both claimed, a century ago, to be "Paris on the Amazon." A significant detail from the rubber-boom times around 1900 was that rich families used to send their laundry to Lisbon or Paris to be washed there instead of in the muddy waters of the Amazon. In Belém, the port of entrance to the region, a department store called "Paris N'America" was inaugurated in 1870, and it still exists today. In Manaus, the former capital of the rubber trade, the magnificent Teatro Amazonas, constructed during the final decade of the nineteenth century, continues to be the major symbol of the region's prosperity. On the ceiling of the auditorium inside this opera house — with its dome of 36,000 vitrified ceramic tiles imported from Europe — there is a painting with a view one would have from the ground of the Eiffel Tower looking up. In other words, it conveys to spectators the illusion of observing, in the middle of the jungle, a stage spectacle in Paris.

Paris on the Amazon? How is this intriguing question of cultural identity seen today by the inhabitants of this "peripheral" region, which has approximately the same size as the whole of Europe? The Amazonian author Márcio Souza (born in 1946) made it the subject of one of his screenplays: *As Folias do Látex* (Rubber Follies), launched in 1976 and remade in 2007 with screenings in Rio and São Paulo.[32] The play focuses on the cycle of rubber exploitation, showing "how the big international economic interest acted in Amazonia, directly or through their native representatives" (*FL*, 11). As the author observes, it was "a historical moment full of contradictions, and the region, by making an enormous effort to alienate its identity, succumbed precisely because of its lack of identity" (*FL*, 12). Let us analyze some significant elements of this question of identity in the form of an intertextual dialogue between Souza's play and Benjamin's *Passagen-Werk*, observing that both authors share the idea that historical processes have a dramatic rather than an epic structure (cf. N7,3) and that dramatic forms are particularly appropriate to express the "höhere Konkretheit" ("higher concreteness") "[des] neue[n] geschichtliche[n] Denken[s]" ("[of] the new historical thinking," S1,6; cf. N1a,2).

Rubber Follies belongs to the genre of *vaudeville,* in the French tradition of the nineteenth century. This kind of light comedy, with songs and dance, just for entertainment, was then very popular; its annual production could amount to more than 200 plays, as Benjamin informs us (d9,3). He used some of them as historical sources, such as *Les embellissements de Paris* (1810; cf. M6a,3); *Les passages et les rues* (1827; cf. A10,3; A10a,1), and *Les filles de marbre* (1853; cf. O7,1; O10a,7). Among the different etymologies of *vaudeville,* Souza chooses that of "voix de la ville." It is indeed by a constellation of voices assembled on a stage in Manaus that he presents the history of Amazonia at the time of the rubber boom. *Vaudeville,* as Souza points out, is a form of theater of "bourgeois irresponsibility"; with its "low subjects and style" it is meant for "a less exigent public" (*FL,* 12). Cultivating an ironic view of history, it takes distance from the "nostalgia of the good old times in Amazonia," as well as from the "politically correct literature," which denounces the misery of the *seringueiros* (rubber workers); its jokes make us laugh instead of shedding tears, but they also draw attention to injustice and social inequity (*FL,* 12–13). Finally, the irreverence of Souza's *vaudeville,* in particular its spirit of *follies,* is a ludic counterpoint to Benjamin's fight against "madness and delusion" with "the axe of reason."

Focusing on the question of identity, let us now look at some examples from *Rubber Follies.* Presented by a master of ceremonies who is more or less the voice of the author, the play is composed of twelve scenes with historical persons as well as with symbolic characters. It starts with the first scientific communication on latex rubber, in 1743, by the French naturalist Charles-Marie de La Condamine, who made the first scientific exploration of the Amazon River. A key scene (*FL,* 51–62), set in the 1880s, shows various human types: the Brazilian colonel, the Englishman, and the American exploiting the rubber business, each in his own manner. While the American makes his investments, considering Manaus a new Klondike, and the Englishman smuggles rubber-tree seeds to Malaysia in order to break Amazonia's monopoly, the colonel, who strolls through the shops of Manaus in the company of several cocottes, declares that his nature is not that of a businessman: "I was born to enjoy the pleasures of life" (*FL,* 56). Another scene (*FL,* 63–73) evokes Eduardo Ribeiro, governor of the state of Amazonas from 1890 to 1896, who dreamed of transforming Manaus into a "Paris of the tropics" and with this in mind launched a huge project of Haussmannization, the nineteenth-century demolition of parts of medieval Paris in order to build the grand boulevards and modernize the city, which figures prominently in the *Passagen-Werk.* The Teatro Amazonas, inaugurated on the last day of his government, 31 December 1896, is the major symbol of that aspiration. Souza's *vaudeville,* however, is not an apology of the local ruling class, as is clear from the following declaration of the colonel, as a representative of the rubber barons: "My money is in London, my soul is in France, and to Brazil I offer my respectful patriotism" (*FL,* 73). Last but not least we need to mention the group of the *Seringueiros* in Souza's drama: they represent the thousands of workers who actually extracted the latex and created the wealth of Amazonia in rubber-boom times.

The best résumé of their work, as of the whole debate on the issue of the identity of the "Paris on the Amazon" is — in accordance with the joking and (self-)ironic spirit of Souza's *vaudeville* — one of the "voices of the city." A text spoken by one of the cocottes offers a concise portrait of the region. It is especially conceived for a foreign public. In order to "divulge our progress" beyond the limits of Brazil, the cocotte plans to travel to Paris and there give a lecture, in the famous Salle Pleyel, so that "Europe will be able to learn more about Amazonia." The issue of identity is sharpened by the form and style of the text. Its naiveté is underlined by its linguistic mixture: the inclusion of Portuguese words in grammatically incorrect French (in this translation: incorrect English). A transformation of the text into correct English would destroy its peculiarity. The incorrect use of the language is a parody of intercultural dialogue and a way to draw our attention to educational inequity. The talk of the cocotte is an ironical comment on the limitations of critique, but it does not refrain from focusing on the use of natural resources, of labor and of public money by the holders of power. To make this final quotation more complete, let us imagine — in the spirit of *vaudeville* — that the scene occurs in Paris in the 1920s and that Walter Benjamin is seated in the auditorium — he who made of the prostitute one of the essential categories for understanding the modern metropolis. Listening to the talk of the cocotte from Manaus, especially when she speaks of the "axe" of the *seringueiro* striking the rubber tree in the primeval forest, Benjamin might then be wondering if this is meant to be a postcolonial interrogation of his European modernism. Here is the text:

> The Estade of Amazonas is large an estade as every gents knows. It holds in its boje [big belly] the grand river known as Amazon River, who holds water capable to finish all the dryness of Ceará. Amazonas holds borrache [latex] which is the product of a tree called bourrachier.
>
> To extract the borrache, the cearence [from the State of Ceará] strikes the bourrachier with the axe and then fincs [fixes] a tigelle [bowl] in the buraque [hole]. The borrache flows and falls in the tigelle. At afternoon the cearence comes and pours the tigelles small in the tigelles grand and takes them to his house. When he holds a portion of grand tigelles full, he sells it to the regaton [merchant who navigates on the river] and passes rest of the year to play violin, balancing in his rede [hammock].

Amazonas is very prosperous, but a plague menaces it from time to time, called nerysm [probably a reference to Silvo Nery, governor of the State of Amazonas from 1900 to 1904]. When it attacks, it chupes [sucks] all its money. Away from this, the Estade of Amazonas goes forward. (*FL,* 108–9).

The discourse of the cocotte, with all its naiveté, draws our attention to an important motive of world history: the idea that the source of wealth consists of the "Ausbeutung der Natur" ("exploitation of nature") by humankind. Benjamin criticized this idea as "mörderisch" ("murderous," J75a) — which, however, did not prevent him from seeing the "primeval forest" as the symbol of a *locus horribilis* instead of intact nature. The evolution of capitalism since then has presented certain motifs of the *Passagen-Werk* in an infernal crescendo, insofar as a positive attitude toward the "exploitation of nature" has become alarmingly widespread in our present time. Since the 1960s the axes that hit the rubber trees around 1900 have been replaced by thousands of chain saws cutting the rainforest down. When we look at the present state of primeval forests on our planet, we are told by specialists that the largest one, the Amazonian rain forest, will have been destroyed by approximately 2080.[33] Benjamin's concern that we "not succumb to the horror that beckons from deep in the primeval forest" will then lack its object. The soil will then be cleared, if not of myth and delusion, definitely of the jungle and its undergrowth, in the full sense of the word. What the author of the *Passagen-Werk* intended to do with the soil of the nineteenth century is actually being done with that of the twenty-first century. The primeval forest (*Urwald*) is being cultivated (*urbar* gemacht) and finally being *urbanized*. The civilization of concrete cement is about to take the place of the forest. So — after all, we finally have reached — Paris on the Amazon?! Yes, but in a sense quite different from the dreams of the rubber-boom times. The primeval forest, fortunately, still exists; it is time to dialogue with it and to include it in our reflection about the shaping of our urban civilization.[34]

Notes

1 See also the contribution of Karl Solibakke in this volume.

2 Walter Benjamin, *Passagens,* ed. Willi Bolle, trans. Irene Aron and Cleonice Mourão. (Belo Horizonte and São Paulo: EdUFMG and Imprensa Oficial do Estado de São Paulo, 2006).

3 Michael Werner and Bénédicte Zimmermann, eds., *De la comparaison à l'histoire croisée* (Paris: Seuil, 2004), especially 15–49.

4 Frantz Fanon, *Les damnés de la terre* (1961; repr., Paris: La Découverte, 2002; in English, *The Wretched of the Earth,* trans. Constance Farrington (New York: Grove, 1963).

[5] Edward W. Said, *Orientalism* (London: Penguin, 1978).

[6] Bill Ashcroft, Gareth Griffiths, and Helen Tiffin, *The Empire Writes Back: Theory and Practice in Post-Colonial Literatures* (London and New York: Routledge, 1989).

[7] Homi Bhabha, *The Location of Culture* (London and New York: Routledge, 1994).

[8] Willi Bolle, *Physiognomik der modernen Metropole: Geschichtsdarstellung bei Walter Benjamin* (Cologne, Weimar, and Vienna: Böhlau, 1994).

[9] Rolf J. Goebel, *Benjamin heute: Großstadtdiskurs, Postkolonialität und Flanerie zwischen den Kulturen* (Munich: Iudicium, 2001).

[10] Fritz Fischer, *Griff nach der Weltmacht: Die Kriegszielpolitik des kaiserlichen Deutschland, 1914/18* (Düsseldorf: Droste, 1961).

[11] The unpublished fragment résumés quoted in this essay are located in the Walter Benjamin Archiv of the Stiftung Archiv der Akademie der Künste in Berlin. I thank the Hamburger Stiftung zur Förderung von Wissenschaft und Kultur for permitting me to publish them, and Erdmut Wizisla for his help.

[12] "Kolonialpoesie" is Benjamin's résumé of fragment J78,1.

[13] The résumé of fragment J64a,2 reads "De Maitre als Theoretiker der Kolonialpolitik" ("De Maitre as theoretician of colonial politics").

[14] Cf. Willi Bolle, "Die Metropole als Hypertext: Zur netzhaften Essayistik in Walter Benjamins 'Passagen-Projekt,'" *German Politics and Society* 23, no. 1 (Spring 2005): 88–101.

[15] In this section I elaborate some elements of a multimedia presentation that I made at the Walter Benjamin Festival, "Now: Das Jetzt der Erkennbarkeit; Orte Walter Benjamins in Kultur, Kunst und Wissenschaft," Berlin, 17–22 Oct. 2006.

[16] Eric Hobsbawn, *The Age of Revolution: Europe, 1789–1848* (London: Weidenfeld & Nicolson, 1962).

[17] The text of this section and of the next one is an improved version of a part of my article "Metrópoli & Mega-urbe: histoire croisée," in *Topografías de la modernidad — El pensamiento de Walter Benjamin*, ed. Dominik Finkelde, T. de la Garza, and F. Mancera (Mexico City: UIA-UNAM, 2007), 235–63.

[18] Variant in N1,4: "Aller Boden mußte einmal von der Vernunft urbar gemacht . . . werden" ("Every ground must at some point have been made arable by reason . . .").

[19] Mário de Andrade, *Paulicéia desvairada* (1922), in *Poesias completas*, ed. Diléa Zanotto Manfio (Belo Horizonte and São Paulo: Itatiaia and EdUSP, 1987), 55–115, here 83. Further references to this work are cited in the text using the abbreviation *PD* and the page number. The texts of the Brazilian authors are quoted in my translation, while the notes refer to the originals.

[20] Lucien Lévy-Bruhl, *Les Fonctions mentales dans les sociétés inférieures*, 9th ed. (1910; repr., Paris: Félix Alcan, 1951).

[21] Claude Lévi-Strauss, *La pensée sauvage* (Paris: Plon, 1962).

22 Sigmund Freud, "Das Unbewußte" (1913), in *Gesammelte Werke*, vol. 10 (Frankfurt am Main: S. Fischer, 1991), 263–303, here 294.

23 Walter Benjamin, "Über einige Motive bei Baudelaire," in *GS* I.2:605–53; *SW* 4:313–55.

24 Mário de Andrade, *A Escrava que não é Isaura: Discurso sobre algumas tendências da poesia modernista* (1924), repr., in *Obra imatura* (Belo Horizonte and São Paulo: Itatiaia and Martins, 1980), 195–300, here 252. Further references to this work are cited in the text using the abbreviation *ENI* and the page number. This text, along with the "Prefácio interessantíssimo" of *Paulicéia desvairada* (*PD*, 59–77), is Mário de Andrade's most important theoretical statement on modern urban poetry.

25 Friedrich Nietzsche, *Die Geburt der Tragödie*, in *Werke*, vol. 1, ed. Karl Schlechta (Frankfurt am Main, Berlin, and Vienna: Ullstein, 1972), 48–49.

26 *The Divine Comedy of Dante Alighieri*, trans. Jefferson Butler Fletcher (New York: Macmillan, 1931), 12.

27 Racionais MC's, *Sobrevivendo no Inferno*, CD (Cosa Nostra Fonográfica and Sonopress, Manaus, 2002). The print versions of the songs of this CD and the other two CDs cited below are on the Web site http://racionais-mcs.lyrics-songs.com/.

28 Racionais MC's, *Racionais MC's*, CD (Cosa Nostra Fonográfica and Sonopress, Manaus, undated).

29 Racionais MC's, *Nada como um dia após o outro dia: Chora agora, ri depois* (Nothing like one day after another day: Cry now, laugh later), 2 CDs (Cosa Nostra Fonográfica and Sonopress, Manaus, 2002)

30 Racionais MC's, *Sobrevivendo no Inferno*, CD.

31 Cf. Mike Davis, "Planet of Slums," *New Left Review* 26 (Mar.–Apr., 2004), 5–34.

32 Márcio Souza, *As Folias do Látex* (1976; repr., Manaus: Valer, 2007). Further references to this work are cited in the text using the abbreviation *FL* and the page number.

33 According to a study carried out by the Hadley Centre, analyzed in the 2007 report of the Intergovernmental Panel on Climate Change (www.ipcc.ch), there is a possibility that the Amazonian ecosystem will completely disappear by 2080.

34 I wish to thank John Dawsey (Universidade de São Paulo) for his assistance in revising an earlier draft of this essay.

11: Benjamin's Gender, Sex, and Eros

Dianne Chisholm

PIVOTAL MOVEMENTS OF BENJAMIN'S THOUGHT are modulated by his critical, if convoluted, attention to gender, sex, and Eros. Images of esoteric love, male impotence, mass prostitution, feminine fashion, utopian
lesbianism, and androgyny and hermaphroditism help formulate Benjamin's larger philosophical preoccupations with language, history, technology, metropolitan culture and society, and even with such messianic
matters as awakening and redemption. They appear as recurrent motifs
that evolve over the course of his oeuvre, from the earliest meditations
on Eros and language in "Metaphysik der Jugend" ("The Metaphysics of
Youth," 1913–14) and on modernity's unprecedented transformation
of sex in "Über Liebe und Verwandtes: (Ein europäisches Problem)"
("On Love and Related Matters: [A European Problem]," 1920), to
illuminations on "esoteric love" and "revolutionary discharge" in "Der
Sürrealismus: Die letzte Momentaufnahme der europäischen Intelligenz" ("Surrealism: The Last Snapshot of the European Intelligentsia,"
1929), and to culminating reflections on the allegorical impotence and
"sexual shock" of "Baudelaire's erotology" in the essays and notes on
Baudelaire (1935–39).

Scholars have noted the pervasiveness and importance of Benjamin's
meditative images and motifs of gender, sex, and Eros, but none have
attempted to bring them all together in one constellation. We might speculate as to why not. First, these images are far from simple: the images
of gender are often ambiguously androgynous, while those of sex (the
sexual, corporeal sexuality) and Eros (esoteric love, the spiritually erotic)
are ambiguously interrelated (in pure union or daemonic mixture). Second, the character, function, and context of these images change over the
course of Benjamin's writing. Third, Benjamin often interpolates these
images and motifs into constellations with other, non-gendered, non-
sexual, and non-erotic themes. His critics thus tend to isolate conjunctions between Eros (and/or gender and/or sex) and some other major
theme of thought. Sigrid Weigel, for example, focuses on "Eros and Language," and she offers an instructive "genealogy" of this relation.[1] Chris
Andre considers the evolving conjunction of Eros and historiography in

Benjamin's writing. He identifies the axiomatic turn in Benjamin's historiographical method as occuring in the 1929 essay on "surrealism," where Benjamin discovers Breton's technique of deploying "esoteric love" to resurrect the lost revolutionary ardor of Paris-past in a "profane illumination" of Paris-present. Andre traces Benjamin's appropriation of this technique and its melancholic (*himnerotic*) remaking into what ultimately becomes the optic of dialectical temporality at work in the Baudelaire essays and *Das Passagen-Werk* (*The Arcades Project*).[2] Irving Wohlfarth identifies, in Benjamin's thought-image of "Zum Planetarium" ("To the Planetarium"), a conjunction of Eros and technology, or catechresis, that he tentatively names "technological Eros," and he reads this catachresis in detail in the context of such metaphysicians of the erotic as Freud, Nietzsche, Bataille, Caillois, and Jünger.

While Weigel, Andre, and Wohlfarth consider the conjunctions of Eros in Benjamin's writing, other critics, and Weigel also, consider conjunctions of gender. Weigel analyzes Benjamin's method of thinking in verbal images, and she shows how images of "the feminine" function as a central feature in the course of his development of the dialectical image.[3] Eva Geulen brings out the centrality of gender in Benjamin's writing, and she calls for a "systematic rethinking of Benjamin's primary philosophical concerns, his theory of language and his philosophy of history, his concepts of experience and materiality — all according to the dimension of gender"[4] To initiate a response to her own call, Geulen outlines "a genealogy of gender" in Benjamin's writing. She focuses not on the feminine *per se* but on the ubiquitous hermaphrodite — that is, the hermaphroditic ambiguity and ambiguous hermaphroditism with which Benjamin generally works through such dialectical oppositions as the spiritual and the material, pure language and instrumental language, messianism and historical materialism, as well as the feminine and the masculine, the erotic (the spiritual) and the sexual.

In their pursuit of a materialist theory of sexual modernity, feminist critics tend to focus on images of gender and sexuality in Benjamin's city writing and to overlook his esoteric eroticism. The notable Benjamin scholar Susan Buck-Morss investigates Benjamin's representation of the female prostitute as the allegory of the (human) commodity. She is the first of many to critique Benjamin's regard for the perception and experience of commodity society from the exclusive point of view of the prostitute's client but never from that of the prostitute herself.[5] Buck-Morss does not, however, consider the esoteric role played by the allegorical prostitute in destroying the commodity's phantasmagorical Eros (advertising's illusory erotic aura) and in "awakening" the city-lover to revolutionary history's unfulfilled utopia of social and sexual emancipation. Benjamin's feminist readers are right to charge Benjamin with misogyny for investigating modernity through a masculinist perspective, yet they give their critique a sharpened dialectical edge when they consider how, in his writing, the female prostitute functions as an agent of deconstruction in the context of commodity fetishism and reified sex. By allegorizing the commodity's total and massive devaluation of "the feminine" or "esoteric love," Benjamin's "prostitute" destroys the commodity's primary fantasy-device of conjuring iconic allusions to divine consummation.

With the negative and positive revelatory capabilities of Benjamin's sex/gender images in mind, Christine Buci-Glucksmann discovers, in Benjamin's Baudelaire studies, a "utopia of the feminine" that is at once "catastrophic," "anthropological," and "transgressive." She reads the "catastrophic" dimension of Benjamin's "prostitute" as *the Trauerspiel of the prostitute-body.*[6] The prostitute-body compares, Buci-Glucksmann argues, with the Baroque allegory, in that it incites a crisis of seeing: where God and salvation once were, humanity now is, in all its mortal anguish and unsalvageable wreckage. Fragmented imagistically into sexual parts for sale and consumption, the prostitute-body accentuates the modern crisis of looking (for valuable exchange) to the point of critical self-illumination (and possible redemption). In her analysis of the "anthropological" dimension of the utopia of the feminine, Buci-Glucksmann excavates historical — Saint-Simonian — sources of feminist androgyny, along with cabalistic and other mystic sources of "divine androgyny," that inspired Benjamin's rereading of Baudelaire's "heroic lesbian." But she does not invoke images of "esoteric love" or its conjunction with language in Benjamin's writing. Conversely, Weigel, who does stress the esoteric conjunction of Eros and language, rejects the idea that Benjamin's images of the feminine amount to a theory of the feminine, utopian or otherwise. Instead Weigel urges us to read Benjamin's images of the feminine and female sexuality as aspects of his textuality, or for "the way in which he works with these images, transforms them into dialectical or thought-images."[7]

Some feminist critics approach Benjamin's images of gender and sexuality to clarify the extent of his masculinism and/or misogyny. Rey Chow, for instance, unveils the problematic equation of demasculinization and feminization in Benjamin's writing, where feminization signifies not a specifically feminine enhancement or empowerment but a diminution of male potency.[8] She also considers Benjamin's images of the big-city (male) subject's "love" for the prostitute/commodity-thing, who is decked out in imitation of the fashion mannequin/corpse as an object of misogynous necrophilia. Benjamin's feminist readers are especially annoyed by his exclusively masculine imaging of the *flâneur*. Janet Wolff calls for a reinvestigation of urban modernity through the imagined, if not actually documented, perspective of the *flâneuse*. Some feminist critics scrutinize Benjamin's constellation of the *flâneur* to refine and advance feminist theory developed elsewhere. Miriam Hansen, for instance, discovers useful critical affinities between Benjamin's concept of distracted perception (technologically-mediated urban field-of-vision) and a specific form of female spectatorship in her elaboration of feminist theories of the gaze.[9] Anne Friedberg uses Benjamin to help discover how the *flâneur's* gaze is transformed into the ironic gaze of feminist post-modern cinema through the historic mediation of the female window-shopper, the primary consumer-subject of the *grands magasins*.[10]

Given Benjamin's emphatic imaging of the prostitute/whore with exclusive attention to the shock experience of modernity's urban male, it is not surprising that feminist critics should abandon their attempt to find incipient feminist theory in his writing. It is surprising, however, given Benjamin's entirely *perverse* imaging of gender, sexuality, and Eros, that queer studies critics pay his work little systematic attention.[11] Queer theory primarily refers to Michel Foucault's deconstructive approach to the discursive panopticon and hygienic imaginary of sexual modernity.[12] Benjamin also offers a method of deconstruction — a critical, allegorical, and dialectical method of deconstructing the sexual phantasmagoria of modern mass marketing that keeps the masses spellbound and mystifies prospects for real social/sexual revolution. But unlike Benjamin's method, Foucault's method works without "revolutionary nihilism" and catastrophic images of "esoteric love," which might seem anachronistically obfuscating. Today's queer studies scholars, after witnessing decades of the commercial selling-out of revolutionary (youth, feminist, anti-racist, gay and lesbian) movements, are redolently cynical about "revolution" in any form, even as a redeemable trope from the past. How could they be anything but radically skeptical about the redemptive "awakening" capabilities of the profane illuminations of esoteric love? Queer critics today regard the prospects of cultural and social transformation that are spearheaded by transgender and transsexual experience as far more compelling than the transfiguring capabilities of Benjamin's androgynous angel of history (despite the great success of Tony Kushner's millennial stage play "Angels of America," wherein Benjamin's figure is evoked for contemporary reconsideration).

Bearing in mind the skepticism of feminist and queer critics, this chapter highlights precisely what might warrant further feminist and queer study, as well as new directions in Benjamin scholarship: namely the unexamined *perversity* with which Benjamin images gender, sex, and Eros. My primary conjectures in this chapter are *that* images and motifs of gender, sex, and Eros appear pervasively in Benjamin's thinking and writing, and in conjunction with such arch themes as language, history, and technology; *that* they do so perversely; and *that* it is through the perverse imaging of gender, sex, and Eros in conjunction with larger philosophical themes that Benjamin formulates his critique and vision of modern society and culture.

My purpose is to assemble, for the first time, a constellation or compendium of Benjamin's motifs of gender, sex, and Eros, and to reveal the optic of perversity through which these motifs allow, individually and collectively, the author and his readers to see and see through the phantasmagorias of capitalist modernity. I then proceed to offer prospects and themes for future research, including first, Benjamin's androgyny, hermaphroditism, and transsexualism in conjunction with Magnus Hirschfeld's sexology; second, urban utopia and transsexual architecture; third, the work of sex in the age of mechanical reproducibility; and fourth, ecotechnological eros and the coming community.

A Brief Compendium of Benjamin's Images and Motifs of Gender, Sex, and Eros

Benjamin's images and motifs of gender, sexuality, and Eros are perverse in the following senses:

1. They resist conventional and traditional ideas and representations of procreative or (re)productive heterosexuality; instead, they present variants of non-procreative, non-productive gender, sex, and Eros.

2. They resist conventional and traditional ideas and representations of "natural" and "normal" (masculine and feminine) gender and/ or (male and female) sex, and they present variant combinations of gender and sex (hermaphroditic, androgynous, transsexual) with ambiguous, positive or negative, critical value.

3. They reject the conventional and traditional division of the spiritual (or intellectual) and the sexual, and they unite the spiritual and the sexual in variant — Platonic, Sapphic, courtly, surreal — images of esoteric love; at the same time, they resist the ("demonic" or "Socratic") merging of the spiritual and the sexual; and ultimately, they figure the splitting of *Eros* from *sexus* in modern life as a catastrophic reduction and profanation of esoteric love.

4. They reveal how avant-garde/surrealist technology might induce "body- and image-space" to "interpenetrate" in such a way that the "revolutionary tensions" of the collective (viewing) body are gathered and raised to the point of "revolutionary discharge"; or they image the erotic-nihilistic power of surrealism to penetrate public space and "innervate" the collective body politically to the point of orgasmic insurgency.

5. They privilege "the love of the female for the female" as the image of pure love, *par excellence;* this is just as much the case in Benjamin's earliest, Platonic, writings, as it is in his Baudelaire studies and in the *Passagen-Werk* (*The Arcades Project*, 1927–40),

although the later writings complicate images of lesbianism with historical materialism.

6. They privilege variant images of "male impotence" as emblems of creative resistance to procreative sex and (re)productive society that represent the moral and industrial status quo of the bourgeois market society.

7. Above all, they privilege images of the female prostitute as the primary figure of resistance to natural and normal procreative sex: in "Berliner Chronik" ("A Berlin Chronicle," 1932) the prostitute figures as the mythic "guardian of the threshold" to the existential frontier beyond the domain of bourgeois morality; in the Baudelaire studies and *Das Passagen-Werk* "she" gives the commodity a human face and is the mass-object/-medium through which the lonely big-city dweller can experience "communion with the masses"; she is also the allegory of the commodity that destroys the mythic aura of urban romance by laying bare the exchange value of bourgeois social/sexual relations; moreover, she combines with images of "male impotence" to resist bourgeois (re)productivity.

8. They privilege the uncanny feminine or female in images that, with defamiliarizing ambiguity, embody the living and the dead, and the human and the machine, such as the fashion- model/mannequin/corpse, the girl/automaton/doll, and the prostitute/commodity/thing.

"The perverse" in Benjamin is not so much a category of gender, sex, or Eros as a way of *seeing*, or an attitudinal perspective. Perverse images of gender, sex, and Eros are the media through which Benjamin reimages and rethinks the social and cultural, and not just sexual, changes wrought by modernity. They are imagistic constructions that function as ironic, allegorical, and dialectical representations of the values of modern commodity society. In his later writing, for instance, "the perverse" functions as an allegorical lens through which the dreamer of bourgeois romance — or the everyday consumer of metropolitan society's commodity dream-world — sees the present for what it actually is: that moment of revolutionary modernity wherein social (sexual) revolution has yet to take place but is rendered impotent by the fetish-fantasies of mass culture. Benjamin draws significantly from psychoanalysis's theory of the unconscious, and, with Freudian inspiration, he acknowledges the latent desire that compels the individual and the collective to become perversely enamored with the commodity's fetish-fantasies. As he perversely reimages (or imagistically re-perverts) them, these fetish-fantasies stand in for the lost object of revolution and beguile modern dreamers with ever heightened illusion (the phantasmagoria of revolutionary fashion) and massive disappointment (cultural melancholia).

Benjamin's "perverse" might be most closely associated with Freud's "uncanny," as a category of unnerving perception and experience. Yet it shares little correspondence with Freud's theories and categories of sexuality. Since Benjamin's perverse images of gender, sex, and Eros function as (or in) "thought-images" or "dialectical images" that rethink and resist contemporary idealizations of things-most-valued, things-worthy-of-love, they should be regarded as critical devices through which to scrutinize sexual, cultural, and social modernity. Freud, on the other hand, delineates sexual categories in an attempt to define human sexuality discursively and thus to institute a new medical-scientific scheme for organizing contemporary clinical and metapsychological understanding of sexual phenomenology. Consequently, Benjamin's "perverse" but not Freud's "sexuality" (nor, for that matter, any Victorian sexology) escapes Foucault's critique of the discursive hypostatization and regimentation of sexuality, since Benjamin (unlike Freud and the sexologists) uses, or demonstrates the use of, language to trouble reified (bourgeois) sexuality. Both Freud and Benjamin understand "perverse sexuality" as any sexuality that does not aim at and result in conjugal and procreative heterosexuality, and while Freud regards homosexuality as perverse but non-pathological, Benjamin perversely ascribes to lesbianism a "heroic" resistance to instrumentalized Eros (compulsory heterosexual love and procreation). Moreover, Benjamin, but not Freud, characterizes anthropological modernity as universally perverse, despite humankind's deluded, if eternal, belief in and overvaluation of the naturalness and normalcy of procreative heterosexuality and heterosexual love.

The images of hermaphroditism that punctuate Benjamin's thinking on how modernity transforms (and transsexualizes) relations between the sexes may receive some inspiration from Freud's theory that adult sexuality derives from an embryonic bisexuality. Benjamin, however, mostly draws his hermaphrodite from symbolic, poetic, mystic, cabalistic, utopian, and other sources in esoteric literature and not from scientific literature that tends to ascribe hermaphroditism to organic, genetic, and psycho-somatic causes. Despite his express fascination with transvestism and transsexuality — as, for instance, in his childhood recollection of a female "prostitute in a very tight-fitting white sailor's suit"[13] — Benjamin indicates no familiarity with groundbreaking research on "sexual intermediaries" conducted by his contemporary and fellow Berliner, Magnus Hirschfeld. It becomes the task of another Benjamin — Harry Benjamin, Hirschfeld's student — to develop and popularize the medical etiology and social recognition of "transsexualism." Benjamin (Walter) demonstrates little interest in the medical-juridical concept and treatment of transsexualism, though the recurrence of transsexual images in his writing invites one to read him in the context of modern sexology to at least understand how Benjamin's writing creatively, critically, and perversely, *diverges* from sexual science.

Benjamin also images libidinal economy as perversely non-productive or as having the potency to strike and thus delay, divert, or destroy (the pace and means of) bourgeois productivity. "Strike and standstill are conceived [in Benjamin's figure of the labor-strike] as 'Vollzug' or consummation, which returns an unexpected potency to impotence," Geulen observes, "indicating that Benjamin's complex sexual economy travels along rather strange paths."[14] We might say that Benjamin's images of sexual economy, and of gender, sex, and Eros, in general, are *queerly* strange. That is, they are queer in the sense that they resist and distort normative representations of love and sexuality, of sex and gender differences. Moreover, they are *strangely* queer in the sense that Benjamin develops their figurative tactics of resistance without reference to or alliance with any minority sexuality movements of the day. In fact, Benjamin's images are perversely asexual and/or esoteric and share little camaraderie with the emerging self-stylizations of the gays, lesbians, bisexuals, transvestites, transsexuals, prostitutes, and dandies with whom he shared an ambiguous love of big-city life. Perhaps this is why few queer studies scholars read queer urban history and literature in light of Benjamin. The last section of this chapter will, however, indicate the implications of Benjamin's "perverse" for queer studies research.

The rest of this section offers a short compendium of Benjamin's perverse images and motifs of gender, sex, and Eros. This compendium, which is neither comprehensive nor exhaustive, is organized in clusters of images and motifs under the rubrics of "esoteric love," "technological eros," "male impotence," "the prostitute," "Baudelaire's erotology," "lesbianism," "homosexuality," "dolls/uncanny Eros," and "hermaphroditism/androgyny/transexualism."

Esoteric Love

Benjamin reflects on modern Eros first in idealist, then surrealist, and, ultimately, in materialist terms with a respective emphasis on emblem, apostrophe, and allegory. In "Metaphysik der Jugend" he speculates on the nature of love and language by imaging "the conversation" between Sappho and her women friends. In this thought-image, Sapphic love is an emblem of esoteric eroticism that transcends natural, procreative love. At the same time, the silent language used in Sapphic communion is emblematic of pure language that transcends the instrumentality or seductiveness of communicative speech. Sapphic language does not just compare to Sapphic love with its non-procreative, non-instrumental purity. Sapphic language and Sapphic love are *united*. The spiritual (mental) and the erotic (bodily) *commune* in Sapphic conversation, where "greatness" finds its expression in "silence" (*SW* 1:10). Sapphic love/language should not be mistaken for a women's language (*SW* 1:9). Only men trust in communicative language and public speaking. Women possess no such trust, and when they speak they only prattle. In Platonic terms, women's language (prattle) is a shadow of a shadow (men's public speech, instrumental communication). Alternatively, Sappho's silent conversation embodies pure language in emblematic communion.

Benjamin reiterates this Sapphic rendering of esoteric love in "Sokrates," where "die tiefste, die herrlichste und erotisch und mythisch höchst vollendete, ja fast strahlende (wenn sie nicht so ganz nächtig wäre) die weib-weibliche ist" (*GS* II.1:130; "the most profound, the most splendid, and the most erotically and mythically perfect, indeed even if the most radiant (if it were not so totally of the night), is the love of the female for the female," *SW* 1:53). Benjamin does not develop his thought on esoteric love until "Surrealism," where he reimages it without the emblematic aura of Sapphism. In "Surrealism," esoteric love appears in the figure of Nadja, the muse-medium through whom André Breton conducts his peripatetic "profane illuminations" about post-revolutionary Paris. According to Benjamin, "she" is less the actual, misfortunate street-walker after whom Breton names his novel and who guides him through familiar streets in a charismatic, defamiliarizing light, than she is an anachronistic invocation of the courtly lady. Breton beholds "esoteric love" as an *apostrophe* to the ideal feminine, whose last incarnation was the beloved of troubadourial fantasy and whose absence in modern times Breton revives with surrealist devices of unconscious projection.

Breton's auspicious liaison with Nadja in their walks about Paris places him in a waking dream wherein repressed and forgotten passions of revolutionary history are illuminated by the aura of esoteric love. "Die Dame ist in der esoterischen Liebe das Unwesentlichste" ("The lady, in esoteric love, matters least") Benjamin writes, "So auch bei Breton. Er ist mehr den Dingen nahe, denen Nadja nahe ist, als ihr selber" (*GS* II.1:299; "So, too, for Breton. He is closer to the things that Nadja is close to than to her," *SW* 2:210). The "things" that Nadja is close to are derelict hotels, cafés, and other public spaces, which, in the uncanny and defamiliarizing light of esoteric love, reveal the unfulfilled consummation of utopian design in epiphanies of "revolutionary nihilism." This apostrophe to esoteric love with its effective "profane illumination" is, according to Benjamin, what a truly revolutionary surrealism aims to produce, and, according to Chris Andre, it is the prototype of historical materialism's dialectical image.[15] In close association with "Nadja" and the haunts of Paris, we might recall the "Asja Lacis Street" in the epigram to *Einbahnstraße* (1928). "Asja Lacis Street" is the essay's other name, which derives from "der die sie / als Ingenieur / im Autor durchbrochen hat" (*GS* IV.1:83; "her who / as an engineer / cut it through the author," *SW* 1:444) — namely, the Latvian revolutionary who was Benjamin's greatest (disappointment in) love. Like "Nadja," "Asja Lacis" names that esoteric love in whose aura the somnolent streets of modernity are illuminated with awakening insights that cut through the urban consciousness of male genius with catastrophic revelation.

Benjamin's last rethinking and reimaging of esoteric love appears in the dialectical image of "love at last sight," as part of his investigations of "Baudelaire's erotology."[16] "Love at last sight" is how esoteric love appears and functions in commodity space decades before that space is interpenetrated by the body- and image-space of revolutionary surrealism. Here the beloved is not the uniquely charismatic Nadja/Asja. "She" is a stranger and a street-walker, or, in any case, an anonymous female passerby who the crowd presents to the lonely man as he drifts around the city and is everywhere beckoned by commodity spectacles. She seduces his attention with her fashionable attire and grace, though she sees him no more than does a fashion model or a storefront mannequin. She has eyes only for fashion, or, like the mannequin/mass-object she imitates, her eyes are like mirrors that do not return but merely reflect his gaze, in a shocking eidetic reduction of hoped-for erotic communion to profane sexual desire. In "love at last sight" we see the total negation of the Sapphic conversation and its silent communion of Eros and language. Instead of bodies and minds caressing one another, disembodied mannequin mirror-eyes turn Eros into stone. "Love at last sight" is an allegory of the decay of esoteric love; it functions only critically, not to invoke ideal love, but to disenchant.

Technological Eros

The last thought-image of *Einbahnstraße*, "Zum Planetarium," presents a constellation of images that evokes what Irving Wohlfarth suggests we regard as a "technological Eros."[17] In this constellation, the spectacle of the First World War is negatively illumined against a radiant antiquity when nature-wooing mankind entertained an ecstatic communal rapport with the cosmos. At the same time, the spectacle of the First World War is negatively illumined against a utopian future when the proletariat will have remastered technology so as to afford humanity a new (pro)creative intercourse with nature (*SW* 1:486–87). This new (pro)creative intercourse with nature foresees not just technological mastery of nature as the imperialists would have it but, above all, political mastery of the relation between nature and man. "Zum Planetarium" advances the idea of a technology that is attuned to the cosmos both more closely and more distantly (with the perfect esoteric balance of closeness to and distance from the Beloved/Other) than previous attempts to commune with or control nature. By cultivating a new "technological eros," humankind replaces imperialism's technological "Taumel der Vernichtung" ("frenzy of destruction"), like that of the First World War, which turned "das

Brautlager in ein Blutmeer" ("the bridal bed into a blood bath") with the "Rausche der Zeugung" (*GS* IV.1:147–48; "ecstasy of procreation," *SW* 1:486–87). Here "procreation" (or pro-creation) refers to the creative intercourse of humankind and nature that a proletarian-mastered technology might conduct. The result would not be the reproduction of the same (anthropological species) but the birth of new, post-human man (*Urmensch*). As such, it is a *perverse* procreation that destroys/dismantles and replaces the Earth-ravaging machine of technological imperialism, in ecstatic techno-communion with the cosmos.

Male Impotence

Images and motifs of male impotence punctuate Benjamin's writing, starting with the appearance in "Sokrates" of the "männlich[e] Genius" ("male genius") who, in the presence of "des Weiblichen" ("the feminine") is creative but not conceptive and who is marked by "Empfängnis ohne Schwangerschaft" (*GS* II.1:131; "conception without pregnancy," *SW* 1:53). Such idealized impotence evolves, and also devolves, in the 1930s into various critical appearances, such as the satirical image of "Hitlers herabgeminderte Männlichkeit" (*GS* VI:103–4; "Hitler's Diminished Masculinity," *SW* 2:792–93), or the misogynous counterimage in the section "Nach der Vollendung" ("After Completion") of "Kleine Kunst-Stücke" (*GS* IV.1:438; "Little Tricks of the Trade," *SW* 2:730), written in 1928, which sets the "männliche Erstgeborene des Werkes" ("male first-born of his work)" well above and apart from procreative female sexuality. "Berliner Chronik" and "Berliner Kindheit um neunzehnhundert" feature images of "impotence before the city" that, though they do not refer to sexual impotence per se, do embody Benjamin's fascination with and fear of accosting prostitutes — those guardians of the threshold who signify ambiguously both the erotic frontier beyond the domain of the bourgeois family and the existential nothingness of reified sexuality.[18] Images of "impotence before the city" are also associated with the *flâneur's* fruitless philandering and wayward genius for getting lost or straying from appointed destinations. It is, however, in the later writing on Baudelaire that the most complex images of male impotence appear. Benjamin's "Baudelaire" reincarnates the creative impotence of male genius, along with Breton's "esoteric love" and recollections of Benjamin's own "impotence before the city." Baudelaire is the city poet whose only love is a prostitute — the beloved-without-aura — in whom the poet recognizes himself (as fallen laureate and kindred streetwalker) and through whom he empathizes with the commodity.

Male impotence amounts to a leitmotif in Benjamin's writing and thus merits more detailed review. To begin with, in "Socrates," the Platonic genius is clearly distinguished from the demonic Socrates, whose pedagogical method is "a mere means to compel conversation" ("ein bloßes Mittel zur Erzwingung der Rede") between himself and his homosexual initiates into conceiving what is foreknown. For Socrates, "geht der Wissende mit dem Wissen schwanger" ("the knower is pregnant with knowledge"). Thus "die sokratische Frage ist nicht zart und so sehr schöpferisch als empfangend, nicht geniushaft. Sie ist . . . eine Erektion des Wissens" ("the Socratic question is neither tender nor so much creative as it is conceptive; it is not genius-like. . . . It is an erection of knowledge"). Socratic love embodies the "furchtbar[e] Herrschaft sexueller Anschauungen im Geistigen" ("terrible domination of sexual views in the spiritual"). Moreover, "Same und Frucht, Zeugung und Geburt nennt seine sympotische Rede in dämonischer Ununterschiedenheit" ("Socrates' talk in the *Symposium* refers to seed and fruit, procreation and birth, in daemonic indistinguishability"). In contrast, genius is "der Zeuge jeder wirklich geistigen Schöpfung" ("the witness to every truly spiritual creation") which is "geschlechtslos und doch von überweltlichem Geschlechte" ("asexual and yet of supramundane sexuality"). If "Sokrates preist . . . die Liebe zwischen Männern und Jünglingen und rühmt sie als das Medium des schöpferischen Geistes" ("Socrates praises the love between men and youths and lauds it as the medium of the creative spirit"), genius lives through the existence of the feminine, which "verbürgt die Geschlechtslosigkeit des Geistigen in der Welt" ("guarantees the asexuality of the spiritual in the world"), for, "wie für das Weib unbefleckte Empfängnis die überschwengliche Idee von Reinheit ist, so ist Empfängnis ohne Schwangerschaft am tiefsten das Geisteszeichen des männlichen Genius" ("just as immaculate conception is, for the woman, the rapturous notion of purity, so conception without pregnancy is most profoundly the spiritual mark of the male genius" (*GS* II.1:130–31; *SW* 1:52–54).

"Male genius" is impotent before the feminine (or the Beloved), who personifies the mystery of the unity of the erotic and the sexual. Socratic love penetrates metaphysical mysteries with a demon desire that forces its dialogue with his philosophical male initiates to conceive uncreatively or to reproduce knowledge foreknown; whereas Platonic love inspires genius to pose (to the feminine/beloved — the Other of/with whom knowledge is sought) "die heilige Frage, die auf Antwort wartet und deren Resonanz erneut in der Antwort wieder auflebt" (*GS* II.1:131; "the holy question which awaits an answer and whose echo sounds in the response," *SW* 1:53). Genius engages conversation without anticipating or arriving at conception (the foreclosure of knowledge), yet creatively re-conceives the question that is born in the answer. Genius engages language in creative conversation in the spirit of pure love, with no preconceptions or foreknowledge in mind. To put it another way, the genius of Platonic love is fruitfully impotent, just as the communion of Sapphic love is inconceivably sexual.

In "Über Liebe und Verwandtes," Benjamin speculates on the trans-formation of love in modernity and on how contemporary male genius might recognize love in such confusing times. In this context, what constitutes male impotence is the loss of "historischen Formen" ("histori-cal forms," such as Platonic love, courtly love), with which the creative man can perceive the *supernatural* unity of the erotic and the sexual in "the feminine," and see through the newly fabricated appearances of modern woman. Since these forms are long since "abgestorben" ("have withered and died"), "unfähig wie nur je scheint der europäische Mann jener Einheit des weiblichen Wesens gegenüberzustehen" (*GS* VI:72–73; "European man is as incapable as ever of confronting that unity in woman," *SW* 1:229–30). This historic incapability is compounded by the fact that "that unity in woman" is now concealed in modern fashion, which, however ephemeral, has induced revolutionary change in the eternal nature of love between the sexes. Modern fashion demo-niacally dresses "that unity in woman" to appear "natural" (as though radiating from the female body itself) only to repel the discerning man with a sense of the grotesquely "unnatural." Accenting the contours of the female body, fashion's hyperbolic sexuality radiates more powerfully than the aura of Eros. In the face of such demoniacal concealment of the spiritual, man is ever more impotent and desiring. To penetrate the mystery of the unity of the erotic and sexual inspired by the veil of com-modity fetishism, he must become like her; he must undergo a "fast planmäßige Metamorphose . . . der männlichen Sexualität in die weibli-che durch den Durchgang durch das Medium des Geistes" (*GS* VI:73; "almost planned metamorphosis of masculine sexuality into feminine sexuality through the medium of the mind," *SW* 1:231). The impotence of male genius is, thus, itself transformed in response to revolutionary fashion's transformation of the eternal feminine. Male genius transsexu-alizes. Only by mentally metamorphosing into the female of urban fash-ion does genius recognize the spirit in which the unity of the erotic and the sexual is fabricated.

Ultimately, it is the image of Baudelaire that assembles the various motifs of male impotence into a constellation of profane, erotic illumi-nation. Baudelaire personifies the male genius who spends his creative impotence on consorting with a prostitute in whom he sees himself, and who, as her *semblable,* empathizes with the commodity. As Benjamin sees her, the prostitute in mass society is twice fallen: first, as a woman who sells her sex for money, and second, as a soul whose social, moral, and spiritual value is reduced to an abstract (bloodless and spiritless) rate of exchange. As a poet, Baudelaire embodies the impossible task of redeem-ing her value in verse that sells. His solution is to join her on the streets and to illumine the world that she traffics. With her eyes, he images the commodity with a human face, and, with his images, he both enchants

and disenchants those other *semblables,* the reader-consumers of his pros-
tituted verse, with the inhumaness of commodity society.

The Prostitute

Another leitmotif of sex is comprised of variant images of the prostitute. Since more critical attention has been paid to Benjamin's prostitute than to his other images of gender, sex, and Eros, coverage here is
brief. From "Metaphysik der Jugend" to the Baudelaire studies, Benjamin images the (female) prostitute in ambiguous alliance with (male)
genius/impotence against the sexual status quo that is brokered by
bourgeois morality and represented by reproductive heterosexuality and
traditional family values.[19] He also images the prostitute to figure his
ambivalence toward the kind of sexual liberation that mass prostitution
affords. She is the "guardian of the threshold" that leads, on the one
hand, to erotic utopia and, on the other, to the void of Eros that trade
in sex guarantees. Benjamin invests the ambiguity and ambivalence of
these images with increasing tension and complexity in the context of
his studies of nineteenth-century Paris. Here the prostitute is not only
the city-dweller and streetwalker *par excellence;* she is also the primary
vehicle of traffic in commodified femininity and (female) sexuality. She
signifies the ultimate embodiment of the usurpation of use value (the
use of sex for the consummation of erotic desire, for procreation) by
exchange value (the cost of sex at a competitive rate).

What Benjamin values most about the prostitute is the shocking
revelation that she presents to Baudelaire, namely that, as he writes in
"Zentralpark" ("Central Park," 1938–39) she is the "Triumph der Allegorie" (*GS* I.2:667; "triumph of allegory," *SW* 4:170) over every classic
and romantic symbol of love that the market has appropriated for its commercial phantasmagoria. Through Baudelaire, Benjamin observes that in
big-city prostitution, the woman herself becomes a "Massenartikel" (*GS*
I.2:686; "mass-produced article," *SW* 4:188). This means that one finds
prostitutes in big cities not only *en masse* but also dressed and circulating
as mass-objects, as human commodities. The big-city prostitute destroys
any semblance of spiritual value by laying bare the monetary meaning of
all social exchange, and by exposing the erotic façade of sexual relations.
She allegorizes the prostitution that every city-goer undertakes when she
or he sells her labor on the mass market, just as she allegorizes the commodification of labor when labor sells out human creativity to sterile,
mechanical reproducibility and priceless work to standardized cost. Benjamin ascribes formidable critical power not to the actual prostitute but to
the allegory of modernity that she presents to (Baudelaire's) genius. The
allegorical triumph that she poses could only appeal to the male genius who
perversely cherishes his impotence (against the procreation of bourgeois

family and bourgeois literary productivity), and who descends into the hell of big-city life with a passion that is satanic and splenetic.

"Baudelaire's Erotology," or "love at last sight"

Benjamin investigates the "Erotologie von Baudelaire" (*GS* I.2:663; "Baudelaire's erotology," *SW* 4:167) in a cluster of images that appear in the Baudelaire essays, and in convolute J of *Das Passagen-Werk* as well as in "Zentralpark." In this cluster we find allegories of prostitution, images of heroic and damned lesbianism, and revelations of male impotence. Of these, Benjamin highlights one that most critically illumines modernity's perception and experience of Eros, namely: that of "love at last sight" or "sexual shock" (*SW* 4:323). The image appears in conjunction with Benjamin's analysis of the sonnet "A une passante" in "The Flâneur" and, later, in "Über einige Motive in Baudelaire" (briefly discussed above under "Esoteric Love" and summarily reviewed here). In this analysis Baudelaire occupies the subjective position of the man whose gaze is momentarily aroused by a woman passerby whom the crowd's animation brings to his attention. She attracts his erotic contemplation with her fashionable appearance. Yet the possibility of love that she so elegantly and strikingly poses literally passes him by. Her eyes, like those of the fashion mannequin, are blank mirrors that do not return his gaze and reflect merely the commodity enchantment of the consumer crowd. The woman's capacity to look (in a communion of eyes) is severed from the market gaze to which her attractiveness appeals. Before this gaze the poet experiences a profane and mortifying seduction, and he is traumatized by "sexual shock." His symptoms express a suffering that could only befall genius, since only genius perceives the severance of "Eros" from "sexus" and the catastrophic splitting of what was once spiritually united.

Lesbianism

Images of lesbianism appear in Benjamin's earliest writings and do not appear again until his later writing. Sapphic love figures emblematically as the highest form of Platonic love in "Metaphysik der Jugend" and in "Sokrates" (see "Esoteric Love" above). In these essays, Sappho and her women-friends commune wordlessly and erotically, in body and in spirit, without the demonic (Socratic) mix of the erotic and the sexual. Against the image of Sapphic "conversation" and its positive idealization of the non-procreative conjunction of *Eros* and language, Benjamin images the dialogue between genius and prostitute and its negative idealization of the conjunction of *sex* and language. The dialogue (which is really two monologues) is that medium in which genius and prostitute meet, in bodies and in words, to *not* engender (children, concepts) and to *negate* reproductive sexuality, maternity, and motherhood (*GS* II.1:94; *SW* 1:8–9).

Sapphic emblems of "pure love" reappear much later and only in convolute S "Malerei, Jugendstil, Neuheit" ("Painting, Jugendstil, Novelty") of *Das Passagen-Werk*, where, accordingly, "Die lesbische Liebe trägt die Vergeistigung bis in den weiblichen Schoß vor. Dort pflanzt sie das Lilienbanner der 'reinen Liebe' auf, die keine Schwangerschaft und keine Familie kennt" ("lesbian love carries spiritualization forward into the very womb of woman. There it raises its lily-banner of 'pure love,' which knows no pregnancy and no family," S8a,3). Jugendstil painting raises the "banner" of lesbianism's purely ornamental eroticism in perverse resistance to technological modernity's industrial and commercial (re)production. The apotheosis of figurative lesbianism in literary modernism is the lesbian of Baudelaire's verse. In "Das Paris des Second Empire bei Baudelaire" ("The Paris of the Second Empire in Baudelaire"), Benjamin confirms that "Die Lesbierin ist die Heroine der modernité" (*GS* I.2:594; "the lesbian is the heroine of *la modernité*," *SW* 4:56), because she reincarnates a classical idea of Eros in an age whose greatness is on the cusp of passing into spiritual and aesthetic decay (*SW* 4:55–56). Yet Baudelaire's lesbian is *paradoxically* heroic: on the one hand, she is an avatar of Greek antiquity's "Hippolyte," Queen of the Amazons; on the other, she is modernism's scandalous, overly-sexualized female (*femme damnée*) whose lust escapes the restraining institutions of marriage and maternity and exudes something unnaturally natural (animal) (*SW* 4:57–58).

Benjamin recognizes that Baudelaire had no knowledge of and no sympathy for actual lesbians, and that his lesbian sources were exclusively literary and reductively sexual (*SW* 4:58) He counters Baudelaire's ignorance of lesbian material and historical reality by tracing extra-literary sources of lesbianism in utopian socialism, thus giving a social and political complexity to its image. He points to Saint-Simonianism, and recovers from Claire Demar's manifesto *Ma loi d'avenir* (My Law with a Future) relevant passages that urge women to free themselves from men and motherhood and fulfill their own creativity. He cites the confession of an unnamed female adherent of Saint-Simon's doctrine, who declares her love for her fellow woman alongside her equal, if different, passion and reverence for her fellow man. Furthermore, Benjamin regards the emergence of the modern lesbian in association with women's entry, for the first time, into the production process outside the home and with the masculinizing tendency of factory work and "höhere[n] Formen der Produktion, auch de[m] politisch[en] Kampf als solche[m]" ("higher forms of production, as well as the political struggle per se"). He views the "Vesuviennes movement" that "stellte der Februarrevolution ein Corps, das sich aus Frauen zusammensetzte" (*GS* I.2:597; "supplied the February Revolution with a corps composed of women," *SW* 4:58) as a material consequence of the industrial transformation of "weiblichen Habitus" ("the feminine habitus"). But while Benjamin compounds the heroic image of Baudelaire's singularly sexual lesbian with social, political, and economic depth, he offers no systematic analysis of how utopian socialist feminism or revolutionary lesbian-feminism may have changed the "feminine habitus."

Homosexuality

Images of male homosexuality appear occasionally in Benjamin's writing, but he does not develop them significantly, and they do not amount to a major theme. Benjamin's most elaborate image of homosexuality appears in "Socrates." Here the love of the female for the female is the ideal emblem of Platonic love, whereas Socratic love is monstrous and daemonic. "Same und Frucht, Zeugung und Geburt nennt seine sympotische Rede in dämonischer Ununterschiedenheit, und stellt im Redner selbst die fürchterliche Mischung vor: Kastrat und Faun" (*GS* II.1:131; "Socrates' talk in the *Symposium* refers to seed and fruit, procreation and birth, in daemonic indistinguishability and presents in the speaker himself the terrible mixture of castrato and faun," *SW* 1:54). Accordingly, "Sokrates preist . . . die Liebe zwischen Männern und Jünglingen und rühmt sie als das Medium des schöpferischen Geistes" (*GS* II.1:131; "Socrates praises the love between men and youths and lauds it as the medium of the creative spirit," *SW* 1:53) and yet, his pedagogical method is coercive: "Durch Haß und Begierde verfolgt er das Eidos und sucht es objektiv zu machen" (*GS* II.1:131; "through hatred and desire, Socrates pursues the *eidos* and attempts to make it objective," *SW* 1:53–54). Benjamin concludes: "In Wahrheit ein Nicht-Menschlicher ist Sokrates, und unmenschlich . . . geht seine Rede über den Eros" (*GS* II.1:131; "In truth, Socrates is a nonhuman, and his discussion of eros is inhumane," *SW* 1:54). Socratic love registers lowest "in der Stufenfolge der Erotik" (*GS* II.1:131; "in the hierarchy of the erotic," SW 1:54).

Sigrid Weigel observes that "it is striking that Benjamin did not, after the caricature of 'Socrates,' devote any systematic attention to male homosexuality."[20] She discovers only two further, marginal, mentions: "in the Proust essay, or, for example, in a short note written in Siena that might be assigned to the motif of the "Eros of distance":[21] "Der Ritus lehrt: die Kirche hat sich nicht durch Überwindung der mann-weiblichen Liebe sondern der homosexuellen aufgebaut. Daß der Priester nicht mit dem Chorknaben schläft — das ist das Wunder der Messe. Dom von Siena 28 Juli 1929" (*GS* VI:204; "The rite teaches us: the Church did not develop on the basis of overcoming male-female love but homosexual love. That the priest does not sleep with the choirboy: that is the miracle of the Mass [Siena Cathedral 28 July 1929]"). Benjamin does, in fact, make another and more extensive mention of homosexuality in a passage of his "Paris Diary" (1930). In this passage he describes his visit to a gay bathhouse, ostensibly to visit the manager, who was an acquaintance of Proust's. He is particularly attentive to the outward appearance of the bathhouse, and of the "erstaunlich schöne Jungen" ("astoundingly beautiful boys"), and he appears to perversely approve of the charming aura of respectable bourgeois family (or boarding school) life with which they masquerade the offensive scenes that take place. At the threshold between charming aura and sexual reality stands the "Ladentisch oder d[ie] Kasse" ("counter, or the till"), where one buys "Badekarten" ("tickets to the baths") and gains entrance to the theater of vice. The descriptive tone of this passage expresses Benjamin's ambivalent fascination with baths' phantasmagoria of subversion and their transsexualizing and dehumanizing transformation of boys into consumable "nuttigen Puppen" (*GS* IV.1:576–77; "tarty dolls," *SW* :344).

Dolls/Uncanny Eros

Images of the doll abound throughout *The Passagen-Werk,* most notably in convolutes A, "Passagen, magasins de nouveauté‹s›, calicots" ("Arcades, *Magasins de Nouveauté,* Sales Clerks"), B, "Mode" ("Fashion"), L, "Traumhaus, Museum, Brunnenhalle" ("Dream House, Museum, Spa"), and Z, "die Puppe, der Automat" ("The Doll, The Automaton"). These images are exclusively feminine, including the little girl's toy doll, the fashion mannequin — whole and partitioned into breasts and legs, and the mechanized feminized automaton or "woman-machine." Of these, images of the fashion mannequin figure most prominently. She is the uncanny assemblage of woman-corpse, woman-machine, woman-commodity, and woman-thing. Fashion mannequins are "die wahren Feen dieser Passagen" ("the true fairies of these arcades," Z1,2) and they enchant the living with the fashionable charm and sartorial allure of the unliving. In the society of the spectacle, the natural female body is dressed in the mannequin's unnatural femininity, whose erotic, sexual, and commercial appeal becomes the model of self-fashioning for female consumers of all classes — for bourgeois women, sales women, and prostitutes alike. What disturbs and fascinates Benjamin most about the mannequin is the phantasmagorical magic with which this prop of visual advertising spellbinds female window-shoppers into seeing and transforming themselves into living dolls geared to dress in poses and apparel that contort the body's organic integrity while accentuating its sexual anatomy. Modernity's woman of fashion is mesmerized into collaborating with the commodity market; she suffers her living body to be made over in conformity with the mannequin's virtual body, like a well-dressed corpse.

As Benjamin notes, new modes of fashion dictate the sexual exhibition of the female body for public consumption. In this arena of women's sexual objectification, as he cites it, mannequins serve as the mass props of consumer persuasion. Lined up in every store window, they solicit the gaze of the individual consumer in overwhelming crowds. The woman who dresses in accord with the mannequins' seductive instruction is recruited into an imaginary sorority of greatest desirability; she joins ranks with the urban masses and embodies their commitment not to revolutionary politics but to fashion revolution. Fashioning herself in this way, the woman consumer conceivably enjoys a communion with the masses not unlike the male client whose communion with the masses is mediated by the fashionably attired prostitute.

Hermaphroditism, Androgyny, and Transsexualism

Images of ambiguous gender and sex appear more frequently in Benjamin's writing than those of straight femininity and masculinity. For example, the lesbian woman of his Baudelaire studies is, in terms of gender, a mannish woman. The demon (Socrates) is at once effeminate "castrato" and phallic "faun." Images of male impotence signify not just a diminished masculinity but a transgendering of the masculine into the feminine — as in the case of Baudelaire, who sees himself in the woman prostitute and who makes his career on the streets as a boulevard poet and street-walker. Genius may be the spirit of masculine sexuality in Platonic love, but in the context of modernity it undergoes a sex change, for only by changing into feminine sexuality can modern genius perceive the spiritual nature of the erotic that the sexual exhibition of modern feminine fashion conceals (or makes seem unnaturally natural). Since it takes masculine genius to know the spirituality of the unity of the erotic and the sexual, and since the feminine is the existential embodiment of this unity, love's revelation must then be androgynous. This is the case whether the love that is revealed is Platonic or modern. If modern then masculine genius must undergo a mental sex change to see the spiritual through the profane sexuality of feminine fashion, and love's revelation is ambiguously en-gendered as transsexual.

In any case, the mix of feminine and masculine attributes in Benjamin's images of androgyny and hermaphroditism is itself ambiguously positive and negative. "Socrates" signifies a negative, demonic hermaphroditism. Likewise, "Baudelaire" signifies a negative, "satanic" transsexualism (in his descent into the female prostitute's body- and image-space). Yet Klee's angel in Benjamin's "Über den Begriff der Geschichte" ("On the Concept of History," 1940)[22] signifies the "divine androgyny" of messianic redemption. Benjamin's androgynous angel, like the androgynous, utopian architecture of Saint-Simonianism, foresees a post-historical unity of the masculine and the feminine, of the creative and the procreative, in the wake of modernity's obsession with catastrophic progress.

Themes for Further Study

Although Benjamin does not outline an incipient *theory* of gender and sexuality, his usefulness for future research in feminist and queer studies should not be dismissed. Conversely, Benjamin scholarship has far from exhausted inquiry into the significance of the prevalence of images and motifs of gender, sex, and Eros in Benjamin's writing, and it has yet to consider that prevalence in the context of contemporary sexology and the history of sexuality. How does Benjamin's imaging of gender, sex, and Eros subvert the panoptic discourse of sex, and with what implications for social/sexual emancipation? Should Benjamin's motifs of gender, sex, and Eros be thought of as "avant-garde" in their own right and not just as critical reflections on surrealist sexualities? If Benjamin's images and motifs of gender, sex, and Eros indicate a "strange" libidinal economy and a general tendency toward illuminating "the perverse," at the same time as they fail to reflect any political or cultural liaison with any sexual liberation movements of the day, then what social meaning can we give this peculiar form of queerness? What new branch of queer studies does Benjamin's "perverse" suggest? These are questions that remain to be asked with systematic research.

The future of Benjamin-inflected research in feminist and queer studies, as well as the future of sexuality-oriented Benjamin scholarship, might begin with the pervasively "perverse" in Benjamin's writing. The pervasiveness of perverse images of gender, sex, and Eros in Benjamin's writings warrants further research by Benjamin scholars into Benjamin's critical (if only negative) relation to the sexology of his day and to the erotic (bohemian, queer) communities of Berlin and Paris on whose margins he conducted his *flâneries*. Susan Buck-Morss has astutely reconstructed the actual route of Benjamin's dilatory *flâneries* to and from the Bibliothèque Nationale. We might also consider how Benjamin's *flâneur*-writing invents and deploys a queer technique of cruising the city of sexual modernity. Then again, Benjamin's pervasively "perverse" imaging of modernity's gender, sex, and Eros offers a critical perspective through which to reorient queer studies and its remarkably singular Foucauldian focus. Some themes for future research in feminist studies, queer studies, and cultural critique, as well as Benjamin studies, are suggested below:

Benjamin's Androgyny, Hermaphroditism, and Transsexualism in the Context of Sexology

Given Benjamin's numerous references to Freud's or Freudian interpretations of sexuality, Freud's theory of bisexuality would suggest the most obvious frame of reference with which to understand Benjamin's most esoteric, most perverse (and perversely complex) images — namely, his androgynous, hermaphroditic, and transsexual images. Given also that

Benjamin was thinking in these images at a time when Magnus Hirschfeld was conducting and publicizing his radically contentious researches on "sexual intermediaries," it is surprising that no one has yet thought to read these images in the context of sexology.

We might first, then, consider how Benjamin's hermaphroditism differs from Freud's bisexuality. Freud argues that the nascent human psyche is bisexual and that it is subsequently structured to conform to normative gender through a multi-phasic Oedipal process of incorporation, identification, projection, castration, and repression. Accordingly, this process rarely forms a psyche that is perfectly feminine or masculine. Bisexuality retains its primacy throughout the process of psychosexual maturation and it persistently finds expression in mature sexuality, chiefly in homosexuality. Female homosexuality, for Freud, is always associated with masculinity in women (feminine female homosexuals fall outside Freud's radar, while Freud regards effeminate male homosexuals with indifference). Benjamin, like Freud, confuses sexuality and gender; he, for instance, discusses lesbianism and the masculinization of female factory workers in the same breath. But Benjamin's "lesbian" comprises a constellation of motifs drawn from nineteenth-century avant-garde culture (including George Sand's transvestism and Proust's Albertine, as well as those mentioned above). Less an en-gendering of the individual psyche, Benjamin's "lesbian" is more a multi-faceted emblazon of perverse femininity in the wake of women's entry into the industrial work force and their emancipation from motherhood, as well as their re-fashioning in apparel of greater physical and social mobility.

Yet even a negative comparison between Benjamin's androgyny, hermaphroditism, and transsexualism and Hirschfeld's sexual intermediaries could illuminate Benjamin's critical and perverse contradictions of the thinking of contemporary sexual science. A leading advocate for the recognition of sexual diversity and minority sexuality — especially homosexuality — Hirschfeld was targeted by German Nazis, who thought his ideas extremely dangerous. Hirschfeld's research radically departed from the received thinking of his predecessor, Richard von Krafft-Ebing, whose *Psychopathia Sexualis* (1877) categorized and pathologized all forms of sexuality that did not aim at procreative heterosexuality, above all "metamorphosis sexualis paranoiaca" (transsexuality). Hirschfeld's book *Transvestites* (1910) differentiates transvestitism from homosexuality and fetishism, and transsexuality (the embodiment of the psychic urge of a person of one sex to "metamorphose" into the other sex) from hermaphroditism (the possession of sexual anatomy of both sexes), though it categorizes transsexuality as a form of psychosis. Decades later Harry Benjamin would, in *The Transsexual Phenomenon* (1966), refine the empirical distinction between "somatopsychic transsexualists" from "psychogenic transvestites."[23] By contrast, *Walter* Benjamin images a "transsexuality" that is neither psychically nor somatically induced, but that instead is a form of cultural metamorphosis that the industry and fashion of the commodity society imposes on gender, sex, and love.

Benjamin scholarship might further investigate Benjamin's insights into the production of new sexual species in relation to research in sexology by Hirschfeld and his followers. How do Benjamin's "androgynous lesbian," "(male-to-female) transsexual genii and literati," "fashion-induced female transvestites," "factory-induced (female-to-male) transsexuals," as well as "daemonic hermaphroditism," and "divine androgyny," compare with Hirschfeld's "sexual intermediaries" as the indices of an emerging anthropology and coming sexual community? How might Benjamin's insights be combined with those of Hirschfeld and others to interrogate what is now, as in Benjamin's time, the newest metropolitan species and most modish form of transsexuality, namely "metrosexuality"?

Transsexual Architecture

Benjamin raises the specter of utopian nineteenth-century architecture that designed, but never actualized, public space for where the sexes might meet — not to exchange sex but to change their sexual (inter)subjectivity. While considering the androgynous nature of Baudelaire's "modern woman in her heroic manifestations,'" Benjamin makes a passing reference to Charles Duveyrier's *La ville nouvelle ou le Paris des Saint-Simoniens,* and specifically to Duveyrier's androgynous design for a temple that was to be the showpiece of the Saint-Simonians' "New City" (*GS* I.2:594; *SW* 4:56). This reference not only identifies a concrete historical source of Baudelaire's androgynous lesbian but also alludes to the materialist faith that inspired utopian architecture. Duveyrier and his Saint-Simonian brethren believed that by constructing androgynous public space for the communion of the masses they could transform a decaying Vitruvian "mancity" into a vital and organic bisexual commonwealth. Elaborations of this design called for the trans-incorporation of female and male structural and functional anatomy into one gigantic building "organism," whose galvanizing space would induce a mass "moralization of the people."[24] The new masses of *citoyenne* and *citoyen* would here be viscerally organized, embodied, and engendered in the collective space of manwomancity (or manwomanicity). As they walked through the temple's internal anatomy, city subjects would undergo a psychic-social sex change from individual men and women into an androgynous body politic. The temple's androgyny would serve as the prime architectural model for androgynizing the city overall. Gone would be all residue of Rome's patriarchal *res publica* that excluded women from functioning equally in social, cultural, and political life.

Utopian architectural androgyny aimed to bring men and women together in one collective space in the spirit of public communion and community-building; it did not aim to fuse, or confuse, the sexes in one body, nor did it embody a "daemonic" mix of the sexual and the spiritual. The "transsexualizing" that such androgynous architecture entails is that of the public body — the body politic — not the individual female or male body. Women are "masculinized" inasmuch as they join men in public works and political union; men are "feminized" inasmuch as they join women in social communion. Such a union, or communion, of separate spheres is in keeping with Benjamin's ethos of "esoteric love." Yet Benjamin raises this specter of utopian androgyny, not in celebration of its idea, but in profane illumination of its never having been actualized. The design remains to be deployed in contemporary architectural engineering. He thus invites historians and futurists of urban culture to consider architecture's ideal and actual, utopian and pragmatic contribution to be the transformation of sexual-social relations in modern society. Queer cultural studies might read Benjamin's notes on architectural androgyny alongside his notes on sartorial androgyny — especially those that evidence how new urban fashions transformed women's physical, sexual, and social mobility.

The Work of Sex in the Age of Technological Reproducibility

Feminists rightly criticize Benjamin for failing to consider the perception and experience of commodity society from the perspective of this exemplary human commodity. The prostitute, for Benjamin, best serves his critical project as the destructive allegory of mass society's self-betrayal and its delusory romance with the commodity fetish. Yet, Benjamin does offer feminists a way of thinking about the prostitute as an exemplary figure of anthropological materialism through which the transformation of industrial-age sex and sexuality is made most concretely and critically perceptible. Benjamin's prostitute is not just a mass victim of mass marketing. Nor is she merely Our Lady of Commodity Seduction dressed in the phantasmagoria of exchange value. She represents the liberation of all women, and all sex and sexuality, from the traditional confines of marriage — at a cost: the mobile woman can put herself on the (sex) market or she will be seen as sexually marketable even when she literally is not. With sexual mobility comes sexual marketability, and not only for women. Sexual mobility and marketability is the social leveler of erotic freedom for all classes of women and all classes of queers — cruising lesbians and gay men, as well as male hustlers and lesbian streetwalkers. In the modern industrial city everyone, not just the bourgeois heterosexual male, is free to cruise the streets in search of a lover-buyer.

In failing to consider the subjectivity of cruising lesbians and gay men, working-class male hustlers, and female and lesbian prostitutes, Benjamin also overlooks the dangers of street violence that accompany and compromise this new sexual mobility. While feminists cover the "danger" aspect of street-walking women from women's perspectives, they might yet consider — with Benjamin in mind — the paradoxes of perception and experience that women suffer and entertain in venturing as marketably "free" sexual agents into the city. How did and do women recognize and negotiate their sexuality in the city's labyrinths of fashion, where they are everywhere bombarded and manipulated by advertising to imitate the seductions of the upscale hooker and her counterpart, the glamour model, not to mention the sartorial, if standardized and often ill-fitting, beckoning of the mannequin-corpse? How do women value their hard-won promiscuity against bourgeois morality that, with duplicity, sanctions accumulation and variation (as in shopping for love) at the same time that it condemns prostitution and public sex, and places supreme value on the unique and original (the fetish one-of-a-kind — "the little woman")?

Feminists and critics of popular culture might appropriate Benjamin's imagistic insights on mass prostitution and fashion for analyzing the role of mass media in both resisting and advancing the reification of sex. How do popular TV programs (like *Sex and the City,* to take the most obvious example) return an aura of romance to street-savvy sex and promiscuity, if not — as Benjaminian insight illuminates — by fetishistically obscuring the difference between sex-workers (who cunningly maneuver the economy of sexual relations without illusion, yet who remain subject to that economy) and free-lovers (who cleverly enjoy trying on serial or multiple affairs as existential subjects, and who, apparently, can see through and rise above the deceptions and seductions of the sex market)? How might a Benjamin-inflected analysis approach the current HBO serial *Big Love,* a cynical episodic exposure of the self-deceptions entertained by a closeted family of Mormon polygamists, whose liberation from the old patriarchal cult is afforded by a zealous adaptation of the entrepreneurial spirit and wholesale consumerism that — despite hiding its illegality and amorality — is more effective than bourgeois society in restoring spiritual aura and family values to the reproductive economy? How do the women of this break-away, assimilating, yet closeted polygamist family symptomatically disavow their status as mass-consumable-object and their sex-work for corporate profit even as they avoid taking their sex to public market? How might Benjamin's allegory of prostitution illuminate this new kind of commodity sex, in which prostitute and mother are wed together and brought into the private sanctuary of the bourgeois-polygamist home?

Analysis of queer culture might also benefit from a Benjamin-inflected approach to the paradoxes embodied and hidden in the "work" of queer urban sex. Such an approach would consider such questions as: how have cruising queers negotiated the streets without blurring the distinction between hustling and cruising — a distinction little valued by libertines of the *ancien regime* but much valued by modernity's queer liberals? What remains of the gay sexual revolution and of the great gay migration to the big city? Or, how can lesbian culture come into existence and sustain itself without doing the work of making lesbianism marketably sexy, and, how, if it *is* successful, does it not sell itself out to the sexual status quo and abolish its heroic resistance to the reproduction of market values? Alternatively, how might the nineteenth-century utopian dream of engendering a women's culture be reconsidered in light of recent historical findings that it was cruising lesbian prostitutes and their consorts and clients who were the first sexually mobile, street-walking women to occupy city space for women?[25]

Eco-Technological Eros

Benjamin's thought-image "Zum Planetarium" (*GS* IV.1:146–48; "To the Planetarium," *SW* 1:486–87) from *Einbahnstraße* augurs a coming age of technology that replaces the "Naturbeherrschung" ("mastery of nature") of imperialist technology with a "Berherrschung vom Verhältnis von Natur und Menschheit" ("mastery of the relation between nature and man."). Imperialist technology achieves its climax in the orgy of destruction of the First World War, whereas the coming technology revels in the prospect of creating a new relation to nature in communion with the cosmos: "Ihr [mankind] organisiert in der Technik sich eine Physis, in welcher ihr Kontakt mit dem Kosmos sich neu und anders bildet als in Völkern und Familien" ("In technology, a *physis* is being organized through which mankind's contact with the cosmos takes a new and different form from that which it had in nations and families"). The war that shattered the "Gliederbau der Menschheit" ("frame of mankind") also revealed the real power of technology to affect the world on a cosmic scale beyond the scope of nature's utility. Does Benjamin allude here to state and Oedipal structures that were so highly naturalized in European modernity? In any case, in the wake of global destruction came the bliss of a mind-blowing perception, namely that "der Schauer echter kosmischer Erfahrung ist nicht an jenes winzige Naturfragment gebunden, das wir 'Natur' zu nennen gewohnt sind" ("the paroxysm of genuine cosmic experience is not tied to that tiny fragment of nature that we are accustomed to call Nature"). Recruited by the betraying ruling class to man the war machine, the proletariat was the body that felt this "paroxysm" most, and that most resisted the pacification of peace time. To Benjamin, the revolts that followed the First World War signal an attempt by the members of the proletariat "den neuen Leib in ihre Gewalt zu bringen" ("to bring the new body under its control"). The planetarium figures as a stage of technological revolution, where the war's proletarian survivors set their sights on a new form of planetary society. Unlike Foucault's panopticon, Benjamin's planetarium looks outward to a planet no longer oppressed by a master anthropology and open to Man's self-overcoming. The planetarium's astronomers, besides being proletarian survivors of an imperialist death-drive, are life-force physicists whose technology evolves symbiotically with the complex machinery of terrestrial vitality. Such a technological becoming might be critically compared with Donna Haraway's reinvention of nature through cyborg assemblages, and Gilles Deleuze and Félix Guattari's empire-breaking, earth-coupling desire-machines.[26] Viewed in constellation with these starships of postmodernity, Benjamin's technological Eros presages the dawn of a "new earth" and a "new people."[27]

Notes

[1] Sigrid Weigel, "Eros and Language: Benjamin's Kraus Essay," in *Benjamin's Ghosts: Interventions in Contemporary Literary and Cultural Theory,* ed. Gerhard Richter (Stanford, CA: Stanford UP, 2002), 278–95.

[2] Chris Andre, "Aphrodite's Children: Hopeless Love, Historiography, and Benjamin's Dialectical Image," *SubStance: A Review of Theory and Literary Criticism* 85 (1998): 105–28.

[3] Sigrid Weigel, "From Gender Images to Dialectical Images in Benjamin's Writings," in *The Actuality of Walter Benjamin,* ed. Laura Marcus and Lynda Nead, trans. Rachel McNicholl (London: Lawrence & Wishart, 1998), 40–54; Sigrid Weigel, "From Images to Dialectical Images: The Significance of Gender Difference in Benjamin's Writings," in *Body- and Image-Space: Re-Reading Walter Benjamin,* trans. Georgina Paul with Rachel McNicholl and Jeremy Gaines (New York: Routledge, 1996), 80–94.

[4] Eva Geulen, "Toward a Genealogy of Gender in Walter Benjamin's Writing," *The German Quarterly* 69.2 (Spring 1996): 161–80, here 62.

[5] Buck-Morss, Susan. "The Flaneur, the Sandwichman and the Whore: The Politics of Loitering," *New German Critique* 39 (Autumn 1986): 99–40.

[6] Christine Buci-Glucksmann, La raison baroque de Baudelaire à Benjamin (Paris: Éditions Galilée, 1984). In English: *Baroque Reason: The Aesthetics of Modernity,* trans. Patrick Camiller (London: Sage, 1994), 99.

[7] See Sigrid Weigel, "Towards a Female Dialectic of Enlightenment: Julia Kristeva and Walter Benjamin," in *Body- and Image-Space: Re-reading Walter Benjamin,* 63–79, here 69, for analysis of the sexual/textual dimensions of Benjamin's writing.

[8] Rey Chow, "Walter Benjamin's Love Affair with Death," *New German Critique* 48 (Autumn 1989): 63–86.

[9] Miriam Hansen, "Benjamin, Cinema and Experience: The Blue Flower in the Land of Technology," *New German Critique* 40 (Winter 1987): 179–224.

[10] Anne Friedberg, "Les flâneurs du mal(1): Cinema and the Postmodern Condition," *PMLA* 106.3 (May 1991): 419–31.

[11] A notable exception is my *Queer Constellations: Subcultural Space in the Wake of the City* (Minneapolis: U of Minnesota P, 2005), which considers the critical and productive inter-implications of Benjamin's perverse erotology and queer studies in urban culture.

[12] Michel Foucault, *The History of Sexuality*, trans. Robert Hurley (New York: Vintage, 1990).

[13] Walter Benjamin, "A Berlin Chronicle," *SW* 2:595–637, here 620.

[14] Geulen, "Toward a Genealogy of Gender," 164.

[15] Andre, "Aphrodite's Children," 112–15.

[16] The motif of "love at last sight" appears in Benjamin's discussion of Baudelaire's sonnet "A une passante" in the section "Der Flaneur ("The Flâneur")" of "Das Paris des Second Empire bei Baudelaire" (1938, unpublished in Benjamin's lifetime; *GS* I.2:546–50; "The Paris of the Second Empire in Baudelaire," *SW* 4:3–94).

[17] The following interpretation of Benjamin's "technological eros" is mine, not Wohlfarth's.

[18] The phrase "impotence before the city" appears in *A Berlin Chronicle* (1932, unpublished in Benjamin's lifetime), *SW* 2:595–637, here 596.

[19] See the dialogue between Genius and Prostitute in "Metaphysik der Jugend" (*GS* II.1:94; *SW* 1:8–9); "Berliner Chronik" and "Berliner Kindheit um 1900" (esp. "Bettler und Huren" ["Beggars and Whores"] in the 1934 version); the Baudelaire studies, and convolute O "Prostitution, Spiel" ("Prostitution, Gambling") of *Das Passagen-Werk*.

[20] Weigel, "Eros and Language," 294.

[21] Weigel may be referring to "Zum Bilde Prousts" ("On the Image of Proust"), where Benjamin briefly considers Proust's attention to "den fremdartigen Abschattungen eines Jupien" (*GS* II.1:318; "the exotic shadings of a Jupien," *SW* 2:243.

[22] *GS* I.2:691; *SW* 4:389–400. See also the contributions of Vivian Liska and Marc de Wilde in this volume.

[23] Richard von Krafft-Ebing, *Psychopathia sexualis* (1893; repr., Boston: Adamant Media Corporation, 2001); Magnus Hirschfeld, *Transvestites: The Erotic Drive to Cross Dress* (1910; repr., New York: Prometheus Books, 2003); Harry Benjamin, *The Transsexual Phenomenon* (New York: Julian P, 1966).

[24] See Syros Papaetros, "Paris Organique — Paris Critique: Urbanism, Spectacle and the SaintSimonians," [*sic*] *Iconomania: Studies in Visual Culture*, 1–29, http://www.humnet.ucla.edu/humnet/arthist/icono/papapetros/simonian.htm.

[25] See Leslie Choquette, "Homosexuals in the City: Representations of Lesbian and Gay Space in Nineteenth-Century Paris," *Journal of Homosexuality* 41.3/4 (2001): 149–67.

[26] Donna Haraway, *Simians, Cyborgs, and Women: The Reinvention of Nature* (New York: Free Association P, 1996); Gilles Deleuze and Félix Guattari, *Mille Plateaux* (Paris: Les Éditions de Minuit, 1980) (in English: *A Thousand Plateaus*, trans. Brian Massumi [Minneapolis: U of Minnesota P, 1987]); Félix Guattari, *Les trois écologies* (Paris: Editions Galilée, 1989) (in English: *Three Ecologies*, trans. Ian Pindar and Paul Sutton [London: Continuum, 2000]).

[27] Gilles Deleuze and Félix Guattari, *What Is Philosophy?* (New York: Columbia UP, 1991), 99.

12: Sonic Dreamworlds: Benjamin, Adorno, and the Phantasmagoria of the Opera House

Adrian Daub

I

IF THERE IS SUCH A THING AS "popular imagination" among cultural theorists, then Walter Benjamin and Theodor Adorno have come to occupy nearly opposite positions in it. Benjamin, the *flâneur,* the collector, the producer of fragments, hero of the academic precariate; Adorno, the professor, the secret (or not-so-secret) systematician, the comfortable resident of the "Grand Hotel 'Abgrund,'" the fuddy-duddy felled by a couple of bare breasts. And yet it is the very lectures at the Frankfurt Institute for Social Research that the infamous *Busenaktion* interrupted[1] that at times find Adorno practicing the hermeneutics commonly associated with Benjamin: distraction, illumination, *flânerie.* It is one such particular moment that forms the basis for this article: Adorno steps into his dead friend's shoes and embarks upon a *flânerie.* He is heading to the opera rather than the cinema, and readers might brace themselves for another denunciation of anything that is not Alban Berg, or another of Adorno's paladins of the musical avant-garde. But Adorno has something different in mind, for he arrives late.

Arriving late as a hermeneutic trick — in an excerpt from his 1958 lectures on dialectics Adorno takes the *flâneur* to the opera. It is a rare moment in Adorno where distraction becomes a "method of attention"[2] and where, as Edmond Jaloux, in a passage quoted by Benjamin in the *Passagen-Werk* (*Arcades Project*), puts it, "le fait seul de tourner à droite ou à gauche constituait déjà un acte essentiellement poétique" ("the mere turning right or left already constitute[s] an essentially poetic act" (M9a,4). This is a step Benjamin's solitary wanderer never took: The *Passagen-Werk* discusses "Die Oper als Zentrum (*GS* V.2:1212; "the opera as center," *AP,* 906) and pays special attention to Haussmann's *Avenue de l'Opéra,* but it stops short of the building itself. Benjamin himself, however, discusses a visit to the opera in his *Moskauer Tagebuch* (*Moscow Diaries*), and applies to it an optic remarkably reminiscent of Adorno's tardiness. He describes a performance of Rimsky-Korsakov's *The Tsar's Bride:*

> Der Administrator empfängt uns. Er . . . führt uns durch alle Räume (im Vestibül ist viel Publikum schon lange vor Anfang versammelt, die von ihren Arbeitsstätten direkt ins Theater kommen) zeigt uns auch den Konzertsaal. Im Vestibül liegt ein außerordentlich auffallender, wenig schöner Teppich. . . . Unsere Plätze sind in der zweiten Reihe. . . . In einer Pause gehen wir ins Vestibül. Es gibt aber drei. Sie sind viel zu lang und ermüden Asja. . . . Am Schluß ist die Beschaffung der Garderobe sehr schwierig. Zwei Theaterdiener bilden mitten auf der Treppe einen Kordon, um den Zustrom der Leute zu den winzigen Garderobenräume zu regeln. (*GS* VI:298)

> [The administrator greets us. [He] shows us through all the rooms (in the vestibule, quite a crowd has gathered long before the beginning of the performance, people who have come from their workplaces directly into the theater) and also the concert hall. In the vestibule, there is an extremely noticeable and unpleasant carpet. . . . Our seats are in the second row. . . . In one of the intermissions we go to the vestibule. But there are three. They are far too long and they tire Asja out. . . . At the end, retrieving our coats proves quite difficult. Two ushers form separate lines on the grand staircase in order to regulate the flow of people into the tiny coat checks.[3]]

I have edited Benjamin's report somewhat, but I have left its most baffling aspect intact: His visit to the opera includes a description of rows of seats, the carpet in the foyer and an exhaustive account of the intermissions — but it entirely leaves out the performance itself. Adorno's *flâneur* similarly performs his "poetic act" by not heading straight into the concert hall but rather loitering (in Benjaminian "irresolution"[4]) in the foyer, the grand staircase or the coat check. Adorno explains this purposeful tardiness as follows:

> [Ich] habe deshalb das Experiment angestellt, über Musik Reflexionen, Betrachtungen anzustellen, die ich "Musik von Außen" nannte, und zwar im wörtlichen und im übertragenen Sinn, also in dem wörtlichen zunächst einmal, Musik sich so anzuhören, wie sie nicht etwa in einem Opernhaus oder in einem Konzertsaal klingt, sondern wie eine Oper klingt, wenn man es etwa versäumt hat, nach dem Ende der Pause sofort in seine Loge sich zurückzubegeben und dann dieses Getöse von außen vernimmt, das Gefühl, dass dabei eine Art Seite der Musik herauskommt, die man sonst nicht sieht, und, allgemeiner gesprochen, war mir aufgegangen, dass über ein Phänomen etwas nur auszusagen ist, wenn man es zugleich gewissermassen von außen ebenfalls sieht und nicht nur von innen . . .

[I therefore performed the experiment of arriving at reflections, observations about music by something I called "music from the outside" ["*Musik von Außen*"], both in the literal and metaphorical senses, literally listening to music not as it sounds in an opera house or a concert hall, but as it sounds when you are late in returning to your box after intermission and you hear this noise from the outside, the feeling that this reveals a side of the music that one usually does not see, and, speaking more generally, I realized that describing a phenomenon involves seeing it as though from the outside and not just from the inside.[5]]

In many respects, then, Benjamin's *Moscow Diaries* find him practicing something along the lines of "music from the outside" — the crucial difference being that he mentions nothing of even the most incidental sounds of the operatic performance. Adorno's aural *flâneur* on the other hand hears bits of music, noise, applause, the shuffling of feet, nothing particularly distinct, one imagines, but rather what the radio listener picks up, tuning in and out of different broadcasts.[6] In his studies on what he dubbed the "radio voice," Adorno claims that this approach is doomed to fundamentally misapprehend music; here, however, he seems to think there is something in music that the latecomer in the foyer may be better attuned to than those sitting diligently in their seats inside.[7] What is it that makes this "experiment" of "music from the outside" theoretically productive, rather than a state to hurry through on the way to one's box? What is it the latecomer gleans from the distant noises of the concert hall, and how do these distant noises come to attain such evidentiary quality? The scene is clearly one important to musical modernity, for we find it recapitulated even in the period's music itself: The first *Nachtmusik* (night music) of Gustav Mahler's seventh symphony, for instance, constitutes itself as something like a *flânerie* past a concert hall.[8] In the words of Hans Heinrich Eggebrecht, "Mahler walks through the town in the evening and takes in all the music he can hear," including snippets of music emanating from an opera house and a music hall.[9]

In what follows, I will seize on this act of auditory *flânerie* as an avenue into the investigation of operatic phantasmagoria, by which I understand a type of illusory performativity that masks its own material conditions of production — a path that can only be followed by relying on both Adorno and Benjamin as guides. In the process Benjamin's notion of *flânerie* and phantasmagoria serve as important landmarks, even though they reveal their one-sided focus on visuality. Benjamin's *flâneur*, so attuned to the visual seduction of the capitalist commodity, is strangely deaf to its siren's call. His maxim isn't simply "Alles ansehen, nichts anfassen" ("Look at everything, touch nothing," M4,7), it also seems to be "look at everything, hear nothing." While Benjamin introduces the term "phantasmagoria" as something of a theoretical *Open, Sesame* of nineteenth-century (visual) culture, architecture, and art, music is left out of his considerations of the term entirely. This is not simply because, as Susan Buck-Morss has argued, "the sense of sight was privileged in this phantasmagoric sensorium of modernity,"[10] but rather because music in general receives astoundingly short shrift in Benjamin — Lutz Koepnick has spoken of a "repression" rooted in Benjamin's "anxieties about the role of the acoustical in the modern world."[11] To be sure, the *Trauerspiel* book (*Ursprung des deutschen Trauerspiels,* Origin of the German Mourning Play, 1928) briefly discusses Richard Wagner, but primarily by way of engaging Friedrich Nietzsche's *Birth of Tragedy;*[12] in the *Passagen-Werk,* on the other hand, Wagner enters the discussion only as seen through the prism of Charles Baudelaire. As a result, when the concept of phantasmagoria is brought to bear on music, and specifically opera, in subsequent scholarship it is not usually in the sense Benjamin gives it, but rather in that of Adorno's influential essay *Versuch über Wagner* (In Search of Wagner).[13]

In discussing opera, Adorno's discourse on phantasmagoria has been used frequently, whereas Benjamin's definition of the same term has been employed primarily to talk about visual culture. Nevertheless, recent scholars have undertaken an analysis of opera that draws on a sense of "phantasmagoria" that is much closer to Benjamin's understanding of the term than Adorno's. This is because they have increasingly probed the *cognitive* technologies of opera in the latter half of the nineteenth century, whether primarily as a visual spectacle or in the shape of modern acoustics. Jonathan Crary, for instance, has argued that Wagner's Bayreuth *Festspielhaus* was intended "to exercise a fuller control over the attentiveness of an audience," contiguous with other forms of nineteenth-century audio-visual spectacle.[14] Crary's discussion of Wagnerian aesthetics owes significantly more of a debt to Benjamin than to Adorno, and indeed an argument can be made that Benjamin's rather intermittent engagements with the problem of Wagner in the *Trauerspiel* book and the *Passagen-Werk* license this sort of reading: After all, the reason why Benjamin mobilizes the Baroque against the total artwork is the latter's allergy against the dispersal and historicity of Baroque aesthetics; and what attracts Benjamin to Baudelaire is precisely his unwillingness to manipulate away the shocks of modernity.[15]

A "Benjaminian" analysis of the "phantasmagoria" of nineteenth-century opera, in the mode of Crary, proceeds from the simple fact that opera in the later nineteenth century constituted not merely an aesthetic problem but also a cognitive one.[16] Questions of attention, of audibility, of illusion were as much a part of Wagner's project as they were of panoramas, world exhibitions, train stations, and shopping arcades — that is, the urban phantasmagoria catalogued in Benjamin's *Passagen-Werk.* Many of these questions circled around the construction of an artistic geography and the concomitant elision of the actual geography of the opera house: What had previously — to work with a Benjaminian conceptual pair — been primarily a semi-porous sphere of attraction and distraction (such as the Italian or French grand opera), was in Wagner's Festspielhaus rapidly transformed into a darkened, autarkic place of contemplation. The doors locked, the lights turned down, all chatter banished, the opera house of the turn of the century resembled earlier ones as much as a modern airliner resembles the deck of a nineteenth-century steamer.

The nineteenth century becomes a period of disciplining the audience. Spectacle makes demands on its spectators, turning them into observers who are expected to surrender entirely to its attractions.[17] Arthur Schopenhauer, for instance, fulminates against women who ruin man's concert-going experience by "continuing their chatter (ihr Geplapper fortsetzen)" even "during the most beautiful passages of the greatest masterpieces (unter den schönsten Stellen der größten Meisterwerke)."[18] The hypermasculine "masterpiece" requires absolute silence and devotion, and the technological reforms of Wagner form only one component of this domination of the audience. Consider for instance Wagner's scathing caricature of an Italian opera house:

> In der Oper versammelte sich in Italien ein Publikum, welches seinen Abend mit Unterhaltung zubrachte; zu dieser Unterhaltung gehörte auch die auf der Scene gesungene Musik, der man von Zeit zu Zeit in Pausen der Unterbrechung der Konversation zuhörte; während der Konversation und der gegenseitigen Besuche in den Logen fuhr die Musik fort, und zwar mit der Aufgabe, welche man bei großen Diners der Tafelmusik stellt, nämlich durch ihr Geräusch die sonst schüchterne Unterhaltung zum lautern Ausbruch zu bringen.[19]

> [In the opera house of Italy there gathered an audience which passed its evenings in amusement; part of this amusement was formed by the music sung upon the stage, to which one listened from time to time in pauses of the conversation; during the conversation and visits paid from box to box the music still went on, with the same office one assigns to table music at grand dinners, namely to encourage by its noise the otherwise timid talk.[20]]

When discussing the Chinese theater in his radio lecture on the "Theaterbrand von Kanton," Benjamin himself invokes the theater of distraction Wagner describes, but he seems to regard it as something altogether positive: "Auf die Feierlichkeit aber pfeifen sie. Denn dazu sind sie viel zu große Theaterkenner, um nicht die Freiheit zu verlangen, jederzeit ihre Meinung über die Vorstellung kundzugeben" (*GS* VII.1:227; "They [the Chinese] entirely ignore the seriousness [of theater]. For they are far too knowledgeable about the theater to deny themselves the freedom to express their opinion during the performance"). The contrast to the (modern, Wagnerian) opera house is obvious: here the audience members, in their pitch-dark space, are being discouraged from any communication, even from looking at each other, except for occasional disciplinary frowns at accidental or thoughtless emissions of sound. The music, on the other hand, with its source hidden from view, becomes acoustically dominant, demanding constant, unremitting attention, visual or auditory. Since, as Crary points out, "Wagner completely eliminated the lateral views of older theater design to achieve a frontal engagement with the stage for every spectator,"[21] we may well think of this transformation as analogous to the passage from a carnevalesque "cinema of attractions"[22] to the modern multiplex. And what Adorno calls "music from the outside" attempts to trace, in Benjaminian fashion, the residue of the great silencing in the opera house.

Wagner's revolution of musical technique is thus inseparable from his revolution of the architecture and technology of the opera house. It will be my contention in what follows that this connection requires the construction of a dialogue between Benjamin and Adorno, in particular relating to their respective deployments of "phantasmagoria." A number of post-Wagnerian composers self-reflectively engage with this new operatic phantasmagoria. I will point to the operas of Franz Schreker (1878–1934) as an instance where the technological-aesthetic conjunction of phantasmagoria is built into the very structure of the artwork itself.

II

In a note in one of the methodological convolutes of the *Passagen-Werk*, Walter Benjamin discusses phantasmagoria as the "concealment of labor." He cites Adorno (whom he still calls "Wiesengrund"[23]) and invokes Wagner as an exemplar: phantasmagoria, he writes, is "ein Konsumgut, in dem nichts mehr daran gemahnen soll, wie es zustandekam" ("a consumer item in which there is no longer anything that is supposed to remind us how it came into being"); at the same time, he cites Adorno's programmatic claim that "Wagners Orchesterkunst . . . hat den Anteil der unmittelbaren Produktion des Tons aus der aesthetischen Gestalt vertrieben" ("Wagner's orchestration has banished the role of the immediate production of sound from the aesthetic totality," X13a). Benjamin's highly compressed montage of citations highlights a set of analogies that grounds the aesthetic theory of the Frankfurt School, but it also indicates that there is much about the terms analogized that remains opaque.[24] Adorno's article on Wagner fundamentally reflects on the social meaning of the autonomy of art; Benjamin's *Passagen-Werk*, of which the note cited above is a part, is not exclusively, or even primarily, concerned with artistic phenomena, and, as we saw, certainly not with music. Benjamin's invocation of his friend's work on Wagner, and his own attempts to grapple with the phantasmagoric "dreamworlds" of the nineteenth century thus sit somewhat awkwardly side-by-side in this note — as they do in much of the scholarship on opera that has drawn on either theorist since. Nevertheless, both thinkers also furnish the resources to resolve this awkwardness, or, perhaps better, to put it to work.

At its most basic, the term "phantasmagoria" refers to the aesthetic equivalent of commodity fetishism: the commodity fetishist invests the commodity with a life it doesn't actually have and ignores the processes (namely labor) of which the commodity is a mere effect. Phantasmagorias similarly dissimulate the aesthetic processes at work in their production; they wear the costume of something that just happens to be there, independent of what is going on behind the scenes. What exactly *is* behind the scenes is, as we will see, subject to some debate: what are the means of production that the phantasmagoria occludes? Used by both Adorno and Benjamin, in *Versuch über Wagner* and the *Passagen-Werk* respectively,[25] the concept has spawned two distinct usages, one in the discussion of music and another in the discussion of media other than music: panoramas, photography, world exhibitions, interior decorations, and so on. While the two deployments of the term bear clear family resemblances, they tend to differ with respect to their relative models of production. Their variance coincides with that between the two senses of the word "aesthetic" — one understands "aesthetic" means of production to refer to something that brings about a *work of art* (the dominant usage since Kant); the other understands "aesthetic" to refer to the production of a sensory experience (the original sense of *aisthesis*). My argument in what follows depends on the fact that *both* of these senses of "phantasmagoria" seize on a factor that informs modernity's staging in the opera house.

The first discourse of phantasmagoria is based strictly on Adorno's usage and is often restricted to Wagner. It reads phantasmagoria as the dominance of things and thing-like qualities — of which the most important musical manifestation is harmony — over the relational and social aspects of production, exemplified in music by motivic development. Adorno's analysis proceeds by showing how a highly modern artistic "technology" paradoxically serves to create an impression of the distant, autochthonous, or mystical, all of which present the aesthetic object as miraculously always already present and thus constitutively repress the question of the production of these aesthetic phenomena.[26] In other words, the archaic façade of the "technology" hides the contingency and produced-ness of the phantasmagoria by insisting that the object is natural or is the reiteration of something that has existed all along.

In a Wagnerian *Gesamtkunstwerk*, in which the traditional modes of producing an opera are all integrated and synchronized, phantasmagoria becomes the driving force behind the artistic form. However, even though libretto, music, *mise-en-scène,* and the architecture of the opera house may be conceived and controlled by one and the same person, the opera cannot fully divest itself of the embarrassing fact that there is still a multitude of hands involved in its production: phantasmagoria is at heart an "impossible object."[27] The reasons for its impossibility reside in the social world: in a contradictory, antinomial world any representation of a fused "whole" belies the ineluctable antagonism underpinning all (bourgeois) reality.[28] Because this reality resists fusion, the *Gesamtkunstwerk* must proceed by means of a violent synthesis: the various elements of the *Gesamtkunstwerk* are made to regurgitate the dictated synthesis to one another, each subordinated to the abstract logic of musical (phantasmagoric) production.[29] Their "wholeness" (as one of Adorno's most famous aphorisms runs) is their *untruth*.[30]

For Adorno it is primarily the denial of time, of development, of newness, that marks Wagnerian music as phantasmagoric,[31] the falsely naturalizing, totalizing, and spatializing in Wagner's compositional technique. But this approach seems to subscribe to a relatively limited view of what constitutes a "technology," focusing on the work of the composer and librettist repressed in phantasmagoria. While this Wagner-focused reading of phantasmagoria is perfectly accurate when it comes to the *work of art,* it gives short shrift to the various technologies that actually contribute to a *performance* of, say, the *Ring of the Nibelung.*[32] Phantasmagoria, in other words, is not merely a concept to be applied to color, tone, texts, or sets — it is also a concept intimately related to the fact that Wagner's operas were performed in Bayreuth and in the many opera houses subsequently styled after it, and that they were performed at a particular point in time, as certain technologies of performance had become available.[33] In Benjamin's words, it is a theater "komplizierter Maschinerien, riesenhafter Statistenaufgeboten, raffinierter Effekten" (*GS* II:697; "of complicated machinery, gigantic human resources, and sophisticated effects"). It is crucial that these technologies enabled not a new work of art but rather a new kind of sensory experience.

III

This emphasis on a new (and particularly modern) kind of sensory experience moves our discussion of the concept closer to Benjamin's understanding of what constitutes "phantasmagoria." For while the *Passagen-Werk* explicitly invokes Adorno's use of the concept with respect to Wagner, it is clear that Benjamin deploys the term differently (albeit analogously). Benjamin follows Marx in reading phantasmagoria as fetishes that divest a world of commodities of its historical contingency and transfigure it into something universal, natural, inevitable.[34] But the suppression of labor in the fetish also translates into an elision of the world of industry in favor of *Feerien* (fairytales), preserved seemingly isolated from the industrializing world that made them possible in the first place. In a modern world characterized by fragmentation and alienation, where a unified experience is virtually impossible, phantasmagorias artificially recreate a sensory totality that suggests a level of (social, metaphysical, and cognitive) cohesion that no longer exists in reality. They create, as Susan Buck-Morss has described it, "a total environment . . . that functioned as a protective shield for the senses" through the "manipulation of the synaesthetic system by control of environmental stimuli."[35] This system reintegrates sensory experiences that have become subject to shock, dispersal, and displacement "under conditions of modernity."

For Benjamin this new kind of experience was primarily *visual* — and his catalogue of phantasmagorias of the nineteenth century concerns most often phenomena in which "dream images" suggest a false totality of *vision*. Nevertheless, when Benjamin alludes to a kind of theater or opera house for which "alles, was ihre Hand berührt, zu Reizen wird" (*GS* II:697; "everything it touches becomes a stimulus," *SW* 2:778), he makes it clear that this conceptual complex can be transferred to the audio-visual spectacle as well. Moreover, there exists in Adorno's oeuvre a more detailed suggestion on how a "Benjaminian" reading of operatic phantasmagoria might proceed: what in his 1958 essay "Die Naturgeschichte des Theaters" ("The Natural History of the Theatre") he labels the "dialectic of the dome."[36] Adorno introduces this dialectic as a means of interrogating what is specifically modern within the (technological-architectural) place of performance by juxtaposing it with the atavistic ritual sublimated within it.

Clearly inspired by Benjamin's *Passagen-Werk*, the "dialectic of the dome" refers to the most material aspects of production: it connects the performative aspect of phantasmagoria to the technological conditions of its performance.[37] Benjamin, in his radio text on the "Theaterbrand von Kanton" ("Theater Fire of Canton"), discusses the theater as "nicht etwa die Stücke, die aufgeführt werden, oder die Schauspieler . . . sondern vor allem die Zuschauer und den Raum selbst" (*GS* VII.1:226; "not the plays that are performed [in the theater], or the actors . . . , but rather the audience and the space itself") — it is precisely this sense of theater that the dialectic of the dome interrogates. Like his hermeneutic in the *Wagner* monograph, Adorno's approach to this dialectic is to read production back into the aesthetic object. Unlike the approach in *Versuch über Wagner*, however, "Die Naturgeschichte des Theaters" no longer conceives of production in terms of color and sonority but rather attempts to describe, in a rather Benjaminian way, how architecture and acoustics conspire to produce a particular kind of synaesthetic experience. The "dialectic of the dome" thus comes to code for a Benjaminian take on opera, arrived at by detour through Adorno's importation of Benjamin's concepts. I take this "dialectic" to stand metonymically for an entire range of applications that come to dominate the post-Wagnerian opera house. The dialectic of the dome inheres in the form of the opera house, but it is only the opera, the *performance,* that releases it.

What makes an opera house phantasmagoric in this sense? First, of course, an opera house depends on shielding its audience from anything lying beyond the experience of the opera — and that "anything," as both Benjamin and Adorno argue, is primarily the social world. The opera (like the autonomous artwork) is to lie beyond the social and economic sphere — even in the very straightforward sense that any opera house worth the price of admission banishes the noise of the street and the bustle of the masses. But why is this experience that the opera house artificially creates "synaesthetic"? Benjamin argues that any fully integrated perception of the human social world is necessarily shattered in the fractured conditions of technological and social modernity. We experience many *things* happening (often enough we *hear* one thing, but are forced to *smell* or *see* ten others), but paradoxically we are no longer capable of what Dewey would call "having an experience."[38] Our sensorium is as dispersed as the life-world to which it is forced to attend.

Arthur Schopenhauer suggested that the shocks of modern life — noise and interruption — prevent the *unification* of the senses in what he calls "spirit."[39] Noise, according to Schopenhauer, prevents the integration of sense data into one point (an object), and the uniting of those sense data at one point (a unified subject).[40] It is here that the connection between Benjamin's cognitive aesthetics of shock on the one hand and the aesthetic project of the *Gesamtkunstwerk* becomes clear. Phantasmagorias technologically will into existence an artificial totality for an experience "der das Schockerlebnis zur Norm geworden ist" (*GS* I.2:614; "for which the shock experience [*Erlebnis*] has become the norm," *SW* 4:318), as Benjamin puts it; similarly, Wagner, in Adorno's view, wills into existence a total work of art unconcerned with the social preconditions of its theatrical production and the distractions of the social world outside. The meaningful and unified experiences increasingly impossible outside the opera house are artistically and artificially reinstated by the musical performance inside. Outside, we are "cheated out of experience,"[41] inside we are rewarded with an experience that, as Benjamin has already told us, is no longer really possible.[42]

The dialectic inherent in the dome of an opera house lies in its double function as "dividing wall and reflector in one."[43] Neither ancient amphitheatres nor Shakespeare's Globe had domes; thus the ritual from which drama of all sorts descends could rise to the heavens (for which, as religious ritual, it was ultimately intended). The dome is, by its very existence, evidence of and index for the disappearance of this totality of sense and meaning. The modern spectators are fragmented, severed from any total sense or sense perception of their world. The dome is also, however, a "reflector." The sounds erstwhile destined for heaven do not go to waste today; instead they are reflected back toward us, the audience. They face us as a technologically produced nature — *our* sounds (the sound humans create) are as greedily consumed as the world outside is drowned out. What is more, the sound that reflects at us may even seem to us to come from heaven anyway — at which point we have mistaken human work, alienated by human means, for a hint of the divine. In fact, one prime factor in the vaunted acoustics of the Bayreuth *Festspielhaus* was the audience itself — the Bayreuth sound "from nowhere" could only be accomplished once the listeners' bodies had in some sense become part of the structure, the technology.[44] As a Bayreuth audience, we are among the very means of production the phantasmagoria hides from us.

One can see how this concept lends itself to the Christian mysticism of Wagner's later works — anyone who has seen a performance of *Parsifal* in which a light show and an invisible choir accompany the unveiling of the grail has been witness to this technological, theatrical manna. Not surprisingly, too, the "dividing wall and reflector" is, in the nineteenth century as today, often adorned with a technological firmament, usually in the shape of a giant chandelier. Adorno's most striking example for this transposition of myth into the technology is nothing other than applause.[45] Applause, he asserts, obviously once had ritual function — maybe a call out for the Gods to honor someone, or, perhaps more sinister, a call for a sacrifice. Today applause comes back at us roaring in all its mythic force, yet disconnected from anything whole. What we experience is nothing but uproarious agreement with each other, a brief identity not with the cosmos but with a (select) crowd of our fellow men.[46]

The opera house functions as what Adorno thematized throughout his philosophy as "identity," which Frederic Jameson has aptly characterized as "repetition as such, the return of sameness over and over again, . . . that is to say, neurosis."[47] The dome of the opera house stymies all forms of openness: first, human openness to difference as present outside the opera house. Second, it stymies cognitive openness to any difference within the opera house, since it "collects" the sounds we are required to hear and subdues the manifold of buzzes and tingles into an experience. And third, it undercuts any awareness or differentiation of who is doing what (since any such awareness may eclipse the self-sufficiency of the hall) and gives us the illusion that what people have produced comes like manna from heaven. It blinds humans to the tautological claustrophobia of their "second" (cultural) nature, and to the very real differences and injustices that persist within it.

All of this, however, could just as well be said of any kind of roof over a theatre or an opera house. The "dialectic of the dome" goes beyond theorizing the roof of the concert hall as "dividing wall and reflector in one," to consider also the specific construction of the dome, as man-made and technological. Identity requires work, and that work consists not merely of passively obviating but rather of actively bundling the elements of the phantasmagoria. The dome has been *made* to actively bundle: it functions as shock-preventer and shock-conductor. I use the word "conductor" here both in the sense of some*thing* passing something else along and in the sense of some*one* conducting a performance.

How can a dome do both? It is the job of the modern opera house to keep certain stimuli from entering the sensory field of each audience member and to amplify others. One might argue that a wall or a well-placed window may perform a similar task, and that is where the second sense of "conductor" comes in: The modern opera house, far from merely swallowing some sounds and allowing others to pass, is in fact actively (even uncannily) engaged in styling, modulating, and inflecting the sensory input of its audience. It carefully determines which stimuli are to reach the senses, when they are to do so, and from where. It is only through this careful management of stimuli that the *syn*aesthetic can enter modern experience — only through active manipulation, in other words, can the senses be brought into congruence. For instance, the Bayreuth phantasmagoria is not just sonic and visual, not simply a matter of acoustics and hidden orchestra — it has been said that only at Bayreuth do you *not hear* the first few bars of the *Rheingold* but *feel* them as they travel up your legs.

Both dome and phantasmagoria gather and order sensory data to suggest a coherent whole rather than a buzzing confusion. Obviously, however, a real synaesthetic experience is rarely possible under conditions of modernity. The phantasmagoria produces a synaesthetic experience technologically: it composes space, time, and sound in order to delude the spectators' sensorium into experiencing modernity whole, when in fact it isn't. Benjamin, whose *Passagen-Werk* is something of a catalogue of the phantasmagoria of the nineteenth century, lists the following examples of such synaesthetic composition: world expositions, panoramas, urban planning, the bourgeois interior. All these are produced for the purpose of shielding the subject from things that might unsettle a (false) unity of experience through newness, disruption, or shock — Adorno and Benjamin are not merely pointing out an *idolatrous* solipsism, but one that is *induced,* often for conservative political purposes.

Since they provide a total experience in a fragmented world, phantasmagorias are marked as much by what they leave out as by what they keep in. Their effect lies in the management of "shocks," as Benjamin describes in his book on Baudelaire (*GS* I.2:613–17, *SW* 4:317–18). It is here that we need to leave Adorno's appropriations of Benjamin entirely and focus on Benjamin's cognitive theory, what Susan Buck-Morss has labeled Benjamin's *anaesthetics.* We are adapted to shocks by being systematically exposed to them in a technologically simulated environment.

The phantasmagoric techno-totality is not so much supposed to drown out the noise of traffic and people; rather, it is ultimately supposed to attune us to them. After all, it doesn't combat noise by silence but with more carefully structured noise.

Not only do phantasmagorias shut us off from reality, then, but they gradually and artfully reconcile us to reality, in spite of our very real alienation from it. This is precisely how a modern opera house works: its greatest work goes into shutting out the world beyond the "magic circle" of stage and audience; within the space of silence thus created, the modern opera can lay out a new geography, an anaesthetic one. The conductor Bruno Walter relates the following story about Gustav Mahler: on a visit, Walter expressed admiration of an alpine panorama, to which the composer replied that there was no need to do so, since "I've composed all this away already."[48] Composing means simulating and erasing that which might lie "behind" the simulation. The anaesthetic, particularly in the case of Wagner, can be extremely noisy, but it provides a composed assault as art or as entertainment, which prepares the audience for the world outside, both because it hardens them to it (makes them ready for it), and because it leads them to ignore it.

Of course, this cognitive autarky of the concert hall somewhat paradoxically enables the unfolding of what Adorno elsewhere calls "symphonic space."[49] Because the membrane between the concert hall on the one hand and the foyer, the coat checks, in short, the building shell itself, have been rendered impermeable, music can now undertake to simulate distance within the confines of the concert hall. Adorno claims that the New German School (by which he means mainly composers influenced by or reacting to Wagner) is guided by the idea of a "distant sound," by which he means something very much like phantasmagoria, in which "Musik verräumlicht innehält" (music becomes static and spatialized).[50] Even on a purely empirical level, the question of distance enters into the compositional as well as the technological equation through Wagner. In Mahler's symphonies, for instance, horns, trumpets, and other instruments routinely chime in from offstage, for instance the distant call of the *postillon*'s horn in the scherzo of the Third Symphony. The horn can be heard from the distance and launches into a duet with the horns on stage; Adorno himself comments that this dialogue "versöhnt . . . das Unversöhnte" (reconciles the unreconciled)[51] — in other words that it creates precisely some kind of falsely coherent (phantasmagoric) space. Just as world exhibitions, according to Benjamin, at once spatialize an "Universum der Waren" ("universe of commodities") and just as Grandville caricatures bestow "Warencharakter aufs Universum" (*GS* V.1:51; "commodity character on the universe," *AP*, 8), Mahler's post-horn dialogue annihilates (real) space, only then to unfold its own simulated space.

IV

This simulated space is of course most readily problematized in narrative forms. In the case of opera, this tends to assert itself as a drive that propels the narrative beyond the confines of the stage. In many operas of the immediate Wagnerian aftermath, the narrative either explicitly thematizes the stage, the backstage area, or even the balconies of the opera house[52] — in particular in the works of the Austrian composer and conductor Franz Schreker (1878–1934), whose chromaticism, overall musical idiom, and acoustics were influenced by Wagner. As Christopher Hailey has pointed out, Schreker's operas are characterized by "powerful musical symbol[s] calculated to play a structural role in the opera."[53] In his *Memnon,* an abortive project from the 1910s, the stage is dominated by a colossus, which at the opera's climax begins to hum as the first rays of the sun hit it. The sets themselves, in other words, are supposed to intervene in the music.

When Adorno refers to a "distant sound" that dominates the post-Wagnerian opera house, he is not simply thinking about a musical concept but is quite concretely alluding to a particular opera, called simply *Der ferne Klang* (The Distant Sound, 1903–10). Its composer, Franz Schreker, relies on an entire catalogue of "distances": the distance of a birdsong "behind the scenes," the vanishing distance of a gypsy combo coming onstage, and the metaphysical distance of the titular "distant sound," which is nothing other than aesthetic manna, sound from nowhere. The very fact that Mahler can have a dialogue with the backstage area, that Schreker can rely on the audience's ability to distinguish between different kinds of distance, is a testament not only to a compositional technique inherited from Wagner but, more importantly, to an operatic architecture descended from Bayreuth (or at least the cognitive programs underpinning it and projects like it). Only once the outside world is absolutely shut out can the audience pick up on something like a "distant sound."

However, as Adorno and Horkheimer make clear in relation to cinema, phantasmagorias never quite deliver the relief they promise; all they can do is offer constant release and defer deliverance *ad infinitum.*[54] This is where Jameson's invocation of identity as neurotic becomes cogent once more: phantasmagorias create a compulsion to repeat in a double sense — first one seeks them out again and again, and second, in their grasp one is doomed (or enticed, rather) to neurotically "reiterate the world," to repeat the way the world has always been.[55] Herbert Marcuse therefore equated identity with Thanatos, the death drive, a drive toward ever-sameness.[56] As Adorno perceived, attending the opera certainly has something in common with a voyage in the belly of a whale, or a return to the womb.[57]

Schreker's *Der ferne Klang* presents its audience with a disturbing allegory of this very link between operatic phantasmagoria and death drive.

Or, put differently, it charts, as Benjamin puts it following Brecht, how the apparatus turns from a means *for* the producer to a means *against* the producer (*GS* II:697). The opera's hero quests for the pure experience of the "distant sound," access to which is obstructed to him in his social *milieu*. The opera stages this obstacle quite literally: a plethora of duets, songs, diegetic ensembles, fairy tales, and even an opera-within-the-opera parade across the stage, acoustically barring unobstructed access to the pure aesthetic transcendence of the distant sound. In this way the *telos* of the opera's narrative is blocked by the opera itself. Its hero, Fritz, is thus recapitulating the desire that has led the audience to the opera in the first place: to escape from the discontinuity and heterogeneity of the everyday life-world into the phantasmagoria of the operatic womb. Not coincidentally, Fritz attains the "distant sound" only in death — the wish for the distant sound is nothing but the death drive.

The very insistence with which identity is produced, however, raises the question — as Jameson again points out — of "what it would take to have the strength to stand the new, to be 'open' to it; but even more: what that new might be, what it might be like, how one would go about conceptualizing and imagining what you can by definition not yet imagine or foresee; what has no equivalent in your current experience."[58] This of course is what Schreker's "distant sound" ultimately encodes: identity as the self-same obscures the new, the clamor on stage frustrates the longing that points beyond the stage.

In modernity we have foreclosed the cultic function of the opera house, in the sense that we do not believe it puts us in touch with divine or cosmic powers. Yet it retains a ritual function, having de-historicized and de-mythified that ritual. For Benjamin the modern era is still marked by its insufficient cleavage from the ritualistic, mythic realities of "pre-history,"[59] to the extent that we still live in prehistory. Technological developments have made the *Ur*-elements of the theatre manageable, but they have not sublated them (in the sense of the Hegelian *Aufhebung*). Just as in modern society instrumental reason enslaves people in the same way that a force of nature might, the technological apparatuses in the opera house divest people of themselves just as an ancient sacrifice might.

Another opera by Schreker explores precisely the power a particular kind of music can exercise over a particular kind of space: *Die Orgel* (The Organ), later retitled *Der singende Teufel* (The Singing Devil, 1924, 1927–28), is dominated by the titular organ, with which the abbot of a monastery attempts to Christianize the heathens. His project of domination comes to naught, however, and the organ-builder hero sets fire to the monastery — from its ashes emerge the otherworldly sounds of the organ in its dying wheeze. Within the opera, the relationship between the transformative powers of ecclesiastical space and those of operatic space is ambiguous: on the one hand, the aesthetic project of domination is depicted negatively, as tyranny (in the case of the abbot) or as naivety (in that of the organ builder); on the other hand, the final sonic phantasmagoria — the dying wheeze of the great organ — seems to elevate the secularized ritual powers of the opera over and against the failed ones of ecclesiastic ritual. While *Der singende Teufel* clearly recognizes the violent, identitarian, and ideological element in its own phantasmagoria, it nevertheless can't help slipping into one final thrilling special effect by which the phantasmagoria, like Baron Münchhausen, pulls itself out of the muck by its own hair.

At the base of Schreker's interrogation of phantasmagoria in *Der singende Teufel* is his insight that the opera house is a secularized temple, the same insight that animates Adorno's "Naturgeschichte des Theaters"; similarly, Benjamin was struck by the architectural and atmospheric similarities of churches and the modern shopping arcades (L1,6; L2,4). Adorno's text lays bare the archaisms of modern opera, not in terms of *musical* form, but rather in terms of the architecture and technology that "put on" an opera in the first place: Benjamin's stopovers in the Moscow theater, namely the lobby ("Foyer"), the orchestra ("Parkett") and of course the dome ("Kuppel"). Since, as we have seen, the modern opera house is "identitarian," that is, it tries precisely to preclude a plurality of readings, Adorno's method of reading for this repressed or sublimated archaism takes the shape of a sort of "double vision." In a post-Wagnerian opera house many things happen at once, but none detract from the one thing we *experience* happening. The way to dislodge this identity is via spatial and bodily dislocation: the modern opera house depends for its "effect" on our bodies being in a certain place, looking a certain way, or holding our attention in one place rather than another.

We offset or subvert phantasmagorias by looking where we are not supposed to, or by physically going where the techno-totality is revealed for a production. We might, as Benjamin does in Moscow, pay attention to the carpeting of the foyer. We might turn around and look precisely where we are not to look — Adorno amusingly picks out the gallery as the locus of a "second stage," from where, in a more "natural" theatrical environment, such as a saloon, someone might actually shoot the piano player. Not by accident did Gustav Mahler ban applause between arias (the "claque") and the constant coming and going of the Vienna *Hofoper*'s aristocratic guests, as well as any conversations during the performance.[60] One might argue that we can still register the aftershocks of this violent disciplining action in any opera or concert performance: does not the persistent coughing in between (or even during) scenes, movements, and acts represent an inarticulate, inchoate protest by the caged creature hidden in the smoking jacket? This coughing is the scream of the bourgeoisie: trapped, constrained, and, most importantly, forced to pay continuous attention to that which it cannot or does not want to pay attention to, the *creature* in the spectator or listener can voice its protest only by bypassing the *subject* ostensibly (and ostentatiously) enjoying the musical performance — it is the throat where it can lodge its complaint, where it can force a *tussis nervosa*.

By partaking unreflectively in rituals older than the institution of the opera, audience and performers alike are caught in a *Zauberkreis,* a magic circle without escape. The only way we can recover, and become aware of, the mythic force of the goings-on is by putting distance between us and them. Anyone who has ever followed the end of a performance from the foyer or the coat check will have experienced the uncanny flip side of the civilized pageant inside: the distant claps, the indistinguishable shouts, the booing, the stamping feet; all of it betrays the atavism that the evening suits and bouquets inside attempt to cover over. Not only the place of ritual smacks of a certain atavism, however; musical performance is ripe with it as well. Adorno compares the soloist, the virtuoso, the star, to an animal trainer or bullfighter. Again, the precarious banishing rituals performed by these high priests of art are obvious only for the non-spectator.

Spatial dislocation allows us to see the theatre as an institution still mired in the irrational, regardless of (or maybe inversely proportional to) the technological means it invests in its own hermetic autarky. The more we are shut out from the "magic circle," the greater our awareness of the archaism, the magic of this circle. And herein lies the paradox: the more opera denies the traditional visual cues of its production, lowering the orchestra into its pit and hiding the elaborate acoustics, combining the sensory manifold of which it consists as a phantasmagoria, the more the mythic, archaic, irrational character of this strange ritual becomes apparent to someone spatially not within the purview of the phantasmagoria. The more perfect the illusion inside, the more evident its irrational antithesis outside.

But, as we saw, while the Benjaminian "dreamworld" of the nineteenth century was consolidating in and around the opera house, a number of operas began interrogating the very phantasmagoric techniques/technologies that the project of the Wagnerian *Gesamtkunstwerk* demanded of them. Of course, the shock effects characteristic of the avant-garde constitute the preferred avenue into the disruption of the total work of art. But even before alienation effects became commonplace, a number of composers instead tried to push phantasmagoria to a point of self-reflexivity, by thematizing near-obsessively the very space operatic phantasmagorias constitutively abjure and deny.

In Schreker's *Der ferne Klang,* the hero, Fritz, is haunted by the titular "distant sound," which always beckons offstage: at times it comes from the orchestra, at others the score indicates that it should emanate from backstage. Fritz composes an opera trying to capture his "distant sound." In the third act we get to hear Fritz's opera from the distance — the action itself takes place in a restaurant near the opera house and bits of music float over, as do the applause and eventual boos. The opera being played, it turns out, sounds exactly like the first act of *Der ferne Klang* itself. Here, then, the audience is itself listening to "music from the outside," in fact it is even listening to itself from the outside — in a restaurant rather than the foyer, but outside the magic circle nonetheless.

If we recall the little vignette Adorno offers in his lectures and his method of listening to "music from the outside," it becomes clear that what he is calling for is that precise dislocation on a theoretical level: what else is "music from the outside," if not listening to oneself listening? Adorno insists that it is only a *double* vantage that makes thought genuinely dialectical: laying claim to an Archimedean point outside the phenomenon in question without thinking through either the "logic of the thing" or one's own implication in it limits one's understanding, just as much as hovering religiously over the brute given "facts" would. Our standpoint outside the "magic circle" of the operatic performance is thus only one aspect of our exploration of the "logic" of the phenomenon. The "thing itself" can only be comprehended if we follow our latecomer into the "magic circle" and watch the opera — albeit while keeping the coat check and the foyer in mind.

Notes

Portions of this article were previously published as "Adorno's Schreker: Charting the Self-Dissolution of the Distant Sound," *Cambridge Opera Journal* 183.3 (2006): 247–71.

[1] Lisa Yun Lee, "The Bare-Breasts Incident," in *Feminist Interpretations of Theodor Adorno*, ed. Renée Heberle (University Park: Pennsylvania State UP, 2006), 113–14.

[2] Ackbar Abbas, "Cultural Studies in a Postculture," in *Disciplinarity and Dissent in Cultural Studies*, ed. Cary Nelson and Dilip Gaonkar (London: Routledge, 1996), 289–312.

[3] All translations in this chapter not otherwise credited are my own.

[4] Susan Buck-Morss, "The Flaneur, the Sandwichman and the Whore: The Politics of Loitering," *New German Critique* 39 (1986): 102.

[5] I am indebted to the Adorno Archives Frankfurt for access to the lecture transcripts (Vo 3179, 153).

[6] This is a connection to which Susan Buck-Morss has pointed already: see "The Flaneur, the Sandwichman and the Whore," 105.

[7] Adorno, "Radio Voice," in *Current of Music: Elements of a Radio Theory* (Frankfurt am Main: Suhrkamp, 2007).

[8] Peter Bevers, "The Seventh Symphony," in *The Mahler Companion*, ed. Donald Mitchell and Andrew Nicholson (Oxford: Oxford UP, 1999), 385.

[9] Hans Heinrich Eggebrecht, *Die Musik Gustav Mahlers* (Munich: Piper, 1982), 50.

[10] Susan Buck-Morss, "Aesthetics and Anaesthetics: Walter Benjamin's Artwork-Essay Reconsidered," *October*, 64 (1992): 24.

[11] Lutz Koepnick, "Benjamin's Silence," in *Sound Matters: Essays on the Acoustics of Modern German Culture,* ed. Lutz Koepnick and Nora Alter (New York: Berghahn Books, 2004), 118.

[12] Eli Friedlander, "On the Musical Gathering of Echoes in the Voice — Walter Benjamin and the *Trauerspiel," Opera Quarterly,* 21, no. 4 (2006): 631–46.

[13] Theodor W. Adorno, *Versuch über Wagner,* in *Die musikalischen Monographien,* vol. 13 of *Gesammelte Werke* (Frankfurt am Main: Suhrkamp, 1973), 7–148.

[14] Jonathan Crary, *Suspensions of Perception* (Cambridge, MA: MIT Press, 1999), 249–51.

[15] Susan Buck-Morss, *The Dialectics of Seeing: Walter Benjamin and the Arcades Project* (Cambridge, MA: MIT Press, 1989), 255.

[16] This is even a point made by Wagner himself: Richard Wagner, "Das Bühnenweihfestspiel in Bayreuth, 1882," in *Schriften und Dichtungen,* vol. 10 (Leipzig: Breitkopf & Härtel, 1911), 307.

[17] Jonathan Crary, *Techniques of the Observer: On Vision and Modernity in the Nineteenth Century* (Cambridge, MA: MIT Press, 1992), 5.

[18] Arthur Schopenhauer, "Ueber die Weiber," in *Parerga und Paralipomena II* (Leipzig: Brockhaus, 1874), 655.

[19] Richard Wagner, "Zukunftsmusik," in *Schriften und Dichtungen,* vol. 7 (Leipzig: Breitkopf & Härtel, 1911), 124–25.

[20] Richard Wagner, "Zukunftsmusik," in *Judaism in Music and Other Essays* (Lincoln: U of Nebraska P, 1995), 332.

[21] Crary, *Suspensions of Perception,* 251.

[22] See Tom Gunning, "The Cinema of Attractions: Early Film, Its Spectator, and the Avant-Garde," in *Theater and Film: A Comparative Anthology,* ed. Robert Knopf (New Haven, CT: Yale UP, 2005), 37–45.

[23] Adorno was born Theodor Wiesengrund, but changed his name to Theodor W[iesengrund]. Adorno (Adorno being his mother's maiden name) upon becoming a naturalized US citizen. Benjamin addresses Adorno throughout his writings as "Wiesengrund."

[24] See Rajeev Patke, "Benjamin on Art and Reproducibility: The Case of Music," in *Walter Benjamin and Art,* ed. Andrew Benjamin (London and New York: Continuum, 2005), 185–208, here 188–89.

[25] Adorno, *Versuch über Wagner,* 82–91.

[26] For the conception of "natural history" that allows Adorno to theorize how history at its most historical can end up *producing* nature, see Theodor W. Adorno, "Die Idee der Naturgeschichte," in *Philosophische Frühschriften,* vol. 1 of his *Gesammelte Schriften* (Frankfurt am Main: Suhrkamp, 1973), 345–65.

[27] See Alastair Williams, "Technology of the Archaic: Wish Images and Phantasmagoria in Wagner," *Cambridge Opera Journal* 9/1 (1997): 78.

[28] "Adorno, *Versuch über Wagner,* 96.

29 In a 1965 essay Adorno outlined how such particular "logics" can function and how they may be subsumed by a totalizing construction ("Über einige Relationen zwischen Musik und Malerei," in *Musikalische Schriften I–III*, vol. 16 of his *Gesammelte Schriften* (Frankfurt am Main: Suhrkamp, 1974), 628–42).

30 Theodor W. Adorno, *Minima Moralia* (Frankfurt am Main: Suhrkamp, 1974), 55.

31 Williams, "Wish Images." Williams utilizes Derrida's reflections on use value and exchange value to critique the blunt juxtapositions Adorno lapses into in his monograph.

32 Cf. David Levin, *Unsettling Opera* (Chicago: U of Chicago P, 2007).

33 In his recent discussion of Benjamin's *Trauerspiel* book and Wagner's *Ring*, albeit in a different context, Samuel Weber has similarly emphasized the importance of place in opera's conception and performance: drama needs to always be performed (rather than ossifying into an external thing, a *work*) and each performance has to call the torpid play back into existence — a ritual character that Wagner understood all too well. However, Weber strangely skirts the fact that Wagner's operas are rarely called "operas," "pieces" ("Stücke") or "theater," and that he in fact explicitly opposes his works to each of these terms — clearly, then, Wagner's relation to the "work" is quite different from that of other dramatists. His *Bühnenfestspiel* is supposed to transcend the "piece"-character of an "ordinary" theater performance (Samuel Weber, *Benjamin's–abilities* [Cambridge, MA: Harvard UP, 2008], 286).

34 Buck-Morss, *The Dialectics of Seeing*, 80.

35 Buck-Morss, "Aesthetics and Anaesthetics," 22.

36 Adorno, "Die Naturgeschichte des Theaters," in *Musikalische Schriften I–III*, 309–20; Theodor W. Adorno, "Natural History of the Theatre," in *Quasi una Fantasia — Essays on Modern Music* (London: Verso, 1998), 65–79.

37 We cannot speak of a strictly "Adornian" use of the concept on the one hand and a strictly "Benjaminian" one on the other (one reason why I associated the two variant conceptualisations of phantasmagoria with two particular *texts* rather than their authors). Adorno imports "phantasmagoria" from Benjamin's vocabulary, along with a good many aspects of Benjamin's philosophy. However, Adorno's reception of Benjamin's aesthetics (including concepts such as "aura" and "phantasmagoria") continued over the better part of three decades after Benjamin's early death, changing considerably with time: see Martin Zenck, "Phantasmagorie — Ausdruck — Extrem," in *Adorno und die Musik*, ed. Otto Kolleritsch (Graz: Universal Edition, 1979), 202–26.

38 John Dewey, *Art as Experience* (New York: Perigee, 2005), 36–59.

39 Schopenhauer, "Ueber Lerm und Geräusch," in *Parerga und Paralipomena II*, 679.

40 As Jonathan Crary notes, "Schopenhauer is one of the earliest to grasp the link between attention and perceptual disintegration" (*Suspensions of Perception*, 55).

41 Walter Benjamin, *Baudelaire: A Lyric Poet in the Era of High Capitalism* (London: New Left Books, 1973), 137.

[42] Benjamin, "On Some Motifs in Baudelaire," *SW* 4:318.

[43] Adorno, "Naturgeschichte des Theaters," 308.

[44] Cosima Wagner, *Tagebücher* (Munich: Piper, 1976/77), 1:998.

[45] Adorno, "Naturgeschichte des Theaters," 309.

[46] That this "crowd," at least in Wagner, constitutes something of a *racial* community is a disturbing possibility I will leave aside in this context. See Marc A. Weiner, *Richard Wagner and the Anti-Semitic Imagination* (Lincoln: U of Nebraska P, 1995).

[47] Fredric Jameson, *Late Marxism — Theodor Adorno or the Persistence of the Dialectic* (London: Verso, 1990), 16.

[48] Bruno Walter, *Gustav Mahler* (Berlin: S. Fischer, 1957), 30.

[49] Theodor W. Adorno, "The Radio Symphony (1941)," in *Essays on Music* (Los Angeles: U of California P, 2002), 257.

[50] Adorno, *Versuch über Wagner*, 82.

[51] Adorno, *Mahler: Eine musikalische Physiognomik, GS* 13:157.

[52] Samuel Weber points out that Benjamin's analysis of the status of "work" in German tragic drama allows us to see this kind of self-reflexivity in Wagner's *Gesamtkunstwerk*: Wagner's tetralogy charts the construction and (necessary) undoing of precisely the kind of "work" he himself is attempting. The very project of self-enclosure and autarky that characterizes the *Gesamtkunstwerk* is thus problematized in the opera's plot (Weber, *Benjamin's –abilities*, 287).

[53] Christopher Hailey, *Franz Schreker, 1878–1934: A Cultural Biography* (Cambridge: Cambridge UP, 1993), 176.

[54] Theodor W. Adorno and Max Horkheimer, *Die Dialektik der Aufklärung* (Frankfurt am Main: Suhrkamp, 1971), 162.

[55] Jameson, *Late Marxism*, 16.

[56] On Wagner's anticipation of Freud's theory of the death drive, see Linda and Michael Hutcheon, "Death Drive: Eros and Thanatos in Wagner's *Tristan and Isolde*," *Cambridge Opera Journal*, 11/3 (1999): 267–93.

[57] Herbert Marcuse, *The Aesthetic Dimension* (Boston, MA: Beacon, 1978).

[58] Fredric Jameson, *Late Marxism*, 16.

[59] Buck-Morss, *Dialectics of Seeing*, 58–71.

[60] See Henry-Louis De La Grange, *Vienna: The Years of Challenge*, vol. 2 of *Gustav Mahler* (Oxford: Oxford UP, 1999), 59–61.

Select Bibliography and List of Further Reading

Alter, Robert. *Necessary Angels: Tradition and Modernity in Kafka, Benjamin, and Scholem.* Cambridge, MA: Harvard UP, 1991.

Benjamin, Andrew, ed. *Walter Benjamin and Art.* London and New York: Continuum, 2005.

———. *Walter Benjamin and History.* London and New York: Continuum, 2005.

Benjamin, Andrew, and Peter Osborne, eds. *Walter Benjamin's Philosophy: Destruction and Experience.* Manchester: Clinamen P, 1993.

Bock, Wolfgang. *Walter Benjamin — Die Rettung der Nacht.* Bielefeld: Aisthesis, 2000).

Bolle, Willi. *Physiognomik der modernen Metropole: Geschichtsdarstellung bei Walter Benjamin.* Cologne, Weimar, and Vienna: Böhlau, 1994.

Brodersen, Momme. *Walter Benjamin: A Biography.* Edited by Martina Derviş. Translated by Malcolm R. Green and Ingrida Ligers. London and New York: Verso, 1996.

Brüggemann, Heinz. *Walter Benjamin über Spiel, Farbe und Phantasie.* Würzburg: Königshausen & Neumann, 2007.

Buck-Morss, Susan. The *Dialectics of Seeing: Walter Benjamin and the Arcades Project.* Cambridge, MA, and London: MIT Press, 1989.

Bürger, Peter. *Theory of the Avant-Garde.* Translated by Michael Shaw. Minneapolis: U of Minnesota P, 1984.

Caygill, Howard, Alex Coles, and Andrzej Klimowski. *Introducing Walter Benjamin.* Cambridge: Icon Books; n.p.: Totem Books, 1998.

Cohen, Margret. *Profane Illumination: Walter Benjamin and the Paris of Surrealist Revolution.* Berkeley, Los Angeles, and London: U of California P, 1993.

Ferris, David S., ed. *The Cambridge Companion to Walter Benjamin.* Cambridge: Cambridge UP, 2004.

Finkelde, Dominik. *Benjamin liest Proust: Mimesislehre, Sprachtheorie, Poetologie.* Munich: Fink, 2003.

Garber, Klaus. *Rezeption und Rettung: Drei Studien zu Walter Benjamin.* Tübingen: Niemeyer, 1987.

Gilloch, Graeme. *Walter Benjamin: Critical Constellations.* Cambridge: Polity, 2002.

Goebel, Rolf J. *Benjamin heute: Großstadtdiskurs, Postkolonialität und Flanerie zwischen den Kulturen.* Munich: Iudicium, 2001.

Handelman, Susan A. *Fragments of Redemption: Jewish Thought and Literary Theory in Benjamin, Scholem, and Levinas.* Bloomington: Indiana UP, 1991.

Hanssen, Beatrice. *Critique of Violence: Between Poststructuralism and Critical Theory.* London: Routledge, 2000.

———, ed. *Walter Benjamin and The Arcades Project.* London and New York: Continuum, 2006.

———. *Walter Benjamin's Other History: Of Stones, Animals, Human Beings, and Angels.* Berkeley: U of California P, 1998.

Hanssen, Beatrice, and Andrew Benjamin, eds. *Walter Benjamin and Romanticism.* London and New York: Continuum, 2002.

Honold, Alexander. *Der Leser Walter Benjamin: Bruchstücke einer deutschen Literaturgeschichte.* Berlin: Vorwerk 8, 2000.

Jacobs, Carol. *In the Language of Walter Benjamin.* Baltimore: Johns Hopkins UP, 1999.

Jacobson, Eric. *Metaphysics of the Profane: The Political Theology of Walter Benjamin and Gershom Scholem.* New York: Columbia UP, 2003.

Jennings, Michael W. *Dialectical Images: Walter Benjamin's Theory of Literary Criticism.* Ithaca, NY: Cornell UP, 1987.

Koepnick, Lutz. *Walter Benjamin and the Aesthetics of Power.* Lincoln and London: U of Nebraska P, 1999.

Lindner, Burkhardt, ed. *Benjamin-Handbuch: Leben — Werk — Wirkung.* Stuttgart and Weimar: Metzler, 2006.

Löwy, Michael, *Fire Alarm: Reading Walter Benjamin's "On the Concept of History."* Translated by Chris Turner. London and New York: Verso, 2005.

Marcus, Laura, and Lynda Nead, eds. *The Actuality of Walter Benjamin.* London: Lawrence & Wishart, 1998.

McCole, John. *Walter Benjamin and the Antinomies of Tradition.* Ithaca, NY: Cornell UP, 1993).

Menke, Bettine. *Sprachfiguren: Name — Allegorie — Bild nach Walter Benjamin.* Munich: Fink, 1991.

Menninghaus, Winfried. *Schwellenkunde: Walter Benjamins Passage des Mythos.* Frankfurt am Main: Suhrkamp, 1986.

———. *Walter Benjamins Theorie der Sprachmagie.* Frankfurt am Main: Suhrkamp, 1980.

Missac, Pierre. *Walter Benjamin's Passages.* Translated by Shierry Weber Nicholsen. Cambridge: MIT Press, 1995.

Nägele, Rainer, ed. *Benjamin's Ground: New Readings of Walter Benjamin.* Detroit, MI: Wayne State UP, 1988.

Opitz, Michael, and Erdmut Wizisla, eds. *Benjamins Begriffe.* Frankfurt am Main: Suhrkamp, 2000.

Osborne, Peter, ed. *Walter Benjamin: Critical Evaluations in Cultural Theory.* London: Routledge, 2004.

Pensky, Max. *Melancholy Dialectics: Walter Benjamin and the Play of Mourning.* Amherst: U of Massachusetts P, 1993.

Richter, Gerhard, ed. *Benjamin's Ghosts: Interventions in Contemporary Literary and Cultural Theory*. Stanford CA: Stanford UP, 2002.

———. *Thought-Images: Frankfurt School Writers' Reflections from Damaged Life*. Stanford, CA: Stanford UP, 2007.

———. *Walter Benjamin and the Corpus of Autobiography*. Detroit, MI: Wayne State UP, 2000.

Santner, Eric L. *On Creaturely Life: Rilke, Benjamin, Sebald*. Chicago: U of Chicago P, 2006.

Scholem, Gershom. *Die Geschichte einer Freundschaft*. Frankfurt am Main: Suhrkamp 1975.

Schulte, Christian, ed. *Walter Benjamins Medientheorie*. Constance: UVK Verlagsgesellschaft, 2005.

Smith, Gary, ed. *On Walter Benjamin: Critical Essays and Recollections*. Cambridge, MA: MIT Press, 1988.

Steiner, Uwe. *Walter Benjamin*. Stuttgart and Weimar: Metzler, 2004.

Unseld, Siegfried, ed. *Zur Aktualität Walter Benjamins: Aus Anlaß des 80. Geburtstags von Walter Benjamin*. Frankfurt am Main: Suhrkamp, 1972.

Van Reijen, Willem, and Herman van Doorn. *Aufenthalte und Passagen: Leben und Werk Walter Benjamins; Eine Chronik*. Frankfurt am Main: Suhrkamp, 2001.

Walter Benjamin Archiv, ed. *Walter Benjamins Archive: Bilder, Texte und Zeichen*. Frankfurt am Main: Suhrkamp, 2006.

Weber, Samuel. *Benjamin's –abilities*. Cambridge, MA, and London: Harvard UP, 2008.

Weigel, Sigrid. *Body- and Image-Space: Re-Reading Walter Benjamin*. Translated by Georgina Paul with Rachel McNicholl and Jeremy Gaines. New York: Routledge, 1996.

———. *Entstellte Ähnlichkeit: Walter Benjamins theoretische Schreibweise*. Frankfurt am Main: Fischer, 1997.

Whybrow, Nicolas. *Street Scenes: Brecht, Benjamin, and Berlin*. Portland, OR: Intellect, 2005.

Witte, Bernd. *Benjamin: Der Intellektuelle als Kritiker*. Stuttgart: Metzler, 1976.

———. *Walter Benjamin: An Intellectual Biography*. Translated by James Rolleston. Detroit, MI: Wayne State UP, 1991.

Wolin, Richard. *Walter Benjamin: An Aesthetic of Redemption*. New York: Columbia UP, 1982.

Notes on the Contributors

WOLFGANG F. BOCK was Professor of the Theory and History of Visual Communications at the Faculty of Art and Design at the Bauhaus-University of Weimar. He is now visiting Professor at the Federal University of Rio de Janeiro (UNIRIO), Brazil. He is the author of *Walter Benjamin — Die Rettung der Nacht: Sterne, Melancholie und Messianismus* (1995); *Bild, Schrift, Cyberspace* (2002); *Medienpassagen* (2006); *Vom Blickvispern der Dinge: Sprache, Erinnerung und Ästhetik bei Walter Benjamin* (2009); and numerous articles on art, media, design, literature, philosophy, and cultural studies. He is coeditor of the *Zeitschrift für kritische Theorie*.

WILLI BOLLE is Professor of Literature at the Universidade de São Paulo/ Brazil. He is the author of *Physiognomik der modernen Metropole: Geschichtsdarstellung bei Walter Benjamin* (1994) and *grandesertão. br — O romance de formação do Brasil* (2004), as well as the editor of *Passagens* (2006), the Brazilian edition of Benjamin's *Passagen-Werk*. His current research project consists of a cultural topography of Brazil, from the megacities (especially São Paulo), through the backlands (sertão) to Amazonia.

DIANNE CHISHOLM is Professor of English at the University of Alberta. She is the author of *Queer Constellations: Subcultural Space in the Wake of the City* (2005) and *H. D.'s Freudian Poetics: Psychoanalysis in Translation* (1992). She is also guest coeditor with Rob Brazeau of a special issue, "The Other City: (De)mystifying Urban Culture," for the *Journal of Urban History* (2002) and has published numerous articles on urban modernism and modernity.

ADRIAN DAUB is Assistant Professor of German at Stanford University. He is the author of *"Zwillingshafte Gebärden": Zur kulturellen Wahrnehmung des vierhändigen Klavierspiels im neunzehnten Jahrundert* (2009), and has published articles on opera, film, performance art, and Frankfurt School Marxism.

DOMINIK FINKELDE teaches at the Munich School of Philosophy — Faculty of Philosophy of the Society of Jesus. He is the author of *Benjamin liest Proust: Mimesislehre, Sprachtheorie, Poetologie* (2003), *Politische*

Eschatologie nach Paulus: Badiou, Agamben, Žižek, Santner (2007), and *Slavoj Žižek zwischen Lacan und Hegel. Politische Philosophie — Metapsychologie — Ethik* (2009). He has written articles on the Weimar Republic, twentieth-century literature, contemporary European philosophy, and museum studies.

Rolf J. Goebel is Professor of German at the University of Alabama in Huntsville. He is the author of *Kritik und Revision: Kafkas Rezeption mythologischer, biblischer und historischer Traditionen* (1986), *Constructing China: Kafka's Orientalist Discourse* (1997), and *Benjamin heute: Großstadtdiskurs, Postkolonialität und Flanerie zwischen den Kulturen* (2001). He is also a coauthor of *A Franz Kafka Encyclopedia* (2005) and has written articles on Kafka, Benjamin, orientalism, representations of urban topographies, especially Berlin, and other topics in modern literature and culture.

Eric Jarosinski is Assistant Professor of German at the University of Pennsylvania. Forthcoming publications include: "The Theoretical Space of Siegfried Kracauer's *Ginster*," in *Spatial Turns,* ed. Jaimey Fisher and Barbara Mennel; "Of Stones and Glass Houses: *Minima Moralia* as a Critique of Transparency," in *Language Without Soil,* ed. Gerhard Richter; and *The Hand of the Interpreter,* coedited with Mena Mitrano. He is currently completing a book manuscript, *Cellophane Modernity,* on metaphors of transparency in modern German culture.

Lutz Koepnick is Professor of German, Film and Media Studies at Washington University in St. Louis. Koepnick is the author of, among other works, *Framing Attention: Windows on Modern German Culture* (2007), *The Dark Mirror: German Cinema between Hitler and Hollywood* (2002), and *Walter Benjamin and the Aesthetics of Power* (1999). He is also the coeditor and coauthor of books and anthologies on new media art and aesthetics, German postwar cinema, the exile of European visual artists in the United States, and the role of sound in modern German culture.

Vivian Liska is Professor of German Literature and director of the Institute of Jewish Studies at the University of Antwerp, Belgium. Her publications include *Die Nacht der Hymnen. Paul Celans Gedichte, 1938–1944* (1993*); Die Dichterin und das schelmische Erhabene: Else Lasker-Schülers* Die Nächte Tino von Bagdads (1997*); Die Moderne — Ein Weib* (2000); and *When Kafka says "We": Uncommon Communities in German Jewish Literature* (2009). She is also the editor of *Contemporary Jewish Writing in Europe* (with Thomas Nolden; 2007), *Modernism* in the ICLA series *History of the European Literatures* (with Astradur Eysteinsson; 2007) and *What Does the Veil Know?* (with Eva Meyer; 2009).

Karl Ivan Solibakke is Research Professor in German Literature and Culture at Syracuse University. He is the author of *Geformte Zeit: Musik als Diskurs und Struktur bei Bachmann und Bernhard* (2005) and coeditor of the *Benjamin Blätter,* a publication series sponsored by the *Internationale Walter Benjamin Gesellschaft.* Solibakke has also published articles on Thomas Bernhard, Elfriede Jelinek, Heinrich Heine, Franz Kafka, and Uwe Johnson as well as on fundamentalism in America.

Marc de Wilde is Assistant Professor of Legal History at the University of Amsterdam. He has written a dissertation on political theology in the work of Walter Benjamin and Carl Schmitt (2008). He has also published articles on legal theory, the concept of sovereignty, and political violence.

Bernd Witte is Professor of German Literature at the Heinrich-Heine-University in Düsseldorf. From 2002 to 2006 he served as Dean of the Division of Humanities. In 2000 he became President of the International Walter Benjamin Society and was recently elected Chair of the Board of the *Freundeskreis des Goethe-Museums Düsseldorf.* Professor Witte has published extensively on a wide variety of literary and cultural topics, ranging from Gellert and Goethe to Benjamin (*Walter Benjamin: An Intellectual Biography,* 1991), Kafka, Celan, and Bachmann. His latest book publications are *Goethe: Das Individuum der Moderne schreiben* und *Jüdische Tradition und literarische Moderne* (both 2007).

Index